Scott J. Dorman

Sams **Teach Yourself**

C# 5.0

in **24** **Hours**

SAMS 800 East 96th Street, Indianapolis, Indiana, 46240 USA

Sams Teach Yourself C# 5.0 in 24 Hours

ISBN-13: 978-0-672-33684-3
ISBN-10: 0-672-33684-7

The Library of Congress Cataloging-in-Publication data is on file.

Printed in the United States of America

First Printing November 2012

Trademarks

All terms mentioned in this book that are known to be trademarks or service marks have been appropriately capitalized. Sams Publishing cannot attest to the accuracy of this information. Use of a term in this book should not be regarded as affecting the validity of any trademark or service mark.

Warning and Disclaimer

Every effort has been made to make this book as complete and as accurate as possible, but no warranty or fitness is implied. The information provided is on an "as is" basis. The author and the publisher shall have neither liability nor responsibility to any person or entity with respect to any loss or damages arising from the information contained in this book.

Bulk Sales

Sams Publishing offers excellent discounts on this book when ordered in quantity for bulk purchases or special sales. For more information, please contact

> **U.S. Corporate and Government Sales**
> **1-800-382-3419**
> **corpsales@pearsontechgroup.com**

For sales outside of the U.S., please contact

> **International Sales**
> **international@pearsoned.com**

Editor-in-Chief
Greg Wiegand

Executive Editor
Neil Rowe

Development Editor
Mark Renfrow

Managing Editor
Kristy Hart

Project Editor
Betsy Harris

Copy Editor
Karen Annett

Indexer
Christine Karpeles

Proofreader
Debbie Williams

Technical Editor
Christopher Wilcox

Publishing Coordinator
Cindy Teeters

Cover Designer
Anne Jones

Compositor
Nonie Ratcliff

Contents at a Glance

Part V: Diving Deeper

Table of Contents

Foreword

At the end of the previous millennium, a small team of designers met in a small conference room on the second floor of Building 41 at Microsoft to create C#, a then brand-new language. The designers wanted the language to be easy to understand but not simplistic, familiar to C++ and Java programmers but not a slavish copy of either, safe by default but not too restrictive, and practical but without abandoning a disciplined, consistent, and theoretically valid design.

After many months of thought, design, research, development, testing, and documentation, C# 1.0 was delivered to the public. It was a pretty straightforward object-oriented language. Many of the details of its design were carefully chosen to ensure that objects could be organized into independently versionable components, but the fundamental concepts of the language all came from ideas developed in object-oriented and procedural languages going back to the 1970s or earlier.

The design team continued to meet three times a week in that same second-floor conference room to build upon the solid base established by C# 1.0. By working with colleagues in Microsoft Research Cambridge and the CLR team across the street, the type system was extended to support parametric polymorphism on generic types and methods. They added "iterator blocks" to make it easier to build collection types. Generic types and iterators had been pioneered by earlier languages such as CLU and Ada in the 1970s and 1980s. They also added anonymous methods; the idea of embedding anonymous methods in an existing method goes all the way back to the foundations of modern computer science in the 1950s.

C# 2.0 was a huge step up from its predecessor, but still the design team was not content. They continued to meet in that same second-floor conference room three times a week. This time, they were thinking about fundamentals. They realized that programmers manipulate data by combining relatively simple operations in complex ways; those operations typically include sorting, filtering, grouping, joining, and projecting collections of data. The concept of a syntactic pattern for "query comprehensions" that concisely describe these operations was originally developed in functional languages such as Haskell but also works well in a more imperative language like C#. And thus LINQ—Language Integrated Query—was born.

After ten years of meeting for six hours a week in the same conference room, the need to teleconference with offsite team members motivated a change of venue to the fifth floor. The design team looked back on the last ten years to see what real-world problems were not solved well by the language, where there were "rough edges," and so on. The increasing need to interoperate with both modern dynamic languages and legacy object models motivated the design of new language features like the "dynamic" type in C# 4.0. And they threw in typesafe covariance on certain generic interfaces for good measure.

Still the design team was not content; they were always looking at real-world developers to see what vexing problems they faced that could be solved with better language tools. They identified *dealing with latency* as a stumbling block for many modern application developers. In a world of multicore machines connected over networks, the milliseconds that elapse between requesting a result and processing it further ought not to be wasted, but it is very difficult to write clear, understandable programs that work well in high-latency environments. This motivated the addition of asynchronous methods in C# 5.0, which enable a program to do useful work while a method is waiting for a high-latency result to become available.

I figured it might be a good idea to do a quick look at the evolution of the C# language here, in the foreword, because this is certainly not the approach taken in this book. And that is a good thing! Authors of books for novices often choose to order the material in the order they learned it, which, as often as not, is the order in which the features were added to the language. What I particularly like about this book is that Scott chooses a sensible order to develop each concept, moving from the most basic arithmetical computations up to quite complex interrelated parts. Furthermore, his examples are actually realistic and motivating while still being clear enough and simple enough to be described in just a few paragraphs.

I've concentrated here on the evolution of the language, but of course the evolution of one language is far from the whole story. The language is just the tool you use to access the power of the runtime and the framework libraries; they are large and complex topics in and of themselves. Another thing I like about this book is that it does not concentrate narrowly on the language, but rather builds upon the language concepts taught early on to explain how to make use of the power afforded by the most frequently used base class library types.

As my brief sketch of the history of the language shows, there's a lot to learn here, even looking at just the language itself. I've been a user of C# for more than ten years and am a member of the design team, and I'm still finding out new facts about the language and learning new programming techniques every day. Hopefully your first 24 hours of C# programming described in this book will lead to your own decade of practical programming and continual learning. As for the design team, we're still trying to figure out what comes next; I'm looking forward to finding out.

Eric Lippert
Seattle, Washington
September 2012

About the Author

Scott J. Dorman is a Microsoft C# MVP, speaker, blogger, and the creator of the WP Requests and WinStore Requests websites. Scott has been involved with computers in one way or another for as long as he can remember, but started professionally in 1993 and has been working with .NET and C# since 2001. Currently, Scott's primary focus is developing commercial software applications using Microsoft .NET technologies. Scott runs a software architecture-focused user group, speaks extensively (including at Microsoft TechEd and community-sponsored code camps), and contributes regularly to online communities such as The Code Project and StackOverflow. Scott also maintains a .NET Framework and C#-focused technology blog at http://geekswithblogs.com/sdorman.

Dedication

This book is first and foremost dedicated to Nathan, whom I hope follows in my footsteps and someday writes books of his own. Thank you for giving me a unique perspective and showing me the world through the eyes of a child.

Acknowledgments

It seems like just yesterday when I finished the previous edition of this book, but it was actually almost two years ago. When I decided to write that first book, I wasn't prepared for just how difficult it was going to be. Even though this edition focuses on what's new in the .NET Framework and the C# language, I reviewed all of the comments and content to see where I could improve and simplify. As always, even though I was the one responsible for the content, I couldn't have done it without the help and support of others. First, I need to thank Brook for giving me the idea of writing that first book and Neil for allowing me to write this next edition. The rest of the editors at Sams, without whom the book would never have been published, were also great to work with. My technical editor Christopher also deserves a huge amount of thanks. Of course, without the entire C#, .NET Framework, and Visual Studio product teams, I wouldn't have had anything to write about in the first place.

I wrote this book for the development community, which has given so much to me. Without its encouragement and support, I wouldn't have been in a position to write this book at all. This includes everyone associated with the Microsoft MVP program and the Microsoft field evangelists, particularly Joe "devfish" Healy, Jeff Barnes, and Russ "ToolShed" Fustino.

Finally, of course, I have to thank Nathan for being so patient and understanding of the many long nights and weekends it took to finish this book. Although he is too young right now to understand why I spent so much time on the computer rather than playing with him, I hope he will appreciate it as he gets older. While the first book introduced him to computers at a very early age, watching me work on this book has only served to strengthen his intellectual curiosity and deepen his growing knowledge of the technical world around him. In spite of all that, I know he will be happy that this is done and I can start spending more playtime with him.

We Want to Hear from You

As the reader of this book, you are our most important critic and commentator. We value your opinion and want to know what we're doing right, what we could do better, what areas you'd like to see us publish in, and any other words of wisdom you're willing to pass our way.

We welcome your comments. You can email or write us directly to let us know what you did or didn't like about this book—as well as what we can do to make our books stronger.

Please note that we cannot help you with technical problems related to the topic of this book, and that due to the high volume of mail we receive, we might not be able to reply to every message.

When you write, please be sure to include this book's title and author, as well as your name and contact information. We will carefully review your comments and share them with the author and editors who worked on the book.

Email: consumer@samspublishing.com

Mail: Sams Publishing
          ATTN: Reader Feedback
          800 East 96th Street
          Indianapolis, IN 46240 USA

Reader Services

Visit our website and register this book at informit.com/register for convenient access to any updates, downloads, or errata that might be available for this book.

Introduction

In late December 1998, Microsoft began working on a new development platform that would result in an entirely new way to create and run next-generation applications and web services. This new platform was called the .NET Framework and was publicly announced in June 2000.

The .NET Framework unified the existing Windows interfaces and services under a single application programming interface (API) and added many of the emerging industry standards, such as Simple Object Access Protocol (SOAP), and many existing Microsoft technologies, such as the Microsoft Component Object Model (COM and COM+) and Active Server Pages (ASP). In addition to providing a consistent development experience, the .NET Framework enabled developers to focus on the application logic rather than on more common programming tasks with the inclusion of one of the largest available class libraries. Finally, by running applications in a managed runtime environment that automatically handled memory allocation and provided a "sandboxed" (or restricted access) environment, many common programming errors and tasks were reduced and, in some cases, eliminated.

Now, more than 10 years later, the .NET Framework continues to evolve by simplifying the everyday "pain points" felt by developers and by supporting emerging industry standards and technologies in a way that is easy to use. The most recent release of the .NET Framework provides unparalleled support for working with asynchronous methods and allows you to easily create new Windows Store apps. All of this while continuing to improve the Visual Studio development environment and associated tools to make our lives as developers easier.

At Microsoft's Professional Developer Conference (PDC) in 2008, one of the themes was "make the simple things easy and the difficult things possible." The .NET Framework achieved that with its first release, and each release after that continues to realize that goal.

The C# (pronounced "See Sharp") programming language was developed with the .NET Framework by Anders Hejlsberg, Scott Wiltamuth, and Peter Golde and was first available in July 2000. Having been written specifically for the .NET Framework, it is considered by many to be the canonical language of the .NET Framework. As a language, C# drew inspiration for its syntax and primary features from Delphi 5, C++, and Java 2. C# is a general-purpose, object-oriented, type-safe programming language used for writing applications of any type. Just as the

.NET Framework continues to evolve, C# also evolves to keep pace with the changes in the .NET Framework and to introduce new language features that continue to make the simple things easy and the difficult things possible.

Although there are more than 50 different programming languages supported by the .NET Framework, C# continues to be one of the most popular and modern general-purpose languages.

Audience and Organization

This book is targeted toward the non-.NET programmer who is venturing into .NET for the first time or an existing .NET programmer trying to learn C#. If you are first learning how to program, this book can help you on your way, but it isn't intended to be a beginning programming book. The book is designed with the purpose of getting you familiar with how things are done in C# and becoming productive as quickly as possible. I take a different approach in this book by using a more holistic view of the language. I chose this approach to give you the most complete understanding of the C# language by focusing on how the current language features enable you to solve problems.

This book is divided into five parts, each one focusing on a different aspect of the language. These parts progress from the simple fundamentals to more advanced topics, so I recommend reading them in order:

▶ Part I, "C# Fundamentals," teaches you about the .NET Framework, the object-oriented programming features of C#, the fundamentals of C# type system, and events. You are also introduced to Visual Studio by building a simple application and finally learn the basics of how to debug an application.

▶ Part II, "Programming in C#," teaches you the fundamentals of programming. You learn how to perform loops and work with strings, regular expressions, and collections. Then we move to more advanced topics, such as exception management and generics. Finally, we finish with anonymous functions (lambdas), query expressions (LINQ), and how to interact with dynamic languages.

▶ Part III, "Working with Data," shows how to interact with the file system and streams, create and query XML documents, and work with databases.

▶ Part IV, "Building an Application Using Visual Studio," starts with building a Windows desktop application using data binding and validation. Next, you learn how to build a Windows Store app, including asynchronous programming, using the async pattern. Finally, you learn how to build an application for the web.

▶ Part V, "Diving Deeper," introduces the advanced concepts of attribute programming, dynamic types, and language interoperability. Next, you learn the fundamentals of how the .NET Framework organizes memory, how the garbage collector works, and how the .NET Framework provides mechanisms for deterministic finalization. Finally, you learn how to use multiple threads and parallel processing.

Throughout the book, I use examples that show real-world problems and how to solve them using C# and the .NET Framework. In Part IV, we actually build some complete applications from scratch that draw on the skills you learned in the previous three parts.

Conventions Used in This Book

This book uses several design elements and conventions to help you prioritize and reference the information it contains.

New terms appear in **bold** for emphasis.

In addition, this book uses various typefaces to help you distinguish code from regular English. Code is presented in a `monospace` font. Placeholders—words or characters that represent the real words or characters you would type in code—appear in *`italic monospace`*. When you are asked to type or enter text, that text appears in **`bold monospace`**.

Some code statements presented in this book are too long to appear on a single line. In these cases, a line continuation character is used to indicate that the following line is a continuation of the current statement.

NOTE

Notes provide useful sidebar information that you can read immediately or circle back to without losing the flow of the topic at hand.

CAUTION

Cautions focus your attention on problems or side effects that can occur under certain situations.

TIP

Tips highlight information that can make your programming more effective.

Source Files

The source files referred to throughout the text can be found on the book's website, www.informit.com/title/9780672336843.

Closing Thoughts

The Microsoft .NET Framework and C# continue to be one of the most powerful yet elegant languages I've worked with and provide many exciting opportunities for developing the next "killer application." You won't be an expert in C# when you finish this book, but I hope you feel comfortable about creating applications in .NET and C#.

The .NET Framework and C#

Learning a new language is like learning to ride a bicycle or drive a car. You must learn the fundamentals first and build your confidence as you progress to more complex actions. When you understand the principles and have the confidence that you can accomplish your goal, suddenly that goal doesn't seem so far out of reach. By the end of this hour, you will have a basic understanding of the .NET Framework, its components and their relationship to each other, and the C# language.

The .NET Framework

The .NET Framework provides developers with the tools and technology to create and run next-generation applications and web services in a way that is language and platform independent. It has a rich class library that supports many common tasks and simplifies many difficult tasks, enabling you to focus your time more effectively on the problem at hand: solving the business needs in the most efficient manner possible. Code written for the .NET Framework is called **managed code**, whereas any other code is called **unmanaged code**.

Just as code written for the .NET Framework is called managed code, the resulting application is called a **managed application**. When a managed application runs, it automatically hosts the common language runtime it was built against. Not only does the .NET Framework provide a number of different runtime hosts, it also provides the tools necessary to write your own. Because of this capability, unmanaged applications such as Internet Information Services (IIS) and Microsoft SQL Server can host their own copy of the common language runtime, enabling them to take advantage of both managed and unmanaged features.

The .NET Framework is designed to do the following:

▶ Provide a runtime environment that simplifies software deployment and reduces the chances of version conflicts.

▶ Enable the safe execution of code.

▶ Use industry standards for all communication to enable integration with non-.NET code.

▶ Provide a consistent developer experience across all types of applications in a way that is language and platform independent.

▶ Provide a runtime environment that minimizes or eliminates the performance problems of scripted or interpreted languages.

To achieve these goals, the .NET Framework has four components.

The Common Language Runtime

The **common language runtime (CLR)** is the core of the .NET Framework and provides a unified type system and a managed runtime environment. Just as your heart provides the pumping action your body needs to function, the common language runtime provides the low-level core services your application needs to function and is said to manage your code. Together they form a foundation for developing and executing applications that are language and platform independent and help eliminate, or at least reduce, many common programming errors.

Common Type System

The unified type system, called the **common type system (CTS)**, enables all .NET languages to share the same type definitions, enabling those types to be manipulated in a consistent manner. This helps ensure correctly written applications by

▶ Removing the possibility that incompatible data can be assigned to a type

▶ Enabling every .NET language to have the same description of a type, regardless of what language was used to define that type

▶ Enforcing a consistent manner in which a language manipulates a type

GO TO ▶ We discuss types a bit later in this hour. **HOUR 3, "UNDERSTANDING C# TYPES,"** provides more detailed information.

Because the common type system specifies the definition of how types look and behave in a language-independent fashion, it must take into account differences in those languages. The common type system provides a minimum set of rules a .NET language (and, consequently, its compiler) must follow, called the **common language specification (CLS)**. This common definition also enables the idea of language integration, which enables you to use a type defined in another language as if it were defined natively in your language.

NOTE

Type Safety and the CTS

The common type system and common language specification form the foundation of the type safety found in the .NET Framework.

This foundation provides the .NET Framework a consistent way to promote type safety but not enforce it. The task of enforcing type safety is left to the individual language compilers and the virtual execution system (which you learn about a bit later in this hour).

Common Intermediate Language

The common type system and common language specification help meet the goal of being language and platform independent, but it does no good if the compiler generates executable object code tied to the hardware platform. To resolve this problem, managed code is partially compiled into a low-level language called **common intermediate language (CIL)**. You can think of common intermediate language like assembly language; it is made up of individual, low-level instructions that represent your code.

An **assembly** is a partially compiled unit, or package, that contains CIL instructions and provides a logical boundary for defining types. Because assemblies are partially compiled, they can be either 32- or 64-bit, depending on the operating system and hardware. This capability truly means that managed applications are platform independent and, at the same time, can take advantage of hardware technology without recompiling or adding special instructions to your code.

TIP

CLS Compliance

Almost all the classes provided by the framework class library are CLS compliant, so any .NET language will have access to the same library. If you are developing your own library, it is suggested that you also ensure that your classes are CLS compliant to allow for the widest adoption and use possible.

Virtual Execution System

The other important part of the common language runtime is the managed runtime environment, called the **virtual execution system (VES)**, which handles the low-level core services your application needs. Just as Java applications require the Java virtual machine (JVM) to run, a managed application requires the CLR and, more specifically, the VES to run.

When a .NET application starts, it is the VES that is responsible for actually loading the CIL code, executing that code, and, ultimately, managing the memory allocations required by the application. In other words, the VES provides the services and infrastructure to abstract both platform and language differences.

As part of the loading and compilation process, the VES performs various validation and verification checks to ensure that the file format, assembly metadata, and CIL are consistent and that the CIL instructions themselves do not allow illegal memory access. This ensures that an application can access only memory or other resources to which it has been explicitly granted access. This restricted environment can be thought of as a **sandbox**.

If the VES provides a runtime environment and executes assemblies containing CIL, are those assemblies interpreted or compiled? Remember, one of the goals for the .NET Framework is to provide a runtime environment that minimizes or eliminates the performance problems of scripted or interpreted languages. This would imply that the CIL code is compiled, but when does that compilation happen?

One of the services the VES provides is the **Just-In-Time (JIT) compiler**. Just-In-Time compilation is the process of taking the partially compiled CIL code and generating executable object code, or native code, at runtime.

TIP
___

Just-In-Time Compilation

The process of Just-In-Time compilation is called **jitting** and the JIT compiler is also called the **jitter**.
___

By compiling the code in this manner, the .NET Framework gains a considerable speed improvement over traditional interpreted languages. Just-In-Time compilation also has benefits over regular (static) compilation, as it can enforce security guarantees at runtime and recompile the code at runtime to gain additional optimizations. The .NET Framework JIT compiler is highly optimized for compiling CIL code into highly efficient object code, runs on demand, and caches the compiled code for future use.

Memory Management and Garbage Collection

Proper memory management is a classic problem in many unmanaged programming languages and is a potential source for some common errors. In these languages, the developer is responsible for allocating and deallocating memory at the correct times. The .NET Framework resolves this problem by controlling these memory allocations and deallocations automatically as part of the VES.

It is this automatic memory management, also known as **garbage collection**, which makes C# (and the other .NET languages) a **garbage-collected language**. Garbage collection frees you from having to worry as much about releasing memory when it is no longer needed. This enables you to create applications that are more stable by preventing many of those common programming errors and focusing your time on the business logic your application requires.

Even with automatic memory management, it is still important to understand how the garbage collector interacts with your program and the types you create. An in-depth discussion on garbage collection is well outside the scope of this book, but we talk a little bit more about it in Hour 23, "Memory Organization and Garbage Collection."

Framework Class Library

Although the CLR forms the core of the .NET Framework, the **framework class library (FCL)** actually gives it substance. The class library is similar to Java's class libraries, the C++ Standard Template Library (STL), Microsoft's Active Template Library (ATL), the Microsoft Foundation Classes (MFC), Borland's Object Windows Library (OWL), or any of the various other class libraries available today.

Just like those class libraries, the FCL is a rich collection of reusable classes, or types, enabling you to achieve a high level of developer productivity by simplifying many common programming tasks.

NOTE

Framework Class Library

The framework class library contains more than 4,000 public classes and is one of the largest class libraries available today. It is the best example in the .NET Framework of making the simple things easy and the hard things possible.

Although it is possible to create an application without using the types provided by the FCL, it is impractical to do so.

Figure 1.1 shows some of the types available in the FCL, grouped by functional area.

At the lowest level are the **base class libraries (BCL)** that serve as the standard runtime for any .NET language and provide types that represent the intrinsic CLR types, collections, streams, string manipulation, basic file access, and a variety of other operations or data structures. The remaining classes in the FCL are focused on specific functional areas, such as providing data access, extensible markup language (XML) support, globalization support, diagnostics, configuration, networking, communication, business workflow support, web applications, and Windows desktop applications, to name just a few.

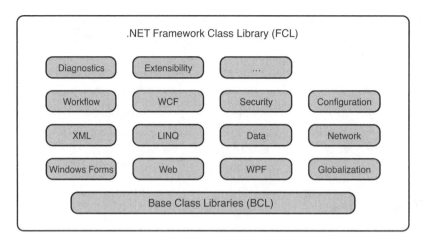

FIGURE 1.1
Framework class library.

Namespaces

With thousands of classes in the .NET Framework class library, there needs to be a way to prevent ambiguity between type names and to provide a convenient hierarchical grouping mechanism. The .NET Framework uses the concept of **namespaces** to accomplish this. A namespace is simply a collection of types and has no effect on the accessibility of a type. Namespaces can be split across multiple assemblies. The .NET Framework uses the hierarchical nature of namespaces to provide a progressive framework, creating a powerful and easy-to-use development platform.

NOTE

Namespaces and Type Names

Namespaces use a dotted syntax to denote a hierarchical grouping, with each level in the hierarchy separated by a dot (.).

Given a type's full name, everything up to the rightmost dot is the namespace, whereas the last part (after the rightmost dot) is the type name. For example, `System.Printing.PrintDriver` is the full name for the `PrintDriver` type in the `System.Printing` namespace.

Namespaces, however, are only conveniences supported by the .NET programming languages. In the CLR, a type is always identified by its full name, which contains both the name of the type and its containing namespace.

Almost 400 namespaces exist in the .NET Framework class library, although you will probably never interact with some of them. As you become more familiar with the class library, you will find certain namespaces that you use more frequently than others, which might be a different set than ones your co-workers or peers use.

Some of the commonly used namespaces are shown in Table 1.1.

TABLE 1.1   Commonly Used Namespaces

Namespace	Description
System	The base, or root, namespace for .NET; contains classes that define the commonly used data types, exceptions, and events
System.Collections.Generic	Contains classes that define various generic collections, enabling you to create strongly typed collections
System.Data	Contains classes that form the majority of the ADO.NET library, enabling you to manage data from multiple data sources
System.Diagnostics	Contains classes that enable you to interact with event logs and performance counters, debug your application, and trace the execution of your code
System.Globalization	Contains classes that represent culture-related information, including the language, country/region, calendars in use, sort order for strings, and format patterns for dates, currency, and numbers
System.IO	Contains classes that enable synchronous and asynchronous reading and writing on data streams and files
System.Linq	Contains classes and interfaces that support queries using Language Integrated Query (LINQ)
System.Net	Contains classes that provide a simple programming interface for many of the protocols used on networks today
System.Security	Contains classes that provide the .NET Framework security system
System.ServiceModel	Contains classes necessary to build Windows Communication Foundation (WCF) services and client applications
System.Text	Contains classes for working with strings and characters
System.Web	Contains classes that enable browser-server communication
System.Windows	Contains several important Windows Presentation Foundation (WPF) base element classes, various classes that support the WPF property system and event logic, and other types more broadly consumed by WPF

Namespace	Description
System.Windows.Controls	Contains classes to create controls that enable a user to interact with an application
System.Windows.Forms	Contains classes for creating Windows-based applications that take full advantage of the rich user interface features available in the Windows operating system
System.Xml	Contains classes that provide standards-based support for processing XML

Parallel Computing Platform

Writing multithreaded and asynchronous applications has always been possible in both managed and unmanaged code; however, it has also been difficult to get correct. The .NET Framework simplifies writing these applications with the **parallel computing platform**, which is a programming model for both managed and unmanaged code that raises the level of abstraction so you no longer need to worry as much about the lower-level concepts, such as threads and locks.

For managed code, the parallel computing platform includes parallel implementations of the common loop instructions, a parallel implementation of LINQ to Objects, and new lock-free and thread-safe collections. Visual Studio also includes diagnostic tools, such as the parallel concurrency analyzer and processor migration analysis that enable you to easily debug and tune your code.

The parallel computing platform simplifies the mechanics of writing code that can effectively take advantage of multiple processors. The decision of what code is right for parallelism still requires analysis and, ultimately, changing the way you think about how to solve a particular problem. We touch on some of these aspects of the parallel computing platform in Hour 24, "Understanding Threads, Concurrency, and Parallelism."

GO TO ▶ HOUR 24, "UNDERSTANDING THREADS, CONCURRENCY, AND PARALLELISM," for more information on multithreaded and parallel programming.

Dynamic Language Runtime

The **dynamic language runtime (DLR)** is an additional runtime environment providing language services and support for dynamic languages. Being built on top of the common language runtime means these dynamic languages can now integrate with other .NET languages. The DLR also enables dynamic features for existing statically typed languages such as C#, enabling them to support consistent expressions when working with dynamic objects from any source.

With the inclusion of the DLR, the support for dynamic languages, and enabling dynamic features in static languages, developers are now free to choose the best language possible to solve the task and be certain that other developers and other .NET languages can easily use the dynamic code they create.

GO TO ▶ HOUR 22, "DYNAMIC TYPES AND LANGUAGE INTEROPERABILITY," for more detailed coverage on integrating with dynamic languages.

TIP

What Is a Dynamic Language?

In a language such as C#, which is statically typed, the compiler attempts to prove type safety, and, if it cannot, generates an error. In a dynamic language, this attempt at proving type safety is not made. In addition, most dynamic languages perform more complex type operations, such as determining the correct method overload, at runtime, whereas C# performs this type of resolution at compile time.

In effect, what would normally be done at compile time in a statically typed language is done at runtime. This includes the idea that you can generate code at runtime (using what is commonly called an `eval` or `repl` loop) that can modify the state of running objects. As a result, dynamic languages enable a great deal of freedom and are most frequently used as scripting languages.

Some common dynamic languages are JScript, JavaScript, Python, and Ruby.

The C# Language

If you are a C, C++, or Java programmer, C# will be immediately familiar because it shares a similar syntax. If you are already familiar with Visual Basic (any version of Visual Basic that runs on the .NET Framework, not Visual Basic 6.0 or earlier), the syntax might seem foreign but the framework class library will be familiar. For those of you who have never worked in any of these languages, you will soon find that developing with C# is easier than many other languages due to the elegant syntax and rich class library.

TIP

Language Inspiration

As a language, C# has drawn inspiration for its syntax and primary features from a number of different languages, including Delphi 5, C++, and Java 2.

The generic type system (which you learn more about in Hour 12, "Understanding Generics") drew from the generic type systems in Eiffel and Ada. Haskell and Lisp were the primary inspirations for query comprehensions in LINQ and lambda expression evaluation (see Hour 13, "Understanding Query Expressions").

C# also added features found in dynamic languages such as Ruby and functional languages like F#.

Like many modern programming languages, C# is an **object-oriented language** and fully supports the object-oriented programming concepts of inheritance, polymorphism, encapsulation, and abstraction. In addition to being an object-oriented language, C# also supports **component-oriented programming**, which enables you to specify units of functionality (components) that are self-contained and self-documenting by presenting a model with properties, methods, events, and metadata about the component. C# has support for these concepts directly in the language, making it a natural process to create and use components.

GO TO ▶ **HOUR 4, "UNDERSTANDING CLASSES AND OBJECTS THE C# WAY,"** for more information on object- and component-oriented programming.

C# has language features enabling developers to take advantage of the advances and improvements made in the CLR. Garbage collection automatically manages memory. **Exception handling** creates a structured and extensible way to detect and recover from errors. As a **type-safe language**, it is impossible to have uninitialized variables, illegally access memory, or store data of one type in a location that can accept only a different type.

GO TO ▶ **HOUR 11, "HANDLING ERRORS USING EXCEPTIONS,"** for more information on exception handling.

In addition, C# also has language features and syntax designed to reduce the amount of boilerplate code you must write, making your code less complex and reducing the chance for making common errors. In some cases, these are nothing more than simple changes in syntax, simplifying complex or error-prone language features, and are readily accessible and easily understood; in other cases, these improvements enable scenarios that are more advanced.

C# continues to evolve with each new release, adding new language features and syntax, always striving to achieve the goal of making the simple things easy, the difficult things possible, and the bad things difficult. As C# adds new capabilities, the simple things become easier, the difficult things become easy, and the things not previously possible become possible.

Types

In C#, **types** describe values. Any time you want to use a value, you need a type. As you saw when you learned about the common type system, a type defines the allowed values and operations supported by those values. Every value in C# is fully described by its exact type and is an **instance** of that exact type. Being fully described means that the type unambiguously defines both the representation of and operations on a value.

Types in C# are divided into value types and reference types. **Value types** describe values that are completely self-contained and include numeric types, enumerated types, and structures. **Reference types**, however, store a reference to a value rather than the actual value.

GO TO ▶ **HOUR 3, "UNDERSTANDING C# TYPES,"** for a more in-depth look at the difference between value and reference types.

C# provides many predefined value types and a few predefined reference types. It also enables you to create your own user-defined types. In upcoming hours, you explore, in more detail, the difference between value types and reference types and how to create your own. For now, however, the most important difference is that a value type is copied "by value" because it contains the actual value, whereas a reference type contains a reference to the actual data.

Statements and Expressions

A **statement** is simply a single, complete program instruction that must end with a semicolon (;). Only specifying a single instruction seems like it would be restrictive, but C# also gives us the idea of a **statement block**, which is simply a group of statements enclosed by "curly" braces ({ and }) . You can use a statement block anywhere you would normally use a single statement.

Because statements end with a semicolon, you are free to use whitespace (such as a space character, tab character, or newline) in a way that helps visually orient your code. The best approach is to adopt a simple and consistent style (if your company or team does not already have one) to make your code easier to read and maintain.

CAUTION

Whitespace

Even though the compiler generally ignores whitespace, the whitespace between a type declaration, its identifier, and any other keywords is important. Without whitespace here, the compiler can't distinguish the keywords.

An **expression** evaluates to a value. If you consider a statement to be a program action, an expression is a computation. Expressions that result in a Boolean value (either `true` or `false`) are most commonly used to test if one or more conditions are true and are called **Boolean expressions**.

Variables and Constants

The simplest definition for a **variable** is that it represents a storage location whose value can change over time. The most common forms of variables are local variables and fields, both of which are defined by providing a type, an identifier, and, optionally, an initial value:

```
int a;
int b = 1;
```

If you are declaring multiple variables of the same type, you can combine the declarations, as follows:

```
int a, b;
```

When a variable is declared inside of a limited scope (such as a method), it is said to be a **local variable** and is accessible by name only from within that scope.

NOTE

Scope, Declaration Space, and Lifetime

Scope can be thought of as a container in which it is legal to refer to a variable by its unqualified name. This is different from the declaration space, in which no two identifiers are allowed to have the same name. If scope defines where you can use a name, declaration space answers where that name is unique.

The lifetime of a variable is closely connected to its scope and defines how long the variable will be accessible. A variable is guaranteed to be alive at least as long as its scope is executing.

You learn about scope and declaration space in more detail in Hour 4.

A **field** is simply a variable that is not declared inside of a limited scope and can be associated with either the type itself, in which case it is a **static variable** (which you can think of as the equivalent to a global variable), or with an instance of the type, in which case it is an **instance variable**. Local variables and fields must be initialized before they are used and are accessible only while the block containing their declaration is executing.

The code in Listing 1.1 shows a Color type that has private instance fields named red, blue, and green and public static fields named White, Red, Blue, and Green.

LISTING 1.1   A Color Class

```
class Color
{
   private byte red;
   private byte blue;
   private byte green;

   public Color(byte red, byte blue, byte green)
   {
      this.red = red;
      this.blue = blue;
      this.green = green;
   }
```

```
    public static Color White = new Color(0xFF, 0xFF, 0xFF);
    public static Color Red = new Color(0xFF, 0, 0);
    public static Color Blue = new Color(0, 0xFF, 0);
    public static Color Green = new Color(0, 0, 0xFF);
}
```

The static fields are initialized at some point before they are used, but afterward, there is nothing to prevent them from being changed. To accommodate the idea of declaring a field that cannot be changed after it has been assigned, C# enables you to create read-only fields.

Listing 1.2 shows the changed lines of the Color class.

LISTING 1.2   A Color Class Using Read-Only Fields

```
class Color
{
    // ...

    public static readonly Color White = new Color(0xFF, 0xFF, 0xFF);
    public static readonly Color Red = new Color(0xFF, 0, 0);
    public static readonly Color Blue = new Color(0, 0xFF, 0);
    public static readonly Color Green = new Color(0, 0, 0xFF);
}
```

GO TO ▶ **HOUR 4, "UNDERSTANDING CLASSES AND OBJECTS THE C# WAY,"** for more information on read-only fields.

TIP

Literal Values and "Magic Numbers"

Literal values are generally numeric values that have special fixed meanings specified directly in code. Over time, the meaning of these literal values can be lost, making that part of the code difficult to maintain. As a result, these literals are often called "magic numbers." By using constants instead of literal values, the meaning is preserved, making the code self-documenting.

How long would it take you to figure out what the number means in the following function?

```
static float Compute(float f1)
{
    return 299792458 / f1;
}
```

Now, if that same function were written using a constant, the meaning of that "magic number" becomes clear:

```
static float Compute(float f1)
{
    const float SpeedOfLight = 299792458;

    return SpeedOfLight / f1;
}
```

In our example, the value 299792458 is a literal value and would therefore be considered a magic number. As you might have guessed, constants are preferred over using just literal values because they have names that can provide more meaning than just a number, and you can guarantee that its value has not changed.

A **constant** represents a value that can be computed at compile time. Constants are associated with the type itself, as if they were static. Like variables, constants can be declared inside of a limited scope or globally. Unlike variables, a constant must always be initialized when it is declared.

A statement that declares a variable or a constant is generally called a **declaration statement** and can appear anywhere within a block.

Identifiers and Keywords

When you declare a variable, field, or constant, you must provide both the data type and a meaningful name called an **identifier**.

Identifiers must follow these rules:

▶ Only letters (uppercase and lowercase), digits, and the underscore character are valid.

▶ An identifier must begin with a letter or the underscore character, although using an underscore (or multiple underscores) as the beginning character for any publicly accessible identifier is considered poor style and should be avoided.

▶ Identifiers must be unique within a given declaration space.

▶ Identifiers are case sensitive.

You should follow these additional guidelines when choosing identifiers:

▶ Identifiers should be easily readable.

▶ Identifiers should not use abbreviations or contractions as part of the name.

▶ Identifiers should convey the meaning or intent as much as possible.

In C#, identifiers are case sensitive. The recommended naming conventions suggest using **camel casing notation**, which capitalizes the first letter of each word except the first word (for example, `bookTitle`) for variable and parameter names and **Pascal casing notation**, which capitalizes the first letter of each word (for example, `BookTitle`) for methods and other identifiers.

TIP

Camel and Pascal Casing

Camel casing is so named because the sequence of letters looks like the humps on a camel's back. Pascal casing was named after the style popularized by the Pascal programming language (and because Anders was the original designer of the Turbo Pascal language).

Microsoft no longer recommends using Hungarian notation or using the underscore character to separate words, both common in other languages.

If you are already familiar with another case-sensitive language, such as C, C++, or Java, this should feel normal to you. However, if you are coming from a language that is not case sensitive, such as Visual Basic, this might take a bit of practice. Fortunately, the Visual Studio 2012 code editor has features that can help make that transition easier.

Because identifiers define the names of specific elements, it is reasonable that the C# language also needs to use identifiers to indicate special meaning to the compiler (and to you). As a result, there are certain identifiers, called **keywords**, which have been reserved for use by the language itself.

There are 77 keywords in C# that are reserved at all times; these are listed in Table 1.2.

TABLE 1.2   C# Keywords

abstract	as	base	bool	break
byte	case	catch	char	checked
class	const	continue	decimal	default
delegate	do	double	else	enum
event	explicit	extern	false	finally
fixed	float	for	foreach	goto
if	implicit	in	int	interface
internal	is	lock	long	namespace
new	null	object	operator	out
override	params	private	protected	public
readonly	ref	return	sbyte	sealed

short	sizeof	stackalloc	static	string
struct	switch	this	throw	true
try	typeof	uint	ulong	unchecked
unsafe	ushort	using	virtual	void
volatile	while			

An additional 26 keywords, known as **contextual keywords**, have special meaning only in limited circumstances, or context. Outside of that context, these keywords can be for your own purposes, although to minimize confusion, you should try to avoid doing so, if possible. The contextual keywords are listed in Table 1.3.

TABLE 1.3   C# Contextual Keywords

add	alias	ascending	async	await
by	descending	dynamic	equals	from
get	global	group	into	join
let	on	orderby	partial	remove
select	set	value	var	where
yield				

Summary

At the beginning of the hour, you looked at the .NET Framework and the components that are part of it. This might have been a little more in-depth than what you were expecting for the first hour, but having at least a basic understanding of why the .NET Framework was created and how it is put together is essential to becoming a well-rounded and successful .NET programmer. From those beginnings, you learned about the C# language and were introduced to statements, expressions, variables, constants, identifiers, and keywords.

Throughout the rest of this book, each hour builds upon what you learn from the previous hours and progresses from learning the fundamentals of C# and how it provides support for both object-oriented and component-oriented programming, all the way to learning about more advanced topics such as multithreading and parallel programming. Along the way, you build a more complete real-world application, from "soup to nuts" as the saying goes, and you build a solid foundation in C# and .NET programming on which you can build larger and more complex applications.

Q&A

Q. What is the .NET Framework?

A. The .NET Framework is a platform enabling developers to create and run next-generation applications and web services in a way that is language and platform independent and helps eliminate, or at least reduce, many common programming errors.

Q. What is the common language runtime (CLR)?

A. The common language runtime (CLR) is the core of the .NET Framework upon which C# runs.

Q. What is the difference between a managed application and an unmanaged application?

A. Code written for the .NET Framework is called managed code, whereas any other code is called unmanaged code.

Q. What is meant by garbage collection and why is it important?

A. Garbage collection is a runtime service provided by the .NET Framework that frees you from having to handle memory allocation and deallocation manually. This enables you to create more stable applications by preventing many of those common programming errors and enables you to focus your time on the business logic your application requires.

Q. What is C#?

A. C# is an object-oriented, type-safe programming language that runs on the .NET Framework.

Q. Are C# programs compiled?

A. Yes, C# programs are compiled at development time to common intermediate language (CIL). At runtime, they are compiled to executable object code by the Just-In-Time (JIT) compiler.

Workshop

Quiz

1. What are the components of the .NET Framework?

2. Why is the common type system important?

3. What is common intermediate language (CIL)?

4. Why is the framework class library important?

5. What does the dynamic language runtime (DLR) provide to C#?

6. Is the following code valid in C#?

```
class Program
{
    static void Main()
    {
        const int LettersInEnglishAlphabet = 26

        system.console.WriteLine(
            "There are {0} letters in the English alphabet.",
            LettersInEnglishAlphabet)
    }
}
```

7. What is the correct interpretation of the following variable declarations?

```
int a, b = 1;
```

8. Which of the following is *not* a valid identifier?

    A. lightHouse

    B. _lighthouse

    C. 22lighthouse

    D. lighthouse2

Answers

1. The .NET Framework has four major components: the common language runtime, framework class library, parallel computing platform, and dynamic language runtime.

2. The common type system is important because it gives every .NET language the same description of a type and defines how that type can be used, which enables language integration.

3. Common intermediate language is the low-level language into which managed code is partially compiled. You can think of common intermediate language like assembly language; it is made up of individual, low-level instructions that represent your code.

4. The framework class library provides a rich set of reusable types available to all .NET languages and enables you to achieve a high level of developer productivity by simplifying many common programming tasks.

5. The DLR enables C# to work with dynamic objects from any source (COM, IronRuby, IronPython, and JavaScript, to name a few) using a consistent syntax.

6. No, the code shown is not valid C# for two reasons. First, none of the statements end in a semicolon (;). Second, the correct type name is `System.Console.WriteLine` not `system.console.WriteLine` because C# is a case-sensitive language.

7. Combining multiple variable declarations and initial value assignments like this is dangerous because it can be ambiguous. The correct interpretation of this statement is equivalent to the following:

```
int a;
int b = 1;
```

8. The correct answer is C. Identifiers cannot start with a number.

Exercises

There are no exercises for this hour.

Introducing Visual Studio

What You'll Learn in This Hour:

▶ Introducing the Visual Studio editions
▶ Writing your first program
▶ Debugging in Visual Studio
▶ Visualizing data
▶ Commenting your code

Visual Studio is a complete **Integrated Development Environment (IDE)** that is actually made up of many different tools designed with one goal: enabling you to create innovative, next-generation applications. At its heart, Visual Studio includes a powerful code editor, language compilers (including support for Visual Basic, C#, C++, and F#), and debugging tools.

Visual Studio also includes much more than that:

▶ Integration with source control systems

▶ Graphical design tools

▶ Tools for Microsoft Office, SharePoint, and cloud development

▶ Testing tools

Although it is entirely possible to write applications using your favorite text editor and the command-line utilities that are part of the .NET Framework software developer kit (SDK), it is not practical to do so. The benefits of the integration of the editing and debugging tools, combined with the productivity enhancements provided by Visual Studio, enable you to easily and effectively write and debug your applications.

In this hour, you are introduced to Visual Studio by writing your first .NET application. You then learn the basics of working with the Visual Studio debugger and how it can be used to help you locate and correct application flaws, or bugs.

Introducing the Visual Studio Editions

Microsoft offers several editions of Visual Studio, some of which must be purchased and some of which are free. You may have one of the Visual Studio products, such as the following:

▶ Ultimate with MSDN

▶ Premium with MSDN

▶ Professional with MSDN

▶ Professional (without MSDN)

▶ Express for Web

▶ Express for Windows 8

▶ Express for Windows Desktop

The Express editions are free and targeted at web, Windows Store apps, and more traditional Windows desktop development. The other four editions are designed for use in a corporate development setting and offer additional features and capabilities.

Throughout this book, most of the examples and screen images are from Express for Windows Desktop (except those in Hour 19, "Building Windows Store Apps," which uses Express for Windows 8). If you run one of the other Visual Studio editions, the screen images may look different.

When Visual Studio starts, you see the Start Page, shown in Figure 2.1, which enables you to access recent projects, create new projects, learn about upcoming product releases, or read the latest development news.

The Start Page is divided into the following sections:

▶ The command section, which shows the New Project and Open Project commands. This section can also show the Connect to Team Foundation Server command, if you have installed one of the Visual Studio with MSDN editions.

▶ The Recent Projects list, which shows the most recently opened projects. Clicking one of the projects opens it in Visual Studio. It is also possible to pin a project, as shown in Figure 2.2, which keeps it in its current position after other projects are opened and closed.

▶ A tabbed content area. The Get Started tab displays a list of Help topics and other resources that can help you learn about the features of Visual Studio. The Latest News tab lists featured articles from the selected RSS feed.

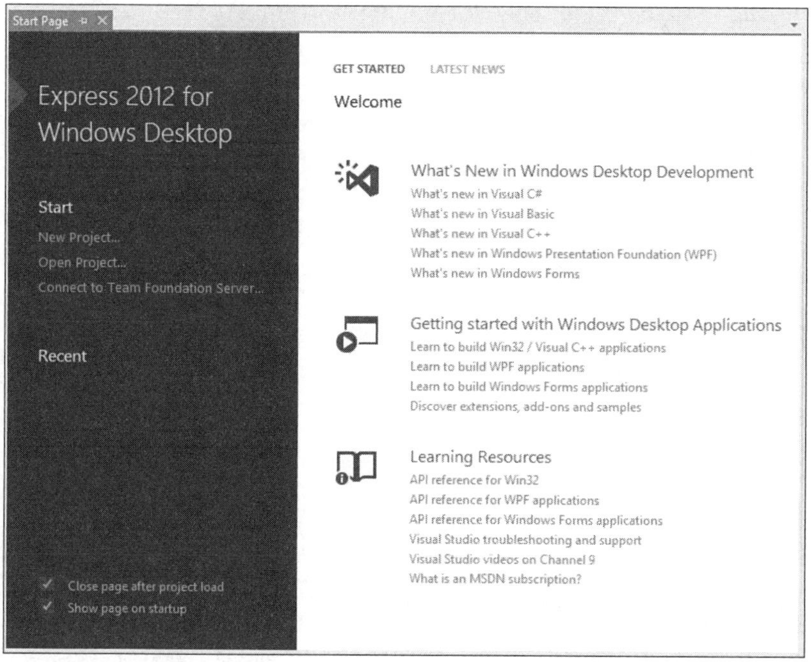

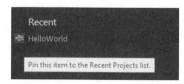

FIGURE 2.1
Express 2012 Start Page.

FIGURE 2.2
Pinning recent projects.

Solutions, Projects, and Items

Visual Studio uses two concepts to help you organize and interact with your source code files called solutions and projects.

A **project** is a collection of source files and related metadata that produce a single assembly when compiled. A **solution** includes one or more projects plus additional files and metadata that define the solution as a whole. Whenever you create a new project, Visual Studio automatically creates a solution for you. When necessary, you can add additional projects to that solution. A project can belong to multiple solutions, and complex applications can require more than one solution.

The Solution Explorer, shown in Figure 2.3, displays the solution, the project (or projects) contained in that solution, and the items for each project, enabling you to easily view and manage these containers and their associated items.

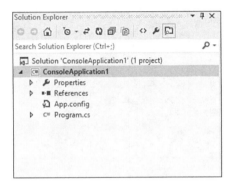

FIGURE 2.3
Solution Explorer.

Most of the time, you interact with the Solution Explorer by double-clicking a project item, such as a code file, to display it in an editor window or through the context menu to add or remove items or projects.

Writing Your First Program

At this point, you should be familiar enough with the C# language and syntax to write your first program. If you haven't already installed Visual Studio, now is the time to do so. As your first introduction to C#, you will continue the tradition of starting with a simple application that displays the message "Hello, world" on the screen.

Creating a Project

Creating the project can be done using the New Project command on the Start Page, the New Project toolbar button, or the application menu. These three locations are shown in Figure 2.4. If you have one of the Visual Studio with MSDN editions installed, the location of the menu item and toolbar button may be slightly different.

This displays the New Project dialog box, shown in Figure 2.5, which enables you to specify the name and type of project.

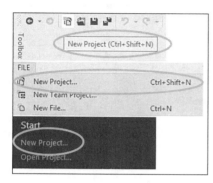

FIGURE 2.4
New Project commands.

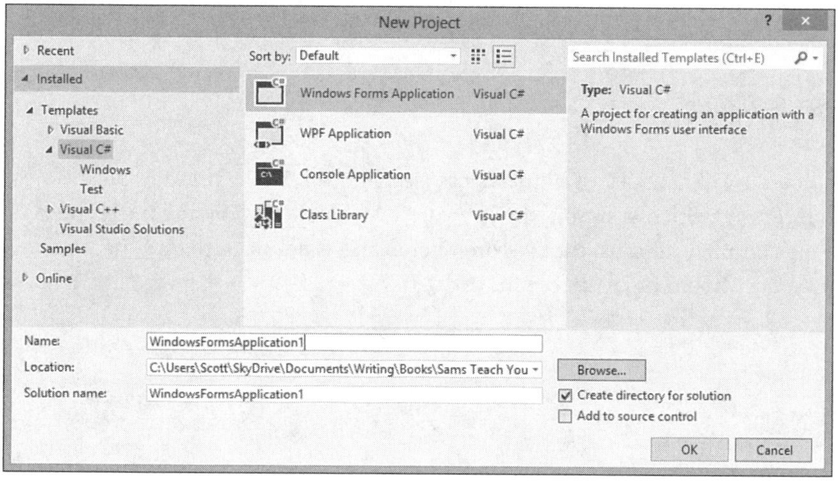

FIGURE 2.5
New Project dialog box.

For this first application, you will create a console application named `ConsoleHelloWorld`. After you select the project type and provide the name, you can click the OK button or double-click the project type. This closes the dialog box, creates the project, and displays the default code for that project, as shown in Figure 2.6.

As you can see, Visual Studio has already done some of the work for us and provided some starting code. Before we start adding our own code, let's examine the code Visual Studio generated for us.

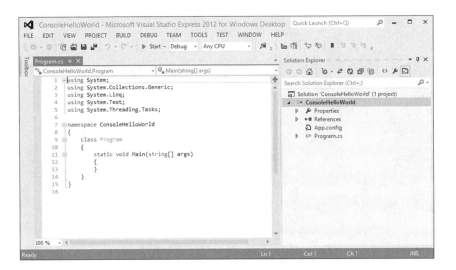

FIGURE 2.6
Default code for a console application.

At the top of the file (lines 1 to 5) is a list of namespaces (see Figure 2.7). Each namespace is included by a `using` directive, which is simply the keyword `using` followed by the namespace. `Using` directives tell the compiler, and us, that we are referencing a namespace and the types declared in that namespace should be available for use.

```
1  using System;
2  using System.Collections.Generic;
3  using System.Linq;
4  using System.Text;
5  using System.Threading.Tasks;
```

FIGURE 2.7
`Using` directives.

Just below the `using` directives (see Figure 2.8), you declare a namespace named ConsoleHelloWorld (line 7) and a class named Program (line 9). Inside this class, we have defined a static function named Main (line 11). You learn about classes and methods in more detail in Hour 4, "Understanding Classes and Objects the C# Way," but for now, think of them as a container whose boundaries are defined by the opening and closing braces.

Adding Program Statements

Now, you can focus on what we need this application to do. Because you are working in a console application, you need a way to interact with the console window that runs our application.

By examining the framework class library, you will find a class named `Console`, which provides methods for displaying messages and receiving user input through the keyboard.

```
 7 ⊟namespace ConsoleHelloWorld
 8  {
 9 ⊟    class Program
10      {
11 ⊟        static void Main(string[] args)
12          {
13          }
14      }
15  }
```

FIGURE 2.8
Default `Program.cs` contents.

To display text in the console window, you need to enter the following statement between the braces that define `Main` (lines 12 and 13):

```
Console.WriteLine("Hello, world");
```

Your file should now look like Figure 2.9.

```
11 ⊟        static void Main(string[] args)
12          {
13              Console.WriteLine("Hello, world");|
14          }
15      }
```

FIGURE 2.9
Adding `Console.WriteLine`.

You could have also written this line using the full type name, which is `System.Console`. It isn't necessary to do so because of the `using` directives included at the beginning of the file. Because these `using` directives tell the compiler that you want to use types declared in that namespace, you can use just the type name. If, however, there were two types with the same name in two included namespaces, the compiler cannot determine which one to use. In that case, you would still need to use the full type name.

At this point, you have a complete "Hello, world" application. Although this might seem like a trivial example, it only appears that way. Keep in mind that a Windows command prompt is not a managed application, so that single line in your C# program encapsulates all the necessary logic to interact with that unmanaged application and direct it to display the text you want. To the C# compiler, that seemingly innocuous line ultimately depends on dozens of types in about a dozen different namespaces, all provided by the framework class library.

Running the Application

If you haven't already done so, run your application by pressing Ctrl+F5. Visual Studio then saves your file (if you haven't already saved it), compiles it to an application named `ConsoleHelloWorld.exe`, and runs it.

NOTE

"Press Any Key to Continue..."

If you use the Start Debugging menu option, the Debug Target toolbar button, or F5, the application will run and then immediately exit. To prevent that from happening, you should use either Ctrl+F5 or the Start Without Debugging menu option, under the DEBUG menu.

When you run without debugging, Visual Studio automatically adds the message "Press any key to continue...". If you don't want to see that message or remember to use Ctrl+F5 each time, you could add the following as the last statement in the `Main` method:

```
Console.ReadLine();
```

This will cause the application to wait until the Enter key is pressed before continuing. Because this is the last line of the method, the application will simply exit.

If you entered everything correctly, you should see the message "Hello, world" in a command window, as shown in Figure 2.10.

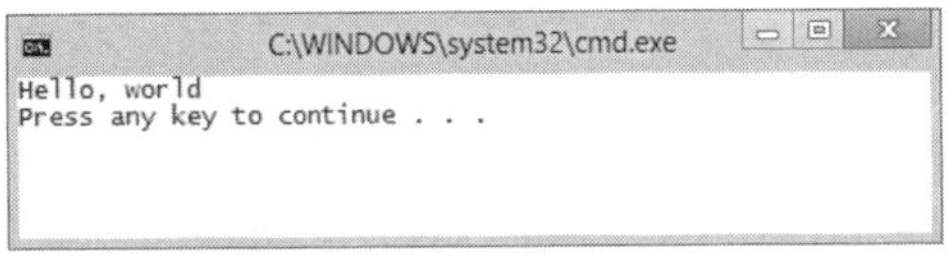

FIGURE 2.10
Hello, world.

Debugging in Visual Studio

The Visual Studio debugger is actually made up of a set of tools that enable you to inspect your application's internal state as it is running. Some of the tasks the debugger enables you to perform are as follows:

- ▶ Examining your code
- ▶ Controlling the execution of your application
- ▶ Evaluating and modifying variables
- ▶ Seeing the variable contents when an exception occurs

All of the debugging tools can be accessed through the Debug menu in Visual Studio, including the different debugger windows and dialog boxes that enable you to see and modify information about your application.

Compiler and Runtime Errors

Errors can occur at any time in your application, including when you write the code. These errors are compiler or build errors, and actually prevent the compiler from successfully compiling your code into an assembly. Runtime errors occur when your application is actually executing in the form of exceptions and are the errors the Visual Studio debugger enables you to locate and diagnose.

One of the basic rules for integer division is that you cannot divide a number by zero. If you attempt to do this at compile time, you see a compiler error, as shown in Figure 2.11.

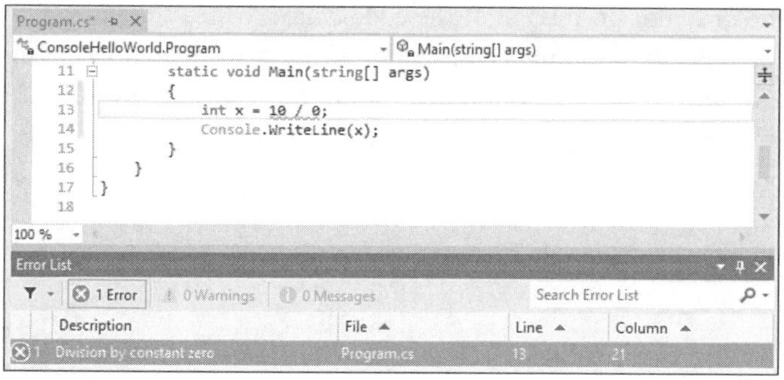

FIGURE 2.11
Compiler error shown in the error list.

To easily find the location of the compiler error, you can double-click the entry in the error list to go directly to that line in the code.

Most likely, this isn't actually what was intended. Instead, you want to divide by a user-provided divisor, as shown in Listing 2.1. This code retrieves a value provided by the user, converts it to an integer value, and then uses it as the divisor.

LISTING 2.1   Dividing Using a User-Provided Divisor

```
static void Main(string[] args)
{
    string input = Console.ReadLine();
    int divisor = Convert.ToInt32(input);
    int x = 10 / divisor;
    Console.WriteLine(x);
}
```

Although this code compiles and runs without any errors, what happens if the divisor entered is zero or, even worse, not numeric at all?

If you are running the application outside of Visual Studio, your application will crash with one of two possible unhandled exceptions:

- ▶ System.DivideByZeroException— Attempted to divide by zero
- ▶ System.FormatException— Input string was not in a correct format

Debugging Your Code

If you run the application inside Visual Studio, however, you get the ability to debug the application at the point the exception occurred, as shown in Figure 2.12.

The Visual Studio debugger suspended (commonly called breaking) program execution at the point the DivideByZeroException occurred. The line that contains the exception is highlighted, by default, in yellow, and the gray bar on the left of the code editor (called the margin) contains a yellow arrow indicating the execution point. The Exception Assistant, shown in detail in Figure 2.13, also appears and shows the type of exception, the exception message, troubleshooting tips, and corrective actions. In this case, the Exception Assistant indicates that you attempted to divide by zero and there are no corrective actions.

GO TO ▶ **HOUR 11, "HANDLING ERRORS USING EXCEPTIONS,"** for more information on exceptions.

NOTE

Breaking on Exceptions

Having your application break on all exceptions might not be the desired behavior during a debugging session. This behavior is configurable, allowing you to break only on certain exceptions, break only on unhandled exceptions, and a few other options.

You can access these settings through the Exceptions choice on the Debug menu.

If you are running Visual Studio Express, instead of the Exception Assistant, you will see an Exception dialog box, as shown in Figure 2.14.

In addition to the Exception Assistant, Visual Studio includes a number of tools that help you identify and eliminate program errors; the primary ones are as follows:

- ▶ Variable windows
- ▶ Breakpoints
- ▶ DataTips
- ▶ Execution control
- ▶ Immediate window

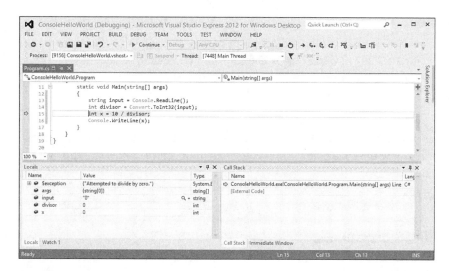

FIGURE 2.12
Visual Studio debugger breaking on an exception.

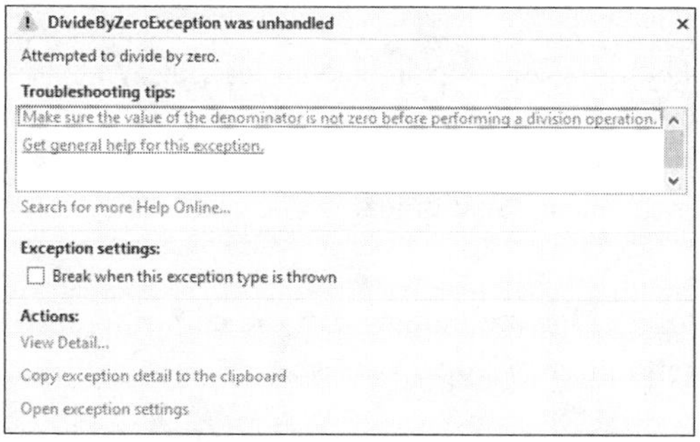

FIGURE 2.13
Exception Assistant.

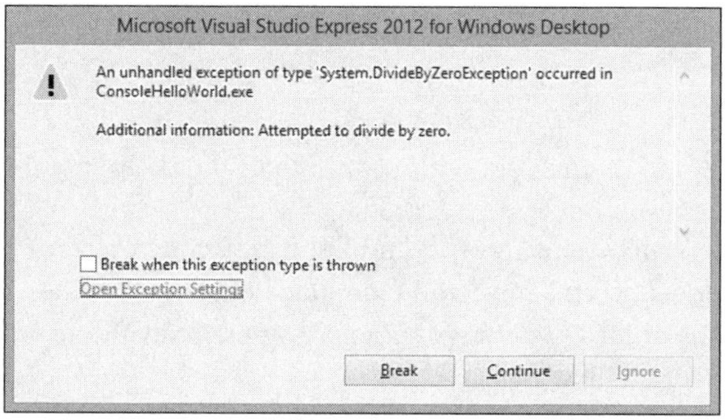

FIGURE 2.14
Exception dialog box.

Variable Windows

Variable windows display the name, value, and data type of variables while you debug. Although seeing the current value of a variable is helpful when you debug, modifying the value of a variable is even more helpful. Fortunately, the variable windows enable you to do just that. By double-clicking in the value column, or using the Edit Value context menu, you can edit the value of that variable.

Visual Studio Express provides two variable windows: the Locals window and the Watch window. These windows appear below the code editor while you debug and can be accessed using the Debug Windows menu.

CAUTION
_____

Visual Studio with MSDN Editions

If you are using one of the Visual Studio with MSDN editions, you have a few extra capabilities not found in the Visual Studio Express editions.

In addition to the Locals and Watch windows, you also have an Autos window, which displays variables used in the current and preceding line of code. Like the Locals window, the debugger also automatically populates the Autos window.

Although the Watch window allows you to examine many variables or expressions, the QuickWatch dialog box enables you to examine a single variable or expression at a time and is useful for quickly seeing a single value or large data structure.

You also have multiple Watch windows, four of them actually, instead of just one.
_____

The Locals window, shown in Figure 2.15, displays all the local variables that are currently in scope. When a value has been modified, it appears in red.

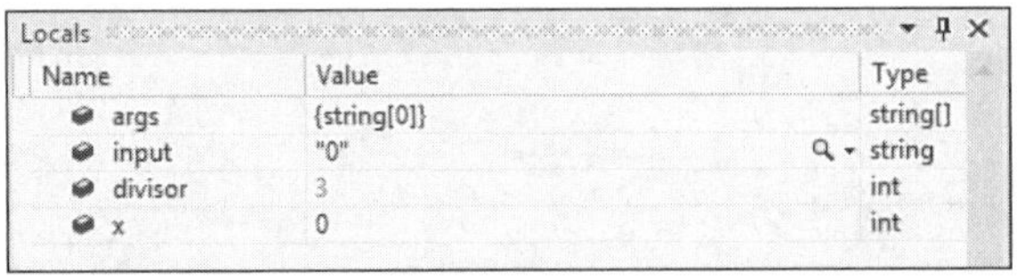

Locals		
Name	Value	Type
args	{string[0]}	string[]
input	"0"	string
divisor	3	int
x	0	int

FIGURE 2.15
Locals window.

The Watch window enables you to enter expressions directly. The simplest expression you can enter is a variable name; however, the debugger accepts most valid language expressions. The expression evaluator does not accept lambdas or LINQ query syntax expressions. To evaluate an expression in the Watch window, you can do the following:

▶ Click on the Name column in an empty row and enter the variable name or expression.

▶ Drag a variable or expression from the code editor to an empty row.

▶ Use the Add Watch context menu from the selected expression.

When an expression has been added to the Watch window, it remains there until you remove it. If the expression is no longer in scope, it displays in a disabled state.

When the Watch window displays a `dynamic` object, a special "Dynamic View" node is added that shows the members of the `dynamic` object but does not enable editing the values.

GO TO ▶ HOUR 22, "DYNAMIC TYPES AND LANGUAGE INTEROPERABILITY," for more information on dynamic types.

NOTE

Expressions with Side Effects

Expressions that change data are said to have side effects. When you enter such an expression into the Watch window, the side effect occurs each time the expression is evaluated by the Watch window. If you are not aware that the expression has side effects, this can lead to unexpected results.

When an expression is known to have side effects, it is evaluated only the first time you enter it. Subsequent evaluations are disabled; however, you can override this behavior by clicking the Update icon (which resembles two green arrows circling in opposite directions within a green circle) that appears next to the value.

Using DataTips

You can also view the current value using a DataTip, which is one of the more convenient ways for viewing information about variables and objects in your program while you are debugging. By placing the mouse pointer over the variable in a source editor while you debug, the DataTip displays, as shown in Figure 2.16. Just as you can in the Locals window, you can edit the value by clicking on the DataTip.

```
int divisor = Convert.ToInt32(input);
int x = 10 / divisor;
Console.WriteLine  divisor 0
```

FIGURE 2.16
DataTip.

By default, DataTips are transient and disappear when you move the mouse cursor away from the variable. DataTips can also be pinned, as shown in Figure 2.17, to a specific location in the source file by clicking the Pin to Source icon (the pushpin on the right side of the DataTip).

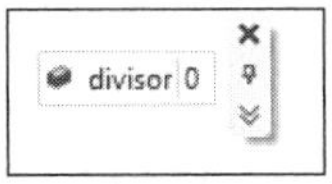

FIGURE 2.17
A pinned DataTip.

Although DataTips are visible only during a debugging session, pinned DataTips display a push-pin icon in the margin of the editor that you can place the mouse cursor over to view the value from the last debugging session, as shown in Figure 2.18.

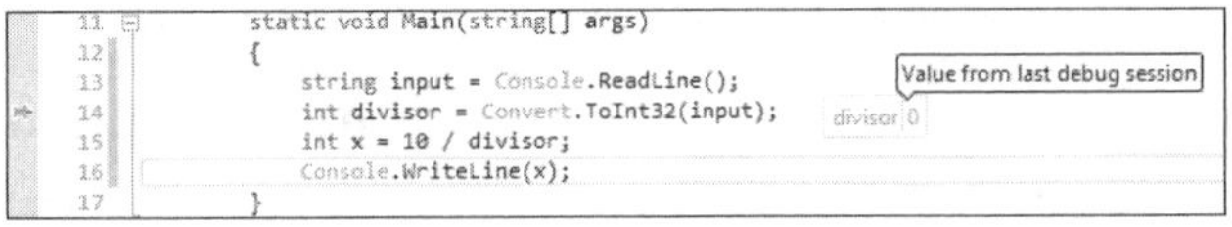

FIGURE 2.18
A pinned DataTip while editing.

By clicking the Unpin from Source icon, you can float the DataTip above any open windows. A pinned or floating DataTip will be visible in the same location for any subsequent debugging sessions, including after restarting Visual Studio.

TIP

Sharing DataTips

You can also export DataTips to an XML file to share with other developers working on the same project.

To export DataTips, click Export DataTips on the DEBUG menu, navigate to the location where you want to save the XML file, provide a name for the file, and click OK. To import DataTips, click Import DataTips on the DEBUG menu and select the appropriate XML file.

Using the Immediate Window

The Immediate window enables you to evaluate expressions, execute statements, print variable values, and many other actions. The Immediate window also supports specific Visual Studio commands in addition to allowing you to execute language statements.

For example, the commands to display the value of the divisor variable at the time the exception occurred are shown in Figure 2.19. You can use the Up and Down arrow keys to cycle through previously entered commands.

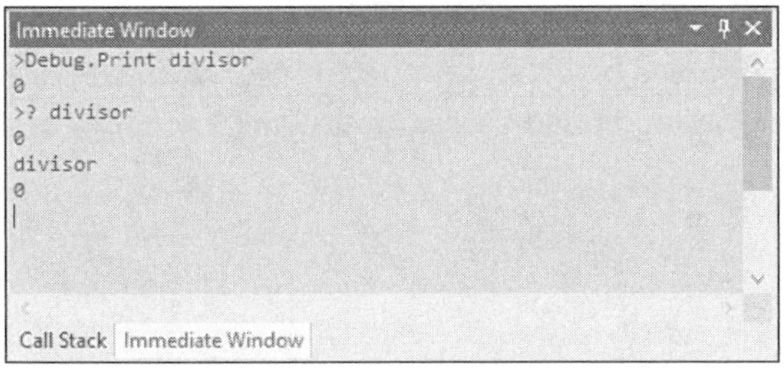

```
Immediate Window                              ▼ ⱷ ×
>Debug.Print divisor
0
>? divisor
0
divisor
0
|
```
Call Stack Immediate Window

FIGURE 2.19
Immediate window.

Understanding Breakpoints

When debugging an application using the Visual Studio debugger, your application is either executing (running) or in Break mode. Break mode occurs when the debugger breaks the program execution as the result of an exception, a user-defined breakpoint, or manually breaking the execution. Most of the debugger features are available only when your application is in Break mode.

To manually break the execution of your program, you can use Break All from the Debug menu. This causes the debugger to stop the execution of all programs running under the debugger.

As the name implies, a breakpoint tells the debugger that your application should break execution at a certain point. When a breakpoint is set, the line is shown in red by default, and a solid red circle displays in the editor margin, as shown in Figure 2.20.

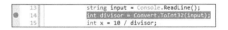

```
 13        string input = Console.ReadLine();
●14        int divisor = Convert.ToInt32(input);
 15        int x = 10 / divisor;
```

FIGURE 2.20
An enabled breakpoint.

There are multiple ways to set a breakpoint. To set a breakpoint on an entire line, you can click the margin next to the line of code, place the mouse cursor over the line of code and use the Insert Breakpoint context menu option, or place the caret (the text cursor represented by the vertical bar) in the line of code and press the F9 key.

After a breakpoint has been set, your application will break at that location every time it is run under a debugger. When you no longer want the breakpoint set, you can remove it by clicking the breakpoint symbol in the margin. You can also place the mouse cursor over the line of code containing the breakpoint and use the Delete Breakpoint context menu option, or place the caret (the text cursor represented by the vertical bar) in the line of code and press the F9 key.

Sometimes, however, you only want to disable a breakpoint. To do this, you can right-click the breakpoint symbol in the margin or place the mouse cursor over the line of code containing the breakpoint, and use the Disable Breakpoint context menu option. You can also place the caret in the line of code and press the Ctrl+F9 keys. A disabled breakpoint, shown in Figure 2.21, is displayed with a red outlined circle in the editor margin and a red border around the line containing the breakpoint.

```
13        string input = Console.ReadLine();
14        int divisor = Convert.ToInt32(input);
15        int x = 10 / divisor;
```

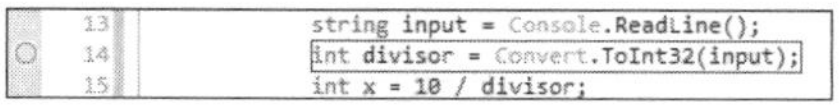

FIGURE 2.21
A disabled breakpoint.

To reenable a breakpoint, right-click the breakpoint symbol in the margin or place the mouse cursor over the line of code containing the breakpoint and use the Enable Breakpoint context menu option. You can also place the caret in the line of code and press the Ctrl+F9 keys.

NOTE

Extra Breakpoint Capabilities

If you use one of the paid Visual Studio editions, you have a few extra breakpoint capabilities not found in the Express editions.

The most apparent one is the ability to create a tracepoint. A tracepoint is a breakpoint, which, by default, does not break program execution but instead performs a custom action. Tracepoints are most commonly used for printing messages when your program reaches a certain point.

In addition to tracepoints, you can also place restrictions on when a breakpoint will actually cause the debugger to break program execution by applying a condition. The debugger evaluates the condition expression when the breakpoint is reached. If the condition is satisfied, the debugger breaks program execution; if not, the program continues to execute. Closely related to conditions, you can also indicate that the breakpoint should occur after it has been hit a certain number of times. By default, execution breaks every time a breakpoint is hit.

Finally, you can use the Breakpoints window to display all the current breakpoints and tracepoints. The Breakpoints window also enables you to label a breakpoint or a group of breakpoints. Labels are useful when you want to mark a related group of breakpoints.

Controlling Program Execution

When an application is in Break mode, one of the most common debugging procedures is to execute code one line at a time. The Visual Studio debugger provides four ways to do this:

▶ Step Into

▶ Step Over

▶ Step Out

▶ Step Into Specific

Step Into and Step Over both instruct the debugger to execute the next line of code. The only difference is that if the line contains a function, Step Over executes the entire function and stops at the first line outside the function. Step Into halts at the first line of code inside the function.

When you are inside a function call and want to return to the calling function, you can use Step Out, which resumes execution until the function returns and then breaks at the first line outside the function.

Sometimes Step Into or Step Over isn't enough, particularly when you have nested function calls. Instead, you want to step into a specific function call at a certain nesting level. To do this, you can use the Step Into Specific context menu, which allows you to choose the function you want to step into.

The currently executing line is shown highlighted in yellow, by default, with a yellow arrow symbol in the margin, as shown in Figure 2.22.

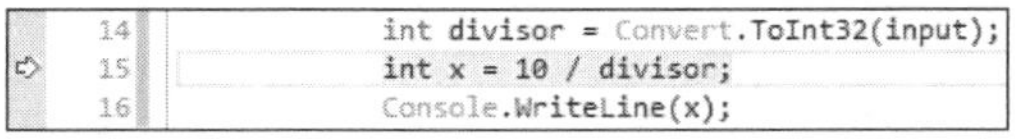

```
14        int divisor = Convert.ToInt32(input);
15        int x = 10 / divisor;
16        Console.WriteLine(x);
```

FIGURE 2.22
The current execution point.

The Step Into, Step Over, Step Out, and Step Into Specific actions all move "forward" in your program execution one line at a time. Sometimes, when you have started debugging you want to execute to a certain point and then break again. You can do this by finding the desired line, adding a new breakpoint, and then continuing execution with the F5 key.

However, this isn't always necessary. You can also continue execution until it reaches the current cursor location. To do this, right-click on a line in the source code editor, and choose the Run To Cursor context menu.

Using the Call Stack Window

Although executing code and working with variables while debugging is certainly powerful, sometimes it is important to know where you have been as well. This information can be viewed through the Call Stack window, shown in Figure 2.23, which displays the name of each function on the stack and the programming language it was written in.

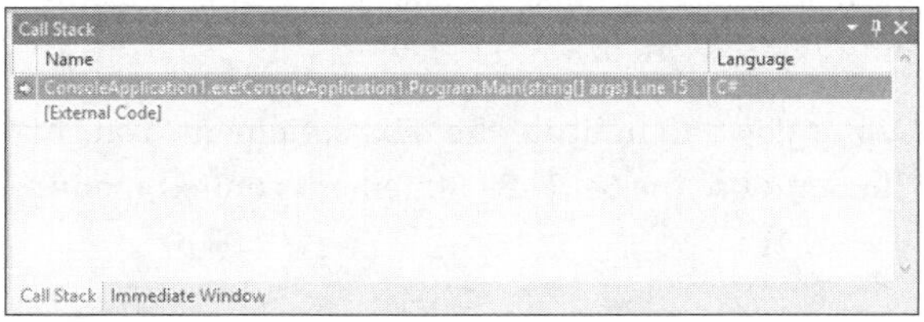

Call Stack	▾ ╫ ×
Name	Language
➡ ConsoleApplication1.exe!ConsoleApplication1.Program.Main(string[] args) Line 15	C#
[External Code]	

Call Stack | Immediate Window

FIGURE 2.23
The Call Stack window.

Again, just as in the code editor, a yellow arrow indicates the stack frame containing the current execution point. The information shown in the Locals and Watch windows are from this frame. By double-clicking another row in the call stack, or right-clicking on another row and choosing Switch To Frame on the context menu, you can change context to another frame on the stack. A green arrow indicates the frame that has the current context and the line of code executed in that frame is highlighted in green, as shown in Figure 2.24.

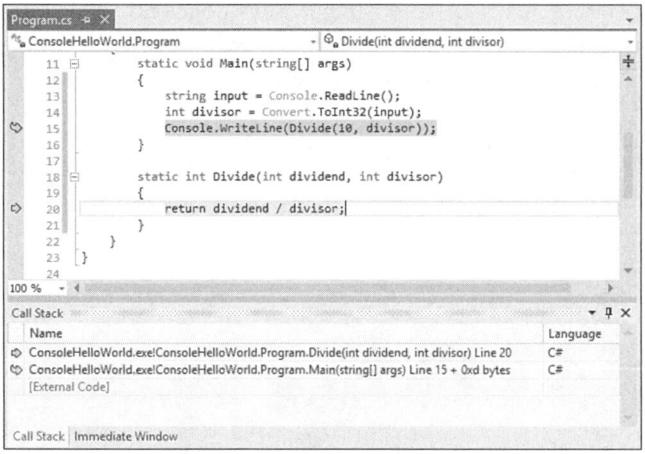

FIGURE 2.24
Switching to another call stack frame.

CAUTION

Switching Call Stack Frames

When you switch to another call stack frame, the current execution point remains in the original frame. When you continue execution or perform one of the Step actions, execution continues from the original frame, not the frame you selected.

Setting the Next Statement

Although switching context to another stack frame is useful, sometimes it is necessary to reexecute a line that has previously executed or even skip over sections of code. This can be accomplished by manually setting the next statement to be executed.

You can do this by moving the yellow arrow up or down to indicate the next statement. You can also place the mouse cursor over the desired line and use the Set Next Statement context menu.

CAUTION

Setting the Next Statement

When you set the next execution statement, you cause the program to jump directly to that location. This means that any instructions between the old and new execution points are not executed. It also means that if the execution point moves backward, any intervening instructions are not undone.

It is also not possible to move the next statement to another function or scope because doing so usually results in call-stack corruption, ultimately causing a runtime error to occur.

Visualizing Data

Seeing the value of a variable while debugging is useful, and as data structures become more complex, this ability becomes ever more powerful. Unfortunately, sometimes a value is better understood when seen using a manner that is more appropriate for its data type or value. For example, a string containing HTML is certainly more easily understood if the data is viewed as it would appear in a web browser, and a string containing XML is more easily understood when you can visually see the XML structure.

Visual Studio includes five standard visualizers:

▶ Text, HTML, and XML visualizers, which all work with string objects

▶ WPF Tree visualizer, for displaying the properties of a WPF object's visual tree

▶ Dataset visualizer, which works for `DataSet`, `DataView`, and `DataTable` objects

NOTE

Visualizers

Many additional visualizers are available for you to download. Installing a new visualizer is as simple as copying the files to the following location (on Windows 7 and later):

`Documents\Visual Studio 2012\Visualizers`

When a data type has a visualizer available, you see a Magnifying Glass icon in the DataTip (as shown in Figure 2.25), variable windows, or the QuickWatch dialog box.

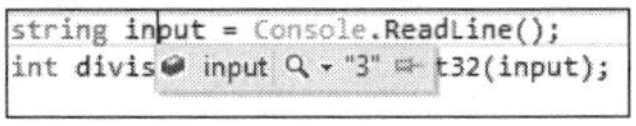

FIGURE 2.25
Debugger visualizers.

By clicking the magnifying glass, you are presented a menu of the available visualizers, shown in Figure 2.26; choosing one displays the value of the variable in the specified visualizer window.

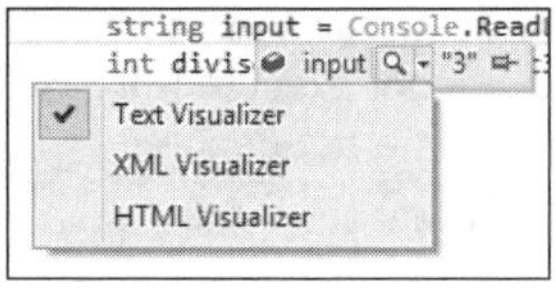

FIGURE 2.26
Menu of available visualizers.

For example, choosing the Text Visualizer displays the visualizer window shown in Figure 2.27.

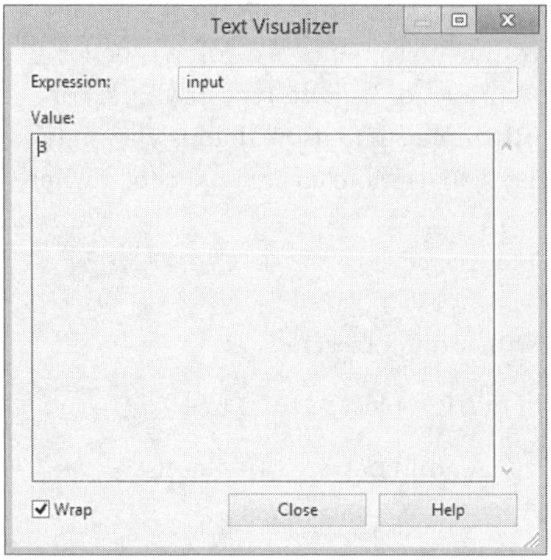

FIGURE 2.27
Text Visualizer.

Commenting Your Code

Although commenting your code isn't actually a feature of the Visual Studio debugger, it is one of the simplest ways to reduce bugs from the start. Good comments make it easier to understand what the code is doing and, more important, why it is doing it a particular way. Comments are meant to be read by programmers and should be clear and precise. A comment that is hard to understand or incorrect isn't much better than having no comment at all.

NOTE

XML Comments

Another form of comment that you should get in the habit of using are **XML comments**. An XML comment generally starts with three forward slashes (///) on each line. Everything after those slashes must be valid and well-formed XML. The simplest XML comment looks like

```
/// <summary>
/// This is a summary comment, typically describing what a
/// method or property does in one or two short sentences.
/// </summary>
```

These comments are most often used to create documentation for your code using external tools such as Sandcastle. Another nice feature of XML comments is that the Visual Studio code editor automatically uses them to generate IntelliSense ToolTips for your own code.

XML comments can also be delimited by starting with the `/**` character sequence and ending with `*/`.

A comment is simply text ignored by the C# compiler. Comments are actually removed from the code text during compilation, so there is no impact to performance. For the compiler to recognize text as a comment, it must start with two forward slashes (//). Everything to the right of the slashes, and including the slashes, is a comment. This means that a comment can be on a line by itself, like this:

```
// This is a full line comment.
```

It can also appear at the end of a line of code, typically called an end-of-line comment, like this:

```
string name; // The name should include both first and last names.
```

NOTE

Delimited Comments

C# also supports a comment style made popular by the C programming language, which requires only a starting (/*) and ending (*/) comment character sequence; everything in between (including the start and end character sequence) is treated as a comment.

Although this comment style can be used for single-line comments, it is more commonly used for multiline comments. For example, a multiline comment using this style would be written as follows:

```
/* This is the start of a comment that spans
* multiple lines but does not require the
* characters at the start of each line. */
```

The C# editor automatically starts each line following the first one with a single asterisk (*) character. Multiline comments can also be easily accomplished by adding the // characters to each line.

Adding clear and precise comments to your code means that you don't have to rely on memory to understand the "what" and "why" of a section of code. This is most important when you look at that code later on, or someone else must look at your code. Because comments become part of the textual content of your code, they should follow good writing principles in addition to being clearly written.

To write a good comment, you should do your best to document the purpose of the code (the why, not how) and indicate the reasoning and logic behind the code as clearly as possible. Ideally, comments should be written at the same time as you write the code. If you wait, you probably won't go back and add them.

NOTE

Unit Tests

Although well-commented code can help with code maintenance, an effective way to both document and verify the functionality of your code is to write unit tests.

There are a variety of unit test frameworks, including the MSTest framework included with Visual Studio. No matter which unit testing framework you choose, the basic premise is similar. You write a unit test separate from your main code that tests a single "unit" (typically a method or property) to ensure that the method reliably produces the correct results under all possible conditions.

Unit tests also enable you to make code changes with confidence that those changes have not changed the expected behavior or result.

Summary

In this hour, you learned the basics of Visual Studio. You also wrote your first C# console application. Whether this was your first managed application as well or simply your first C# application, these first steps are laying the foundation for what comes later. This might have seemed like a trivial example—after all, how exciting is it to print the words "Hello, world" on the screen—but it is just the beginning.

Later, you learned how to use the Visual Studio debugging tools to diagnose and help fix application runtime errors. You learned about the importance of providing meaningful code comments and the differences between compile time and runtime errors.

Finally, you learned about the different tools the Visual Studio debugger makes available, including the variable windows and the Immediate window. You also learned how you can control program execution and set breakpoints to stop program execution at specific locations.

Q&A

Q. What is the purpose of a breakpoint?

A. A breakpoint suspends the execution of your application at a specific point.

Q. What is the difference between the Locals window and the Autos window?

A. The Locals window displays variables that are local to the current scope, typically the currently executing procedure or function. The Autos window displays variables only for the currently executing and the preceding statement.

Workshop

Quiz

1. What characters are used to indicate a single-line comment?

2. What does the yellow arrow in the code editor margin or call stack window indicate?

3. Can the value of a variable be modified while debugging?

Answers

1. Two forward slash (//) characters are used to indicate a single-line comment.

2. The yellow arrow indicates the next statement to be executed.

3. Yes, the value of a variable can be modified through the Locals, Autos, Watch, and Immediate windows. It can also be modified through a DataTip.

Exercises

1. Explore what else is available in the System.Console class by changing the "Hello, world" application to ask for your name and output "Hello, name.", where name is text entered while the program is running.

2. Implement the code shown in Figure 2.24, but change lines 2 and 3 of the Main method so that the Divide method looks like the following:

```
int divisor = -1;

if (Int32.TryParse(input, out divisor))
{
    try
    {
        Console.WriteLine(Divide(10, divisor));
    }
    catch (DivideByZeroException ex)
    {
        Console.WriteLine(ex.Message);
    }
}
```

Understanding C# Types

What You'll Learn in This Hour:

▶ An overview of types
▶ The C# predefined types
▶ Other commonly used types
▶ Working with operators
▶ Default values
▶ Null and nullable types
▶ Casting and conversion

In Hour 1, "The .NET Framework and C#," you were introduced to the fundamentals of the .NET Framework and C#, including the framework class library, the common language runtime, and the idea of automatic memory management. You briefly learned about namespaces and types and then moved on to statements, expressions, variables, constants, identifiers, and keywords. From those humble beginnings, you then built a simple C# application and learned about debugging in Hour 2, "Introducing Visual Studio."

Building on what you have already learned, this hour introduces you to the predefined types offered by C# and the different operations that you can perform using them. You then learn about value and reference types. After that, you see nullable types and learn about type conversion.

At the end of this hour, you should have a thorough understanding of the C# types, including the difference between value, reference, and nullable types. You will also have written some more advanced applications that can store and manipulate simple data.

An Overview of Types

C# is both a type-safe and statically typed language. Being statically typed requires you to inform the compiler of the data type for any variable you create. In return, the compiler guarantees that you can only store a compatible data type in that variable, making it type safe. This combination helps prevent common programming errors, leading to a more stable and secure application.

Types are divided into three main categories:

▶ Value types

▶ Reference types

▶ Type parameters

GO TO ▶ **HOUR 12, "UNDERSTANDING GENERICS,"** for more information on type parameters.

TIP

Pointers

There is actually a fourth category of type, called a pointer, which is not part of the core C# language. A pointer type contains the actual location (called an address) of an item in memory. Pointers also allow arithmetic operations as if the value were a number. Although pointers are powerful, they can also be difficult to use correctly and safely.

There are times, however, when using pointers might be required. Fortunately, almost all those times are situations that are more advanced and not something that we need to worry about on a regular basis. Some of those situations can include directly interacting with the underlying operating system or implementing an extremely time-critical algorithm.

To allow the flexibility (and danger) of pointers, C# enables you to write *unsafe* code in which it is possible to create and operate on pointers. When using unsafe code and pointers, be aware that the garbage collector does not track pointers, so you must handle the memory allocation and deletion yourself. In a way, it's like writing C code in a C# program.

By disallowing pointer types except in explicit unsafe code blocks, C# can eliminate an entire category of common errors, making it a much safer language.

Put simply, a value type is completely self-contained and copied "by value." This means that variables of a value type directly contain their data, and it is not possible for operations on one to affect the other. Value types are further categorized into structures, enumerated types, and nullable types.

A reference type contains a reference to the actual data, meaning it is possible for two variables to reference the same object, allowing the possibility that operations on one will affect the other. Reference types are further categorized into classes, arrays, interfaces, and delegates.

Unified Type System

Despite this division between types, C# has a **unified type system**, enabling the value of any non-pointer type to be treated as an object. This gives value types the benefits a reference type has without introducing unnecessary overhead and makes it possible to call object methods on any value, even predefined value types.

The C# Predefined Types

The C# language predefines a set of types that map to types in the common type system. If you are familiar with another programming language, the names of these types might be different, but you can easily see the correlation. All the predefined types are value types except for `object` and `string`. The predefined types are shown in Table 3.1.

TABLE 3.1 Predefined C# Types

Keyword	Aliased Type	Description	Range
bool	Boolean	Logical Boolean	`true` or `false`
byte	Byte	Unsigned 8-bit integer	0 to 255
char	Char	A single 16-bit Unicode character	U+0000 to U+FFFF
decimal	Decimal	A 128-bit data type with 28–29 significant digits	$(-7.9 \times 10^{28}$ to $7.9 \times 10^{28})$ / $(10^0$ to $28)$
double	Double	Double-precision 64-bit floating point up to 15–16 digits	$\pm 5.0 \times 10^{-324}$ to $\pm 1.7 \times 10^{308}$
float	Single	Single-precision 32-bit floating point up to 7 digits	$\pm 1.5 \times 10^{-45}$ to $\pm 3.4 \times 10^{38}$
int	Int32	Signed 32-bit integer	-2^{31} to $2^{31} - 1$
long	Int64	Signed 64-bit integer	-2^{63} to $2^{63} - 1$
sbyte	SByte	Signed 8-bit integer	–128 to 127
short	Int16	Signed 16-bit integer	–32,768 to 32,767
uint	UInt32	Unsigned 32-bit integer	0 to 4,294,967,295
ulong	UInt64	Unsigned 64-bit integer	0 to 18,446,744,073,709,551,615
ushort	UInt16	Unsigned 16-bit integer	0 to 65,535
object	Object	Base type of all other value and reference types, except interfaces	N/A
string	String	A sequence of Unicode characters	N/A

By including a type to directly represent Boolean values (values that are either `true` or `false`), there is no ambiguity that the value is intended to be a Boolean value as opposed to an integer value. This helps eliminate several common programming errors, making it easier to write self-documenting code.

TIP

Boolean Values

In C, Boolean values are represented as an integer value, and it is left up to the programmer to decide if 0 means `true` or `false`. Typically, C programs define named constants representing the integer values of 0 and 1 to help eliminate this ambiguity, but this still allows any integer value to be used.

The `decimal` type provides at least 28 significant digits and is designed to have no representation error over a wide range of values frequently used in financial calculations. The range of values the `double` type can represent with no representation error is a set used primarily in physical calculations.

The `object` type is the underlying base type for all the other reference and value types. The `string` type represents a sequence of Unicode code units and cannot be changed once given a value. As a result, values of type `string` are **immutable**.

C# also has some special types, the most common being the `void` type. The `void` type indicates the absence of a type. The `dynamic` type is similar to `object`, with the primary difference being all operations on that type will be resolved at runtime rather than compile time.

NOTE

`System.Object`

All the value types and the class, array, and delegate reference types derive from `object`. Interface types can derive only from other interface types, but they are convertible to `object`.

Type parameter types actually do not derive from anything, but they are still convertible to `object`.

Unsafe pointer types neither derive from nor are convertible to `object` because they are outside the normal type rules for C#.

All this actually means that every nonpointer type in C# is convertible to, but might not derive from, `object`.

NOTE

Predefined Types and CLS Compliance

All the predefined types are CLS-compliant except the unsigned integer types and the `sbyte` type. You can use these types and still be CLS-compliant as long as they are not publicly accessible. If you do need to make one of these types publicly accessible, they can safely map to a CLS-compliant type:

- ▶ `sbyte` maps to `short`.
- ▶ `uint` normally maps to `long` but can be mapped to `int` when the original value is less than 2,147,483,647.5.
- ▶ `ulong` normally maps to `decimal` but can be mapped to `long` when the original value is less than 9,223,372,036,854,775,807.5.
- ▶ `ushort` normally maps to `int` but can be mapped to `short` when the original value is less than 32,767.5.

Although void and dynamic are types, var represents an **implicitly typed** variable and tells the compiler to determine the real type based on the assigned data.

CAUTION

Var **Is Not Short for** Variant

When the `var` type was first introduced, many people thought it was equivalent to the Visual Basic `Variant` type. A `Variant` is a type that can be used to represent any other data type and is not strongly typed. A `var` type is still strongly typed because it is replaced with a real data type during compilation. Even so, overusing it can decrease the understandability of your code, so use it carefully.

TRY IT YOURSELF ▼

Working with the Predefined Types

Now that you are familiar with the predefined types, let's see how to use them. By following these steps, you write an application that creates some local variables and displays their values. Then you create an implicitly typed variable and verify that it actually creates a strongly typed variable:

1. Create a new console application.

2. In the `Main` method of the `Program.cs` file, enter the following code:

```
int i = 20;
float f = 20.2f;
string s = "Hello, world...again";

Console.WriteLine("This is an {0} value: {1}", i.GetTypeCode(), i);
Console.WriteLine("This is a {0} value: {1}", f.GetTypeCode(), f);
Console.WriteLine("This is a {0} value: {1}", s.GetTypeCode(), s);
```

3. Run the application by pressing Ctrl+F5; you should see the following in the console window, as shown in Figure 3.1.

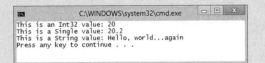

FIGURE 3.1
Output of working with predefined types.

4. Press any key to close the console and return to Visual Studio.

5. Enter the following code in the `Main` method, just after the previous code:

```
var v = 20;
Console.WriteLine("This is also an {0} value: {1}", v.GetTypeCode(), v);
```

6. Hover the mouse cursor over the `var` keyword until the ToolTip is displayed, which confirms that `v` is actually an `int`, as shown in Figure 3.2.

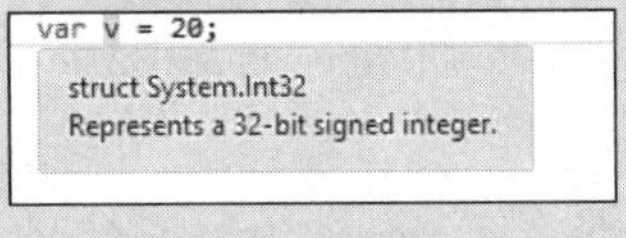

```
var v = 20;
    struct System.Int32
    Represents a 32-bit signed integer.
```

FIGURE 3.2
ToolTip showing a `var` as an `int`.

7. Press Ctrl+F5 again to run the application, and you should now see an additional line appear:

```
This is also an Int32 value: 20
```

8. Press any key to close the console and return to Visual Studio.

9. Enter the following line in the `Main` method:

```
v = "hello";
```

10. You should immediately notice a red "squiggly" line under the statement you just entered and an error message stating that you `Cannot implicitly convert type 'string' to 'int'`. This error occurs because the compiler has already assigned `v` to be of type `int` and the strong-typing capabilities of C# prevent you from assigning a `string` value to the same variable, which is an incompatible type.

11. Remove the line you entered from step 9 so your program compiles again.

Other Commonly Used Types

In addition to the standard predefined types, the .NET Framework provides types for other commonly used values. These types do not have aliases in C# like the predefined types but allow the same operations.

Date and Time

Working with date and time values is done with the `DateTime` structure, which enables you to create values that represent a date and a time, just a date, or just a time value. The two most common ways to create a new `DateTime` value are to use one of the various constructor overloads or one of the four static parse methods: `Parse`, `ParseExact`, `TryParse`, or `TryParseExact`.

The `DateTime` structure provides several properties; the most common are shown in Table 3.2.

TABLE 3.2   Common `DateTime` Properties

Property	Description
Date	Gets the date component of the current instance
Day	Gets the day of the month represented by the current instance
DayOfWeek	Gets the day of the week represented by the current instance
Hour	Gets the hour component of the date represented by the current instance
Minute	Gets the minute component of the date represented by the current instance
Month	Gets the month component of the date represented by the current instance
Now	Gets a `DateTime` object that is set to the current date and time, in the local time zone
TimeOfDay	Gets the time of day for the current instance
Today	Gets the current date
UtcNow	Gets a `DateTime` object that is set to the current date and time, in Coordinated Universal Time (UTC)
Year	Gets the year component of the date represented by the current instance

When adding or subtracting date or time values, you can use instance methods, which return a new `DateTime` value rather than modifying the original one. The common `DateTime` arithmetic methods are shown in Table 3.3.

TABLE 3.3 Common `DateTime` Arithmetic Methods

Method	Description
AddDays	Adds or subtracts the specified number of days
AddHours	Adds or subtracts the specified number of hours
AddMinutes	Adds or subtracts the specified number of minutes
AddMonths	Adds or subtracts the specified number of months
AddYears	Adds or subtracts the specified number of years

It is also possible to subtract two `DateTime` values using the subtraction operator, which results in a `TimeSpan` instance. A `TimeSpan` represents an interval of time measured as a positive or negative number of days, hours, minutes, seconds, and fractions of a second. To ensure consistency, time intervals are measured in days. You can also add a `TimeSpan` to or subtract a `TimeSpan` from a `DateTime`, both of which result in a new `DateTime` value.

The common methods and properties of `TimeSpan` are shown in Table 3.4.

TABLE 3.4 Common `TimeSpan` Members

Name	Description
Add	Adds the specified `TimeSpan` to the current instance
Days	Gets the days component of the time interval represented by the current `TimeSpan`
FromDays	Returns a `TimeSpan` that represents a specified number of days
FromHours	Returns a `TimeSpan` that represents a specified number of hours
FromMilliseconds	Returns a `TimeSpan` that represents a specified number of milliseconds
FromMinutes	Returns a `TimeSpan` that represents a specified number of minutes
FromSeconds	Returns a `TimeSpan` that represents a specified number of seconds
Hours	Gets the hours component of the time interval represented by the current `TimeSpan`
Milliseconds	Gets the milliseconds component of the time interval represented by the current `TimeSpan`
Minutes	Gets the minutes component of the time interval represented by the current `TimeSpan`
Seconds	Gets the seconds component of the time interval represented by the current `TimeSpan`

Name	Description
Subtract	Subtracts the specified TimeSpan from the current instance
TotalDays	Gets the value of the current TimeSpan expressed as whole and fractional days
TotalHours	Gets the value of the current TimeSpan expressed as whole and fractional hours
TotalMilliseconds	Gets the value of the current TimeSpan expressed as whole and fractional milliseconds
TotalMinutes	Gets the value of the current TimeSpan expressed as whole and fractional minutes
TotalSeconds	Gets the value of the current TimeSpan expressed as whole and fractional seconds

Globally Unique Identifiers (GUIDs)

A GUID is a 128-bit integer value that can be used whenever a unique identifier is required that has a low probability of being duplicated. The System.Guid structure enables you to create and compare GUID values. The common members are shown in Table 3.5.

TABLE 3.5   Common Guid Members

Name	Description
CompareTo	Compares the current instance to the specified Guid
Empty	Represents a read-only instance of a Guid whose value is guaranteed to be all zeros
NewGuid	Creates a new instance of the Guid structure
Parse	Converts the string representation of a GUID into the equivalent Guid instance
TryParse	Converts the string representation of a GUID into the equivalent Guid instance, indicating if the conversion was successful

Uniform Resource Identifiers (URIs)

A uniform resource identifier (URI) is a compact representation of a resource available on the intranet or the Internet and can be an absolute URI (like a web page address) or a relative URI that must be expanded with respect to a base URI.

The Uri class enables you to create new URI values and access the parts of a URI, and provides methods for working with URIs, such as parsing, comparing, and combining. Some of the common members are shown in Table 3.6.

TABLE 3.6   Common Uri Members

Name	Description
AbsoluteUri	Gets the absolute URI
Compare	Compares the specified parts of two Uri instances using the specified comparison rules
EscapeUriString	Converts a URI string to its escaped representation
IsFile	Gets a value indicating whether the specified Uri is a file URI
LocalPath	Gets a local operating-system representation of a filename
MakeRelativeUri	Determines the difference between two Uri instances
TryCreate	Creates a new Uri but does not throw an exception if the Uri cannot be created

An instance of the Uri class is immutable. To create a modifiable URI, use the UriBuilder class. The UriBuilder class enables you to easily change the properties of a URI without creating a new instance for each modification. All the properties shown in Table 3.7 are common to both Uri (where they are read-only) and UriBuilder except for the Uri property, which is only available on UriBuilder.

TABLE 3.7   Common Uri and UriBuilder Properties

Name	Description
Fragment	Gets or sets the fragment portion of the URI
Host	Gets or sets the hostname or IP address of a server
Password	Gets or sets the password associated with the user who accesses the URI
Path	Gets or sets the path to the resource defined by the URI
Port	Gets or sets the port number of the URI
Query	Gets or sets any query information included in the URI
Scheme	Gets or sets the scheme name of the URI
Uri	Gets the Uri instance constructed by the specified UriBuilder instance
UserName	Gets or sets the username associated with the user who accesses the URI

Listing 3.1 shows how to use the `UriBuilder` class.

LISTING 3.1 Working with `UriBuilder`

```
Uri immutableUri = new Uri("http://www.example.com");
Console.WriteLine(immutableUri);

UriBuilder mutableUri = new UriBuilder(immutableUri);
Console.WriteLine(mutableUri);

mutableUri.Scheme = "https";
mutableUri.Host = "www.example.com";
mutableUri.Path = "exampleFile.html";
Console.WriteLine(mutableUri);
```

Big Integers and Complex Numbers

The `System.Numerics.BigInteger` type represents an arbitrarily large integer value that has no theoretical upper or lower bound. When a `BigInteger` instance has been created, you can use it just as you would any of the other integer types, enabling you to perform basic mathematical operations and comparisons. Listing 3.2 shows some of the ways you can use the `BigInteger` type.

LISTING 3.2 Working with `BigInteger`

```
BigInteger b1 = new BigInteger(987321.5401);
BigInteger b2 = (BigInteger)435623411897L;
BigInteger b3 = BigInteger.Parse("435623411897");

Console.WriteLine(BigInteger.Pow(Int32.MaxValue, 2));
Console.WriteLine(b2 == b3);
Console.WriteLine(BigInteger.GreatestCommonDivisor(b1, b2));
```

The `System.Numerics.Complex` type represents a complex number, in the form of a + bi, where a is the real part, and b is the imaginary part and allows you to

▶ Compare two complex numbers to determine equality.

▶ Perform arithmetic operations, such as addition, subtraction, multiplication, and division; other numerical operations, such as raising a complex number to a specific power; finding the square root or getting the absolute value; and trigonometric operations, such as calculating the cosine of an angle represented by a complex number.

Listing 3.3 shows some of the ways you can use the `Complex` type.

LISTING 3.3 Working with `Complex`

```
Complex c1 = new Complex(10, 2);
Complex c2 = 3.14;
Complex c3 = Complex.FromPolarCoordinates(5, 0.25);
Complex c4 = (Complex)10.2m;

Console.WriteLine(c1);
Console.WriteLine(c2);
Console.WriteLine(Complex.Sqrt(c3));
Console.WriteLine(Complex.Exp(c4));
```

Working with Operators

C# supports a wide variety of operators, but we only cover the more commonly used ones. An **operator** is a special symbol that indicates which operation to perform in an expression. All the C# predefined types support operators, although not all types support the same operators.

Table 3.8 shows all the C# operators in order of precedence. Within each category, operators have equal precedence.

TABLE 3.8 Operators and Operator Precedence in C#

Category	Operators
Primary	`x.y f(x) a[x] x++ x--` new typeof checked unchecked `->`
Unary	`+ - ! ~ ++x --x (T)x` true false & sizeof
Multiplicative	`* / %`
Additive	`+ -`
Shift	`<< >>`
Relational and Type Testing	`< > <= >=` is as
Equality	`== !=`
Logical AND	`&`
Logical XOR	`^`
Logical OR	`|`

Category	Operators
Conditional AND	&&
Conditional OR	||
Conditional	?:
Assignment	= += -= *= /= %= &= |= ^= <<= >>=
Null-Coalescing	??
Lambda	=>

Arithmetic and Assignment Operators

You have already seen the assignment operator (=) in many of the previous examples. This operator simply stores the value of the right operand in the variable indicated by its left operand. Both operands must be the same type or the right operand must be implicitly convertible to the type of the left operand.

C# provides arithmetic operators that support the standard mathematical operations of addition (+), subtraction (-), multiplication (*), and division (/). Subtle differences exist between the behavior of the C# arithmetic operators and the arithmetic rules you learned in school. In particular, integer division behaves a bit differently depending on the data types you are dividing. When dividing one integer by another, the result is an integer. Any remainder is discarded, and the result is rounded toward zero. To obtain the remainder of an integer division, you must use the modulus operator (%).

C# also supports a compound assignment operator, which combines an arithmetic operation and an assignment in a single operator. A corresponding operation (+=,-=, *=, /=) exists for each of the standard arithmetic operators and the modulus operator (%=), which combine addition, subtraction, multiplication, division, and modulus division with assignment.

For example, suppose you need to increment a variable by one. Using the standard arithmetic operators, such an action would typically look like this:

```
i = i + 1;
```

However, by using the addition compound assignment operator, this operation could be performed like this:

```
i += 1;
```

NOTE

Increment and Decrement Operators

Taking this simplification even further, you can increment or decrement a value by 1 using the increment (++) and decrement (--) operators.

These operators support two different notations: a postfix notation, where the operator occurs after the variable, and a prefix notation, where the operator occurs before the variable. For example, to increment the value of an integer i by 1 and decrement the value of an integer j by 1 using both the postfix and prefix notation you would use the following:

```
int i = 1;
i++;
++i;

int j = 3;
j--;
--j;
```

The only difference between them is the result of the operation, not when the operation occurs. Typically, the result of the postfix notation is the value of the variable before the operation while the result of the prefix operation is the result of the variable after the operation. In both cases, the variable itself has the same value after the operation.

▼ TRY IT YOURSELF

Arithmetic Operators

To examine how the assignment, addition, compound assignment, and increment and decrement operators behave, follow these steps.

1. Create a new console application.

2. In the Main method of the Program.cs file, enter the following code:

```
int i = 20;
Console.WriteLine("i = {0}", i);

i = i + 1;
Console.WriteLine("i = {0}", i);

i += 2;
Console.WriteLine("i = {0}", i);

i -= 3;
Console.WriteLine("i = {0}", i);
```

3. Run the application by pressing Ctrl+F5; you should see the following lines in the console window, as shown in Figure 3.3.

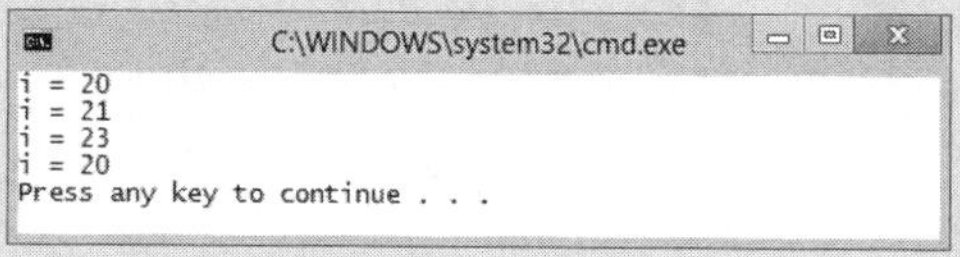

```
[C:\WINDOWS\system32\cmd.exe]
i = 20
i = 21
i = 23
i = 20
Press any key to continue . . .
```

FIGURE 3.3
Output of working with the arithmetic operators.

4. Press any key to close the console and return to Visual Studio.

Relational Operators

The relational operators, shown in Table 3.9, are used when comparing two values and result in a Boolean value.

TABLE 3.9 Relational Operators in C#

Name	Operator	Expression	Result
Equals	==	x == 20	true
		y == 30	false
Not equals	!=	x != 20	false
		y != 30	true
Greater than	>	x > y	true
		y > x	false
Greater than or equals	>=	x >= y	true
		y >= x	false
Less than	<	x < y	false
		y < x	true
Less than or equals	<=	x <= y	false
		y <= x	true

Assuming x = 20 *and* y = 10.

In many programming languages, the assignment and equality operators are easily confused because they use the same symbol. This confusion can result in accidental assignments, which remains one of the more common programming mistakes today. To help minimize the possibility for confusion, C# defines a different operator for equality (==).

Logical Operators

The logical operators, shown in Table 3.10, evaluate Boolean expressions that result in either true or false.

TABLE 3.10 Logical Operators in C#

Name	Operator	Expression	Result
And (Conditional)	&&	(x == 20) && (y == 30)	false; both expressions must be true
And (Logical)	&	(x == 20) & (y == 30)	false; both expressions must be true
Or (Conditional)	¦¦	(x == 20) ¦¦ (y == 30)	true; either or both expressions must be true
Or (Logical)	¦	(x == 20) ¦ (y == 30)	True; either or both expressions must be true
Or (Exclusive)	^	(x == 20) ^ (y == 30)	true; the expressions are both different
Not	!	!(x == 30)	true; the expression must be false

Assuming x = 20 *and* y = 10.

The rules for the logical operators can be easily summarized, assuming an x and y that are Boolean expressions, as shown in Table 3.11.

NOTE

Short-Circuit Evaluation

In C#, the conditional operator perform **short-circuit evaluation**, or minimal evaluation, which means that additional expressions are evaluated only if the first expression would not result in the entire expression being false. The logical operators do not perform short-circuit evaluation.

When short-circuit evaluation is in effect, if the first expression of an AND operator is false, it is not necessary to evaluate any additional expressions because the entire expression will be false. Similarly, if the first expression of an OR operator is true, it is not necessary to evaluate any additional expressions because the entire expression will be true. It is only when the first expression is not sufficient to determine the result of the entire expression that the additional expressions will be evaluated.

TABLE 3.11   Logical Operators Truth Table

X	Y	X && Y	X ¦¦ Y	X ^ Y
true	true	true	true	false
true	false	false	true	true
false	true	false	true	true
false	false	false	false	false

Relational and Logical Operators

By following these steps, you verify the expressions shown in Table 3.9 and Table 3.10:

1. Create a new console application.

2. In the `Main` method, declare two integer variables named `x` and `y` and initialize them to 20 and 10, respectively.

3. Using the expressions from Table 3.9 and Table 3.10, write a series of `Console.WriteLine` statements using the following format, where *expression* is replaced with the correct expression from the tables:

   ```
   Console.WriteLine("expression: {0}", expression);
   ```

4. Run the application by pressing Ctrl+F5, and observe that the results match what is shown in the results column of both tables.

Conditional Operator

The conditional operator (also called a **ternary operator**, or **ternary if**, because it takes three terms) is useful for writing concise expressions and evaluates a condition returning one of two values depending on the result.

The conditional operator has the following form:

```
condition ? consequence : alternative
```

When `condition` is `true`, the `consequence` is evaluated and becomes the result. However, when `condition` is `false`, the `alternative` is evaluated and becomes the result instead.

CAUTION

Common Problems with the Ternary Operator

This operator is right-associative, different than most of the other operators, which are left-associative. This means an expression like

```
a ? b : c ? d : e
```

is evaluated as

```
a ? b : ( c ? d : e )
```

The type of the conditional expression is determined only from the types of the `consequence` and `alternative`, not from the type to which it is being assigned.

Ultimately, this requires that the `consequence` and `alternative` be of the same type, which means an expression like

```
object x = b ? 0 : "hello";
```

won't compile because the types of the `consequence` and `alternative` are `int` and `string`.

Although this code isn't practical and should probably never be used outside of this example, the correct way to write this would be

```
object x = b ? (object)0 : (object)"hello";
```

Default Values

You learned earlier that C# does not allow you to use an uninitialized variable, which means the variable must have a value before you use it. Although this idea of **definite assignment** helps reduce errors, because it is enforced by the compiler, it can be cumbersome if you have to explicitly provide a default value for every field.

To alleviate this burden, fields, or member variables, are always initially assigned with an appropriate default value. Table 3.12 shows the default value for the different predefined data types.

TABLE 3.12 Default Values

Type	Default
sbyte, byte, short, ushort, int, uint, long, ulong	0
char	'\x0000'
float	0.0f
double	0.0d
decimal	0.0m

Type	Default
bool	false
object	null
string	null

As you can see, for the integral value types, the default value is zero. The default value for the char type is the character equivalent of zero and `false` for the `bool` type. The `object` and string types have a default value of `null`, representing a **null reference** that literally is one that does not refer to any object.

Null and Nullable Types

These default values mean that a value type cannot be `null`, which at first glance might seem reasonable. However, it presents certain limitations when you work with databases, other external data sources, or other data types that can contain elements that might not be assigned a value. A classic example of this is a numeric field in a database that can store any integer data or might be undefined.

Nullable types provide a solution to this problem. A **nullable type** is a value type that can represent the proper value range of its underlying type and a `null` value. Nullable types are represented by the syntax `Nullable<T>` or `T?` where T is a value type. The preferred syntax is `T?`. You assign a value to a nullable type just as you would a non-nullable type:

```
int  x = 10;
int? x = 10;
int? x = null;
```

To access the value of a nullable type, you should use the `GetValueOrDefault` method, which returns the assigned value, or, if the value is `null`, the default value for the underlying type. You can also use the `HasValue` property, which returns `true` if the variable contains an actual value, and the `Value` property, which returns the actual value or results in an exception if the value is `null`.

All nullable types, including reference types, support the null-coalescing operator (`??`), which defines the default value to be returned when a nullable type is assigned to a non-nullable type. If the left operator is `null`, the right operator is returned; otherwise, the left operator is returned. Listing 3.4 shows how the null-coalescing operator can be used.

LISTING 3.4   Null-Coalescing Operator

```
int? x = null;
Console.WriteLine(x ?? -1);

x = 3;
Console.WriteLine(x ?? -1);

string s = null;
Console.WriteLine(s ?? "Undefined");
```

▼ TRY IT YOURSELF

Working with Nullable Types

To examine how to work with nullable types, follow these steps. You create a nullable int, making use of HasValue, Value, and GetValueOrDefault() and the implicit conversion between a nullable int and a non-nullable int:

1. Create a new console application.

2. In the Main method, declare an integer variable named x and initialize it to 10. Then declare a nullable integer named nx and initialize it to null.

3. Enter the following statements:

```
Console.WriteLine("nx has a value? {0}", nx.HasValue);
Console.WriteLine("x == nx: {0}", x == nx);
Console.WriteLine("x != nx: {0}", x != nx);
```

4. Now, set nx equal to 20, and enter the following statements:

```
Console.WriteLine("nx has a value? {0}", nx.HasValue);
Console.WriteLine("nx has the value {0}", nx.Value);
Console.WriteLine("x == nx: {0}", x == nx);
Console.WriteLine("x != nx: {0}", x != nx);
```

5. Set nx equal to null and enter the following statements:

```
Console.WriteLine("nx = {0}", nx ?? -1);
Console.WriteLine("nx = {0}", nx.GetValueOrDefault());
Console.WriteLine("nx = {0}", nx.GetValueOrDefault(-2));
```

6. Finally, set nx equal to 10 and enter the following statements:

```
Console.WriteLine("nx = {0}", nx ?? -1);
Console.WriteLine("nx = {0}", nx.GetValueOrDefault());
Console.WriteLine("nx = {0}", nx.GetValueOrDefault(-2));
```

7. Run the application by pressing Ctrl+F5 and observe that the output is the same, as shown in Figure 3.4.

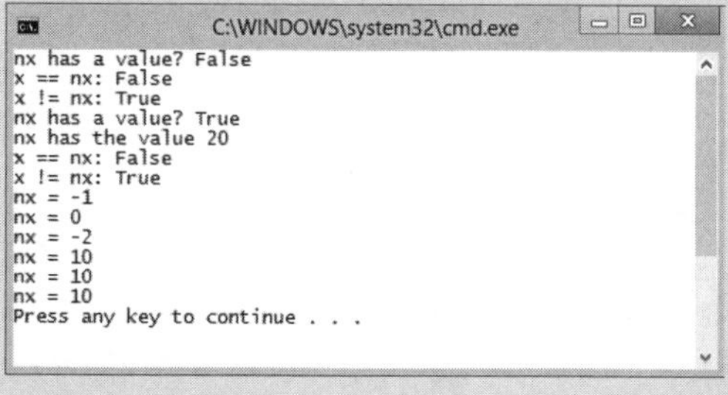

```
C:\WINDOWS\system32\cmd.exe
nx has a value? False
x == nx: False
x != nx: True
nx has a value? True
nx has the value 20
x == nx: False
x != nx: True
nx = -1
nx = 0
nx = -2
nx = 10
nx = 10
nx = 10
Press any key to continue . . .
```

FIGURE 3.4
Output of working with nullable types.

8. Press any key to close the console and return to Visual Studio.

Casting and Conversion

Put simply, a conversion allows an expression to be treated as being a specific type and is typically used to treat an expression of one type as being of a different type. Conversion can be either implicit or explicit, which determines if an explicit cast is required.

All of the predefined types support implicit conversions, shown in Table 3.13, that always succeed. These implicit conversions are allowed because when converting from the original numeric type to the new numeric type, no magnitude can be lost. An explicit conversion is required when there is the possibility of precision being lost as the result of the conversion operation and it requires you to specify the type to which you are converting the original value.

NOTE

Implicit Conversion

A loss of precision may occur when converting from `int`, `uint`, `long`, or `ulong` to `float` and from `long` or `ulong` to `double`. These conversions will, however, never lose magnitude. All of the other implicit numeric conversions never lose any information.

TABLE 3.13 Implicit Conversions on the Predefined Types

From	To								
	short	ushort	int	uint	long	ulong	float	double	decimal
sbyte	✓		✓		✓		✓	✓	✓
byte	✓	✓	✓	✓	✓		✓	✓	✓
short			✓		✓		✓	✓	✓
ushort			✓	✓	✓	✓	✓	✓	✓
int					✓		✓	✓	✓
uint					✓	✓	✓	✓	✓
long							✓	✓	✓
ulong							✓	✓	✓
char		✓	✓	✓	✓	✓	✓	✓	✓
float								✓	

For example, an int value can be implicitly converted to a long while the opposite, converting a long to an int, is explicit and requires an explicit cast. The form of an explicit cast is (T)e, where T is the destination (or result) type and e is the expression or variable being cast.

```
int i = 36;
long j = i; // Implicit conversion from int to long.
int j = (int)j; // Explicit conversion from long to int.
```

Boxing and Unboxing Conversions

What happens when you need a value type to act like a reference type? Earlier you learned that, as part of the unified type system, all value types are convertible to object. When a value type variable needs to be used as a reference type, an object "box" is automatically created and the value is copied into the box. When an object box is changed back to its original value type, the value is copied out of the box and into the variable. Once boxed, operations on the boxed variable do not affect the unboxed (original) variable and vice versa.

The following code shows an example of an implicit conversion where the integer variable i is implicitly boxed to an object variable named boxed. That object variable is then explicitly converted back into an integer variable named j.

```
int i = 36;
object boxed = i; // Implicit boxing conversion from int to object.
int j = (int)boxed; // Explicit unboxing conversion from object to int.
```

One of the problems with explicit conversion is that, if you are not careful, you can end up with code that compiles but fails at runtime. An explicit conversion effectively tells the compiler that you are certain the conversion will succeed, and if it doesn't, a runtime error is acceptable.

To reduce the possibilities of an explicit conversion failing at runtime, C# provides the `as` operator, which looks like `e as T`, where e is an expression and T must be either a reference or nullable type. The `as` operator tells the compiler that there is sufficient reason to believe the conversion will succeed and attempt to convert the value to the specified type. If the conversion was successful, the converted value as `T` is returned; otherwise a `null` is returned.

To take advantage of the `as` operator, the previous code can be rewritten like this:

```
int? i  = 36;
object boxed = i;
int? j = boxed as int?;
```

NOTE

Boxing and Unboxing Operations

Although conversions between value types and reference types are usually called **casts** because they use the C# `cast` operator, the CIL instructions are `box` and `unbox`. As a result, these conversions are also called boxing and unboxing operations.

A boxing conversion is always implicit and converts a value type to a reference type. An unboxing conversion is always explicit and converts a boxed value type (a reference type) back to a value type.

Boxing and unboxing operations are expensive in terms of resources and overhead, so you should try to avoid them whenever possible and ensure that you use the correct type to solve your problem.

TRY IT YOURSELF ▼

Conversions

By following these steps, you explore how to use conversions by converting a value type to a reference type. The application demonstrates how operations on value types, reference types, and boxed value types affect each other:

1. Create a new console application.

2. In the `Main` method, declare an integer variable named i and initialize it to 36. Then declare an `object` named `boxed` and initialize it to i.

3. Enter two `Console.WriteLine` statements to display the value of i and the value of `boxed`.

4. Increment the value of `boxed` by 2, making use of an explicit cast.

5. Duplicate the two `Console.WriteLine` statements entered from step 3 to verify that the value of `i` has not changed while the value of `boxed` has.

6. Now, increment the value of `i` by 1 and duplicate the two `Console.WriteLine` statements from step 3 to verify that the value of `i` has changed while the value of `boxed` has not.

7. Set the value of `i` to the new value of `boxed`, again using an explicit cast.

8. Finally, declare two nullable integers named `h` and `j`, initializing `h` to `null` and `j` to `i` and an object named `jboxed` initialized to `j`.

9. Enter the following code:

```
Console.WriteLine("h has a value? {0}", h.HasValue);
h = jboxed as int?;
Console.WriteLine("h now has the value {0}", h.Value);
```

10. Run the application using Ctrl+F5 and observe that the output matches what is shown in Figure 3.5.

```
C:\WINDOWS\system32\cmd.exe
i = 36
boxed = 36
i = 36
boxed = 38
i = 37
boxed = 38
i = 38
boxed = 38
h has a value? False
h now has the value 38
Press any key to continue . . .
```

FIGURE 3.5
Output of boxing, unboxing, and casts.

11. Press any key to close the console and return to Visual Studio.

Summary

Continuing to build your C# foundation, you have explored the predefined types provided by C# and learned about the rich set of operations you can perform on them. You then learned about value and reference types, including how you can treat a value type as a reference type and how to create a nullable type.

You have written a few more simple C# applications to explore how these concepts work. Although these applications might not be glamorous, they help to complete your foundation, enabling you to build applications that are more advanced. As your foundation in C# grows, the examples and exercises expect you to do more work.

Q&A

Q. What does being statically typed mean?

A. C# is a statically typed language, so you must always inform the compiler of the data type for any variable you create. In return, the compiler guarantees that you can store only compatible data in that variable.

Q. Does C# have pointers?

A. C# does have pointer types, although they are not part of the core language. Pointers are available only in the context of unsafe code.

Q. Why is the unified type system in C# important?

A. By providing a unified type system, C# enables the value of any type to be treated as an `object` without unnecessary overhead.

Q. Are all the predefined types CLS-compliant?

A. No, the unsigned integer types and the sbyte type are not CLS-compliant. There are CLS-compliant types that can be used in place of these types, if necessary.

Q. Is a variable declared using `var` strongly typed?

A. Yes, a variable declared using `var` is still strongly typed because you let the compiler fill in the real type during compilation. `var` is not equivalent to the Visual Basic `Variant` type.

Q. What is the difference between a value type and a reference type?

A. Value types directly contain their data, whereas reference types contain a reference to their data.

Q. Can value types be `null`?

A. All value types are either nullable or non-nullable. A nullable value type can be either `null` or a value of its underlying non-nullable type. A non-nullable value type cannot be `null`.

Q. Why should you avoid boxing and unboxing operations when possible?

A. You should avoid boxing and unboxing operations when possible because they are expensive in terms of resources and overhead.

Workshop

Quiz

1. What are the three primary groups C# types are divided into?

2. Which predefined type is useful for financial calculations and why?

3. What is a base type for all the predefined types?

4. Why is the inclusion of a distinct `bool` type important?

5. Is all string and character data stored as Unicode?

6. What are the implications of strings being immutable?

7. What is the difference between a prefix increment and a postfix increment operation?

8. Can the null-coalescing operator (`??`) be used with reference types and nullable value types?

9. Explain what happens during a boxing operation.

10. Can a `long` be implicitly converted to an `int`?

Answers

1. Types in C# are divided into reference types, value types, and type parameter types.

2. The `decimal` type is useful for financial calculations because it eliminates many representation errors commonly found with other floating-point types.

3. All the predefined types and everything in C# ultimately derive from the `object` type.

4. By including a distinct `bool` type, C# helps eliminate several common programming errors by eliminating the ambiguity that can arise when using an integer 0 or 1 value.

5. Yes, all strings and characters in C# are stored as Unicode code units, allowing them to be localized.

6. Because strings are immutable, they cannot be changed after given a value. This means that any string concatenation operations result in creating an entirely new string object to hold the new value. Performing a large number of these operations in a repetitive fashion over a short period of time can lead to significantly increased memory usage and should be done using a `StringBuilder` instead.

7. In a prefix increment operation, the result is the value of the variable before the increment; in a postfix increment operation, the result is the incremented value assigned back to the variable.

8. Yes, the null-coalescing operator can be used with any type that can contain a `null`, including objects.

9. A boxing operation occurs when a value type is used as a reference type and involves creating a new instance to hold the boxed value. Operations on a boxed object do not affect the original value.

10. No, a `long` cannot be implicitly converted to an `int` because it would lose precision; it can, however, be explicitly converted.

Exercises

1. Write a console application that generates the truth table shown in Table 2.12.

2. Write a console application that demonstrates the difference between value types and reference types. The application should declare two integer variables and two object variables of type `LightHouse`. For the object variables, create a new class file named `LightHouse.cs` and replace the generated code for `LightHouse` with the following code:

```
public class LightHouse
{
    public int NumberOfLights = 1;
    public int RevolutionsPerMinute = 30;
}
```

3. Expand the console application you wrote in the Arithmetic Operators Try It Yourself exercise to explore how the postfix and prefix increment and decrement operators behave.

Understanding Classes and Objects the C# Way

What You'll Learn in This Hour:

- ▶ Object-oriented programming
- ▶ Component-oriented programming
- ▶ Classes in C#
- ▶ Scope and declaration space
- ▶ Nested classes
- ▶ Partial classes
- ▶ Static classes
- ▶ Object initializers

A class is the fundamental programming concept in C#, defining both representation and behavior in a single unit. Classes provide the language support required for object-oriented and component-oriented programming and are the primary mechanism you use to create user-defined types. Traditionally, object-oriented programming languages have used the term *type* to refer to behavior, whereas value-oriented programming languages have used it to refer to data representation. In C#, it is used to mean both data representation and behavior. This is the basis of the common type system and means two types are assignment-compatible if, and only if, they have compatible representations and behaviors.

In this hour, you learn the basics of both object-oriented and component-oriented programming. When you understand these concepts, you move on to creating a class in C# and examining how it fulfills the goals of object-oriented and component-oriented programming. You learn about the different accessibility models, how to create and use properties and methods, and about optional and named parameters.

Object-Oriented Programming

Before we start talking about classes in detail, you need to understand the benefits of object-oriented programming and understand how it relates to C#. Object-oriented programming helps you think about the problem you want to solve and gives you a way to represent, or **model**, that problem in your code. If you do a good job modeling the problem, you end up with code that's easy to maintain, easy to understand, and easy to extend.

As previously mentioned, classes are the fundamental programming concept in C#, defining both representation and behavior in a single unit. Put another way, a **class** is a data structure that combines data storage with methods for manipulating that data. Classes are simply another data type that becomes available to you in much the same way any of the predefined types are available to you. Classes provide the primary mechanism you use to create user-defined types.

NOTE

Maintainable Code

There is, of course, more to creating code that's easy to maintain, understand, and extend than just getting the model correct. The implementation also has to be correct, readable, and correctly organized.

The four primary concepts of object-oriented programming are encapsulation, abstraction, inheritance, and polymorphism. In this hour, you learn about encapsulation and abstraction. In the next hour, you learn about inheritance and polymorphism.

Encapsulation and Abstraction

Encapsulation enables a class to hide the internal implementation details and to protect itself from unwanted changes that would result in an invalid or inconsistent internal state. For that reason, encapsulation is also sometimes referred to as **data hiding**.

As an example of encapsulation at work, think about your car. You start your car in the morning by inserting a key and turning it (or simply pushing a button, in some cases). The details of what happens when you turn the key (or push the button) that actually causes the engine to start running are hidden from you. You don't need to know about them to start the car. It also means you can't influence or change the internal state of the engine except by turning the ignition key.

By hiding the internal details and data, you create a public interface or **abstraction** representing the external details of a class. This abstraction describes what actions the class can perform and what information the class makes publicly available. As long as the public interface does not change, the internal details can change in any way required without having an adverse effect on other classes or code that depends on it.

By keeping the public interface of a class small and by providing a high degree of fidelity between your class and the real-world object it represents, you help ensure that your class will be familiar to other programmers who need to use it.

Let's look at our car example again. By encapsulating the details of what happens when you start your car and providing an action, `StartCar`, and information, such as `IsCarStarted`, we have defined a public interface, thereby creating an abstraction (or at least a partial abstraction, because cars do much more than just start) of a car.

Component-Oriented Programming

Component-oriented programming is a technique of developing software applications by combining preexisting and new components, much the same way automobiles are built from other components. Software components are self-contained, self-describing packages of functionality containing definitions of types that expose both behavior and data.

C# supports component-oriented programming through the concepts of properties, methods, events, and attributes (or metadata), allowing self-contained and self-describing components of functionality called assemblies.

Classes in C#

Now that you have a basic understanding of object-oriented and component-oriented programming, it is time to see how C# enables these concepts to become reality by using classes. You have actually already used classes in the examples and exercises from the previous two hours.

Classes in C# are reference types that implicitly derive from `object`. To define a class, you use the `class` keyword. Look at the application you built at the end of Hour 2, "Introducing Visual Studio." Everything you did was inside a class named `Program`.

The **body** of the class, defined by the opening and closing braces, is where you define the data and behavior for the class.

Scope and Declaration Space

We briefly mentioned scope and declaration space in Hour 1, "The .NET Framework and C#," saying that scope defines where you can use a name, whereas declaration space focuses on where that name is unique. Scope and declaration space are closely related, but there are a few subtle differences.

A more formal definition is that **scope** is an enclosing context or region that defines where a name can be used without qualification.

In C#, both scope and declaration space is defined by a statement block enclosed by braces. That means namespaces, classes, methods, and properties all define both a scope and a declaration space. As a result, scopes can be nested and overlap each other.

If scope defines the visibility of a name and scopes are allowed to overlap, any name defined in an outer scope is visible to an inner scope, but not the other way around.

In the code shown in Listing 4.1, the field age is in scope throughout the entire body of Contact, including within the body of F and G. In F, the use of age refers to the field named age.

LISTING 4.1 Scope and Declaration Space

```
class Contact
{
   public int age;

   public void F()
   {
      age = 18;
   }

   public void G()
   {
      int age;
      age = 21;
   }
}
```

However, in G, the scopes overlap because there is also a local variable named age that is in scope throughout the body of G. Within the scope of G, when you refer to age, you are actually referring to the locally scoped entity named age and not the one in the outer scope. When this happens, the name declared in the outer scope is **hidden** by the inner scope.

Figure 4.1 shows the same code with the scope boundaries indicated by the dotted and dashed rectangles.

Declaration space, on the other hand, is an enclosing context or region in which no two entities are allowed to have the same name. In the Contact class, for example, you are not allowed to have anything else named age in the body of the class, excluding the bodies of F and G. Likewise, inside the body of G, when you redeclare age, you aren't allowed to have anything else named age inside the declaration space of G.

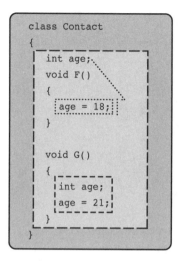

FIGURE 4.1
Nested scopes and hiding.

You learn about method overloading a bit later in this hour, but methods are treated a little differently when it comes to declaration spaces. If you consider the set of all overloaded methods with the same name as a single entity, the rule of having a unique name inside a declaration space is still satisfied.

TRY IT YOURSELF ▼

Working with Scope

To explore the differences between scope and declaration space, follow these steps. Keep Visual Studio open at the end of this exercise because you will use this application later.

1. Create a new console application.

2. Add a new class file named `Contact.cs` that looks like Listing 4.1.

3. In G, add a `Console.WriteLine` statement at the end of the method that prints the value of `age`.

4. In the `Main` method of the `Program.cs` file, enter the following code to create a new instance of the `Contact` class and print the current value of `age`:

```
Contact c = new Contact();
Console.WriteLine(c.age);
c.F();
Console.WriteLine(c.age);
c.G();
Console.WriteLine(c.age);
```

5. Run the application using Ctrl+F5 and observe that the output matches what is shown in Figure 4.2.

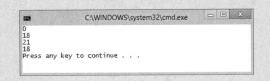

FIGURE 4.2
Working with scope.

Accessibility

Accessibility enables you to control the visibility, or accessibility, of an entity outside of its containing scope. C# provides this through **access modifiers**, which specify constraints on how members can be accessed outside the boundary of the class and, in some cases, even constrain inheritance. A particular class member is **accessible** when access to that member has been allowed; conversely, the member is **inaccessible** when access has been disallowed.

These access modifiers follow a simple set of contextual rules that determine when certain types of accessibility are permitted:

- ▶ Namespaces are not allowed to have any access modifiers and are always `public`.

- ▶ Classes default to `internal` accessibility but are allowed to have either `public` or `internal` declared accessibility. A **nested class**, which is a class defined inside of another class, defaults to `private` accessibility but can have any of the five kinds of declared accessibility.

- ▶ Class members default to `private` accessibility but can have any of the five kinds of declared accessibility.

These rules also define the default accessibility, which occurs when a member does not include any access modifiers.

NOTE

Explicitly Declaring Accessibility

Although C# provides reasonable default access modifiers, you should always explicitly declare the accessibility of your class members. This prevents unintended ambiguity, indicates that the choice was a conscious decision, and is self-documenting.

The access modifiers supported by C# are shown in Table 4.1.

TABLE 4.1 Access Modifiers

Modifier	Description
public	Access is not limited.
protected	Access is limited to the containing class or types derived from the containing class.
internal	Access is limited to the containing assembly.
protected internal	Access is limited to the containing assembly or types derived from the containing class.
private	Access is limited to the containing class only.

CAUTION

Protected Internal

Be careful when using protected internal accessibility because it is effectively protected or internal. C# does not provide a concept of protected and internal.

Fields and Constants

Fields are variables that represent data associated with a class. In other words, a field is simply a variable defined in the outermost scope of a class. If you recall from Hour 1, a field can be either an instance field or a static field, and for both types of field, you can specify any of the five access modifiers. Typically, fields are private, which is the default.

If a field, no matter whether it is an instance or static field, is not given an initial value when it is declared, it is assigned the default value appropriate for its type.

Similar to fields, constants can be declared with the same access modifiers. Because a constant must have a value that can be computed at compile time, it must be assigned a value as part of its declaration. One benefit of requiring a value that can be computed at compile time is that a constant can depend on other constants. A constant is usually a value type or a string literal because the only way to create a non-null value of a reference type other than string is to use the new operator, which is not permitted.

NOTE

Constants Should Be Constant

When creating constants, you should be sure that the value is something that is logically constant forever. Good constants are things that never change, such as the value of Pi, the year Elvis was born, or the number of items in a mol.

If you need to create a field that has constant-like behavior but uses a type not allowed in a constant declaration, you can use a static read-only field instead by specifying both the `static` and `readonly` modifiers. A read-only field can be initialized only as part of its declaration or in a constructor.

▼ TRY IT YOURSELF

Working with Fields

By following these steps, you explore how to create a class containing data and how to provide access to that data. If you closed Visual Studio, repeat the previous exercise first. Keep Visual Studio open at the end of this exercise because you will use this application later.

1. Create a new console application.

2. Add a new class file named `Contact.cs`. Inside the body of the class, declare three private fields named `firstName`, `lastName`, and `dateOfBirth` of type `string`, `string`, and `DateTime`, respectively.

3. Add the following method to the class. You learn more about methods later in this hour and more about the `StringBuilder` class in Hour 9, "Using Strings and Regular Expressions":

```
public override string ToString()
{
    StringBuilder stringBuilder = new StringBuilder();
    stringBuilder.AppendFormat("Name: {0} {1}\r\n", this.firstName,
        this.lastName);
    stringBuilder.AppendFormat("Date of Birth: {0}\r\n", this.dateOfBirth);
    return stringBuilder.ToString();
}
```

4. In the `Main` method of the `Program.cs` file, enter the following:

```
Contact c = new Contact();
Console.WriteLine(c.ToString());
```

5. Run the application using Ctrl+F5 and observe that the output matches what is shown in Figure 4.3.

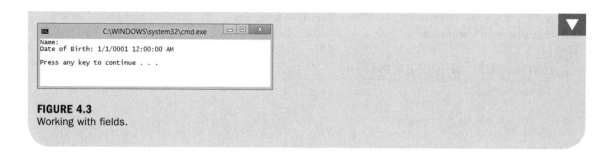

FIGURE 4.3
Working with fields.

Properties

If fields represent state and data but are typically private, there must be a mechanism that enables the class to provide that information publicly. Knowing the different accessibility options allowed, it would be tempting to simply declare the class fields to have `public` accessibility.

This would allow us to satisfy the rules of abstraction, but this would then violate the rules of encapsulation because the fields could be directly manipulated. How, then, is it possible to satisfy both the rules of encapsulation and abstraction? What is needed is something accessed using the same syntax as a field but that can define different accessibility than the field itself. Properties enable us to do exactly that. A property provides a simple way to access a field, called the **backing field**, which can be publicly available while still allowing the internal details of that field to be hidden. Just as fields can be static, properties can also be static and are not associated with an instance of the class.

Although fields declare variables, which require storage in memory, properties do not. Instead, properties are declared with accessors that enable you to control whether a value can be read or written and what should occur when doing so. The `get` accessor enables the property value to be read, whereas the `set` accessor enables the value to be written.

Listing 4.2 shows the simplest way to declare a property. When using this syntax, known as **automatic properties**, you omit the backing field declaration and must always include both the `get` and `set` accessor without a declared implementation, which the compiler provides.

LISTING 4.2   Declaring an Automatic Property

```
class Contact
{
    public string FirstName
    {
        get;
        set;
    }
}
```

In fact, the compiler transforms the code shown in Listing 4.2 into code that looks roughly like that shown in Listing 4.3.

LISTING 4.3   Declaring a Property

```
class Contact
{
   private string firstName;

   public string FirstName
   {
      get
      {
         return this.firstName;
      }
      set
      {
         this.firstName = value;
      }
   }
}
```

CAUTION

Automatic Properties

Automatic properties are convenient, especially when you implement a large number of properties. This convenience does come at a slight cost, however.

Because you don't provide a body for the accessors, you can't specify any logic that executes as part of that accessor, and both accessors must be declared using the automatic property syntax. As a result, if at some point later you realize that you need to provide logic for either of the accessors, you need to add a backing field and the appropriate logic to both accessors.

Fortunately, this change doesn't affect the public interface of your class, so it is safe to make, although it might be a bit tedious.

The get accessor uses a return statement, which simply instructs the accessor to return the value indicated. In the set accessor of the code in Listing 4.3, the class field firstName is set equal to value, but where does value come from? From Table 1.3, you know that value is a contextual keyword. When used in a property set accessor, the value keyword always means "the value that was provided by the caller" and is always typed to be the same as the property type.

Read-Only and Write-Only Properties

For explicitly declared properties, you are allowed to omit either accessor. By including only the `get` accessor, you create a read-only property. To create the equivalent of a read-only property using automatic properties, you would declare the `set` accessor to be `private`.

By including only the `set` accessor, or declaring the `get` accessor to be `private`, you create a write-only property. In practice, you should avoid write-only properties.

By default, the property accessors inherit the accessibility declared on the property definition itself. You can, however, declare a more restrictive accessibility for either the `get` or the `set` accessor.

You can also create calculated properties that are read-only and do not have a backing field. These calculated properties are excellent ways to provide data derived from other information.

Listing 4.4 shows a calculated `FullName` property that combines the `firstName` and `lastName` fields.

LISTING 4.4   Declaring a Calculated Property

```
class Contact
{
   private string firstName;
   private string lastName;

   public string FullName
   {
      get
      {
         return firstName + " " + lastName;
      }
   }
}
```

Because properties are accessed as if they were fields, the operations performed in the accessors should be as simple as possible. If you need to perform more complex operations or perform an operation that could be time consuming or expensive (resource consuming), it might be better to use a method rather than a property.

CAUTION

Properties with Side Effects

The debugger automatically calls property `get` accessors to display results, so properties with side effects can cause unwanted behavior during debugging. In fact, the debugger assumes that property getters follow the best practices, which means they are as follows:

1. Fast
2. Side-effect free
3. Never throw exceptions

▼ TRY IT YOURSELF

Working with Properties

To modify the `Contact` class to allow access to the private data using properties, and to use automatic and calculated properties, follow these steps. If you closed Visual Studio, repeat the previous exercise first. Be sure to keep Visual Studio open at the end of this exercise because you will use this application later.

1. Open the `Contact.cs` file.

2. Add a new public property named `DateOfBirth` that enables reading and writing to the `dateOfBirth` field.

3. Remove the `firstName` and `lastName` fields and create a `FirstName` and `LastName` property as automatic properties.

4. Add a calculated property named `FullName`, which combines the values of the `FirstName` and `LastName` properties. This should be similar to the calculated property shown in Listing 4.4.

5. Modify the `ToString` method to make use of the new `FullName` property instead of performing the string concatenation directly.

6. In the `Main` method of the `Program.cs` file, enter the following code after the `Console.WriteLine` statement:

   ```
   c.FirstName = "Jim";
   c.LastName = "Morrison";
   c.DateOfBirth = new DateTime(1943, 12, 8);
   Console.WriteLine(c.ToString());
   ```

7. Run the application using Ctrl+F5, and observe that the output matches what is shown in Figure 4.4.

FIGURE 4.4
Working with properties.

Methods

If fields and properties define and implement data, methods, which are also called **functions**, define and implement a behavior or action that can be performed. The `WriteLine` action of the `Console` class you have been using in the examples and exercises so far is an example of a method.

Listing 4.5 shows how to add a method to the `Contact` class that verifies an email address. In this case, the `VerifyEmailAddress` method specifies `void` as the return type, meaning that it does not return a value.

LISTING 4.5   Declaring a Method

```
class Contact
{
    public void VerifyEmailAddress(string emailAddress)
    {
    }
}
```

Listing 4.6 shows the same method declared to have a `bool` as the return type.

LISTING 4.6   Declaring a Method That Returns a Value

```
class Contact
{
    public bool VerifyEmailAddress(string emailAddress)
    {
        return true;
    }
}
```

A method declaration can specify any of the five access modifiers. In addition to the access modifiers, a method can also include the `static` modifier. Just as static properties and fields are not associated with an instance of the class, neither are static methods. The `WriteLine` method is actually a static method on the `Console` class.

Methods can accept zero or more parameters, or input, declared by the **formal parameter list**, which consists of one or more comma-separated parameters. Each parameter must include both its type and an identifier. If a method accepts no parameters, an empty parameter list must be specified.

Parameters are divided into three categories:

▶ **Value parameters**—The most common. When a method is called, a local variable is implicitly created for each value parameter and assigned the value of the corresponding argument in the argument list.

▶ **Reference parameters**—Do not create a new storage location but represent the same storage location as the corresponding argument in the argument list. Reference parameters are declared using the `ref` keyword, which must be present both in the parameter list and the argument list.

▶ **Output parameters**—Similar to reference parameters but require the `out` keyword to be present in both the parameter and invocation lists. Unlike reference parameters, they must be given a definite value before the method returns.

NOTE

Parameter Arrays

Parameter arrays, declared with the `params` keyword, can be thought of as a special case of value parameters and declare a single parameter that can contain zero or more arguments of the given type in the argument list.

A method's formal parameter list can include only a single parameter array, in which case it must be the last parameter in the list. A parameter array can also be the only parameter.

For a method to actually perform its desired action on the object, it must be invoked, or called. If the method requires input parameters, those values must be provided in an **argument list**, and if the method provides an output value, that value can also be stored in a variable.

The argument list is normally a one-to-one relationship with the parameter list, meaning that for each parameter, you must provide a value of the appropriate type in the same order when you call the method.

NOTE

Methods as Input

Methods that return a value and properties can also be used as input to other methods, as long as the return value type is compatible with the parameter type. This capability greatly increases the usefulness of both methods and properties, allowing you to chain method or property calls to form behaviors that are more complex.

Looking at the `VerifyEmailAddress` method that has a `void` return type from the earlier examples, you would call the method like this:

```
Contact c = new Contact();
c.VerifyEmailAddress("joe@example.com");
```

However, for the `VerifyEmailAddress` method defined to return a `bool`, you would call the method like this:

```
Contact c = new Contact();
bool result = c.VerifyEmailAddress("joe@example.com");
```

Just as you do with the parameter list, if a method invocation requires no arguments, you must still specify an empty list.

Method Overloading

Ordinarily, two entities cannot have the same name within a declaration space, except for overloaded methods. When two or more methods have the same name in a declaration space but have different method signatures, they are **overloaded**.

The **method signature** is made up of the method name and the number, types, and modifiers of the formal parameters and must be different from all other method signatures declared in the same class; the method name must be different from all other nonmethods declared in the class.

CAUTION

Method Signatures

The return type is not part of the method signature, so methods cannot differ only in return type.

Although the formal parameter list is part of the method signature, methods cannot differ based on a parameter being a `ref` or `out` parameter. When determining uniqueness for the purposes of method overload resolution, the `ref` or `out` attribute of the parameter is not considered.

Overloaded methods can vary only by signature. More appropriately, they can vary only by the number and types of parameters. Consider the `Console.WriteLine` method you have already used; there are 19 different overloads from which you can choose.

Overloading methods is common in the .NET Framework and enables you to give the users of your class a single method with which they interact and provide different input. Based on that input, the compiler figures out which method should actually be used.

CAUTION

Overloads with Different Return Types

Because method signatures do not include the return type, it is possible for overloaded methods to have different return types. Even though this might be legal C# code, you should avoid it to minimize the possibility for confusion.

Method overloading is useful when you want to provide several different possibilities for initiating an action, but method overloading can become unwieldy when there are many options. An example of method overloading is shown in Listing 4.7.

LISTING 4.7   Method Overloading

```
public void Search(float latitude, float longitude)
{
    Search(latitude, longitude, 10, "en-US");
}

public void Search(float latitude, float longitude, int distance)
{
    Search(latitude, longitude, distance, "en-US");
}

public void Search(float latitude, float longitude, int distance, string culture)
{
}
```

▼ TRY IT YOURSELF

Working with Methods

Continuing to expand the `Contact` class, add the `VerifyEmailAddress` and `Search` methods by following these steps. If you closed Visual Studio, repeat the previous exercises first. Be sure to keep Visual Studio open at the end of this exercise because you will use this application later.

1. Open the `Contact.cs` file.

2. Add the `VerifyEmailAddress` method shown in Listing 4.6 so that it returns true if the email address entered is "joe@example.com".

3. Add the overloaded methods shown in Listing 4.7.

4. In the last overloaded `Search` method, enter a `Console.WriteLine` call that prints the values of the parameters.

5. In the `Main` method of the `Program.cs` file, enter the following code after the last `Console.WriteLine` statement:

```
c.Search(37.479444f, -122.450278f);
c.Search(37.479444f, -122.450278f, 50);
c.Search(37.479444f, -122.450278f, 50, "en");

Console.WriteLine(c.VerifyEmailAddress("joe@example.com"));
Console.WriteLine(c.VerifyEmailAddress("jim@example.com"));
```

6. Run the application using Ctrl+F5 and observe that the output matches what is shown in Figure 4.5.

```
C:\WINDOWS\system32\cmd.exe
Name:
Date of Birth: 1/1/0001 12:00:00 AM

Name: Jim Morrison
Date of Birth: 12/8/1943 12:00:00 AM

latitude 37.47944, longitude -122.4503, distance 10, culture en-US
latitude 37.47944, longitude -122.4503, distance 50, culture en-US
latitude 37.47944, longitude -122.4503, distance 50, culture en
True
False
Press any key to continue . . .
```

FIGURE 4.5
Working with methods.

Optional Parameters and Named Arguments

Optional parameters enable you to omit that argument in the invocation list when calling a method. Only value parameters can be optional, and all optional parameters must appear after required parameters, but before a parameter array.

To declare a parameter as optional, you simply provide a default value for it. The modified `Search` method using optional parameters is shown here:

```
public void Search(float latitude, float longitude, int distance = 10, string
culture = "en-US");
```

The `latitude` and `longitude` parameters are required, whereas `distance` and `culture` are both optional. The default values used are the same values provided by the first overloaded `Search` method.

Looking at the Search method overloads from the previous section, it should become clear that the more parameters you have the more overloads you need to provide. In this case, there are only a few overloads, but that is still more than providing a single method with optional parameters. Although overloads are the only option in some cases, particularly those that don't imply a reasonable default for a parameter, often you can achieve the same result using optional parameters.

NOTE

Optional and Required Parameters

A parameter with a default argument is an optional parameter, whereas a parameter without a default argument is a required parameter.

Optional parameters are also particularly useful when integrating with unmanaged programming interfaces, such as the Office automation application programming interfaces (APIs), which were written specifically with optional parameters in mind. In these cases, the original API call might require a large number of arguments (sometimes as many as 30), most of which have reasonable default values.

A method that contains optional parameters can be invoked without explicitly passing arguments for those parameters, allowing the default arguments to be used instead. If, however, the method is invoked and provides an argument for an optional parameter, that argument is used instead of the default.

Listing 4.8 shows an example of calling the Search method, allowing the default values to be used.

LISTING 4.8 Using Optional Parameters

```
Search(27.966667f, 82.533333f, 3);
Search(27.966667f, 82.533333f, 3, "en-GB");
Search(27.966667f, 82.533333f);
```

Although optional parameters allow you the flexibility to omit arguments, you can't skip one that is "in the middle." In other words, you cannot omit arguments between the commas, meaning you could not call the Search method like this:

```
Search(27.966667f, 82.533333f, , "en-GB");
```

To resolve this situation, C# enables any argument to be passed by name, whereby you are explicitly indicating the relationship between the argument and its corresponding parameter. Using named arguments, the different method calls in Listing 4.8 and the illegal call just shown could be written as shown in Listing 4.9.

LISTING 4.9   Using Named Arguments

```
Search(latitude: 27.966667f, longitude: 82.533333f, distance: 3);
Search(latitude: 27.966667f, longitude: 82.533333f, distance: 3, culture: "en-GB");
Search(latitude: 27.966667f, longitude: 82.533333f);
Search(27.966667f, 82.533333f, culture: "en-GB");
Search(latitude: 27.966667f, longitude: 82.533333f, culture: "en-GB");
```

All these calls are equivalent. The first three calls are the same as the calls in Listing 4.8 except that each parameter is explicitly named. The last two calls show how we can omit an argument in the middle of the parameter list and are also the same, although one uses a mixture of named and positional arguments.

NOTE

Named and Positional Arguments

Arguments that are not passed by name are called positional arguments. Positional arguments are the most common.

Named arguments are most often used with optional parameters, but they can be used without them as well. Unlike optional parameters, named arguments can be used with value, reference, and output parameters. You can also use named arguments with parameter arrays, but you must explicitly declare a new array to contain the values, as shown here:

```
Console.WriteLine(String.Concat(values: new string[] { "a", "b", "c" }));
```

As you can see from the `Search` method, by enabling you to explicitly indicate the name of an argument, C# provides an additional (and powerful) way to help write fully describing and self-documenting code.

TIP

Changing the Order of Arguments

Arguments are always evaluated in the order they are specified. Although not generally needed, named arguments enable you to change the order an argument appears in the invocation list:

```
Search(longitude: 82.533333f, latitude: 27.966667f);
Search(latitude: 27.966667f, longitude: 82.533333f);
```

▼ TRY IT YOURSELF

Working with Optional Parameters and Named Arguments

To modify the `Search` methods previously defined to use optional parameters rather than over-loads, follow these steps. If you closed Visual Studio, repeat the previous exercises first. Be sure to keep Visual Studio open at the end of this exercise because you will use this application later.

1. Open the `Contact.cs` file.

2. Remove the first two `Search` methods, leaving only the method containing all four parameters, and modify that method so that `distance` and `culture` are optional, using `10` and `"en-US"` as the default values.

3. Run the application using Ctrl+F5 and observe that the output matches what is shown in Figure 4.6.

```
C:\WINDOWS\system32\cmd.exe

Name:
Date of Birth: 1/1/0001 12:00:00 AM

Name: Jim Morrison
Date of Birth: 12/8/1943 12:00:00 AM

latitude 37.47944, longitude -122.4503, distance 10, culture en-US
latitude 37.47944, longitude -122.4503, distance 50, culture en-US
latitude 37.47944, longitude -122.4503, distance 50, culture en
True
False
latitude 27.96667, longitude 82.53333, distance 3, culture en-US
latitude 27.96667, longitude 82.53333, distance 3, culture en-GB
latitude 27.96667, longitude 82.53333, distance 10, culture en-US
latitude 27.96667, longitude 82.53333, distance 10, culture en-GB
latitude 27.96667, longitude 82.53333, distance 10, culture en-GB
Press any key to continue . . .
```

FIGURE 4.6
Working with optional parameters and named arguments.

4. In the `Main` method of the `Program.cs` file, change the calls to the `Search` method to use different combinations of named parameters and observe the output after each change.

Instantiating a Class

Unlike the predefined value types in which you could simply declare a variable and assign it a value, to use a class in your own programs, you must create an **instance** of that class.

Remember, even though you create new objects directly using the `new` keyword, the virtual execution system is responsible for actually allocating the memory required, and the garbage collector is responsible for deallocating that memory.

Instantiating a class is accomplished using the `new` keyword, like this:

```
Contact c = new Contact();
```

A newly created object must be given an initial state, which means any fields declared must be given an initial value either by explicitly providing one or accepting the default values (see Table 3.12 from Hour 3, "Understanding C# Types").

Sometimes this level of initialization is sufficient, but often it won't be. To provide additional actions that occur during initialization, C# provides an **instance constructor** (sometimes just called a constructor), which is a special method executed automatically when you create the instance.

A constructor has the same name as the class but it cannot return a value, which is different from a method that returns `void`. If the constructor has no parameters, it is the **default** constructor.

NOTE

Default Constructors

Every class must have a constructor, but you don't always have to write one. If you don't include any constructors, the C# compiler creates a default constructor for you. This constructor won't actually do anything, but it will be there.

Because the compiler only generates the default constructor if you don't provide any additional constructors, it is easy to break the public interface of your class by adding an additional constructor that has parameters and forgetting to also explicitly add the default constructor. As a result, it is a good idea to always provide a default constructor rather than letting the compiler generate it for you.

The default constructor (or any constructor) can have any of the accessibility modifiers, so it is entirely possible to create a private default constructor. This is useful if you want to allow your class to be created but want to ensure that certain information is always provided when the object is instantiated.

Listing 4.10 shows the default constructor for the `Contact` class.

LISTING 4.10   Declaring a Default Constructor

```
public class Contact
{
    public Contact()
    {
    }
}
```

Just as it is possible to overload regular methods, it is also possible to overload constructors. The signature for a constructor is the same as it is for a regular method, so the set of overloaded constructors must also vary by signature.

Some reasons for providing specialized constructors follow:

▶ There is no reasonable initial state without parameters.

▶ Providing an initial state is convenient and reasonable for the type.

▶ Constructing the object can be expensive, so you want to ensure that the object has the correct initial state when it is created.

▶ A nonpublic constructor restricts who can create objects using it.

Looking at the `Contact` class you have been using, it would certainly be useful if you provided values for the `firstName`, `lastName`, and `dateOfBirth` fields when creating a new instance. To do that, you would declare an overloaded constructor like the one shown in Listing 4.11.

LISTING 4.11   Declaring a Constructor Overload

```
public class Contact
{
    public Contact(string firstName, string lastName, DateTime dateOfBirth)
    {
        this.firstName = firstName;
        this.lastName = lastName;
        this.dateOfBirth = dateOfBirth;
    }
}
```

In the constructor overload from Listing 4.11, you assigned the value of the parameter to its corresponding private field.

Typically, although not always, when a class contains multiple constructors, those constructors are chained together. To chain constructors together, you use a special syntax that uses the `this` keyword.

NOTE

The `this` Keyword

The `this` keyword refers to the current instance of the class. It is similar to the `Me` keyword in Visual Basic, a `self` identifier in F#, the `__self__` attribute in Python, and `self` in Ruby.

The common uses of `this` follow:

▶ To qualify members hidden by similar names

▶ To pass an object as a parameter to other methods

▶ To specify which constructor should be called from another constructor overload

▶ To indicate the extended type in an extension method

Because static members exist at the class level and are not associated with an instance, you can't use the `this` keyword.

In Listing 4.11, the `this` keyword is used to distinguish between the class field and the parameter because both have the same name.

Listing 4.12 shows the `Contact` class with both constructors from Listing 4.10 and Listing 4.11 using constructor chaining.

LISTING 4.12   Constructor Chaining

```
public class Contact
{
   public Contact()
   {
   }

   public Contact(string firstName, string lastName, DateTime dateOfBirth)
      : this()
   {
      this.firstName = firstName;
      this.lastName = lastName;
      this.dateOfBirth = dateOfBirth;
   }
}
```

One benefit of constructor chaining is that you can chain in any constructor provided by the class, not just the default constructor. When you use constructor chaining, it is important to understand the order in which the constructors execute. The constructor chain is followed until it reaches the last chained constructor, and then constructors will be executed in order going back out of the chain. Listing 4.13 shows a class, C, with three constructors, each chained through to the default constructor.

LISTING 4.13   Chained Constructor Order of Execution

```
public class C
{
   string c1;
   string c2;
   int c3;
```

```
public C()
{
    Console.WriteLine("Default constructor");
}

public C(int i, string p1) : this(p1)
{
    Console.WriteLine(i);
}

public C(string p1) : this()
{
    Console.WriteLine(p1);
}
}
```

Figure 4.7 shows the sequence in which each constructor would execute when instantiated using the second constructor (the one that takes an int and a string as input).

```
C c = new C(3, "C2");
```

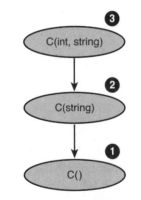

FIGURE 4.7
Constructor chaining sequence.

Static Construction

Instance constructors, like you have just seen, implement the actions required to initialize instances of the class. In some cases, a class might require specific initialization actions to occur at most once and before any instance members are accessed.

To accomplish this, C# provides a **static constructor**, which has the same form as the default constructor with the addition of the `static` modifier instead of one of the access modifiers. Because static constructors initialize the class, you cannot directly call a static constructor.

A static constructor executes at most once and will be executed the first time an instance is created or the first time any of the static class members are referenced.

Nested Classes

A **nested class** is one that is fully enclosed, or nested, inside another class declaration. Nested classes are a convenient way to allow an outer class to create and use objects without making them accessible outside of that class. Although nested classes can be convenient, they are also easy to overuse, which can make your class more difficult to work with.

Nested classes implicitly have at least the same access level as the containing class. For example, if the nested class is `public` but the containing class is `internal`, the nested class is implicitly `internal` as well, and only members of that assembly can access the nested class. However, if the containing class is `public`, the nested class follows the same accessibility rules as a non-nested class.

You should consider implementing a class as a nested class if it has no standalone significance and can be logically contained by another class or members of the class need to access private data of the containing class. Nested classes should generally not be public because they are for the internal use of the containing class.

Partial Classes

Partial classes enable you to split the declaration of a class into multiple parts, typically across multiple files. Partial classes are implemented in exactly the same way as normal classes but contain the keyword `partial` just before the `class` keyword. When working with partial classes, all the parts must be available during compilation and have the same accessibility to form the complete class.

Code-generation tools, such as the visual designers in Visual Studio, which generate a class for you representing the visual control being designed, use partial classes extensively. The machine-generated code is added to one part of the partial class, allowing you to modify the other part of the partial class without concern that your changes will be lost when the machine-generated portion is regenerated.

Partial classes can also be used in other scenarios that don't involve machine-generated code. Large class declarations can benefit from using partial classes; however, this can sometimes mean that your class is trying to do too much and would be better split into multiple classes.

TIP

Nested Classes with Partial Classes

Even though C# does not require a single class per file, like Java, it is often helpful to follow that structure. When using nested classes, this isn't possible unless the containing class is a partial class.

Static Classes

So far, you have seen the `static` modifier applied to constructors, fields, methods, and properties. You can also apply the `static` modifier to a class, which defines a static class. A static class can have only a static constructor, and as a result, it is not possible to create an instance of a static class. For that reason, static classes most commonly contain utility or helper methods that do not require a class instance to work.

Static classes can contain only static members, but those members are not automatically static. You must explicitly include the `static` modifier; however, you can declare any static member as `public`, `private`, or `internal`.

CAUTION

Implicit Static Members

Static classes can contain only static members, but those members are not automatically static. You must explicitly include the `static` modifier; however, you can declare any static member as `public`, `private`, or `internal`.

Extension Methods

Extension methods are regular static methods, but the first parameter includes the `this` modifier and represents the type instance being extended, typically called the **type extension parameter**. Extension methods must be declared in a non-nested, nongeneric static class.

When the namespace containing an extension class is in scope through a `using` directive, the extension methods appear as if they were native instance methods on the extended type. This allows them to be called in a natural and intuitive manner.

Because an extension method is nothing more than a specially marked static method, it does not have any special access to the type being extended and can work only with the public interface of the extended type. It also enables you to call the extension method in the more traditional way by referring to its fully qualified name.

NOTE

Access to Internals

An extension method defined in the same assembly as the type being extended also has access to internal members of that type.

GO TO ▶ **HOUR 12, "UNDERSTANDING GENERICS,"** for more information on generic classes.

Although an extension method matching the signature of an actual method on the type can be defined, it will not be visible. The compiler ensures that during method resolution, any actual class methods take precedence over extension methods. This ensures that an extension method cannot change the behavior of a standard class method, which would cause unpredictable, or at least unexpected, behavior.

TRY IT YOURSELF ▼

Working with Extension Methods

By following these steps, you add an extension method on the `DateTime` class and modify the `Contact` class to use this new extension method. If you closed Visual Studio, repeat the previous exercises first.

1. Create a new file named `Extensions.cs` in the BusinessLogic project.

2. Make the `Extensions` class static and create a new extension method named `GetFullName` that extends `Contact` and uses the same logic as you used for the `FullName` property.

3. Remove the `FullName` property in the `Contact` class and modify the `ToString` method to use this new extension method.

4. Run the application using Ctrl+F5 and observe that the output matches what is shown in Figure 4.8.

```
C:\WINDOWS\system32\cmd.exe
Name:
Date of Birth: 1/1/0001 12:00:00 AM

Name: Jim Morrison
Date of Birth: 12/8/1943 12:00:00 AM

latitude 37.47944, longitude -122.4503, distance 10, culture en-US
latitude 37.47944, longitude -122.4503, distance 50, culture en-US
latitude 37.47944, longitude -122.4503, distance 50, culture en
True
False
latitude 27.96667, longitude 82.53333, distance 3, culture en-US
latitude 27.96667, longitude 82.53333, distance 3, culture en-GB
latitude 27.96667, longitude 82.53333, distance 10, culture en-US
latitude 27.96667, longitude 82.53333, distance 10, culture en-GB
latitude 27.96667, longitude 82.53333, distance 10, culture en-GB
Press any key to continue . . .
```

FIGURE 4.8
Results of working with extension methods.

Object Initializers

You have seen how to create constructors for your class that provide a convenient way to set the initial state. However, as with method overloading, the more fields you require to be set, the more overloaded constructors you might need to provide. Although constructors support optional parameters, sometimes you want to set properties when you create the object instance.

Classes provide an object initialization syntax that enables you to assign values to any publicly accessible fields or properties as part of the constructor call. This allows a great deal of flexibility and can significantly reduce the number of overloaded constructors you need to provide.

Listing 4.14 shows code similar to what you wrote in the "Working with Properties" Try It Yourself exercise, followed by code using an object initializer. The code generated by the compiler in both cases is almost the same.

Listing 4.14   Object Initializers

```
Contact c1 = new Contact();
c1.FirstName = "Jim";
c1.LastName = "Morrison";
c1.DateOfBirth = new DateTime(1943, 12, 8);
Console.WriteLine(c1.ToString());

Contact c2 = new Contact
    {
        FirstName = "Jim",
        LastName = "Morrison",
        DateOfBirth = new DateTime(1943, 12, 8)
    };

Console.WriteLine(c2.ToString());
```

As long as there are no dependencies between fields or properties, object initializers are an easy and concise way to instantiate and initialize an object at the same time.

Summary

At this point, you should have a good understanding of how classes in C# provide a language implementation for object-oriented programming. You learned how scope affects the visibility of members in a class and how you can change accessibility using the different access modifiers. From there, you built a class and instantiated an instance of that class. You then learned about methods and properties, including method overloading, optional, and named parameters. Finally, you learned about nested and partial classes.

Departing from the simple examples you worked with in the previous hours, the samples and exercises in this hour focused on building more real-world classes.

Q&A

Q. What are the four primary principles of object-oriented programming?

A. The four primary principles of object-oriented programming are encapsulation, abstraction, inheritance, and polymorphism.

Q. Why are encapsulation and abstraction important?

A. By using encapsulation and abstraction, you can change internal implementation details without affecting already-written code that uses that class.

Q. What is method overloading?

A. Method overloading is creating more than one method of the same name in a given type. Overloaded methods must have different signatures.

Q. How do properties enable a class to meet the goals of encapsulation?

A. A property provides a simple way to access a field that can be publicly available while still allowing the internal details of that field to be hidden.

Q. What are partial classes?

A. A partial class contains the keyword `partial` on all class declarations and is typically split across multiple source code files.

Q. What is the benefit of using extension methods?

A. Using extension methods enables additional functionality to be added to an existing type without requiring the use of inheritance. This additional functionality can then be used in a natural and intuitive way.

Workshop

Quiz

1. What are the five access modifiers available in C#?
2. What is the default accessibility for a class?
3. What is a constructor?
4. Can the default constructor of a class have parameters?

5. Using the code shown in Listing 4.13, what is the output of the following statement?

```
C c = new C(3, "C2");
```

6. When can a read-only field be assigned?

7. What is method overloading?

8. Are there limitations when using automatic properties?

9. What is a nested class?

10. Can extension methods access private members of the type being extended?

11. What happens when the new operator is executed?

Answers

1. The five access modifiers available in C# are `public`, `protected`, `internal`, `protected internal`, and `private`.

2. Classes default to `internal` accessibility but are allowed to have either `public` or `internal` declared accessibility. Nested classes default to `private` accessibility but are allowed to have any accessibility.

3. A constructor is a special method that is executed automatically when you create an object to provide additional initialization actions.

4. No, the default constructor of a class must always have no parameters.

5. The output of the statement is

```
Default Constructor
C2
3
```

6. A read-only field can be initialized only as part of its declaration or in a constructor.

7. Method overloading is creating more than one method of the same name that differs only by the number and type of parameters.

8. Automatic properties do not provide a way to access the implicit backing field, do not enable you to specify additional statements that execute as part of the `get` or `set` accessor, and do not enable a mixture of regular and automatic syntax.

9. A nested class is one that is fully enclosed inside another class declaration.

10. Because extension methods are simply static methods, they do not have any special access to the type they extend. However, an extension method defined in the same assembly as the type being extended also has access to internal members of that type.

11. The two primary actions that occur when the new operator is executed are (1) memory is allocated from the heap and (2) the constructor for the class is executed to initialize the allocated memory.

Exercises

1. Add a class to the `PhotoViewer` project provided as part of the book downloads. This
    class should be named `Photo` and be in the `PhotoViewer` namespace. The class should
    have the following private fields and a read-only property to retrieve the value of those
    fields:

Data Type	Field Name
bool	exists
BitmapFrame	image
Uri	source

    Add the following constructor:

    ```
    public Photo(Uri path)
    {
        if (path.IsFile)
        {
            this.source = path;
        }
    }
    ```

Inheritance, Interfaces, and Abstract Classes

What You'll Learn in This Hour:

▶ Inheritance and polymorphism
▶ Abstract classes and members
▶ Working with interfaces

In the last hour, you learned how classes in C# provide the language support required for object-oriented and component-oriented programming through encapsulation and abstraction. Although these aspects of object-oriented programming are important, they don't provide a good mechanism for expressing a hierarchical relationship between specialized variations of a class.

Inheritance provides a natural way to express such relationships. Through inheritance, you can create a completely new class that inherits the characteristics and behaviors from its parents. Polymorphism, which is the capability of a type to be used like another type, is a natural result of inheritance.

In this hour, you learn how C# provides support for inheritance and polymorphism through the use of abstract classes and interfaces. You also learn how C# enables you to prevent a class from being extended.

Inheritance and Polymorphism

Just as children inherit characteristics and behaviors from their parents, classes can inherit characteristics and behavior as well. **Inheritance**, also called derivation, in object-oriented programming enables a new class to be created (called a child or **derived class**) that inherits the characteristics and behaviors from its parents (called base classes).

Inheritance enables you to reduce the apparent complexity of a problem into manageable parts. These parts form conceptual layers that provide increasing amounts of specialization or generalization, depending on your point of view, describing in a natural way the hierarchical nature of certain problems expressed using an "is-a" relationship.

CAUTION

Multiple Inheritance

The general idea of inheritance is simple. However, many object-oriented programming languages enable derived classes to inherit from multiple parents, called multiple inheritance.

Multiple inheritance does not change the requirement that the classes have an "is-a" relationship and can be a powerful mechanism, but that power can also result in considerable complexity in the implementation. It can also cause ambiguity when trying to understand the derivation chain of a class because a class with two parents enables two different inheritance paths to a particular base class.

To remove the possible ambiguity and because the number of scenarios for which multiple inheritance is the only appropriate solution is rather small, C# only allows single inheritance.

Typically, specialization is when the new class has additional data or behavior that is not part of the inherited (base) class. Specialization can also occur when the base class specifies that only an action or behavior exists but does not implement that behavior. It is then the responsibility of the derived classes to provide the implementation.

By creating a new type derived from an existing type, you inherit characteristics and behaviors from the parent type. Inheritance also enables derived classes to make several changes from their base class. The derived class can do the following:

▶ Add new private data.

▶ Add new behavior.

▶ Redefine existing behavior.

Again, taking the car example from the last hour, Figure 5.1 shows a possible inheritance chain for a car. A car is a four-wheel vehicle, which in turn is a vehicle. The vehicle is the base, or root, class and provides behavior and data common for all vehicles. As we go down the hierarchy, we find the four-wheel and two-wheel vehicle base classes, which are specializations of vehicle that add additional behavior and data. Finally, we find the car, truck, and motorcycle classes, which are derived classes that might also add additional behavior and data.

In object-oriented programming, **polymorphism** is the capability of one type to be used like another type. Typically, there are two ways this is achieved:

▶ One type inherits (or derives) from another type, enabling it access to the same actions and public data as its parent.

▶ Both types implement a compatible public interface, enabling the same actions and public data but possibly different implementations.

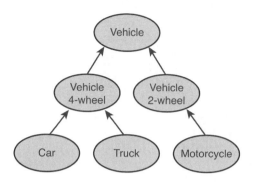

FIGURE 5.1
A class diagram.

Looking at the class diagram in Figure 5.1, it should be clear that although a car and a truck are clearly not the same type, either of those could be substituted for a four-wheel vehicle because they both inherit from that class. Likewise, although a motorcycle could not be substituted for a four-wheel vehicle, it could, along with a car or a truck, be substituted for a vehicle.

As you can see, polymorphism relies heavily on the ideas presented in encapsulation, abstraction, and inheritance. Without these aspects, it would be virtually impossible for one class to be substituted for another.

NOTE

Polymorphism

Polymorphism is one of those words that might sound like it is complicated, but it really isn't. Polymorphism is a natural and common occurrence. The word is the combination of the Greek words poly (meaning many) and morphe (meaning shape or form), literally meaning many shapes or forms.

Inheritance is easily accomplished in C# by providing the name of the class being inherited on the class declaration. Listing 5.1 shows the hierarchy described by Figure 5.1 in code.

LISTING 5.1   A Class Hierarchy in Code

```
public class Vehicle { }

public class FourWheeledVehicle : Vehicle { }

public class TwoWheeledVehicle : Vehicle { }
```

```
public class Car : FourWheeledVehicle { }

public class Truck : FourWheeledVehicle { }

public class Motorcycle : TwoWheeledVehicle { }
```

This type of inheritance is also called **implementation inheritance** because you are actually inheriting an implementation from the parent class. Now that you have a code representation of the hierarchy, how would you go about using it?

CAUTION

Designing Class Hierarchies

The one thing that inheritance does not enable is removing data or behaviors. If you find that you need to remove behavior or data from one of your derived classes, it is most likely because your class hierarchy is not designed correctly.

Designing class hierarchies is not always an easy task and usually takes several attempts to get it right. The best approach is to spend a little more time thinking about the relationships between objects you know and those that might be needed later. If your class hierarchy is overly shallow (not a lot of inheritance) or overly deep (a lot of inheritance), you might want to rethink the relationships.

Remember, not everything in a class hierarchy must be related to one another. It's perfectly acceptable to have a hierarchy that is conceptually made up of several smaller ones.

In C#, an expression assigned to a variable must be known to be compatible with the type of that variable. This means the following code is not allowed:

```
Car c = new Car();
Truck t = c;
```

This should make sense, as a truck is not the same thing as a car. However, logically both a truck and a car are a FourWheeledVehicle and, in turn, a Vehicle so the following code is allowed:

```
Car c = new Car();
Truck t = new Truck();
Vehicle v1 = c;
Vehicle v2 = t;
```

NOTE

Upcasting and Downcasting

The process of casting a derived class to one of its base classes is called upcasting. Casting from a base class to one of its derived classes is called downcasting.

Even though c and v1 both refer to the same Car object, there is an important distinction. When you access c, you are doing so through a variable declared to be of type Car, allowing you access to the members defined by Car and by its base class FourWheeledVehicle, and subsequently Vehicle. However, when you access v1, you are doing so through a variable declared to be of type Vehicle that allows you access only to those members defined by Vehicle.

Think of it this way: A car knows that it is a vehicle and therefore enables access to anything a vehicle can do, but a vehicle knows nothing of a car and can therefore allow you access only to what it knows.

Although you can move upward in the class hierarchy (going from a more derived class to a less derived one), you cannot move downward. For example, the following is not allowed:

```
Vehicle v1 = new Vehicle();
Car c = v1;
```

This might be surprising at first until you remember that a Vehicle could represent any one of five different types. As a result, it is not possible to implicitly assign an expression of a more general type to a variable of a more specific one.

To achieve this, you must explicitly tell the compiler that you want to downcast the base class to the derived class. In this case, you would want to write:

```
Vehicle v1 = new Vehicle();
Car c = (Car)v1;
```

Although this code is legal, it does pose a problem. What would happen if you wrote the following instead?

```
Vehicle v1 = new Vehicle();
Vehicle v2 = new Truck();
Car c = (Car)v2;
```

This code is still legal and will compile without error, but will result in an InvalidCastException at runtime, saying that you cannot cast an object of type Truck to type Car.

GO TO ▶ HOUR 11, "HANDLING ERRORS USING EXCEPTIONS," for more information on exceptions.

The way around this problem is to follow the "trust but verify" philosophy. This simply means that you trust that the code will compile and run, but you verify that the variable of the base class type is actually the correct derived type before performing the cast. Listing 5.2 shows a variety of ways you can accomplish "trust but verify."

LISTING 5.2   "Trust but Verify" Code

```
Car c = new Car();
Truck t = new Truck();
Vehicle v1 = c;
Vehicle v2 = t;

if (typeof(Car).IsAssignableFrom(v1.GetType()))
{
    c = (Car)v1;
    Console.WriteLine(c.GetType());
}

if (v1 is Car)
{
    c = (Car)v1;
    Console.WriteLine(c.GetType());
}

c = v1 as Car;
if (c != null)
{
    Console.WriteLine(c.GetType());
}
```

The first method uses the underlying type system in C# to determine if the type `Car` (the result of the `typeof(Car)` call) is assignable from the type of `v1` (the result of the `v1.GetType()` call), and, if so, explicitly casts `v1` to `Car`. A base class is always assignable from one of its derived classes.

The second method is somewhat simpler and asks the type system if `v1` is a `Car`, and if so, explicitly casts `v1` to `Car`.

The third method is the simplest option, and says if `v1` is convertible to `Car` then perform the conversion and return the result; otherwise, return `null`.

▼ TRY IT YOURSELF

Simple Class Inheritance and Polymorphism

To implement the class hierarchy shown in Listing 5.1 and explore how inheritance and polymorphism behave, follow these steps. Keep Visual Studio open at the end of this exercise because you will use this application later.

1. Create a new console application.

2. Add a new class file named `Vehicles.cs` and implement the basic class hierarchy shown in Listing 5.1.

3. In the `Main` method of the `Program.cs` file, enter the following code:

```
Vehicle v1 = new Vehicle();
Car c1 = (Car)v1;
```

4. Run the application by pressing Ctrl+F5. You should encounter an `InvalidCastException`, as shown in Figure 5.2.

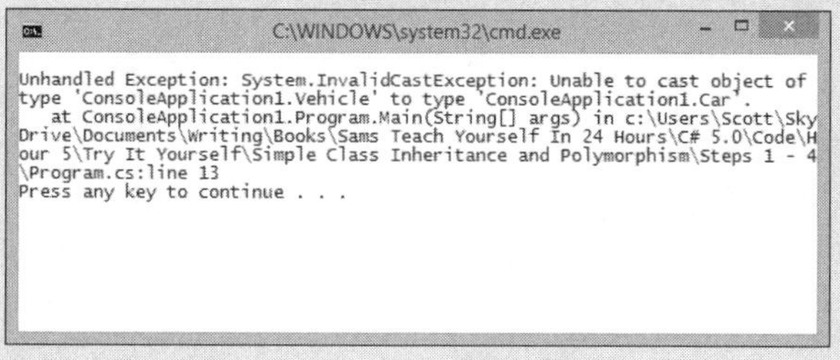

FIGURE 5.2
Result showing an `InvalidCastException`.

5. Remove the statements you previously entered from step 2, and replace it with the code shown in Listing 5.2.

6. Run the application again by pressing Ctrl+F5 and observe that the output matches what is shown in Figure 5.3.

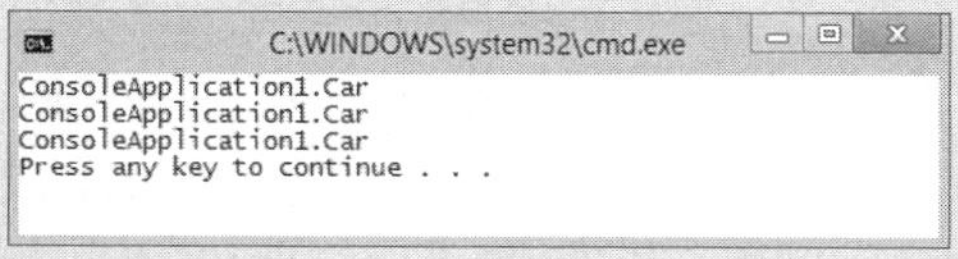

FIGURE 5.3
Result of working with class inheritance and polymorphism.

Listing 5.3 shows a modified version of the code hierarchy from Listing 5.1, providing constructors for some of the derived classes that call one of the base class constructors.

CAUTION

Constructor Chaining and Default Constructors

If you don't explicitly chain a base class constructor, the compiler tries to chain the default constructor.

The problem here is that not all classes have a public default constructor, in which case forgetting to explicitly chain the correct base class constructor can result in a compiler error.

LISTING 5.3   **Constructors in Derived Classes**

```
public class Vehicle
{
    private Vehicle() { }

    public Vehicle(int wheels)
    {
        Console.WriteLine("The number of wheels requested is {0}", wheels);
    }
}

public class FourWheeledVehicle : Vehicle
{
    public FourWheeledVehicle() : base(4) { }
}

public class TwoWheeledVehicle : Vehicle
{
    public TwoWheeledVehicle() : base(2) { }
}

public class Car : FourWheeledVehicle { }

public class Truck : FourWheeledVehicle { }

public class Motorcycle : TwoWheeledVehicle { }
```

▼ TRY IT YOURSELF

Constructor Chaining

By following these steps, you modify the class hierarchy you created in the previous section to explore constructor chaining. If you closed Visual Studio, repeat the previous exercise first. Be sure to keep Visual Studio open at the end of this exercise because you will use this application later.

1. Open the file named `Vehicles.cs`.

2. Modify the classes to reflect the code shown in Listing 5.3.

3. In the `Main` method of the `Program.cs` file, replace the code with code to create a new car, motorcycle, truck, and three-wheeled vehicle.

4. Run the application using Ctrl+F5 and observe that the output matches what is shown in Figure 5.4.

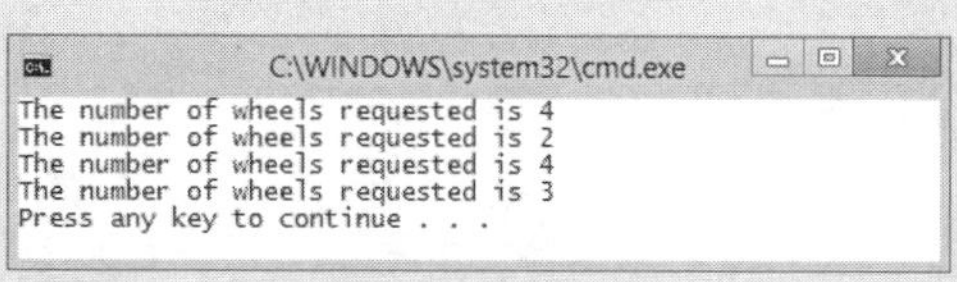

FIGURE 5.4
Result of working with constructor chaining.

Working with Inherited Members

Sometimes a derived class needs to have a method or property with the same name but a different behavior, accomplished using **member overriding**.

To keep things as clear as possible, C# requires the use of two different keywords to override a class member. In the base class, the member declaration must contain the `virtual` keyword, whereas in the derived class, the member declaration must contain the `override` keyword.

Typically, virtual members are simple in the behavior they implement—if they provide a behavior at all. Their purpose is to ensure that in all cases, the derived classes will have the member available and that it will perform some nominal default behavior. The expectation is that the derived classes will override the virtual member with a more appropriate and specific behavior.

Just as you can with constructors, you can use the `base` keyword to access the original implementation. The `base` keyword behaves similarly to the `this` keyword, except it refers to the immediate base class rather than the current class.

Member overriding has certain restrictions:

▶ The overriding member declaration cannot change the accessibility declared by the virtual member.

▶ Neither a virtual nor overridden member can be declared as `private`.

▶ Both declarations must have the same signature.

▶ The overridden member cannot contain the `new`, `static`, or `virtual` modifiers.

CAUTION

Default Virtual Members

Whereas some object-oriented languages, such as Java, default to making members virtual, C# does not. This means that you must be explicit about the possibility of a member being overridden by including the `virtual` keyword because only members declared as virtual can be overridden.

▼ TRY IT YOURSELF

Overriding Base Class Members

Follow these steps to modify the classes you previously created to create virtual and overridden class members. If you closed Visual Studio, repeat the previous exercise first. Be sure to keep Visual Studio open at the end of this exercise because you will use this application later.

1. Open the file named `Vehicles.cs`.

2. Modify the `Vehicle` class to include a virtual `Operate` method that simply prints the word *Default* to the console.

3. Modify the `FourWheeledVehicle` and `TwoWheeledVehicle` classes to override the `Operate` method, and print "Driving a four-wheeled vehicle" and "Riding a two-wheeled vehicle," respectively, after the call to `base.Operate()`.

4. Modify the `Car` class to also override the `Operate` method, but this time replace the call to `base.Operate()` with a `Console.WriteLine` statement that prints "Driving a car."

5. In the `Main` method of the `Program.cs` file, add a call to `Operate` after each instance created. Follow that with a `Console.WriteLine()` to print an empty line.

6. Run the application using Ctrl+F5 and observe that the output matches what is shown in Figure 5.5.

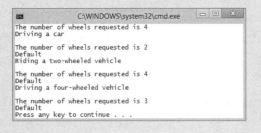

FIGURE 5.5
Result showing how overriding base class members behave.

As you saw from the previous exercise, an overridden member is implicitly `virtual` and can be further overridden by subsequent derived classes. You did this when you implemented the override for `Drive` in the `Car` class, even though `FourWheeledVehicle` already overrode `Drive`. Normally this behavior is desirable; however, there might be times when you want to prevent it from occurring.

CAUTION

Member Hiding

In addition to member overriding, C# also allows you to hide a base class member. This is typically done when you need to redefine a nonvirtual base class member and is achieved by adding the `new` keyword in front of the new definition. Because member hiding is based on the signature, you can use member hiding to change the return type of the member as well.

Hiding base class members is something that can produce unexpected, or at least unintended, results. Although hiding base class members can sometimes be intentional in the derived class, it is often a result of a change to the base class (which you might or might not have control of) that causes you to unintentionally hide a base class member or an incorrectly designed class hierarchy.

As a result, when a base class member is hidden, the compiler generates a warning to let you know. If you are sure that is what you want to do, you should use the `new` keyword on the derived member. The use of the `new` keyword does not remove the need to be cautious when hiding base class members; it simply makes it explicit.

You can prevent further inheritance for a class member or a class by **sealing** it. To seal a class member, you include the `sealed` keyword in addition to the `override` keyword. To seal a class, you simply include the `sealed` keyword.

For example, to seal the `FourWheeledVehicle.Operate` method from the "Overriding Base Class Members" Try It Yourself, you would add the sealed keyword to the method signature, as shown in the following:

```
public class FourWheeledVehicle : Vehicle
{
   public FourWheeledVehicle() : base(4) { }

   public sealed override void Operate()
   {
      base.Operate();
      Console.WriteLine("Driving a four-wheeled vehicle");
   }
}
```

Similarly, if you wanted to prevent further derivation from the `TwoWheeledVehicle` class, you would add the sealed keyword to the class definition, as shown here:

```
public sealed class TwoWheeledVehicle : Vehicle
{
   public TwoWheeledVehicle() : base(2) { }

   public override void Operate()
   {
      base.Operate();
      Console.WriteLine("Riding a two-wheeled vehicle");
   }
}
```

NOTE

Sealing Classes

Designing classes properly for inheritance can be a lot of work, so you have three choices:

▶ Leave the class unsealed but do the work to make it safely inheritable, which might end up being unnecessary if no one ever inherits from your class.

▶ Leave the class unsealed but don't do the work. This puts the burden on the consumer for understanding how your class can be safely extended.

▶ Seal the class. If you are reasonably certain no one will need to inherit from your class, it is probably the best option. It is always possible to unseal the class later, which should have no breaking impact on code that is already using it. Sealing a class also allows certain additional runtime optimizations to occur during JIT compilation.

Abstract Classes and Members

Although inheriting from a class provides a lot of benefit, there are times when you need to provide derived classes with a standard implementation and need to guarantee that a derived class provides an implementation for a particular property or method, or it simply makes sense to have a class that can have no instances. If you think back to the vehicle hierarchy, there are simply no objects that are "vehicles" that are not also some more specific kind of vehicle. To achieve these goals, C# provides the `abstract` modifier that can be applied to both classes and class members.

By declaring a class as `abstract`, you prevent it from being instantiated directly. As a result, abstract classes typically have `protected` constructors rather than `public` ones. If you don't provide a default constructor, the compiler creates a protected default constructor for you. An abstract class can contain virtual, nonvirtual, and abstract members. An abstract member is declared with the `abstract` modifier but does not provide an implementation. Listing 5.4 shows an example of the `Vehicle` class as an abstract class containing an abstract method named `Operate`.

TIP

Static Classes

The compiler actually implements static classes as `sealed abstract` classes, preventing them from being instantiated or inherited.

LISTING 5.4 The Abstract Vehicle Class

```
public abstract class Vehicle
{
    int wheels;
```

```
    protected Vehicle() { }

    public Vehicle(int wheels)
    {
        this.wheels = wheels;
    }

    public abstract void Operate();
}
```

Unlike virtual members, which a derived class can optionally override, abstract members must be overridden in a **concrete** (nonabstract) **derived class**. If the derived class is also abstract, it does not need to override a base class abstract member. Because an abstract member has no implementation until overridden in a derived class, it is not possible for that overridden member to call the same member from the base class.

Using Abstract Classes

By following these steps, you explore how to create an abstract class, and use it as a base class for derived classes. If you closed Visual Studio, repeat the previous exercise first. Be sure to keep Visual Studio open at the end of this exercise because you will use this application later.

1. Open the file named `Vehicles.cs`.

2. Modify the `Vehicle` class so that it is an abstract class and make the `Operate` method an abstract method.

3. Correct the resulting compiler errors.

4. Run the application using Ctrl+F5 and observe that the output matches what is shown in Figure 5.6.

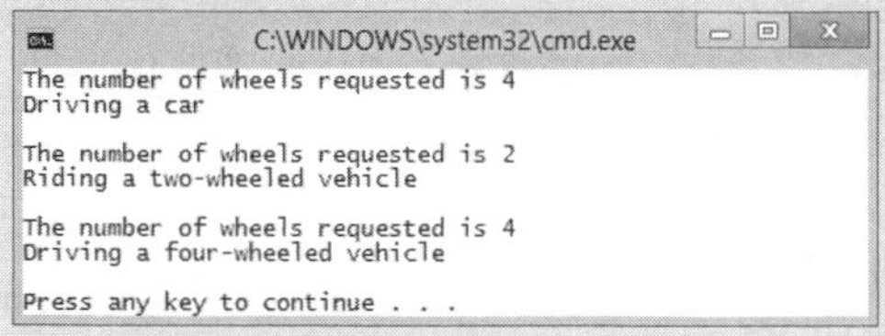

FIGURE 5.6
Result of working with abstract classes.

Working with Interfaces

Because C# does not enable you to inherit from multiple base classes, you need to carefully choose that base class. Fortunately, C# provides an alternative that does enable multiple inheritance. An interface defines a set of common characteristics and behaviors, in the form of public properties and methods, that all derived classes are guaranteed to implement. Think of an interface as a partial type definition, or a type description.

Like abstract classes, an interface cannot be directly instantiated and can have methods, properties, and events. Interfaces cannot contain fields, constructors, or a destructor.

CAUTION

Interfaces Are Not Contracts

It is common to say that an interface defines a contract that any derived classes must implement. This is only true in the sense that the inherited interface defines the method signatures and properties guaranteed to be available on the derived class.

In no way does this provide any guarantee of a specific implementation. It is entirely possible to satisfy the interface while providing no useful implementation whatsoever. The interface simply requires any class inheriting it to have specific properties and methods.

You declare an interface in much the same way as declaring a class, substituting the keyword `interface` for the `class` keyword. An interface can be `internal`, `public`, `protected`, or `private`; however, if you don't explicitly indicate the accessibility, interfaces default to `internal` accessibility. All interface members are automatically `public` and cannot specify an access modifier. Because interface members are also automatically `abstract`, they cannot provide an implementation.

When a class inherits an interface, called **interface inheritance** or **interface implementation**, it inherits only the member names and signatures because the interface doesn't provide an implementation. This means the derived class must provide an implementation for all members defined by that interface. To inherit an interface, you provide the name of the interface just as if you were inheriting a class. You can inherit from multiple interfaces simply by providing a comma-separated list of interface names.

NOTE

Inheriting Both a Base Class and Interfaces

C# uses a positional notation to indicate the base class and the interfaces in the inheritance list. If a class inherits from both a base class and one or more interfaces, the base class is always listed first.

You can also "mix and match" inheritance, meaning that you can inherit from only a base class, inherit only one or more interfaces, or inherit from both a base class and one or more interfaces. If a base class inherits from an interface, any classes that derive from that base class inherit that implementation.

Although interfaces cannot inherit from a class, they can inherit from other interfaces. Interface inheritance simply means that to satisfy one interface, you must also satisfy the other inherited interfaces. This enables you to create highly specialized interfaces and then aggregate those interfaces together to form a larger interface. This is particularly useful if you have multiple unrelated classes that need to implement similar functionality, such as saving data to a compressed ZIP file. The behavior and characteristics related to this could be defined by interfaces, which could then be included as part of other interfaces that define your business objects.

TIP

Interfaces and Extension Methods

In the context of interfaces, extension methods become even more powerful as you can also extend interfaces. Doing this allows all types that implement that interface to gain the extension method. In fact, the entire Language Integrated Query (LINQ) functionality for the generic collections is implemented this way.

When an interface inherits from another interface, the derived interface defines only members that are new; it does not redefine the members of the inherited interfaces. When a class implements this aggregated interface, it must provide implementations for members defined in all the interfaces.

Where the real power and flexibility of using interfaces shine is when used in combination with abstract classes. Because interface methods are implicitly abstract, an abstract class does not need to provide an implementation for an interface member. Instead, it can provide its own abstract member for the interface member. In that case, any derived classes must override it and provide an implementation.

Looking at the vehicle hierarchy from Listing 5.1, what would it take to introduce the concept of emergency vehicles, such as fire trucks, police cars, and police motorcycles? You could introduce a new class, called EmergencyVehicle, but it isn't entirely clear where this new class fits in the existing hierarchy because it would need to be a base class at the same level as FourWheeledVehicle and TwoWheeledVehicle, and any concrete classes would want to inherit from EmergencyVehicle and Truck, Car, or Motorcycle. You already know this type of multiple inheritance is not possible, but how would this change if you used interfaces instead?

▼ TRY IT YOURSELF

Working with Interfaces

These steps explore how to use both interfaces and base classes to create a flexible class hierarchy. If you closed Visual Studio, repeat the previous exercise first.

1. Create a new interface named `IVehicle` that defines a method named `Operate` and modify the `Vehicle` class to inherit from it. The `IVehicle.Operate` method should have the same signature as the `Vehicle.Operate` method.

2. Create a new interface named `IEmergencyVehicle` that inherits from `IVehicle` and provides a void method named `SoundSiren` that takes no parameters.

3. Create three new classes named `PoliceCar`, `PoliceMotorcycle`, and `FireTruck` that derive from the appropriate base class and implement the `IEmergencyVehicle` interface. For the implementation of `SoundSiren`, simply print a message to the console.

4. In the `Main` method of the `Program.cs` file, replace the existing code with code that will:

    a. Create a new instance of a `Car`, assigned to a variable named `car`, and call the `Operate` method.

    b. Assign a new instance of `PoliceCar` to `car` and call the `Operate` method.

    c. Create a new instance of `PoliceCar` named `policeCar` and assign `car` to it. You need to cast `car` to be of type `PoliceCar`.

    d. Call `SoundSiren` on `policeCar`.

5. Run the application using Ctrl+F5, and observe that the output matches what is shown in Figure 5.7.

```
C:\WINDOWS\system32\cmd.exe
The number of wheels requested is 4
Driving a car
The number of wheels requested is 4
Driving a car
Police Car
Press any key to continue . . .
```

FIGURE 5.7
Result of working with interfaces.

When you implemented the interfaces from the last exercise, you used **implicit interface implementation,** in which the class simply declares public members that match those defined by the interface. This is the most common form of interface implementation.

What happens if the class implements multiple interfaces that specify a member with the same signature, as shown in Listing 5.5?

LISTING 5.5   Multiple Interface Inheritance

```
interface IVehicle
{
   void Operate();
}

interface IEquipment
{
   void Operate();
}

class PoliceCar : IVehicle, IEquipment
{
   public void Operate()
   {
   }
}
```

In this case, the compiler makes the public method match both interface members. If this isn't what you intended, you must use **explicit interface implementation**, as shown in Listing 5.6, which requires that you fully qualify the name of the member being implemented. In explicit interface implementation, you do not provide an access modifier because the implementing member is implicitly public but only explicitly through the interface.

LISTING 5.6   Multiple Explicit Interface Inheritance

```
interface IVehicle
{
   void Operate();
}

interface IEquipment
{
   void Operate();
}

class PoliceCar : IVehicle, IEquipment
{
   void IVehicle.Operate()
   {
   }

   void IEquipment.Operate()
   {
   }
}
```

This means that the implementing class must be converted, either implicitly or explicitly, to that interface to have access to the member. As a result, explicit interface implementation has the effect of hiding members from casual use.

Summary

You have now completed your understanding of how C# classes provide a language implementation for object-oriented programming. You learned how class inheritance enables polymorphic objects, chaining base class constructors, and how to override or hide inherited class members. You also learned about abstract classes, and learned how to prevent a class or class member from further inheritance by sealing. Finally, you learned about interfaces and interface implementation.

Q&A

Q. Does C# support multiple inheritance?

A. No, C# supports only single inheritance, enabling a class to inherit from only a single parent, or base, class.

Q. What is polymorphism?

A. Polymorphism is the ability of one type to be used like another type.

Q. What is upcasting and downcasting?

A. The process of casting a derived class to one of its base classes is called upcasting. Casting from a base class to one of its derived classes is called downcasting.

Q. What is member hiding?

A. Member hiding enables a derived class to have a member with the same name as a base class member with exactly the same behavior.

Q. What is a virtual member?

A. A virtual member contains the `virtual` modifier in the base class and might or might not provide default behavior. Derived classes can override a virtual member and provide more appropriate specific behavior.

Q. Is it possible to prevent a class from being inherited?

A. Yes, classes marked with the sealed modifier cannot be inherited.

Q. What is an interface?

A. An interface defines a set of common characteristics and behaviors that all derived classes are guaranteed to implement but cannot contain any implementation, and all interface members must be public. Interfaces do not guarantee an implementation, only that the inheriting class must also contain members matching the signature of the interface members.

Q. Does C# support multiple interface inheritance?

A. Yes, C# supports inheriting from multiple interfaces. Interfaces can also inherit from other interfaces.

Q. Can extension methods be used to extend interfaces?

A. Yes, extension methods can be used to extend interfaces in exactly the same way they are used to extend classes.

Workshop

Quiz

1. Why is class inheritance also called implementation inheritance?

2. What is the correct way to hide an inherited member?

3. What are the restrictions on member overriding?

Answers

1. Class inheritance is also called implementation inheritance because the derived class inherits the implementation of the base class.

2. To hide an inherited member, you should use the `new` keyword on the derived member to explicitly indicate that the base class member is being hidden.

3. Member overriding has the following restrictions:

   ▶ The overriding member declaration cannot change the accessibility declared by the virtual member.

   ▶ Neither a virtual nor overridden member can be declared as `private`.

   ▶ Both declarations must have the same signature.

   ▶ The overridden member cannot contain the `new`, `static`, or `virtual` modifiers.

Exercises

1. Add a public constructor to the `Photo` class in the `PhotoViewer` project that accepts a `string` parameter named `path`. This constructor should contain an empty body and call the `Photo(Uri)` constructor you previously added. Next, add an override for the `ToString` method that returns the result of calling `source.ToString()`.

2. Add a public interface named `IPhoto` that mimics the current public class members of the `Photo` class. Change the `Photo` class to implement this new interface.

Creating Enumerated Types and Structures

What You'll Learn in This Hour:

▶ Enumerated types
▶ Working with structures

In the last few hours, you have been introduced to the basics of how types in C# work, including the predefined types and nullable types, and how classes in C# provide language syntax for object-oriented programming. You also saw how classes enable you to create your own types to represent real-world data. There are still two classifications of value types in C# that we have not talked about: the enumerated type and the structure.

Although classes are the primary mechanism you use to create new types, they do not provide a way to create types that are restricted in value nor do they enable you to create new value types. There are already many predefined enumerated types and structures in C#, but you have the ability to create your own. You have actually already used structures without knowing it because every value type is a structure.

In this hour, you explore enumerated types, looking at what they are and why they are useful. Next, you discover the benefits (and drawbacks) to structures, including how to create your own structures. You are also introduced to some of the structures included in the base class library and see how to use them.

Enumerated Types

An enumerated type, also called an **enumeration** (or just an **enum** for short), is simply a way to create a numeric type restricted to a predetermined set of valid values with meaningful names for those values. Although this might sound simple, enums are actually powerful. By defining a set of valid values, enumerations easily enable you to represent real-world concepts and information in such a way that the compiler understands the underlying values, whereas the programmer understands the higher-level meaning. This enables code that is self-describing and unambiguous.

Many things in the real world conceptually represent enumerations: the days of the week, months of the year, seasons, oceans, and compass directions, to name a few. Let's use the days of the week as an example.

You could represent the days of the week in your code using the integer values 0 through 6 to represent Sunday through Saturday, respectively. Unfortunately, those integer values don't convey much meaning to someone who looks at your code for the first time, or even to you later on when you need to maintain that code. It is also ambiguous because those integer values now have multiple meanings, and it is not always clear if you mean the integer value 0 or Sunday when you see it in code.

Using an integer to represent the days of the week also allows you to assign any valid integer value, not just the ones you expect. Enumerations solve these problems by enabling you to define the set of valid values and give them symbolic names. Think of enumerations as defining a discrete set of constants that are available only through a "container" name.

To define an enumeration, you must use the enum keyword followed by an identifier. You then define the set of legal values inside the body of the enumeration, each separated by a comma (,). Keep in mind that the identifiers used for the named values must follow the same rules defined for variable identifiers. The days of the week enum would look like what is shown in Listing 6.1.

NOTE

Enum Values

The comma after the last value is optional, but it's a good idea to include it so that it is easier to add values to the enum at a later time.

LISTING 6.1 A Simple Enumeration

```
public enum Days
{
    Sunday,
    Monday,
    Tuesday,
    Wednesday,
    Thursday,
    Friday,
    Saturday,
}
```

Whenever you need to refer to a day of the week, you can refer to it by name using the enumeration name and value. For instance, to refer to Wednesday, you would use `Days.Wednesday` and not just `Wednesday`.

NOTE

Multiple Named Values

You can also have more than one named value represent the same numeric value. This is useful in situations where multiple names could represent the same concept. To do this, you simply add that name as a new enumeration value and set it equal to the named value it represents, as shown here:

```
public enum Days
{
    Sunday,
    Monday,
    Tuesday,
    Wednesday,
    HumpDay = Wednesday,
    Thursday,
    Friday,
    Saturday,
}
```

Remember, enumerations are a form of named constants restricted to numeric values only, so it makes sense that each of the named values defined corresponds to a numeric value. In Listing 6.1, those numeric values were not defined. By default, when you define an enumeration, the compiler assigns the first value of the enumeration the integer value 0. The remaining values get a sequentially increasing number from the previous value. The `Days` enumeration could have been written and is equivalent to the code shown in Listing 6.2.

LISTING 6.2   A Simple Enumeration Specifying Values

```
public enum Days
{
    Sunday = 0,
    Monday = 1,
    Tuesday = 2,
    Wednesday = Sunday + 3,
    Thursday = Sunday + 4,
    Friday = 5,
    Saturday = 6,
}
```

Enumerations also support most of the standard operators that you can use on integer values, although not all of them are actually meaningful. The most common operations you perform with enumerations are equality and inequality tests. Because enumerations are value types, you can declare a nullable enumeration as well.

NOTE

The Zero Value

Generally it is best to always provide a zero value named None. If that's not appropriate for the context of the enumeration, the most common default value should be assigned the zero value.

TIP

Underlying Enumeration Types

All the values contained in an enumeration must be of the same data type, called the **underlying type**. By default, the underlying type for enumerations is int, but any of the predefined integer types can be used: byte, short, int, long, sbyte, ushort, uint, or ulong.

To give your enumeration a different underlying type, you specify it after the identifier, like this:

```
enum Days : byte
{
    Sunday,
    Monday,
    Tuesday,
    Wednesday,
    Thursday,
    Friday,
    Saturday,
}
```

Keep in mind, however, that the underlying type determines the overall range of valid values you can choose from when defining the enumeration. In this case, the Days enumeration can have only values from 0 to 255.

▼ TRY IT YOURSELF

Working with Enumerations

To implement the Days enumeration and explore how to use it, follow these steps. Keep Visual Studio open at the end of this exercise because you will use this application later.

1. Create a new console application.

2. Add a new code file named Days.cs, and implement the Days enumeration.

3. In the `Main` method of the `Program.cs` file, declare a local variable of type `Days` named `days` and assign an initial value of `Days.Sunday`.

4. Enter a `Console.WriteLine` statement that displays the enumerated value and integer value of the `days` variable. To get the integer value, you need to cast the variable to an `int`.

5. Run the application by pressing Ctrl+F5, and observe that the output matches what is shown in Figure 6.1.

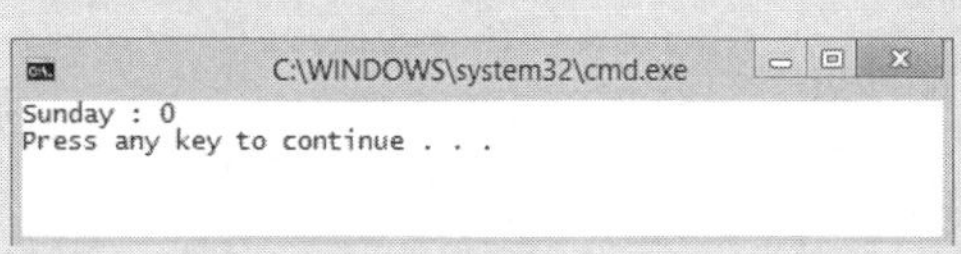

FIGURE 6.1
Displaying a named enumerated value.

6. Now set `days` to `Days.Saturday + 1`.

7. Run the application again by pressing Ctrl+F5, and observe that the output matches what is shown in Figure 6.2.

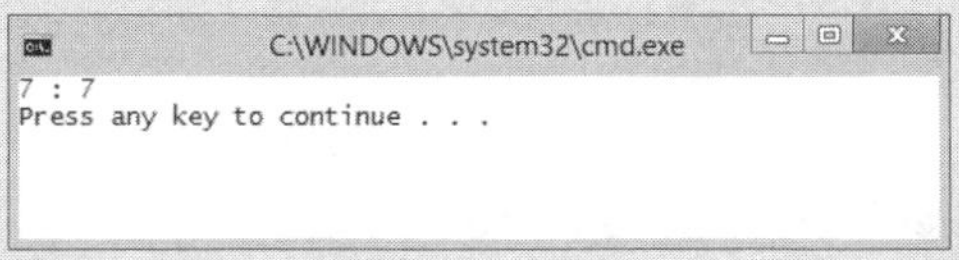

FIGURE 6.2
Displaying an enumerated value that is not in the enumerated type.

You should notice that both the enumerated value and the numeric value are 7. This is because there is no named value that represents the numeric value 7, so the runtime has no choice but to treat it directly as a number. This is a good reason why you should avoid performing arithmetical operations on enumerations.

Understanding Flags Enumerated Types

So far you have looked at enumerations that represent discrete values, but that isn't always the case in the real world. Taking the days of the week example a bit further, you might decide that the users of your application need to specify any combination of the days of the week.

Enumerations also provide the capability to combine values in **flags enumerations**. When using a flags enumeration, you can create new combined values by using the logical OR operation.

Taking the Days enumeration, you can turn it into a flags enumeration, as shown in Listing 6.3.

LISTING 6.3 A Flags Enumeration

```
[Flags]
public enum Days
{
    None = 0,
    Sunday = 0x001,
    Monday = 0x002,
    Tuesday = 0x004,
    Wednesday = 0x008,
    Thursday = 0x010,
    Friday = 0x020,
    Saturday = 0x040,
}
```

To allow the values of a flags enumeration to be combined, all the values must be powers of two. This is necessary because when multiple values are combined, there must still be a way to identify which discrete values make up that combination. As a result, when defining a flags enumeration, you must always specify the values.

NOTE

The Flags Attribute

Another difference between a regular enum and a flags enum is the use of the Flags attribute, which specifies additional metadata about the enumeration.

The Flags attribute also changes the string representation of the enumeration value (from the ToString method) when used with a value made by combining other values.

Although you are not required to use the Flags attribute, it is strongly recommended because it provides a clear indication of intent, not just to the compiler but also to other programmers.

Unlike simple enumerations in which the zero value can be either None or the most common default, flags enumerations should always name the zero value None, and it should always mean that all flags are not set.

▼ TRY IT YOURSELF

Working with Flags Enumerations

By following these steps, you modify the Days enumeration to be a flags enumeration and add some of the commonly used combinations. If you closed Visual Studio, repeat the previous exercise first.

1. Modify the `Days` enumeration to the one shown in Listing 6.3.

2. Add the following combinations:

   a. `Weekend = Sunday ¦ Saturday`

   b. `Workdays = Monday ¦ Tuesday ¦ Wednesday ¦ Thursday ¦ Friday`

3. Set the value of the `days` variable in the `Main` method to the combination:

   `Days.Saturday ¦ Days.Sunday`

4. Enter the following statements to determine if the `days` variable has a specific flag set:

   ```
   Console.WriteLine(days.HasFlag(Days.Saturday));
   Console.WriteLine(days.HasFlag(Days.Friday));
   ```

5. Run the application by pressing Ctrl+F5, and observe that the output matches what is shown in Figure 6.3.

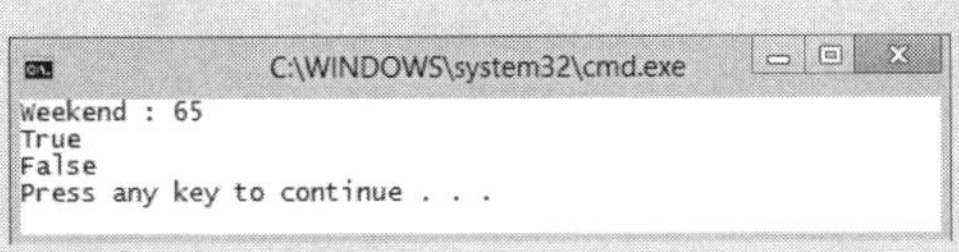

```
C:\WINDOWS\system32\cmd.exe
Weekend : 65
True
False
Press any key to continue . . .
```

FIGURE 6.3
Result of using `HasFlag` and a named enumerated value.

6. Set the value of the `days` variable to the combination:

   `Days.Weekend ¦ Days.Friday`

7. Run the application by pressing Ctrl+F5, and observe that the output matches what is shown in Figure 6.4.

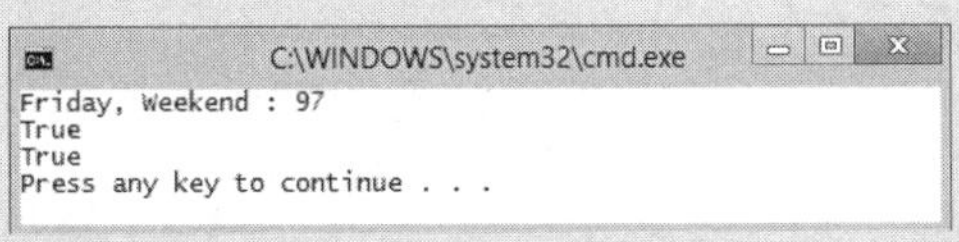

```
C:\WINDOWS\system32\cmd.exe
Friday, Weekend : 97
True
True
Press any key to continue . . .
```

FIGURE 6.4
Result of using `HasFlag` and an unnamed enumerated value.

Working with Structures

Structures, also called **structs**, are intended to be lightweight alternatives to classes when you need a simple user-defined type. Structures are similar to classes and can contain all the same members as a class but are value types rather than reference types. Structures are different, however, from classes in the following ways:

▶ Structures don't support inheritance. Structures implicitly inherit from `System.ValueType` (which, in turn, inherits from `System.Object`). Structures can inherit from interfaces, just as classes can.

▶ Structures are implicitly sealed, which means you cannot inherit from a structure.

▶ A structure cannot have a destructor or declare a default constructor and initialize instance fields. If a structure provides any constructors, all the fields must be assigned in that constructor call.

NOTE

Structures Included in the Base Class Library

All the primitive data types except for `string` and `object` are implemented as structures. The .NET Framework provides more than 200 public structures. Some of the commonly used structures follow:

▶ `System.DateTime`

▶ `System.DateTimeOffset`

▶ `System.Guid`

▶ `System.TimeSpan`

▶ `System.Drawing.Color`

▶ `System.Drawing.Point`

▶ `System.Drawing.Rectangle`

▶ `System.Drawing.Size`

In C#, structures are declared in the same way as classes, except the `struct` keyword is used in place of the `class` keyword.

Defining Struct Methods

Just as classes can define methods, structs can as well. These methods can be either static or instance methods; although, it is more common for structs to contain static public methods and private instance methods.

Operator Overloading

Because structs are user-defined value types, you cannot use most of the common operators, such as the equality operator, on variables defined as one of your own structs. This is a significant limitation, but fortunately, C# provides a way to resolve this through the concept of operator overloading.

If you think of operators simply as specially named methods, operator overloading is simply a special form of method overloading. To declare an overloaded operator, you define a `public static` method whose identifier is the keyword `operator` and the actual operator symbol you are declaring. In addition, at least one parameter of the operator you are overloading must be the same as the containing type. The overloadable operators are defined in Table 6.1.

CAUTION

Language Interoperability

Not all .NET languages support operator overloading, so if you create types that you want to use from other languages, they should be CLS-compliant and should provide alternatives that correspond to any overloaded operators defined.

TABLE 6.1 Overloadable Operators

Category	Operators
Unary	`+ - ! ~ ++ -- true false`
Multiplicative	`* / %`
Additive	`+ -`
Shift	`<< >>`
Relational	`< > <= >=`
Logical	`& ¦ ^`
Equality	`== !=`

The compound operators are conspicuously missing from this list, but if you recall that these operators perform both an arithmetic action and an assignment together, by overloading the appropriate arithmetic operator, you allow the corresponding compound assignment operator to use your new overloaded operator.

Typically, operators should always be overloaded in symmetrical groups. For example, if you overload the equality operator, you should also overload the inequality operator. The only exceptions to this symmetrical overloading guideline are the one's complement operator (~) and the not operator (!). The logical symmetrical groups that should be followed for operator overloading are shown in Table 6.2.

NOTE

Operator Overloading in Classes

Classes also support operator overloading and all of the same "rules" apply. Operators should be overloaded in symmetrical groups and, if your class is CLS-compliant, you should provide alternatives to the overloaded operators as well.

TABLE 6.2 Symmetric Operator Overload Groups

Category	Operator Groups
Unary	`+      -`
	`++    --`
	`true false`
Multiplicative	`*  /  %`
Additive	`+  -`
Shift	`<<  >>`
Relational	`<    >`
	`<=  >=`
Logical	`&  ¦  ^`
Equality	`==  !=  Equals  GetHashCode`

Conversion Operators

In much the same manner as user-defined structs enable you to overload operators to support common operations on your data, you can also influence the casting and conversion process by creating overloaded conversion operators. Again, if you think of conversion and casting as specially named functions, conversion overloading is also a special form of method overloading.

CAUTION

Implicit or Explicit Conversion

Implicit conversions are widening conversions because nothing from the original value is lost because of the conversion. Explicit conversions are narrowing conversions because there is the possibility that data from the original value can be lost because of the conversion.

When defining your own conversion operators, you should keep these behaviors in mind. If the conversion you define has the possibility of losing data as a result, it should be defined as an explicit conversion. If the conversion is safe, meaning there is no possibility of losing data, it should be defined as an implicit conversion.

You have already seen how the built-in numeric types have both implicit conversions, which require no special syntax, and explicit conversions, which do. You can overload these implicit and explicit conversions for your own types by declaring your own conversion operators, which follow similar rules to declaring operator overloads.

To declare a conversion operator, you define a `public static` method whose identifier is the keyword `operator` and whose return type is the type to which you are converting. The type you convert from is the single parameter to the conversion operator.

If you want to declare an implicit conversion, use the keyword `implicit` before the `operator` keyword; otherwise, use the keyword `explicit` to declare an explicit conversion. Conversion operators are sometimes used with operator overloading to reduce the number of operator overloads you must define.

TRY IT YOURSELF ▼

Operator Overloading in Structs

By following these steps, you implement a custom struct to represent degrees in Celsius and Fahrenheit:

1. Create a new console application.

2. Add a new code file named `Celsius.cs`, which defines a struct that looks like this:

```
struct Celsius
{
    private float degrees;

    public float Degrees
    {
        get
        {
            return this.degrees;
        }
    }

    public Celsius(float temperature)
    {
        this.degrees = temperature;
    }

    public static Celsius operator +(Celsius x, Celsius y)
    {
        return new Celsius(x.Degrees + y.Degrees);
    }

    public static implicit operator float(Celsius c)
    {
        return c.Degrees;
    }
}
```

3. Add another code file named `Fahrenheit.cs` that defines a struct similar to `Celsius` but is named `Fahrenheit`.

4. In both structs, define an operator overload for the `-` operator. Follow the same pattern as the `+` operator overload.

5. In both structs, define an implicit conversion operator that converts from `float` to the appropriate struct type. Follow the same pattern as the implicit conversion operator that converts from the struct type to `float`.

6. Next, define an explicit conversion operator in each struct that converts from one to the other. Use the following formulas for the conversion:

> ▶ Celsius to Fahrenheit: `(9.0f / 5.0f) * c.Degrees + 32`

> ▶ Fahrenheit to Celsius: `(5.0f / 9.0f) * (f.Degrees - 32)`

7. In the `Main` method of `Program.cs`, enter the following:

```
Fahrenheit f = new Fahrenheit(100.0f);
Console.WriteLine("{0} fahrenheit = {1} celsius", f.Degrees, (Celsius)f);


Celsius c = 32f;
Console.WriteLine("{0} celsius = {1} fahrenheit", c.Degrees, (Fahrenheit)c);


Fahrenheit f2 = f + (Fahrenheit)c;
Console.WriteLine("{0} + {1} = {2} fahrenheit", f.Degrees, (Fahrenheit)c,
f2.Degrees);


Fahrenheit f3 = 100f;
Console.WriteLine("{0} fahrenheit", f3.Degrees);
```

8. Run the application using Ctrl+F5, and observe that the output matches what is shown in Figure 6.5.

FIGURE 6.5
Results of working with a custom struct.

Clearly, this is not useful because some of the values display using the type name.

9. Add an override for the `ToString()` method that returns the result of calling `this.Degrees.ToString()`.

10. Run the application using Ctrl+F5 and observe that the output matches what is shown in Figure 6.6.

```
C:\WINDOWS\system32\cmd.exe
100 fahrenheit = 37.77778 celsius
32 celsius = 89.6 fahrenheit
100 + 89.6 = 189.6 fahrenheit
100 fahrenheit
Press any key to continue . . .
```

FIGURE 6.6
Results after overriding the `ToString` method.

Construction and Initialization

Just as classes must be given an initial state, so must structs. For classes, this must always occur through a class constructor; however, because structs are value types, you can create a `struct` variable without calling a constructor. For example, we could have created a new `NumberStruct` variable like this:

```
NumberStruct ns1;
```

This creates the new variable but leaves the fields in an uninitialized state. The result is that if you try to access a struct field, you receive a compiler error. By calling the constructor, as you see in Listing 6.4, you guarantee that the fields will be initialized.

Another aspect of struct initialization is that you are not allowed to assign one struct variable to another if the source (the one on the right side of the assignment) is not fully initialized. This means that the following is legal:

```
NumberStruct ns1 = new NumberStruct();
NumberStruct ns2 = ns1;
```

However, the following is not:

```
NumberStruct ns1;
NumberStruct ns2 = ns1;
```

CAUTION

Custom Default Constructors

Unlike classes, structs cannot have a custom default constructor, and you cannot initialize fields in a struct outside of a constructor. As a result, when a struct is created, all the fields are initially set to a zero value.

You can provide overloaded constructors and make use of constructor chaining. However, when you provide overloaded constructors, all the fields must be initialized by your constructor either explicitly or through a chained constructor.

The interesting thing to note is that you can still chain in the default constructor if the zero value is acceptable for the other fields.

Listing 6.4 shows the similarities and differences between structs and classes.

LISTING 6.4 **Comparing Structs and Classes**

```
struct NumberStruct
{
    public int Value;
}

class NumberClass
{
    public int Value = 0;
}

class Test
{
    static void Main()
    {
        NumberStruct ns1 = new NumberStruct ();
        NumberStruct ns2 = ns1;
        ns2.Value = 42;

        NumberClass nc1 = new NumberClass ();
        NumberClass nc2 = nc1;
        nc2.Value = 42;

        Console.WriteLine("Struct: {0}, {1}", ns1.Value, ns2.Value);
        Console.WriteLine("Class: {0}, {1}", nc1.Value, nc2.Value);
    }
}
```

Because both `ns1` and `ns2` are of the `NumberStruct` value type, they each have their own storage location, so the assignment of `ns2.Number` does not affect the value of `ns1.Number`. However, because `nc1` and `nc2` are both reference types, the assignment of `nc2.Number` does affect the value of `nc1.Number` because they both contain the same reference.

CAUTION

Properties or Public Fields

There is some debate concerning structs and properties. Some feel that properties should always be used, even in simple types like structs, whereas others feel it is acceptable for structs to simply make their fields public.

Although using public fields is easier, it allows your value type to be mutable, which is usually not desirable. When defining your own structs, remember that they are value types and, just as strings are immutable, they should be immutable as well. To do this, you should provide constructors allowing the private fields to be set and read-only properties for retrieving the values.

The output produced is shown in Figure 6.7.

FIGURE 6.7
The differences between a class and a struct.

Summary

Enumerated types and structures complete a significant portion of your programming foundation. Now that you know about classes, structures, and enumerated types, you have all the tools to create your own specialized data types for your business applications. Enumerated types enable you to define a set of discrete named values, whereas structures enable you to define your own lightweight value types.

Q&A

Q. Why are enumerated types useful?

A. An enumerated type enables you to define a discrete set of numeric values that can be given easily understood names (identifiers). This enables your code to be more self-documenting but also helps to ensure correctness.

Q. Can enumerated type values be combined to identify values not present in the original enumerated type?

A. This can be accomplished using a flags enumeration, in which all explicit values must be unique powers of two. Values can be combined using the bitwise `or` operator to form new values that are not present in the original enumeration.

Q. Are structures value or reference types?

A. Even though structures can be thought of as lightweight classes, they are actually value types.

Workshop

Quiz

1. What are the possible underlying types of an enumerated type?

2. What is the default type for an enumeration if one is not explicitly specified?

3. What does providing the `Flags` attribute do?

4. Do structures support inheritance?

5. Can you overload operators for a structure?

6. Can structures have a custom default constructor?

Answers

1. Enumerations can be based only on the following types: `byte`, `short`, `int`, `long`, `sbyte`, `ushort`, `uint`, or `ulong`.

2. If you don't explicitly specify the type for an enumeration, it is based on the `int` type.

3. By providing the `Flags` attribute on an enumeration, you clearly communicate that it is permissible for the values of the enumeration to be combined to form new values. It also changes the runtime behavior of the `ToString` method to display the constituent values when called on a combined value.

4. Structures do not support class inheritance, but they do support interface implementation inheritance.

5. Yes, structures support operator overloading.

6. No, structs do not enable a custom default constructor. You can provide additional over-loaded constructors, but all fields must be initialized when the constructor is finished.

Exercises

1. Add a public `enum` named `ColorRepresentation` to the `Exif` project folder. This `enum` should have the following named values:

```
Uncalibrated
sRGB
```

2. Add the following code to the `ExifMetadata` struct found in the `Exif` project folder.

```
public ColorRepresentation ColorRepresentation
{
    get
    {
        ColorRepresentation value = Exif.ColorRepresentation.Uncalibrated;
        if (this.colorRepresentation.HasValue)
        {
            if (!String.IsNullOrWhiteSpace(Enum.GetName(typeof(ColorRepresentation),
                this.colorRepresentation)))
            {
                value = (ColorRepresentation)this.colorRepresentation;
            }
        }

        return value;
    }
}
```

3. Add a private field to the `Photo` class named `exifMetadata` and whose data type is `PhotoViewer.Exif.ExifMetadata`. Add a read-only property named `ExifMetadata` to the interface and provide a class implementation that returns the `exifMetadata` field.

Events and Event Handling

What You'll Learn in This Hour:

▶ Understanding events
▶ Subscribing and unsubscribing
▶ Publishing an event
▶ Raising an event

C# is inherently an imperative programming language, which enables you to describe how to accomplish tasks using procedures (methods). Procedural programming defines the exact statements that will be executed and the order in which they will be executed. This type of programming is most often found in command-line or noninteractive programs because of the generally limited amount of user interaction.

In contrast, event-driven programming is a programming style in which the program flow is determined by events. Events are simply anything of interest, such as user actions (mouse clicks or key presses) or messages from other programs or parts of the same program. In C#, the class that raises, or sends, the event is the **publisher**, and the classes that receive, or handle, the event are **subscribers**. Although you can use events for a variety of reasons, they are most commonly used to signal user actions in a graphical user interface, such as keyboard-related events (keys pressed) and mouse-related events (mouse movement, button clicks, and so on).

In this hour, you learn the basics of event-driven programming, including how to define your own events, initiate and respond to events, and send data through events.

Understanding Events

Events follow a publish/subscribe model where the publisher determines when an event is raised. The subscribers determine the action taken in response to that event. Events can have multiple subscribers, in which case the event handlers are invoked synchronously when the event is raised. If an event has no subscribers, it is never actually raised. Subscribers can handle multiple events from multiple publishers.

NOTE

Delegates

In traditional programming terms, an event is a form of a callback, which enables a method to be passed as an argument to other methods. In C#, these callbacks are referred to as delegates. Event handlers are actually nothing more than methods invoked through delegates.

You can think of delegates as being similar to C or C++ function pointers or Delphi closures and are a type-safe and secure means of writing a callback. Delegates run under the caller's security permissions, not the declarer's permissions.

A delegate type simply defines a method signature and any method with a compatible signature can be associated with a delegate. One key difference between delegate signatures and regular method signatures is that the return type is included in the signature and the use of the `params` modifier in the parameter list is allowed.

Subscribing and Unsubscribing

When you are interested in responding to an event published by another class, you subscribe to that event by defining an event handler method whose signature matches the event delegate signature. You then use the addition assignment operator (+=) to attach the event handler to the event. Listing 7.1 shows how you would subscribe to an event based on the `ElapsedEventHandler` delegate.

LISTING 7.1   Subscribing to an Event

```
var timer = new System.Timers.Timer(1000);
timer.Elapsed += TimerElapsedHandler;

private void TimerElapsedHandler(object sender, System.Timers.ElapsedEventArgs e)
{
    MessageBox.Show("The timer has expired.");
}
```

The first parameter of the event handler method should always be an `object` parameter named `sender` that represents the object that raised the event. The second parameter represents the data passed to the event handler method. This should always be an `EventArgs` type or a type derived from `EventArgs` named e. The event handler method should always have a `void` return type.

The method name can be anything you want, but it is best to be consistent and use a name that is the combination of the name of the object providing the event, the name of the event being handled, and the word Handler.

Although subscribing to events in this manner is common for many classes, Visual Studio makes it easy to subscribe to events, especially those published by any of the user interface controls.

These steps show how to subscribe to a button's `Click` event in a Windows Presentation Foundation (WPF) application:

1. Make sure the button is selected and click the Events tab on the top of the Properties window in Design view, as shown in Figure 7.1. If you don't see the Properties window, right-click the form or control to which you are going to handle an event and select Properties.

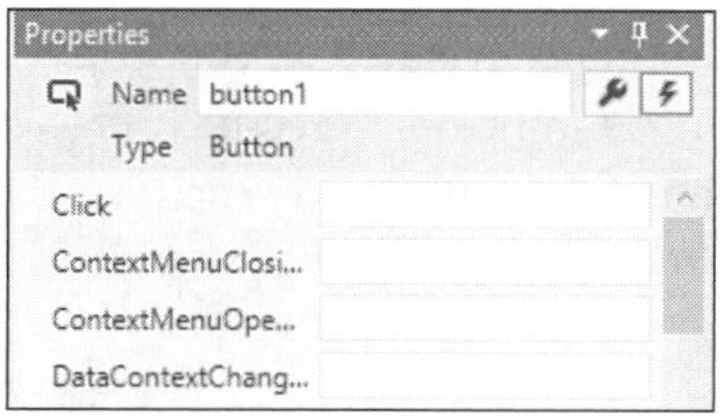

FIGURE 7.1
The Properties window.

2. Double-click the event you will be handling. This causes Visual Studio to create an empty event handler method in your code, shown in Figure 7.2.

```
private void button1_Click(object sender, RoutedEventArgs e)
{
    |
}
```

FIGURE 7.2
The generated event handler method.

Visual Studio also attaches the event handler for you, as shown in Figure 7.3. For WPF applications, this is done in the XML markup, or XAML, which describes the control.

```
<Window x:Class="EventsWpf.MainWindow"
        xmlns="http://schemas.microsoft.com/winfx/2006/
        xmlns:x="http://schemas.microsoft.com/winfx/200
        Title="MainWindow" Height="350" Width="525">
    <Grid>
        <Button Content="Button" Click="button1_Click"
    </Grid>
</Window>
```

FIGURE 7.3
Attaching the event handler in XAML.

If you create a Windows Forms–based application, the process is similar but instead of attaching the event handler in the XAML, Visual Studio would attach the event handler in the `InitializeComponent` method of your form, as shown in Figure 7.4.

```
this.button1.Text = "button1";
this.button1.UseVisualStyleBackColor = true;
this.button1.Click += new System.EventHandler(this.button1_Click);
```

FIGURE 7.4
Attaching the event handler in code.

When you double-click the event, Visual Studio uses a default naming convention. If you want to use a different event handler method name, simply type the name in the text area next to the event, and press the `Enter` key to cause Visual Studio to create the event handler method. If you double-click the control itself rather than the event, Visual Studio creates an event handler method for the default event of the control.

▼ TRY IT YOURSELF

Subscribing to Events

To subscribe to events published by a user interface control in a Windows Forms application and a WPF application, follow these steps:

1. Open the `Hour7` solution in Visual Studio.

2. Open `Form1.cs` in the `EventsWinForms` project by double-clicking the file.

3. In the Design view for `Form1`, select the button and add an event handler for the `Click` event.

4. In the generated event handler method, add the following statement:

   `MessageBox.Show("You pressed the button.");`

5. Run the application by pressing Ctrl+F5. When you click the button, you should see the following dialog box appear, as shown in Figure 7.5.

FIGURE 7.5
`MessageBox` from the event handler.

6. Open `MainWindow.xaml` in the `EventsWpf` project by double-clicking the file.

7. In the Design view for `MainWindow`, select the button and add an event handler for the `Click` event. In the generated event handler method, add the same statement you added in step 4.

8. Run the application by right-clicking the project in the Solution Explorer window and selecting the Start New Instance option from the Debug menu, as shown in Figure 7.6.

Set as StartUp Project		
Debug	▶	▶ Start new instance
ᛁᛝ Add Solution to Source Control...		↳• Step Into new instance

FIGURE 7.6
Solution Explorer context menu.

9. When you click the button, you should see the following dialog box appear, as shown in Figure 7.7.

FIGURE 7.7
`MessageBox` from the event handler.

When you no longer want your event handler invoked when the event is raised, you must unsubscribe from the event. You should also unsubscribe from events before you dispose of the subscriber object. If you don't unsubscribe from the events, the publishing object continues to hold a reference to the delegate that represents the subscriber's event handler, which prevents the garbage collector from deallocating your subscriber object.

To unsubscribe from an event, you either remove the attribute from the XAML markup or use the subtraction assignment operator (`-=`), as shown here:

```
timer.Elapsed -= TimerElapsedHandler;
```

Anonymous Methods

In the previous examples, you attached a named method as the event handler delegate. You can also use the addition assignment operator to attach an anonymous method to the event. An anonymous method provides a way to write an unnamed inline statement block that can be executed in a delegate invocation.

The code shown in Listing 7.1 is shown here using an anonymous method instead of a named delegate:

```
var timer = new Timer(1000);
timer.Elapsed += delegate(object sender, ElapsedEventArgs e)
{
    MessageBox.Show("The timer has expired.");
}
```

Although using an anonymous method for an event handler provides a lot of convenience, it does not provide an easy way to unsubscribe from the event.

Publishing an Event

Events can be published by both classes and structs (although they are more commonly found in classes) using a simple event declaration. Events can be based on any valid delegate type; however, the standard practice is to base your events on the EventHandler and EventHandler<T> delegates. These are delegate types predefined in the .NET Framework specifically for defining events.

The first decision you need to make when defining your own events is whether you need to send custom data with your event. The .NET Framework provides the EventArgs class, which the predefined event delegate types support. If you need to send custom data with your event, you should create a new class that derives from EventArgs. If you don't need to send custom data, you can use the EventArgs type directly, but cannot change it later without breaking compatibility. As a result, you should always create a new class that derives from EventArgs, even if it is initially empty, to provide the flexibility later on to add data.

Listing 7.2 shows an example of a custom EventArgs derived class.

LISTING 7.2 A Custom EventArgs Derived Class

```
public class CustomEventArgs : System.EventArgs
{
    private object data;

    public CustomEventArgs(object data)
    {
```

```
      this.data = data;
   }

   public object Data
   {
      get
      {
         return data;
      }
   }
}
```

The most common way of declaring your event is using a fieldlike syntax. If you have no custom `EventArgs` class, you would use the `EventHandler` delegate type, shown in Listing 7.3.

Listing 7.3   A Simple Event Declaration

```
public class Contact
{
   public event EventHandler AddressChanged;
}
```

If you do have a custom `EventArgs` class, you would use the generic `EventHandler<T>` delegate, substituting your own `EventArgs` class for the `T`, as shown in Listing 7.5.

GO TO ▶ HOUR 12, "UNDERSTANDING GENERICS," for more information on generics.

NOTE

Using Event Properties

Although the fieldlike event definition is the most common, it might not always be the most efficient, particularly for classes with a large number of events. Consider a class with a large number of events. It is reasonable that only a few events have subscribers. Using the field declaration style, you create one field per event, which results in a lot of unnecessary overhead.

To solve this problem, C# also enables defining events with a property-like syntax, as shown in Listing 7.4.

LISTING 7.4   Event Declaration Using Event Properties

```
1.    public class Contact
2.    {
3.        private EventHandlerList events = new EventHandlerList();
4.        private static readonly object addressChangedEventKey = new object();
5.
6.        public event EventHandler AddressChanged
```

```
 7.      {
 8.          add
 9.          {
10.              events.AddHandler(addressChangedEventKey, value);
11.          }
12.          remove
13.          {
14.              events.RemoveHandler(addressChangedEventKey, value);
15.          }
16.      }
17.  }
```

Line 3 declares an `EventHandlerList` specifically designed to contain a list of event delegates. This enables you to use a single variable that contains an entry for every event that has a subscriber. Next, line 4 declares a static read-only `object` variable named `addressChangedEventKey` that represents the key used for the event in the `EventHandlerList`. Finally, lines 6 through 16 declare the actual event property.

This syntax should be familiar to you because it is almost the same syntax for defining a property. The difference is that rather than `get` and `set` accessors, you have `add` and `remove` accessors. The `add` accessor simply adds the input delegate instance to the list, whereas the `remove` accessor removes it. Both of the accessors use the predefined key for the event property to add and remove instances from the list.

Now that you understand the basics of publishing an event, a convenient and consistent way to describe when the event occurs is to categorize them as pre-events and post-events.

Post-events are the most common type of event and occur after the state of the object has changed. Pre-events, also called **cancelable events**, occur before the state of the object changes and provide the capability to cancel the event. These events use the `CancelEventArgs` class to store event data. The `CancelEventArgs` class simply adds a `Cancel` property your code can read and write. If you create or own cancelable events, you should derive your own custom event data class from the `CancelEventArgs` class.

Raising an Event

Defining an event isn't of much use if no mechanism is in place to initiate that event. Event initiation is called **raising**, or **firing**, an event and follows a standard pattern. By following a pattern, it becomes easier to work with events because the structure is well defined and consistent.

Listing 7.5 builds on the example in Listing 7.3 and shows the complete event handler mechanism.

LISTING 7.5   The Complete Event Handler

```
1.  public class Contact
2.  {
3.      public event EventHandler<AddressChangedEventArgs> AddressChanged;
4.
5.      private string address;
6.
7.      protected virtual void OnAddressChanged(AddressChangedEventArgs e)
8.      {
9.          EventHandler<AddressChangedEventArgs> handler = AddressChanged;
10.         if (handler != null)
11.         {
12.             handler(this, e);
13.         }
14.     }
15.
16.     public string Address
17.     {
18.         get { return this.address; }
19.         set
20.         {
21.             this.address = value;
22.             AddressChangedEventArgs args =
23.             new AddressChangedEventArgs(this.address);
24.             OnAddressChanged(args);
25.         }
26.     }
27. }
```

Line 3 declares the event, using the `EventHandler<T>` delegate. Lines 7 through 14 declare a protected virtual method used to raise the event. By making this method `protected` and `virtual`, any derived classes have the capability to handle the event by overriding the method rather than subscribing to the event. This is a more natural and convenient mechanism for derived classes. Finally, lines 22 through 24 declare a new `EventArgs` class and raise the event. If the event did not have custom data, you could have used the `EventArgs.Empty` field to represent an empty `EventArgs`.

NOTE

Raising an Event When Using Event "Properties"

If you use the property-like syntax, the method used to actually raise the event needs to be a bit different to retrieve the event handler from the handler list, as shown here:

```
protected virtual void OnAddressChanged(AddressChangedEventArgs e)
{
    var handler = events[addressChangedEventKey] as
        EventHandler<AddressChangedEventArgs>;

    if (handler != null)
    {
        handler(this, e);
    }
}
```

By convention, the name of the event raiser method starts with "On" followed by the name of the event. For nonstatic events on unsealed classes, this method should be declared as a `protected virtual` method. For static events, nonstatic events on sealed classes, or events on structs, the method should be public. This method should always have a `void` return type and take a single parameter, named e, which should be typed to the appropriate `EventArgs` class.

The content of this method also follows a standard pattern, which makes a temporary copy of the event (line 9) to avoid the possibility of a race condition occurring if the last subscriber unsubscribes immediately after the null check (line 10) and before the event is raised (line 12).

GO TO ▶ HOUR 24, "UNDERSTANDING THREADS, CONCURRENCY, AND PARALLELISM," for more information on race conditions.

CAUTION

Multithreading and Events

This pattern only prevents one possible type of race condition, whereby the event becomes `null` after the check and is only relevant if the code is multithreaded. There are complexities that must be safeguarded against when writing multithreaded events, such as ensuring that any necessary state is still present in a thread-safe manner before executing code that relies on that state.

▼ TRY IT YOURSELF

Publishing and Raising Events

By following these steps, you explore how to publish and raise events:

1. Open the `PublishAndRaise` project in Visual Studio.

2. Add a class named `AddressChangedEventArgs`. This class should follow the same pattern as shown in Listing 7.2.

3. Add a class named `Contact` that looks like the one shown in Listing 7.5.

4. Run the application by pressing Ctrl+F5. The output should look like Figure 7.8. Make sure to set the `PublishAndRaise` project as the startup project.

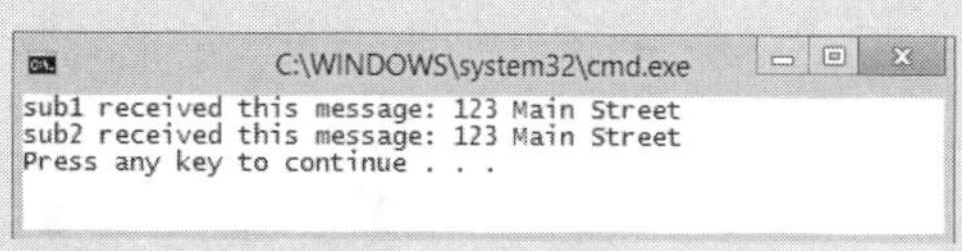

FIGURE 7.8
Results of subscribing to an event.

Summary

In this hour, you learned how C# enables you to create highly interactive applications by raising and responding to events. You also learned that events are not just about user interaction through a graphical user interface but that events also provide a rich and sophisticated notification system that your classes can use.

Through the Visual Studio editor, you have seen how easy it is to create your own event handlers for responding to events initiated through the user interface.

Q&A

Q. What is a delegate?

A. A delegate is a type-safe and secure way of writing a callback, similar to a C++ function pointer or Delphi closure. Using a delegate allows you to encapsulate a reference to a method. The code that calls the referenced method does not need to know at compile time which method will be invoked. Delegates run under the caller's security permissions, not the declarer's permissions.

Q. What is an event?

A. An event is any external stimulus to a program, such as user actions (mouse clicks or key presses), messages from other programs, or parts of the same programs.

Q. What is the `EventArgs` class?

A. The `EventArgs` class stores data for an event. Although it can be used directly, it is best to derive a new class for your event, even if it is initially empty.

Q. What are the two types of event?

A. The two types of event are pre-events and post-events. Pre-events are cancelable events raised before the state of the object changes. Post-events are raised after the state of the object has changed.

Workshop

Quiz

1. What is the most common way to declare an event and what are the drawbacks of using it?

2. Using a property-like syntax to declare an event requires what two accessor members?

3. The standard pattern for raising an event requires a method with what accessibility for non-static events on an unsealed class?

4. Looking at the `OnAddressChanged` method declared in Listing 7.5, why is a copy of the event delegate made?

Answers

1. The most common way to define an event is to use the fieldlike syntax. For classes with a large number of events, particularly when it is reasonable that only a small number of those events will have subscribers, this syntax creates one field per event and results in a lot of unnecessary overhead.

2. The property-like syntax for declaring an event uses an `add` and `remove` accessor. The `add` accessor simply adds the input delegate to the list, whereas the `remove` accessor removes it.

3. For nonstatic events on unsealed classes, the method should be declared as a `protected virtual` method, which enables any derived classes the capability to handle the event using an override.

4. A temporary copy of the delegate is made to avoid one possible race condition where the event is reset to null, causing a runtime error when the event is invoked.

Exercises

1. Extend the application you wrote in the "Publishing and Raising Events" Try It Yourself exercise to add a cancelable `AddressChanging` event. If the event is canceled, do not actually change the value of the `address` variable. Modify the `AddressChangedEventArgs` class to contain the old and new value of the address, which will be printed by the event handler in the `subscriber` class.

HOUR 8
Controlling Program Flow

What You'll Learn in This Hour:

▶ Understanding the selection statements
▶ Iteration statements
▶ Jump statements

At its heart, C# is a procedural programming language, so statements are executed sequentially in the order they appear in the source code. This execution order is referred to as **program flow**. As you might imagine, following only a strict execution order would provide little flexibility. What is missing is a way to control or change what statements are executed based on the result of testing conditions. C# provides **control flow statements** that change the order of execution.

All the control flow statements have the same basic characteristics; they select any number of statements to be executed based on a given set of conditions. These statements are grouped into three main categories, described by their primary behavior. Selection statements and jump statements are most closely related. They both select a statement that will be executed only once, whereas iteration statements repeatedly execute that statement. Jump statements are unconditional, but selection and iteration statements enable conditions to restrict which statements will be executed and how many iterations the execution will occur.

In this hour, you learn the syntax for each of the different control flow statements, learn how they behave, and how to write and test conditions that control program flow. More important, you learn the differences between them and when one type of control flow statement should be used over another.

Understanding the Selection Statements

Selection statements are perhaps the most common form of control flow statements available. They enable a single statement (from a number of possible statements) to be executed based on the value of an expression.

The `if` Statement

The most basic selection statement is the `if` statement, which selects a statement based on the result of a Boolean expression.

The basic syntax for an `if` statement is

```
if ( boolean-expression )
   embedded-statement
```

A slightly more advanced syntax is

```
if ( boolean-expression )
   consequence-statement
else
   alternative-statement
```

If the result of `boolean-expression` evaluates to `true`, control is transferred to the consequence-statement. If the result of `boolean-expression` evaluates to `false` and an `else` portion is present, control is transferred to the `alternative-statement`. When control reaches the end of the statement executed, it is then transferred to the next statement.

The statement executed can be any valid statement, including another `if` statement. In this syntax, the second statement is said to be a nested `if` statement.

In the code shown in Listing 8.1, "`y <= 10`" displays if the condition (`y > 10`) evaluates to `false` and the condition (`x > 10`) evaluates to `true`.

LISTING 8.1   Nested `if` Statements

```
int x = 20, y = 10;

if (x > 10)
{
   if (y > 10)
   {
      Console.WriteLine("y > 10");
   }
   else
   {
      Console.WriteLine("y <= 10");
   }
}
```

CAUTION

The "Mismatched Else" Problem

A common problem when writing `if` statements is known as the "mismatched else" problem, where the formatting of the code does not match the actual control flow:

```
int x = 20, y = 10;

if (x > 10)
    if (y > 10)
        Console.WriteLine("y > 10");
else
    Console.WriteLine("y <= 10");
```

The code here visually looks like the `else` is the alternative of `if (x > 10)`. In reality, it is actually the alternative of `if (y > 10)`.

To help prevent this problem, it is a good idea to always use braces to make it clear which `else` goes with which `if`.

If you need to check a series of exclusive conditions, it is possible to cascade `if` statements by joining an `if` statement to the `else` portion of a previous `if` statement. In such a series, all the `if` statements will be executed in sequence until one of them evaluates to `true`.

Listing 8.2 shows a cascaded `if` statement. If the condition `(x > 10)` evaluates to `true`, "x > 10" displays. If the condition `(x < 10)` evaluates to `true`, "x < 10" displays; otherwise, "x = 10" displays.

LISTING 8.2   A Cascaded `if` Statement

```
int x = 20, y = 10;

if (x > 10)
{
    Console.WriteLine("x > 10");
}
else if (x < 10)
{
    Console.WriteLine("x < 10");
}
else
{
    Console.WriteLine("x = 10");
}
```

▼ TRY IT YOURSELF

Working with the `if` Statement

To see how the `if` statement works, follow these steps. Keep Visual Studio open at the end of this exercise because you will use this application later.

1. Open the `SelectionStatements` project in Visual Studio.

2. Open `Form1.cs` by right-clicking the file and selecting the View Code context menu choice.

3. In the code editor, locate the method named `CheckGuess`, which looks like

   ```
   private Result CheckGuess(decimal guess)
   {
       Result result;
       return result;
   }
   ```

4. Modify the `CheckGuess` method so that the appropriate value of `Result` is returned based on the number passed as the method argument.

5. Look at the `buttonCheckGuess_Click` method, examining the nested `if` statement it contains.

6. Run the application by pressing F5. Enter guesses and watch how the program responds based on your guess.

The `switch` Statement

Switches can be thought of as the natural progression from cascaded `if` statements. They provide similar functionality but are more compact and flexible. The `switch` statement selects a statement list based on a label that corresponds to the value of the expression.

The syntax of a `switch` statement is

```
switch ( expression )
{
    case constant-expression :
        statement-list
        break;

    default :
        statement-list
        break;
}
```

The body of the `switch` is the **switch-block** and contains one or more switch-sections. Each **switch-section** contains at least one label followed by a statement-list.

The type of `expression` establishes the **governing type** of the `switch` and can be `sbyte`, `byte`, `short`, `ushort`, `int`, `uint`, `long`, `ulong`, `char`, the nullable version of those types, the `string` type, or an enumerated type. The `expression` is evaluated only once.

The label for a switch-section must be a constant expression that is unique within the same switch-block and be implicitly convertible to the governing type. For switches whose governing type is `string` or a nullable type, a case label of `null` is permitted.

CAUTION

Switches on `string`

The evaluation of `expression` is case sensitive, so a switch-section will only be executed if its label exactly matches.

If the value of `expression` matches one of the constants in a case label, control is transferred to the first statement after that label. If no matching case is found, control is transferred to the first statement after the `default` label, if present; otherwise, control is transferred to the next statement after the `switch`.

In Listing 8.3, if the condition `(x == 0)` or `(x == 1)` evaluates to `true`, the value of `x` displays; otherwise, "Invalid" displays.

LISTING 8.3   A Simple `switch` Statement

```
int x = 4;

switch (x)
{
    case 0:
        Console.WriteLine("x = " + x);
        break;

    case 1:
        Console.WriteLine("x = " + x);
        break;

    default:
        Console.WriteLine("Invalid");
        break;
}
```

You might have noticed that the code for case 0 and case 1 is identical. To eliminate this redundancy, you can provide a list of labels with no intervening statements.

CAUTION

Fall Through

Unlike other programming languages, such as C and C++, switch statements in C# do not allow fall through of switch-sections, which occurs when execution starts in one switch-section and continues through to another switch-section.

To prevent fall through, C# requires all switch-sections to end in a statement with an unreachable endpoint, of which an unconditional jump statement is one example. The most common is the break statement.

By not allowing such fall-through behavior, C# eliminates a common bug found in C and C++ programs and allows the order of the switch-sections to be changed without affecting the behavior of the statement.

Listing 8.4 shows the same switch statement from Listing 8.3 but uses case fall through. Because there are no intervening statements, the "no fall-through rule" is not violated, and control is transferred to the first statement after the last label in the list.

LISTING 8.4   A switch Statement Using Case Fall Through

```
int x = 4;

switch (x)
{
   case 0:
   case 1:
      Console.WriteLine("x = " + x);
      break;

   default:
       Console.WriteLine("Invalid");
       break;
}
```

NOTE

Scope

Scope within a switch statement is bounded by the entire switch-block, not each switch-section. This means that any local variables or constants declared inside a switch-section are local to the entire switch-block, not just that switch-section.

If you need to restrict scope to within a specific switch-section, you can create an additional nested scope by enclosing the statement list in curly braces.

Working with the `switch` Statement

To see how the `switch` statement works, follow these steps. If you closed Visual Studio, repeat the previous exercise first.

1. In the code editor, locate the method named `buttonCheckGuess_Click`. This method contains a nested `if` statement that determines which `Label` controls to display based upon the return value of the `CheckGuess` method.

2. Modify the `buttonCheckGuess_Click` method so that it uses a `switch` statement over the return value of the `CheckGuess` method rather than the nested `if` statements.

3. Run the application by pressing F5. Enter guesses and watch how the program responds based on your guess, which should be identical to the behavior from the previous exercise.

Iteration Statements

Although selection statements enable one-time execution of a statement based on the value of an expression, iteration statements, also called **looping** statements, repeatedly execute the same statement. Iteration statements evaluate their expression each time, or **iteration**, through the loop. A **top-tested loop** evaluates the expression before the statement executes, whereas a **bottom-tested loop** evaluates the expression after the statement executes.

To terminate the loop early, without reevaluating the expression, you can use any of these jump statements: `break`, `goto`, `return`, or `throw`. The `continue` statement passes control to the next iteration.

The `while` Statement

A `while` statement is a top-tested loop that repeatedly executes an embedded statement until the `boolean-expression` evaluates to `false`. Because the expression is evaluated before each iteration, the statement can be executed zero or more times.

The syntax for a `while` statement is

```
while ( boolean-expression )
   embedded-statement
```

If the result of evaluating `boolean-expression` is `true`, control is transferred to the embedded-statement. When the statement finishes executing, control is transferred to the start of the loop, where the expression is reevaluated.

If the result of evaluating `boolean-expression` is `false`, control is transferred to the next statement after the `while` statement. If the result of the `boolean-expression` is initially `false`, the `embedded-statement` never executes.

In Listing 8.5, the statements inside the body of the loop execute until `i` is greater than or equal to 10. If the `i++;` statement were not included in either the body of the loop or as part of the `boolean-expression`, the loop would execute forever.

LISTING 8.5   The `while` Statement

```
int i = 0;
while (i < 10)
{
    Console.WriteLine(i);
    i++;
}
```

▼ TRY IT YOURSELF

Working with the `while` Statement

By following these steps, you see how the `while` statement works. Keep Visual Studio open at the end of this exercise because you will use this application later.

1. Open the `IterationStatements` project in Visual Studio.

2. Open `Form1.cs` by right-clicking the file and selecting the View Code context menu choice.

3. In the code editor, modify the `PowersOfTwoWhileLoop` method so that it executes the following statements in a `while` loop.

   ```
   this.textBoxOutput.AppendText(String.Format("{0}^2 = {1}\r\n", i,
       Math.Pow(i, 2)));
   i++;
   ```

4. Run the application by pressing F5. Enter a maximum value, select the While radio button, and click the Generate button.

The `do` Statement

A `do` statement also repeatedly executes an embedded statement until the `boolean-expression` evaluates to `false`. Unlike the `while` statement, a `do` statement is a bottom-tested loop, so the `embedded-statement` is executed once before the `boolean-expression` is evaluated. This means it is guaranteed to execute at least one time.

The syntax for a do statement is

```
do
    embedded-statement
while ( boolean-expression );
```

If the result of evaluating `boolean-expression` is `true`, control is transferred to the beginning of the loop where the `embedded-statement` is executed again. If the result of evaluating `boolean-expression` is false, control is transferred to the next statement after the do statement.

In Listing 8.6, the statements inside the body of the loop execute if `i` is less than 10. Just as in the `while` statement, if the `i++;` statement were not included in either the body of the loop or as part of the `boolean-expression`, the loop would execute forever.

Listing 8.6   The do Statement

```
int i = 0;
do
{
    Console.WriteLine(i);
    i++;
}
while (i < 10);
```

TRY IT YOURSELF ▼

Working with the do **Statement**

To see how the do statement works, follow these steps. If you closed Visual Studio, repeat the previous exercise first. Be sure to keep Visual Studio open at the end of this exercise because you will use this application later.

1. In the code editor, modify the `PowersOfTwoDoLoop` method so that it executes the following statement in a do loop:

   ```
   this.textBoxOutput.AppendText(String.Format("{0}^2 = {1}\r\n", i,
       Math.Pow(i, 2)));
   ```

2. Run the application by pressing F5. Enter a maximum value, select the Do radio button, and click the Generate button.

3. Explore what happens if you remove the increment statement from the body of the loop and instead place it as part of the `while` condition.

The `for` Statement

The `for` statement is possibly the most misunderstood iteration statement because it looks the most complex; however, it still provides the same basic behavior of the other iteration statements. It also repeatedly executes an embedded statement until a specified expression evaluates to `false`.

The syntax of a `for` statement is

```
for ( initializer ; condition ; iterator )
   embedded-statement
```

The `for` statement is most commonly used for sequential processing and iterating over arrays.

What makes a `for` statement look complex is the three different expressions, or sections, all of which are optional. Each section must be separated by a semicolon, even when it is omitted.

The initializer can be either a single local variable initialization or a comma-separated list of local variable initialization statements. Any local variables declared in the initializer are scoped to the condition, iterator, and embedded statement.

TIP

Initializer Declaration Space

Think of the entire `for` statement as being defined inside "invisible braces" that define the local variable declaration space for the `initializer`.

The condition must be a Boolean expression. If you omit the condition, the expression defaults to `true`.

Finally, the iterator can be either a single expression or a comma-separated list of expressions that usually change the corresponding local variables declared in the initializer.

CAUTION

Infinite Loops

Just as it is possible to create an infinite loop using a `while` statement, you can create a `for` statement that runs forever by omitting all three sections in the declaration:

```
for ( ; ; ;)
{
   Console.WriteLine("line");
}
```

If you look at the `while` statement from Listing 8.5 again, you should see some elements that look similar to the different sections of the `for` statement. A `while` statement and a `for` statement are interchangeable; the `for` statement is a more compact way to write the same code. Figure 8.1 shows a comparison between a `while` statement and a `for` statement, which should make the relationship between them clear.

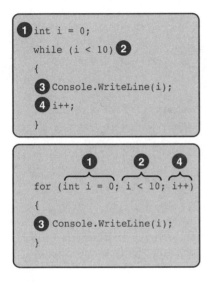

FIGURE 8.1
Comparison of a `for` and `while` statement.

Looking at the sequence of events that occur when a `for` statement executes, it is the same sequence as a `while` statement:

1. The initializer is executed, if present. If there are multiple expressions, they are executed in the order they are written. The initializer is executed once at the beginning of the statement.

2. If `condition` evaluates to `true`, control is transferred to the embedded statement.

3. The embedded statement is executed.

4. The statements in the iterator are evaluated, if present, and the condition is reevaluated. If `condition` evaluates to `false`, control is transferred to the next statement after the `for` statement.

▼ TRY IT YOURSELF

Working with the `for` Statement

By following these steps, you see how the `for` statement works. If you closed Visual Studio, repeat the previous exercise first. Be sure to keep Visual Studio open at the end of this exercise because you will use this application later.

1. In the code editor, modify the `PowersOfTwoForLoop` method so that it executes the following statement in a `for` loop:

    ```
    this.textBoxOutput.AppendText(String.Format("{0}^2 = {1}\r\n", i,
        Math.Pow(i, 2)));
    ```

2. Run the application by pressing F5. Enter a maximum value, select the For radio button, and click the Generate button.

3. Explore what happens if you change the initializer and the iterator expressions.

The `foreach` Statement

The `foreach` statement executes a statement for each element in an array or collection. Unlike a `for` statement, a `foreach` statement cannot be used to add or remove items from the source collection.

The syntax of a `foreach` statement is

```
foreach ( type identifier in expression )
    embedded-statement
```

If `expression` is an array type, an implicit conversion to `IEnumerable` is performed; otherwise, the collection must implement either `IEnumerable` or `IEnumerable<T>` or provide an appropriate `GetEnumerator` method.

NOTE

Iteration Variable

The type and identifier of a `foreach` statement is the **iteration variable** and corresponds to a read-only local variable scoped only to the embedded statement.

As the iteration progresses through the elements in the collection, the iteration variable represents the current element.

The `foreach` statement is the only iteration statement that does not contain a condition to be evaluated. The embedded statement continues to execute for all the elements in the collection or a jump statement has terminated the loop. For a collection or single-dimensional array, the elements are traversed in increasing order starting with index 0. If `expression` is a multidimensional array, the elements are traversed in increasing order, starting with the rightmost dimension, then the next left dimension, and then continuing to the left.

If the collection contains no elements, the embedded statement is not executed.

The code in Listing 8.7 displays each character of a string on a single line.

LISTING 8.7 The `foreach` Statement

```
string s = "This is a test.";

foreach (char c in s)
{
    Console.WriteLine(c);
}
```

TRY IT YOURSELF ▼

Working with the `foreach` Statement

To see how the `foreach` statement works, follow these steps:

1. In the code editor, modify the `PowersOfTwoForEachLoop` method so that it executes the following statement in a `foreach` loop:

   ```
   this.textBoxOutput.AppendText(String.Format("{0}^2 = {1}\r\n", i,
       Math.Pow(i, 2)));
   ```

2. Run the application by pressing F5. Enter a maximum value, select the Foreach radio button, and click the Generate button.

Jump Statements

Jump statements are different from selection and iteration statements because they unconditionally and immediately transfer control to a new location, called the **target** of the jump statement.

NOTE

The `goto` Statement

Although not commonly used, C# does provide a `goto` statement, which transfers control to a statement marked by a label. The `goto` statement can also target a specific `case` or the `default` case in a `switch` statement.

The syntax for a `goto` statement is

```
goto identifier;
goto case constant-expression;
goto default;
```

For example, the following code will transfer control to the `default` case when `x` = 0 and when `x` = 1 will transfer control to the line of code immediately following the Finish label after executing the code specified by case 1.

```
int x = 4;

switch (x)
{
   case 0:
      goto default;

   case 1:
      Console.WriteLine("x = " + x);
      goto Finish;

   default:
       Console.WriteLine("Invalid");
       break;
}

Finish:
   Console.WriteLine("End");
```

Just as with the `break` and `continue` statements, any statements in the same block appearing after the `goto` statement are not executed.

The use of a `goto` statement is strongly discouraged in everyday practice because it is easy to misuse and can result in code that is difficult to read and maintain. Code that makes heavy use of `goto` statements is often referred to as "spaghetti" code because of the resemblance the program flow has to a plate of spaghetti.

The `break` Statement

The `break` statement is used to exit the nearest `switch`, `while`, `do`, `for`, or `foreach` statement. If multiple statements are nested within each other, only the innermost statement is exited.

Listing 8.8 shows the same `for` statement from Figure 8.1 using a `break` statement that causes the loop to terminate after four iterations.

LISTING 8.8 The break Statement

```
for (int i = 0; i < 10 ; i++)
{
    Console.WriteLine(i);
    if (i == 3)
    {
        break;
    }
}
```

Working with the break Statement

By following these steps, you see how the break statement works within different iteration statements. Keep Visual Studio open at the end of this exercise because you will use this application later.

1. Open the JumpStatements project in Visual Studio.

2. Open Form1.cs by right-clicking the file and selecting the View Code context menu choice.

3. In the code editor, modify the following methods to include a break statement when the loop iteration counter equals the breakAfter parameter after the power of two has been calculated:

    ▶ PowersOfTwoBreakDoLoop

    ▶ PowersOfTwoBreakForLoop

    ▶ PowersOfTwoBreakForEachLoop

    ▶ PowersOfTwoBreakWhileLoop

4. Run the application by pressing F5. Enter a break iterations value, select one of the radio buttons, and click the Generate button.

5. Change the location of the break statement so that it occurs before the power of two has been calculated.

6. Run the application again by pressing F5. Enter a break iterations value, select one of the radio buttons, and click the Generate button. You should notice that for the same iteration statement and break iterations values chosen in step 4, the output is different.

The continue Statement

The continue statement starts a new iteration of the nearest while, do, for, or foreach statement. If multiple statements are nested within each other, the continue statement applies only to the innermost statement. Any statements between `continue` and the end of the loop body are skipped.

It is important to realize that a `continue` statement causes the expression, or the iterator section of a `for` statement, to be reevaluated.

Listing 8.9 shows the same `for` statement from Figure 8.1 using a `continue` statement that causes the first three iterations to be skipped.

LISTING 8.9   The continue Statement

```
for (int i = 0; i < 10 ; i++)
{
    if (i < 3)
    {
        continue;
    }

    Console.WriteLine(i);
}
```

▼ TRY IT YOURSELF

Working with the `continue` Statement

To see how the `continue` statement works within different iteration statements, follow these steps. If you closed Visual Studio, repeat the previous exercise first.

1. In the code editor, modify the following methods to include a `continue` statement when the loop iteration counter is less than the `skip` parameter before the power of two has been calculated:

   ▶ PowersOfTwoContinueDoLoop

   ▶ PowersOfTwoContinueForLoop

   ▶ PowersOfTwoContinueForEachLoop

   ▶ PowersOfTwoContinueWhileLoop

2. Run the application by pressing F5. Enter a skip iterations value, select one of the radio buttons, and click the Generate button.

3. Change the location of the `continue` statement so that it occurs after the power of two has been calculated.

4. Run the application again by pressing F5. Enter a skip iterations value, select one of the radio buttons, and click the Generate button. Because the `continue` statement occurs after, it has no effect on the iterations.

The `return` Statement

You have already seen the `return` statement in Hour 4, "Understanding Classes and Objects the C# Way," when you learned about methods and properties. The `return` statement causes control to return to the caller of the member containing the `return` statement. A `return` statement can be used with an expression, as you saw from the examples in Hour 4, in which case it can be used only in a class member that has a non-void return type. A `return` statement can also be used without an expression, in which case it can be used only in a class member that has a void return type, including constructors and finalizers.

Summary

In this hour, you moved away from foundational aspects and learned how to control your application by making decisions, repeating sections of code under certain conditions, and unconditionally jumping to different sections of code.

Knowing how to control the flow of an application is the most central concept in programming. These seemingly simple flow control statements provide the most power and flexibility the C# language has to make an application behave in ways that solve a specific problem.

Q&A

Q. What are the types of control flow statements available in C#?

A. C# provides three types of control flow statements:

▶ Selection statements, which enable for the selection of a single statement to be executed based on the value of an expression from a number of possible statements.

▶ Iteration statements, which repeatedly execute the same statement based on the value of an expression evaluated at each iteration.

▶ Jump statements, which unconditionally transfer control to a new location.

Q. What is the difference between the `while` and `do` statements?

A. The `while` statement provides a top-tested loop, whereas the `do` statement provides a bottom-tested loop. This means that the embedded statement in a `while` loop might execute zero or more times, whereas the embedded statement in a `do` loop executes at least one time.

Workshop

Quiz

1. Does the `switch` statement enable the same code to be used for multiple cases?

2. Can a `switch` statement have more than one default case?

3. How many times will the following `while` statement execute?

```
int i = 10;
while (i < 10)
{
    Console.WriteLine(i);
    i++;
}
```

4. How many times will the following `do` statement execute?

```
int i = 10;
do
{
    Console.WriteLine(i);
    i++;
} while (i < 10)
```

5. What will this `for` statement do?

```
for (int i = 0; ; i++)
{
    Console.WriteLine(i);
}
```

   A. Generate a compiler error.

   B. Print the value of i one time.

   C. Do nothing.

   D. Print the value of i forever.

6. Are the three components of a `for` statement required?

7. Can the identifier declared in a `foreach` statement be used outside the scope of the iteration?

8. When a `jump` statement has been reached, will the statements occurring after the `jump` statement be executed?

9. Are `jump` statements supported within the embedded statement of the iteration statements?

Answers

1. Yes, the same code can be used by multiple cases if they are specified sequentially and contain no intervening statements.

2. No, a `switch` statement can have only one default case.

3. The statement will not execute because the condition is tested first and fails because `i` is equal to 10.

4. The statement will execute once. At the end of the first iteration, the condition is tested and fails because `i` is equal to 10.

5. The correct answer is D. By omitting the condition section of the `for` loop, it continues processing forever because there is no termination condition.

6. No, each component in a `for` statement is optional.

7. This is called the iteration variable and is equivalent to a read-only local variable that is scoped to the embedded statement.

8. No. A `jump` statement unconditionally transfers control to a new location so any statements that appear after the jump statement within the same scope will not be executed.

9. Yes, all the iteration statements support using `jump` statements within the embedded statement.

Exercises

1. Add a `Refresh` method to the `IPhoto` interface with the following signature:

```
void Refresh()
```

   Implement this method in the `Photo` class. The method should contain a single `if` statement. For the `boolean-expression`, test to determine that `this.source` is not `null`. For the `consequence-statement`, use the following code:

```
this.image = BitmapFrame.Create(this.source);
this.exifMetadata = new ExifMetadata(this.source);
this.exists = true;
```

   For the `alternative-statement`, use the following code:

```
this.image = null;
this. exifMetadata = new ExifMetadata();
this.exists = false;
```

   In the `PhotoViewer(Uri)` constructor, add a call to `Refresh()` after the statement that sets the `source` field.

HOUR 9
Using Strings and Regular Expressions

What You'll Learn in This Hour:

▶ Strings

▶ Mutable strings using `StringBuilder`

▶ Type formatting

▶ Regular expressions

As computer programming has evolved from being primarily concerned with performing complex numeric computations to providing solutions for a broader range of business problems, programming languages have shifted to focus more on string data and the manipulation of such data. String data is simply a logical sequence of individual characters. The `System.String` class, which encapsulates the data manipulation, sorting, and searching methods you most commonly perform on strings, enables C# to provide rich support for string data and manipulation.

TIP

String **or** string?

In C#, `string` is an alias for `System.String`, so they are equivalent. Use whichever naming convention you prefer, although the common use is to use `string` when referring to the data type and `String` when accessing static members of the class.

In this hour, you learn to work with strings in C#, including how to manipulate and concatenate strings, extract substrings, and build new strings. After you understand the basics, you learn how to work with regular expressions to perform more complex pattern matching and manipulation.

Strings

A string in C# is an immutable sequence of Unicode characters that cannot be modified after creation. Strings are most commonly created by declaring a variable of type `string` and assigning to it a quoted string of characters, known as a **string literal**, as shown here:

```
string myString = "Now is the time.";
```

NOTE

String Interning

If you have two identical string literals in the same assembly, the runtime only creates one `string` object for all instances of that literal within the assembly. This process, called **string interning**, is used by the C# compiler to eliminate duplicate string literals, saving memory space at runtime and decreasing the time required to perform string comparisons.

String interning can sometimes have unexpected results when comparing string literals using the equality operator:

```
object obj = "String";
string string1 = "String";
string string2 = typeof(string).Name;

Console.WriteLine(string1 == string2); // true
Console.WriteLine(obj == string1); // true
Console.WriteLine(obj == string2); // false
```

The first comparison is testing for value equality, meaning it is testing to see if the two strings have the same content. The second and third comparisons use reference equality because you are comparing an `object` and a `string`. If you were to enter this code in a program, you would see two warnings about a "Possible Unintended Reference Comparison" that further tells you to "Cast the Left Hand Side to Type 'string'" to get a value comparison.

Because string interning applies only to literal string values, the value of `string2` is not interned because it isn't a literal. This means that `obj` and `string2` actually refer to different objects in memory, so the reference equality fails.

These string literals can include special **escape sequences** to indicate nonprinting characters, such as a tab or new line that begin with the backslash character (\\). If you want to include the backslash character as part of the string literal, it must also be escaped. Table 9.1 lists the defined C# character escape sequences.

TABLE 9.1   C# Character Escape Sequences

Escape Sequence	Description
\'	Single quote, used for character literals.
\"	Double quote, used for string literals.
\\	Backslash.
\0	Unicode character 0.
\a	Alert (char 7).
\b	Backspace (char 8).
\f	Form feed (char 12).
\n	New line (char 10).
\r	Carriage return (char 13).
\t	Horizontal tab (char 9).
\v	Vertical quote (char 11).
\uxxxx	Unicode escape sequence for a character with a hexadecimal value xxxx. Also a variable-length version can contain 1 to 4 numeric values.
\uxxxxxxxx	Unicode escape sequence for a character with a hexadecimal value of xxxxxxxx, used for generating Unicode surrogates.

Another option for creating string literals are **verbatim string literals**, which start with the @ symbol before the opening quote. The benefit of verbatim string literals is that the compiler treats the string exactly as it is written, even if it spans multiple lines or includes escape characters. Only the double-quote character must be escaped, by including two double-quote characters, in verbatim string literals so that the compiler knows where the string ends.

When the compiler encounters a verbatim string literal, it translates that literal in to the properly escaped string literal. Listing 9.1 shows four different strings. The first two declarations are equivalent, although the verbatim string literal is generally easier to read. The second two declarations are also equivalent, where `multipleLines2` represents the translated string literal.

LISTING 9.1   String Literals

```
string stringLiteral = "C:\\Program Files\\Microsoft Visual Studio 10\\VC#";
string verbatimLiteral = @"C:\Program Files\Microsoft Visual Studio 10\VC#";

string multipleLines = @"This is a ""line"" of text.
And this is the second line.";
string multipleLines2 =
   "This is a \"line\" of text.\nAnd this is the second line.";
```

NOTE

The `ToString` Method

Strings can also be created by calling the `ToString` method. Because `ToString` is declared by `System.Object`, every `object` is guaranteed to have it; although, the default implementation is to simply return the name of the class. All the predefined data types override `ToString` to provide a meaningful string representation.

Empty Strings

An empty string is different from an unassigned string variable (which is `null`) and is a string containing no characters between the quotes (`""`).

NOTE

`String.Empty` or `""`

There is no practical difference between `""` and `String.Empty`, so which one you choose ultimately depends on personal preference, although `String.Empty` is generally easier to read.

The fastest and simplest way to determine if a string is empty is to test if the `Length` property is equal to 0. However, because strings are reference types, it is possible for a string variable to be `null`, which would result in a runtime error when you tried to access the `Length` property. Because testing to determine if a string is empty is such a common occurrence, C# provides the static method `String.IsNullOrEmpty`, shown in Listing 9.2.

LISTING 9.2 The `String.IsNullOrEmpty` Method

```
public static bool IsNullOrEmpty(string value)
{
    if (value != null)
    {
        return (value.Length == 0);
    }

    return true;
}
```

It is also common to consider a string that contains only whitespace characters as an empty string as well. You can use the static `String.IsNullOrWhiteSpace` method, shown in Listing 9.3.

LISTING 9.3   The `String.IsNullOrWhiteSpace` Method

```
public static bool IsNullOrWhiteSpace(string value)
{
    if (value != null)
    {
        for (int i = 0; i < value.Length; i++)
        {
            if (!char.IsWhiteSpace(value[i]))
            {
                return false;
            }
        }
    }

    return true;
}
```

Using either `String.IsNullOrEmpty` or `String.IsNullOrWhiteSpace` helps ensure correctness, readability, and consistency, so they should be used in all situations where you need to determine if a string is `null`, empty, or contains only whitespace characters.

String Manipulation

The `System.String` class provides a rich set of methods and properties for interacting with and manipulating strings. In fact, `System.String` defines more than 40 different public members.

Even though strings are a first-class data type and string data is usually manipulated as a whole, a string is still composed of individual characters. You can use the `Length` property to determine the total number of characters in the string. Unlike strings in other languages, such as C and C++, strings in C# do not include a termination character. Because strings are composed of individual characters, it is possible to access specific characters by position as if the string were an array of characters.

Working with Substrings

A substring is a smaller string contained within the larger original value. Several methods provided by `System.String` enable you to find and extract substrings.

To extract a substring, the `String` class provides an overloaded `Substring` method, which enables you to specify the starting character position and, optionally, the length of the substring to extract. If you don't provide the length, the resulting substring ends at the end of the original string.

The code in Listing 9.4 creates two substrings. The first substring will start at character position 10 and continue to the end of the original string, resulting in the string "brown fox". The second substring results in the string "quick".

LISTING 9.4   **Working with Substrings**

```
string original = "The quick brown fox";
string substring = original.Substring(10);
string substring2 = original.Substring(4, 5);
```

Extracting substrings in this manner is a flexible approach, especially when combined with other methods enabling you to find the position of specific characters within a string.

The `IndexOf` and `LastIndexOf` methods report the index of the first and last occurrence, respectively, of the specified character or string. If you need to find the first or last occurrence of any character in a given set of characters, you can use one of the `IndexOfAny` or `LastIndexOfAny` overloads, respectively. If a match is found, the index (or more intuitively, the offset) position of the character or start of the matched string is returned; otherwise, the value –1 is returned. If the string or character you are searching for is empty, the value 0 is returned.

CAUTION

Zero-Based Counting

When accessing a string by character position, as the `IndexOf`, `LastIndexOf`, `IndexOfAny`, and `LastIndexOfAny` methods do, C# starts counting at 0 not 1. This means that the first character of the string is at index position 0. A better way to think about these methods is that they return an offset from the beginning of the string.

▼ TRY IT YOURSELF

Working with Substrings

To implement the code shown in Listing 9.4 and see how to create substrings, follow these steps. Keep Visual Studio open at the end of this exercise because you will use this application later.

1. Create a new console application.

2. In the `Main` method of the `Program.cs` file, enter the statements shown in Listing 9.4, followed by statements to print the value of each string.

3. Run the application using Ctrl+F5 and observe that the output matches what is shown in Figure 9.1.

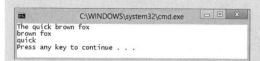

FIGURE 9.1
Results of working with substrings.

4. Modify the two substring calls to use `IndexOf` and `IndexOfAny`, respectively, to produce the same output as shown in Figure 9.1.

String Comparison

To perform string comparisons to determine if one string is equal to or contains another string, you can use the `Compare`, `CompareOrdinal`, `CompareTo`, `Contains`, `Equals`, `EndsWith`, and `StartsWith` methods.

There are 10 different overloaded versions of the static `Compare` method, enabling you to control everything from case sensitivity, culture rules used to perform the comparison, starting positions of both strings being compared, and the maximum number of characters in the strings to compare.

CAUTION
_____

String Comparison Rules

By default, string comparisons using any of the `Compare` methods are performed in a case-sensitive, culture-aware manner. Comparisons using the equality (`==`) operator are always performed using ordinal comparison rules.
_____

You can also use the static `CompareOrdinal` overloads (of which there are only two) if you want to compare strings based on the numeric ordinal values of each character, optionally specifying the starting positions of both strings and the maximum number of characters in the strings to compare.

The `CompareTo` method compares the current string with the specified one and returns an integer value indicating whether the current string precedes, follows, or appears in the same position in the sort order as the specified string.

The `Contains` method searches using ordinal sorting rules, and enables you to determine if the specified string exists within the current string. If the specified string is found or is an empty string, the method returns `true`.

NOTE

Changing Case

Even though the string comparison methods enable ways to perform string comparisons that are not case sensitive, you can also convert strings to an all-uppercase or all-lowercase representation. This is useful for string comparisons but also for standardizing the representation of string data.

The `StartsWith` and `EndsWith` methods (there are a total of six) determine if the beginning or ending of the current string matches a specified string. Just as with the `Compare` method, you can optionally indicate what culture rules should be used and if the search should be case sensitive.

▼ TRY IT YOURSELF

String Comparison

To perform different string comparisons, follow these steps. If you closed Visual Studio, repeat the previous exercise first. Be sure to keep Visual Studio open at the end of this exercise because you will use this application later.

1. In the `Main` method of the `Program.cs` file, enter the following statements:

```
Console.WriteLine(original.StartsWith("quick"));
Console.WriteLine(substring2.StartsWith("quick"));
Console.WriteLine(substring.EndsWith("fox"));
Console.WriteLine(original.CompareTo(original));
Console.WriteLine(String.Compare(substring2, "Quick"));
Console.WriteLine(original.Contains(substring2));
```

2. Run the application using Ctrl+F5 and observe that the output matches what is shown in Figure 9.2.

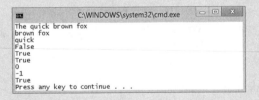

FIGURE 9.2
Results of performing with string comparisons.

The standard way to normalize case is to use the `ToUpperInvariant` method, which creates an all-uppercase representation of the string using the casing rules of the invariant culture.

To create an all-lowercase representation, it is preferred that you use the `ToLowerInvariant` method, which uses the casing rules of the invariant culture. In addition to the invariant methods, you can also use the `ToUpper` and `ToLower` methods, which use the casing rules of either the current culture or the specified culture, depending on which overload you use.

Modifying Parts of a String

Although performing string comparisons is common, sometimes you need to modify all or part of a string. Because strings are immutable, these methods actually return a new string rather than modifying the current one.

To remove whitespace and other characters from a string, you can use the `Trim`, `TrimEnd`, or `TrimStart` methods. `TrimEnd` and `TrimStart` remove whitespace from either the end or beginning of the current string, respectively, whereas `Trim` removes from both ends.

To expand, or pad, a string to be a specific length, you can use the `PadLeft` or `PadRight` methods. By default, these methods pad using spaces, but they both have an overload that enables you to specify the padding character to use.

The `String` class also provides a set of overloaded methods enabling you to create new strings by removing or replacing characters from an existing string. The `Remove` method deletes all the characters from a string starting at a specified character position and either continues through the end of the string or for a specified number of positions. The `Replace` method simply replaces all occurrences of the specified character or string with another character or string by performing an ordinal search that is case sensitive but not culture sensitive.

TRY IT YOURSELF ▼

Modifying Parts of a String

To use the `Replace` and `Remove` methods, follow these steps:

1. In the `Main` method of the `Program.cs` file, remove all the `Console.WriteLine` statements, leaving only the string variable declarations.

2. Enter `Console.WriteLine` statements that will print the string created by:

   ▶ Replacing all `'o'` characters with `'x'` characters in `original`

   ▶ Removing all characters after index position 4 in `original`

   ▶ Removing five characters after index position 4 in `original`

3. After each `Console.WriteLine` statement you entered, enter another `Console.WriteLine` statement that prints the current value of `original`.

▼   **4.** Run the application using Ctrl+F5, and observe that the output matches what is shown in Figure 9.3.

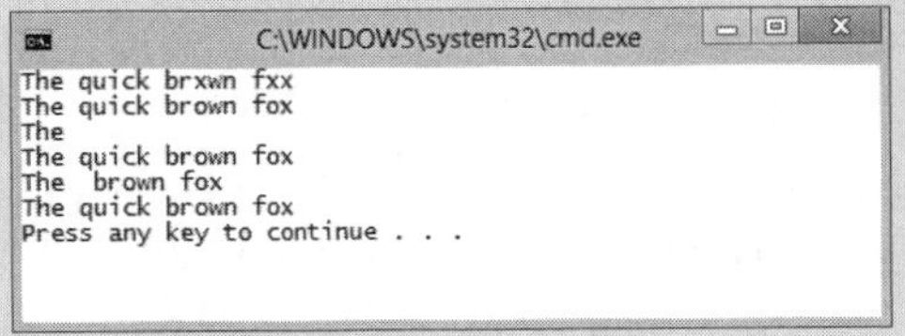

```
C:\WINDOWS\system32\cmd.exe
The quick brxwn fxx
The quick brown fox
The
The quick brown fox
The  brown fox
The quick brown fox
Press any key to continue . . .
```

FIGURE 9.3
Results of string modification.

String Concatenation, Joining, and Splitting

You have already seen several ways to create new strings from string literals and from substrings, but you can also create new strings by combining existing strings in a process called string concatenation.

String concatenation typically occurs two different ways. The most common is to use the overloaded addition (+) operator to combine two or more strings. You can also use one of the nine different overloads of the Concat method, which enables you to concatenate an unlimited number of strings. Both of these methods are shown in Listing 9.5.

TIP

String Concatenation Using Addition

The addition operator actually just calls the appropriate overload of the Concat method.

LISTING 9.5   String Concatenation

```
string string1 = "this is " + " basic concatenation.";
string string2 = String.Concat("this", "is", "more", "advanced", "concatenation");
```

Closely related to concatenation is the idea of joining strings, which uses the Join method. Unlike the Concat method, Join concatenates a specified separator between each element of a given set of strings.

If joining a string combines a set of strings, the opposite is splitting a string into an undetermined number of substrings based on a delimiting character, accomplished by using the Split method, which accepts either a set of characters or a set of strings for the delimiting set.

Listing 9.6 shows an example of joining a string and then splitting it based on the same delimiting character. First, an array of 10 strings is created and then joined using # as the separator character. The resulting string is then split on the same separator character and each word is printed on a separate line.

LISTING 9.6   Joining and Splitting Strings

```
string[] strings = new string[10];
for (int i = 0; i < 10; i++)
{
    strings[i] = String.Format("{0}", i * 2);
}

string joined = String.Join("#", strings);
Console.WriteLine(joined);

foreach (string word in joined.Split(new char[] { '#' }))
{
    Console.WriteLine(word);
}
```

Mutable Strings Using `StringBuilder`

Because strings are immutable, every time you perform any string manipulation, you create new temporary strings. To allow mutable strings to be created and manipulated without creating new strings, C# provides the `StringBuilder` class. Using string concatenation is preferred if a fixed number of strings will be concatenated. If an arbitrary number of strings will be concatenated, such as inside an iteration statement, a `StringBuilder` is preferred.

`StringBuilder` supports appending data to the end of the current string, inserting data at a specified position, replacing data, and removing characters from the current string. Appending data uses one of the overloads of either the `Append` or `AppendFormat` methods.

The `Append` method adds text or a string representation of an object to the end of the current string. The `AppendFormat` method supports adding text to the end of the current string by using composite formatting. Because `AppendFormat` uses composite formatting, you can pass it a format string, which you learn about in the next section.

GO TO ▶ We discuss composite formatting a bit later in this hour.

Listing 9.7 shows the same example of joining and splitting strings shown in Listing 9.6 but uses a `StringBuilder` rather than a `string` array.

LISTING 9.7   Using `StringBuilder`

```
StringBuilder stringBuilder = new StringBuilder();
for (int i = 0; i < 10; i++)
{
    stringBuilder.AppendFormat("{0}#", i * 2);
}

// Remove the trailing '#' character.
stringBuilder.Remove(stringBuilder.Length - 1, 1);

string joined = String.Join("#", stringBuilder.ToString());
Console.WriteLine(joined);

foreach (string word in joined.Split(new char[] { '#' }))
{
    Console.WriteLine(word);
}
```

To insert data, one of the `Insert` overloads should be used. When you insert data, you must provide the position within the current `StringBuilder` string where the insertion will begin. To remove data, you use the `Remove` method and indicate the starting position where the removal begins and the number of characters to remove. The `Replace` method, or one of its overloads, can be used to replace characters within the current `StringBuilder` string with another specified character. The `Replace` method also supports replacing characters within a substring of the current `StringBuilder` string, specified by a starting position and length.

NOTE

`StringBuilder` **Capacity**

Internally, the `StringBuilder` string is maintained in a buffer to accommodate concatenation. The `StringBuilder` needs to allocate additional memory only if the buffer does not have enough room to accommodate the new data.

The default size, or capacity, for this internal buffer is 16 characters. When the buffer reaches capacity, additional buffer space is allocated for an additional amount of characters as specified by the capacity. `StringBuilder` also has a maximum capacity, which is `Int32.MaxValue`, or 231, characters.

The length of the current string can be set using the `Length` property. By setting the `Length` to a value that is larger than the current capacity, the capacity is automatically changed. Similarly, by setting the `Length` to a value that is less than the current capacity, the current string is shortened.

Type Formatting

Formatting allows you to convert an instance of a class, structure, or enumeration value to a string representation. Every type that derives from `System.Object` automatically inherits a parameterless `ToString` method, which, by default, returns the name of the type. All the pre-defined value types have overridden `ToString` to return a general format for the type.

Because getting the name of the type from `ToString` isn't generally useful, you can override the `ToString` method and provide a meaningful string representation of your type. Listing 9.8 shows the `Contact` class overriding the `ToString` method.

LISTING 9.8   Overriding `ToString`

```
class Contact
{
   private string firstName;
   private string lastName;

   public override string ToString()
   {
      return firstName + " " + lastName;
   }
}
```

CAUTION

Overriding `ToString`

Before you start adding `ToString` overrides to all your classes, be aware that the Visual Studio debugging tools use `ToString` extensively to determine what values to display for an object when viewed through a debugger.

The value of an object often has multiple representations, and `ToString` enables you to pass a format string as a parameter that determines how the string representation should appear. A format string contains one or more format specifiers that define how the string representation should appear.

Standard Format Strings

A standard format string contains a single format specifier, which is a single character that defines a more complete format string, and an optional precision specifier that affects the number of digits displayed in the result. If supported, the precision specifier can be any integer value from 0 to 99. All the numeric types, date and time types, and enumeration types support a set of predefined standard format strings, including a "G" standard format specifier, which represents a general string representation of the value.

The standard format specifiers are shown in Table 9.2.

TABLE 9.2 Standard Format Specifiers

Format Specifier	Description
"G", "g"	Represents a general string representation.
	For all numeric types, results in the most compact of either fixed-point or exponential notation. The precision specifier indicates the number of significant digits.
	For all date and time types, represents the general date/time pattern. "G" represents the long time pattern, whereas "g" is the short time pattern.
	For enumeration types, displays the enumeration entry as a string value, if possible, and otherwise displays the integer value of the current instance. If the enumeration is defined with the Flags attribute set, the string values of each valid entry are concatenated together, separated by commas. If the Flags attribute is not set, an invalid value is displayed as a numeric entry.
"X", "x"	For integral types, results in a hexadecimal string. The precision specifier indicates the number of digits in the result string.
	For enumeration types, displays the enumeration entry as a hexadecimal value. The value is represented with leading zeros as necessary, to ensure that the value is a minimum eight digits in length.
"D", "d"	For integral types, results in a string of integer digits with an optional negative sign. The precision specifier indicates the minimum number of digits.
	For enumeration types, displays the enumeration entry as an integer value in the shortest representation possible.
"E", "e"	Supported only by numeric types. Results in the exponential notation representation of the value. The precision specifier indicates the number of decimal digits, and the default is 6.
"F", "f"	For all numeric types and results in a string of integral and decimal digits with an optional negative sign. The precision specifier indicates the number of decimal digits.
	For date and time types, represents the full date/time pattern. "F" represents the long time pattern, whereas "f" is the short time pattern.
	For enumeration types, displays the enumeration entry as a string value, if possible. If the value can be completely displayed as a summation of the entries in the enumeration (even if the Flags attribute is not present), the string values of each valid entry are concatenated together, separated by commas. If the value cannot be completely determined by the enumeration entries, the value is formatted as the integer value.

Format Specifier	Description
"N", "n"	Supported only by numeric types. Results in a string of integral and decimal digits, group separators, and a decimal separator with an optional negative sign. The precision specifier indicates the desired number of decimal places.
"P", "p"	Supported only by numeric types. Results in the number multiplied by 100 and displayed with a percent symbol. The precision specifier indicates the desired number of decimal places.
"R", "r"	Supported only by Single, Double, and BigInteger. Results in a string that can round-trip to an identical number. The precision specifier is ignored.
"M", "m"	Supported only by date and time types. Represents the month/day pattern.
"O", "o"	Supported only by date and time types. Represents the round-trip date/time pattern.
"R", "r"	Supported only by date and time types. Represents the RFC 1123 pattern.
"s"	Supported only by date and time types. Represents the sortable date/time pattern.
"t"	Supported only by date and time types. Represents the short time pattern.
"T"	Supported only by date and time types. Represents the long time pattern.
"u"	Supported only by date and time types. Represents the universal sortable date/time pattern.
"U"	Supported only by date and time types. Represents the universal full date/time pattern.
"Y", "y"	Supported only by date and time types. Represents the year/month pattern.

Using the standard format strings to format a Days enumeration value is shown in Listing 9.9.

LISTING 9.9 Standard Format Strings

```
Days days = Days.Monday;
string[] formats = { "G", "F", "D", "X" };
foreach (string format in formats)
{
   Console.WriteLine(days.ToString(format));
}
```

Just as you can override the ToString method, you can define standard format specifiers for your own classes as well by defining a ToString(string) method, which should support the following:

▶ A "G" format specifier that represents a common format. Your override of the parameter-less ToString method should simply call ToString(string) and pass it the "G" standard format string.

▶ A format specifier that is equal to a null reference that should be considered equivalent to the "G" format specifier.

Listing 9.10 shows an updated Celsius struct from Hour 6, "Creating Enumerated Types and Structures," that supports format specifiers to represent the value in degrees Fahrenheit and degrees Kelvin.

LISTING 9.10   Overriding ToString to Support the Standard Format Strings

```
struct Celsius
{
   public float Degrees;

   public Celsius(float temperature)
   {
      this.Degrees = temperature;
   }

   public override string ToString()
   {
      return this.ToString("C");
   }

   public string ToString(string format)
   {
      if (String.IsNullOrWhiteSpace(format))
      {
         format = "C";
      }

      format = format.ToUpperInvariant().Trim();

      switch(format)
      {
         case "C":
            return this.Degrees.ToString("N2") + " °C";

         case "F":
            return (this.Degrees * 9 / 5 + 32).ToString("N2") + " °F";

         case "K":
            return (this.Degrees + 273.15f).ToString("N2") + " °K";
```

```
        default:
            throw new FormatException();
        }
    }
}
```

Custom Format Strings

Custom format strings consist of one or more custom format specifiers that define the string representation of a value. If a format string contains a single custom format specifier, it should be preceded by the percent (%) symbol so that it won't be confused with a standard format specifier.

All the numeric types and the date and time types support custom format strings. Many of the standard date and time format strings are aliases for custom format strings. Using custom format strings also provides a great deal of flexibility by enabling you to define your own formats by combining multiple custom format specifiers.

The custom format specifiers are described in Table 9.3.

TABLE 9.3 Custom Format Specifiers

Format Specifier	Description
"0"	Supported only by numeric types. The zero is replaced with the corresponding digit if one is present; otherwise, zero appears in the result.
"#"	Supported only by numeric types. The pound sign is replaced with the corresponding digit if one is present; otherwise, no digit appears in the result.
"."	Supported only by numeric types. Determines the location of the decimal separator in the result.
","	Supported only by numeric types. As a group separator, it inserts a localized group separator character between each group. As a number scaling specifier, it divides each number by 1,000 for each comma specified. To be used as a number scaling specifier, it must be immediately to the left of the explicit or implicit decimal point.
"%"	Supported only by numeric types. Multiplies a number by 100 and inserts a localized percent symbol in the result.
"‰"	Supported only by numeric types. Multiplies a number by 1,000 and inserts a localized per mille symbol in the result. The ‰ symbol is the Unicode symbol U+2030.

Format Specifier	Description
`"E0"`, `"E+0"`, `"E-0"`, `"e0"`, `"e+0"`, `"e-0"`	Supported only by numeric types. If followed by at least one 0, formats the result using exponential notation. The case of `"E"` or `"e"` indicates the case of the exponent symbol in the result and the number of zeros determines the minimum number of digits in the exponent. A plus sign (+) indicates that a sign character always precedes the exponent, whereas a minus sign (–) indicates that a sign character precedes only negative exponents.
`;`	Supported only by numeric types. Defines sections with separate format strings for positive, negative, and zero numbers. If only one section is included, which is the default, the format string applies to all values. If two sections are included, the first section applies to all positive values and zeros, whereas the second applies to negative values. If three sections are included, the first applies to positive values, the second to negative values, and the third to zeros.
`"d"`	Supported only by date and time types. The day of the month, from 1 through 31.
`"dd"`	Supported only by date and time types. The day of the month, from 01 through 31.
`"ddd"`	Supported only by date and time types. The abbreviated name of the day of the week.
`"dddd"`	Supported only by date and time types. The full name of the day of the week.
`"g"`, `"gg"`	Supported only by date and time types. The period or era.
`"h"`	Supported only by date and time types. The hour, using a 12-hour clock from 0 to 11.
`"hh"`	Supported only by date and time types. The hour, using a 12-hour clock from 00 to 11.
`"H"`	Supported only by date and time types. The hour, using a 24-hour clock from 0 to 23.
`"HH"`	Supported only by date and time types. The hour, using a 24-hour clock from 00 to 23.
`"K"`	Supported only by date and time types. Time zone information.
`"m"`	Supported only by date and time types. The minute, from 0 through 59.
`"mm"`	Supported only by date and time types. The minute, from 00 through 59.
`"M"`	Supported only by date and time types. The month, from 1 through 12.
`"MM"`	Supported only by date and time types. The month, from 01 through 12.
`"MMM"`	Supported only by date and time types. The abbreviated name of the month.
`"MMMM"`	Supported only by date and time types. The full name of the month.

Format Specifier	Description
`"s"`	Supported only by date and time types. The second, from 0 through 59.
`"ss"`	Supported only by date and time types. The second, from 00 through 59.
`"t"`	Supported only by date and time types. The first character of the AM/PM designator.
`"tt"`	Supported only by date and time types. The AM/PM designator.
`"y"`	Supported only by date and time types. The year, from 0 to 99.
`"yy"`	Supported only by date and time types. The year, from 00 to 99.
`"yyy"`	Supported only by date and time types. The year, with a minimum of three digits.
`"yyyy"`	Supported only by date and time types. The year as a four-digit number.
`"yyyyy"`	Supported only by date and time types. The year as a five-digit number.
`"z"`	Supported only by date and time types. Hours offset from UTC, with no leading zeros.
`"zz"`	Supported only by date and time types. Hours offset from UTC, with a leading zero for single-digit values.
`"zzz"`	Supported only by date and time types. Hours and minutes offset form UTC.
`":"`	Supported only by date and time types. The time separator.
`"/"`	Supported only by date and time types. The date separator.
`'string'`, `"string"`	Literal string delimiter. The enclosed characters should be copied to the result unchanged.
`\`	The escape character that causes the next character to be interpreted as a literal character rather than a custom format specifier.
Other	All other characters are copied to the result string unchanged.

Listing 9.11 displays a `DateTime` instance using two different custom format strings.

LISTING 9.11   Custom Format Strings

```
DateTime date = new DateTime(2013, 3, 22);

// Displays 3
Console.WriteLine(date.ToString("%M"));

// Displays Monday March 22, 2013
Console.WriteLine(date.ToString("dddd MMMM dd, yyyy"));
```

Composite Formatting

You have already seen composite formatting in some of the previous examples using `Console.WriteLine` and `StringBuilder.AppendFormat`. Methods that use composite formatting accept a composite format string and a list of objects as parameters. A composite format string defines a template consisting of fixed text and indexed placeholders, called format items, which correspond to the objects in the list. Composite formatting does not allow you to specify more format items than there are objects in the list, although you can include more objects in the list than there are format items.

The syntax for a format item is as follows:

```
{index[,alignment][:formatString]}
```

The matching curly braces and `index` are required.

The `index` corresponds to the position of the object it represents in the method's parameter list. Indexes are zero-based but multiple format items can use the same index, and format items can refer to any object in the list, in any order.

The optional `alignment` component indicates the preferred field width. A positive value produces a right-aligned field, whereas a negative value produces a left-aligned field. If the value is less than the length of the formatted string, the `alignment` component is ignored.

The `formatString` component uses either the standard or custom format strings you just learned. If the `formatString` is not specified, the general format specifier `"G"` is used instead.

In Listing 9.12, the first format item, `{0:D}`, is replaced by the string representation of `date` and the second format item `{1}` is replaced by the string representation of `temp`.

LISTING 9.12   Composite Formatting

```
Celsius temp = new Celsius(28);

// Using composite formatting with String.Format.
string result = String.Format("On {0:d}, the high temperature was {1}.",
DateTime.Today, temp);
Console.WriteLine(result);

// Using composite formatting with Console.WriteLine.
Console.WriteLine("On {0:dddd MMM dd, yyyy}, the high temperature was {1}.",
DateTime.Today, temp);
```

Regular Expressions

Often referred to as patterns, a regular expression describes a set of strings. A regular expression is applied to a string to find out if the string matches the provided pattern, to return a substring or a collection of substrings, or to return a new string that represents a modification of the original.

TIP

Regular Expression Compatibility

Regular expressions in the .NET Framework are designed to be compatible with Perl 5 regular expressions, incorporating the most popular features of other regular expression implementations, such as Perl and awk, and including features not yet seen in other implementations.

Regular expressions are a programming language in their own right and are designed and optimized for text manipulation by using both literal text characters and metacharacters. A literal character is one that should be matched in the target string, whereas metacharacters inform the regular expression parser, which is responsible for interpreting the regular expression and applying it to the target string, how to behave, so you can think of them as commands. These metacharacters give regular expressions their flexibility and processing power. The common metacharacters used in regular expressions are described in Table 9.4.

TABLE 9.4 Common Regular Expression Metacharacters

Metacharacter	Description
.	Matches any single character except newline ($\n$).
[ ]	Matches a single character contained within the brackets. A range of characters can be specified using the – character.
[^]	Matches a single character not contained with the brackets.
^	Indicates matching should start at the beginning of the line.
$	Indicates matching should end at the end of the line.
\w	Matches a word character. This is equivalent to the pattern [a-zA-Z_0-9].
\W	Matches a nonword character.
\s	Matches a space character. This is equivalent to [\n\r\t\f].
\S	Matches a nonspace character.
\d	Matches a decimal digit. This is equivalent to [0-9].
\D	Matches a nondigit.

Metacharacter	Description
*	Matches the preceding element zero or more times.
+	Matches the preceding element one or more times.
?	Matches the preceding element zero or one times.
{n}	Matches the preceding element exactly n times.
{n,}	Matches the preceding element at least n times.
{n,m}	Matches the preceding element at least n times but no more than m times.
¦	(Alternation operator) Matches the expression either before or after the operator.
( )	Defines an unnamed capturing group.
(?<name>) (?'name')	Defines a named capturing group.
(?<number>) (?'number')	Defines a numbered capturing group.

The Regular Expression Classes in C#

Regular expressions are implemented in the .NET Framework by several classes in the `System.Text.RegularExpression` namespace that provide support for parsing and applying regular expression patterns and working with capturing groups.

The `Regex` Class

The `Regex` class provides the implementation of the regular expression parser and the engine that applies that pattern to an input string. Using this class, you can quickly parse large amounts of text for specific patterns and easily extract and edit substrings.

The `Regex` class provides both instance and static members, allowing it to be used two different ways. When you create specific instances of the `Regex` class, the expression patterns are not compiled and cached. However, by using the static methods, the expression pattern is compiled and cached. The regular expression engine caches the 15 most recently used static regular expressions by default. You might prefer to use the static methods rather than the equivalent instance methods if you extensively use a fixed set of regular expressions.

The `Match` and `MatchCollection` Classes

When a regular expression is applied to a string using the `Match` method of the `Regex` class, the first successful match found is represented by an instance of the `Match` class. The `MatchCollection` contains the set of `Matches` found by repeatedly applying the regular expression until the first unsuccessful match occurs.

The Group and Capture Classes

The Match.Groups property represents the collection of captured groups in a single match. Each group is represented by the Group class, which contains a collection of Capture objects returned by the Captures property. A Capture represents the results from a single subexpression match.

String Validation Using Regular Expressions

One of the most common uses of regular expressions is to validate a string by testing if it conforms to a particular pattern. To accomplish this, you can use one of the overloads for the IsMatch method. Listing 9.13 shows using a regular expression to validate United States Zip+4 postal codes.

LISTING 9.13   Validation Using Regular Expressions

```
string pattern = @"^\d{5}(-\d{4})?$";
Regex expression = new Regex(pattern);

Console.WriteLine(expression.IsMatch("90210")); // true
Console.WriteLine(expression.IsMatch("00364-3276")); // true
Console.WriteLine(expression.IsMatch("3361")); // false
Console.WriteLine(expression.IsMatch("0036-43275")); // false
Console.WriteLine(expression.IsMatch("90210-")); // false
```

Using Regular Expressions to Match Substrings

Regular expressions can also be used to search for substrings that match a particular regular expression pattern. This searching can be performed once, in which case the first occurrence is returned, or it can be performed repeatedly, in which case a collection of occurrences is returned.

Searching for substrings in this manner uses the Match method to find the first occurrence matching the pattern or the Matches method to return a sequence of successful nonoverlapping matches.

Summary

Continuing to move further away from the foundational aspects of programming, in this hour, you learned how C# enables you to work with string data. This included how to perform string comparisons, create mutable strings, and how to use regular expressions.

Q&A

Q. Are strings immutable?

A. Yes, strings in C# are immutable, and any operation that modifies the content of a string actually creates a new string with the changed value.

Q. What does the @ symbol mean when it precedes a string literal?

A. The @ symbol is the verbatim string symbol and causes the C# compiler to treat the string exactly as it is written, even if it spans multiple lines or includes special characters.

Q. What are the common string manipulation functions supported by C#?

A. C# supports the following common string manipulations:

▸ Determining the string length

▸ Trimming and padding strings

▸ Creating substrings, concatenating strings, and splitting strings based on specific characters

▸ Removing and replacing characters

▸ Performing string containment and comparison operations

▸ Converting string case

Q. What is the benefit of the `StringBuilder` class?

A. The `StringBuilder` class enables you to create and manipulate a string that is mutable and is most often used for string concatenation inside a loop.

Q. What are regular expressions?

A. Regular expressions are a pattern that describes a set of strings that are optimized for text manipulation.

Workshop

Quiz

1. What is string interning and why is it used?

2. Using a verbatim string literal, must an embedded double-quote character be escaped?

3. What is the recommended way to test for an empty string?

4. What is the difference between the `IndexOf` and `IndexOfAny` methods?

5. Do any of the string manipulation functions result in a new string being created?

6. What will the output of the following statement be and why?

```
int i = 10;
Console.WriteLine(i.ToString("P"));
```

7. What will the output of the following statement be and why?

```
DateTime today = new DateTime(2009, 8, 23);
Console.WriteLine(today.ToString("MMMM"));
```

8. What will the output of the following `Console.WriteLine` statements be?

```
Console.WriteLine("|{0}|", 10);
Console.WriteLine("|{0, 3}|", 10);
Console.WriteLine("|{0:d4}|", 10);

int a = 24;
int b = -24;

Console.WriteLine(a.ToString("##;(##)"));
Console.WriteLine(b.ToString("##;(##)"));
```

9. What is the benefit of using a `StringBuilder` for string concatenation inside a loop?

10. What does the following regular expression pattern mean?

```
[\w-]+@([\w-]+\.)+[\w-]+
```

Answers

1. String interning is used by the C# compiler to eliminate duplicate string literals to save space at runtime.

2. The double-quote character is the only character that must be escaped using a verbatim string literal so that the compiler can determine where the string ends.

3. The recommended way to test for an empty string is to use the static `String.IsNullOrEmpty` method.

4. The `IndexOf` method reports the index of the first occurrence found of a single character or string, whereas the `IndexOfAny` method reports the first occurrence found of any character in a set of characters.

5. Yes, because strings are immutable, all the string manipulation functions result in a new string being created.

6. The output will be "1,000.00 %" because the `"P"` numeric format specifier results in the number being multiplied by 100 and displayed with a percent symbol.

7. The `"MMMM"` custom date and time format specifier represents the full name of the month, so the output will be "August".

8. The output will be as follows:

```
¦10¦
¦ 10¦
¦0010¦
24
(24)
```

9. Because the `StringBuilder` represents a mutable string, using it for string concatenation inside a loop prevents multiple temporary strings from being created during each iteration to perform the concatenation.

10. This is a simple regular expression for parsing a string as an email address. Broken down, it means "Match any word character one or more times followed by the @ character followed by a group containing any word character one or more times followed by a period (.) character, where that group is repeated one or more times, followed by any word character one or more times."

Exercises

1. Create a new console application and implement the `Celsius` struct shown in Listing 9.10. In the `Main` method, implement the code shown in Listing 9.12.

2. Create a new console application and in the `Main` method implement the code shown in Listing 9.13. Then implement a `Validate` method that is called from the `Main` method. The `Validate` method should use the static `RegEx.IsMatch` method to validate a string parameter as a phone number. The necessary regular expression pattern to match a phone number in the form of 555-555-5555 should look like:

```
^[2-9]\d{2}-\d{3}-\d{4}$
```

HOUR 10
Working with Arrays and Collections

What You'll Learn in This Hour:

▶ Single and multidimensional arrays

▶ Indexers

▶ Generic collections

▶ Collection initializers

▶ Collection interfaces

▶ Enumerable objects and iterators

The majority of problems solved by computer programs involve working with large amounts of data. Sometimes there is a lot of individual and unrelated datum, but many times, there are large amounts of related datum. C# provides a rich set of collection types that enable you to manage large amounts of data.

An array is the simplest type of collection and is the only one that has direct language support. Although the other collection types offer more flexibility than arrays, including the ability to create your own specialized collections, they are generally used in similar ways.

In this hour, you learn to work with different types of arrays, including multidimensional and jagged arrays. When you understand how to work with arrays, you move to using some of the different collection classes provided by the .NET Framework, of which there are more than 40 different classes, base classes, and interfaces.

Single and Multidimensional Arrays

An array is a numerically indexed collection of objects that are all the same type. Although C# provides direct language support for creating arrays, the common type system means that you are implicitly creating a type of System.Array. As a result, arrays in C# are reference types, and the memory allocated to refer to the array itself is allocated on the managed heap. However, the elements of the array, which are the individual items contained in the array, are allocated based on their own type.

In its simplest form, the declaration of a variable of array type looks like this:

```
type[] identifier;
```

NOTE

Arrays

Arrays in C# are different from arrays in C because they are actually objects of type `System.Array`. As a result, C# arrays provide the power and flexibility afforded by classes through properties and methods with the simple syntax offered by C style arrays.

The `type` indicates the type of each element that will be contained in the array. Because the type is declared only once, all the elements in the array must be of that same type. The square brackets are the **index operator** and tell the compiler that you are declaring an array of the given type; they are the only difference between an array declaration and a regular variable declaration. In contrast to other languages, such as C, the size of a dimension is specified when the array is instantiated rather than when it is declared.

To create an array that can contain five integer values, you can specify it like this:

```
int[] array = new int[5];
```

CAUTION

Array Sizes

In C#, the size of an array, obtained through the `Length` property, is the total number of elements in all the dimensions of the array, not the upper bound of the array.

Because C# uses a zero-based indexing scheme for arrays, the first element in an array is at position 0. Therefore, the following statement declares an array of five elements with indices 0 through 4:

```
int[] array = new int[5];
```

The length of the array is 5, but the upper bound is 4.

This type of array declaration creates a single-dimensional rectangular array. The length of each row in a rectangular array must be the same size. This restriction results in a rectangular shape and is what gives rectangular arrays their name. To declare a multidimensional rectangular array, you specify the number of dimensions, or **rank** of the array, using commas inside the square brackets. The most common multidimensional arrays are two-dimensional arrays, which can be thought of as rows and columns. An array cannot have more than 32 dimensions. For example, to create a two-dimensional array that represents a 5 x 2 table of integer values, you can specify it like this:

```
int[,] array = new int[5, 2];
```

In addition to rectangular multidimensional arrays, C# also supports jagged arrays. Because each element of a jagged array is an array itself, each row of the array does not need to be the same size like it does for a rectangular array.

NOTE

Jagged Rectangular Arrays

In the following code, you create a two-dimensional array a with six elements (three rows of two elements) and a one-dimensional array j whose elements are a one-dimensional array with one, two, and three elements, respectively:

```
int[,] a = {
  {10, 20},
  {30, 40},
  {50, 60} };

int[][] j = {
  new[] {10},
  new[] {20, 30},
  new[] {40, 50, 60} };
```

When you try to make a jagged array of rectangular arrays is when things can get confusing. What is the type of the following?

```
int[,][] j2;
```

This is actually a two-dimensional array (three rows of two elements) whose elements are each a one-dimensional array. To initialize such an array, you would write

```
j2 = new int[3,2][];
```

For this reason, it is almost always better if you can use one of the generic collections. It is completely clear that List<int[,]> means a list of two-dimensional arrays, whereas List<int>[,] means a two-dimensional array whose elements are List<int>.

The type system requires that all variables be initialized before use and provides default values for each data type. Arrays are no different. For arrays containing numeric elements, each element is initially set to 0; for arrays containing reference types, including string types, each element is initially null. Because the elements of a jagged array are other arrays, they are initially null as well.

Array Indexing

For arrays to be useful, it is necessary to access specific elements of the array. This is done by enclosing the numeric position of the desired element in the index operator. To access an element of a multidimensional or a jagged array, both index locations must be provided.

▼ TRY IT YOURSELF

Array Indexing

By following these steps, you see how to access an array by index:

1. Create a new console application.

2. In the `Main` method of the `Program.cs` file, declare an integer array named `array` of five elements.

3. Write a `for` statement that initializes each element of the array to its index position times 2.

4. Write another `for` statement that prints the value of each element so that it follows this format, where `index` and `value` correspond to the array index and the value at that index:

   ```
   array[index] = value
   ```

5. Run the application using Ctrl+F5 and observe that the output matches what is shown in Figure 10.1.

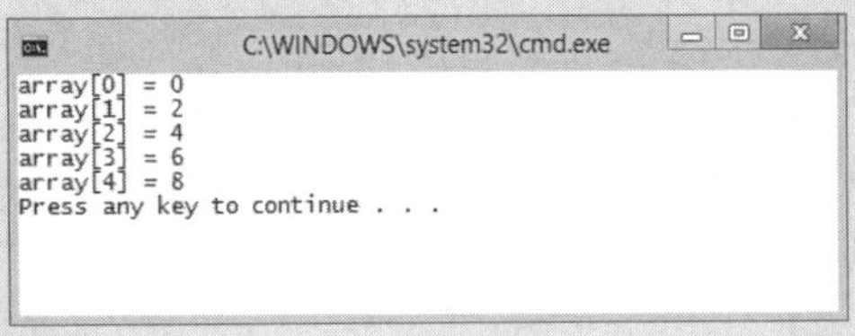

```
C:\WINDOWS\system32\cmd.exe
array[0] = 0
array[1] = 2
array[2] = 4
array[3] = 6
array[4] = 8
Press any key to continue . . .
```

FIGURE 10.1
Results of working with array indexers.

Array Initialization

Using the `new` operator creates an array and initializes the array elements to their default values. In this case, the rank specifier is required for the compiler to know the size of the array. When declaring an array in this manner, additional code must be written.

Listing 10.1 shows what you should have written for step 3 of the previous exercise.

LISTING 10.1   Traditional Array Initialization

```
class Program
{
   static void Main()
   {
      int[] array = new int[5];
      for(int i = 0; i < array.Length; i++)
      {
         array[i] = i * 2;
      }
   }
}
```

Fortunately, C# provides a shorthand form that enables the array declaration and initialization to be written so that the array type does not need to be restated. This shorthand notation is called an **array initializer** and can be used for local variable and field declarations of arrays, or immediately following an array constructor call. An array initializer is a sequence of variable initializers separated by a comma and enclosed by curly braces. Each variable initializer is an expression or a nested array initializer when used with multidimensional arrays.

When an array initializer is used for a single-dimensional array, it must consist of a sequence of expressions that are assignment-compatible with the element type of the array. The expressions initialize elements starting at index 0, and the number of expressions determines the length of the array being created.

Listing 10.2 shows how to use a simple array initializer that results in the same initialized array as shown in Listing 10.1.

LISTING 10.2   Array Initialization

```
class Program
{
   static void Main()
   {
      int[] array = {0, 2, 4, 6, 8};
   }
}
```

Although array initializers are useful for single-dimensional arrays, they become powerful for multidimensional arrays that use nested array initializers. In this case, the levels of nesting in the array initializer must be equal to the number of dimensions in the array. The leftmost dimension is represented by the outermost nesting level, and the rightmost dimension is represented by the innermost nesting level.

For example, the statement

```
int[,] array = { {0, 1}, {2, 3}, {4, 5}, {6, 7}, {8, 9} };
```

is equivalent to the following:

```
int[,] array = new int[5, 2];
array[0, 0] = 0; array[0, 1] = 1;
array[1, 0] = 2; array[1, 1] = 3;
array[2, 0] = 4; array[2, 1] = 5;
array[3, 0] = 6; array[3, 1] = 7;
array[4, 0] = 8; array[4, 1] = 9;
```

The `System.Array` Class

The `System.Array` class is the base class for arrays, but only the runtime and compilers can explicitly derive from it. Despite this restriction, there are more than 25 different static methods available for you to use. These methods operate primarily on one-dimensional arrays, but because those are the most common type of array, this restriction generally isn't very limiting. The more common methods are shown in Table 10.1.

TABLE 10.1 Common Static Methods of `System.Array`

Name	Description
BinarySearch	Searches a one-dimensional sorted array for a value using a binary search algorithm.
Clear	Sets a range of elements in the array to zero, false, or null, depending on the element type.
Exists	Determines whether the specified array contains elements that match the conditions specified.
Find	Searches for an element that matches the conditions defined and returns the first occurrence within the entire array.
FindAll	Retrieves all the elements that match the conditions defined.
ForEach	Performs the specified action on each element in the array.
Resize	Changes the size of an array to the specified new size, if necessary. If the size stays the same, nothing changes, and if the size is larger, a new array is created and the elements are copied from the old array into the new one.
Sort	Sorts the elements in the specified array.
TrueForAll	Determines whether every element in the array matches the conditions defined.

Indexers

You have seen how useful and simple accessing arrays can be through the index operator. Although it is not possible to override the index operator, your own classes can provide an indexer that enables them to be indexed in the same way as an array.

Indexers are declared in a similar manner as properties, but there are some important differences. The most important differences are as follows:

▶ Indexers are identified by signature rather than by name.

▶ Indexers must be an instance member only.

The signature for an indexer is the number and types of its formal parameters. Because indexers are identified by signature, it is possible to include overloaded indexers as long as their signatures are unique within the class.

To declare an indexer, you use the following syntax:

```
type this [type parameter]
{
    get;
    set;
}
```

The modifiers allowed for an indexer are `new`, `virtual`, `sealed`, `override`, `abstract`, and a valid combination of the four access modifiers. Remember, because an indexer must be an instance member, it is not allowed to be `static`. The formal parameter list for an indexer must contain at least one parameter, but can contain more than one separated by a comma. This is similar to the formal parameter list for methods. The type for the indexer determines the type of the object returned by the `get` accessor.

An indexer should always provide a `get` accessor (although it isn't required) but does not need to provide a `set` accessor. Indexers that provide only a `get` accessor are read-only indexers because they do not allow assignments to occur.

TRY IT YOURSELF ▼

Indexers

To create an indexer for a custom class, follow these steps.

1. Create a new console application.

2. Add a new class file named `IndexerExample.cs`, and replace the contents with this code:

```
class IndexerExample
{
    private string[] array = new string[4] { "now", "is", "the", "time" };

    public int Length
    {
        get
        {
            return this.array.Length;
        }
    }

    public string this[int index]
    {
        get
        {
            return this.array[index];
        }
        set
        {
            this.array[index] = value;
        }
    }
}
```

3. In the `Main` method of the `Program.cs` file, declare a new variable of type `IndexerExample` named `example1`.

4. Write a `for` statement that prints the value of each element so that it follows this format, in which `index` and `value` correspond to the array index and the value at that index:

   ```
   index[index] = value
   ```

5. Run the application using Ctrl+F5, and observe that the output matches what is shown in Figure 10.2.

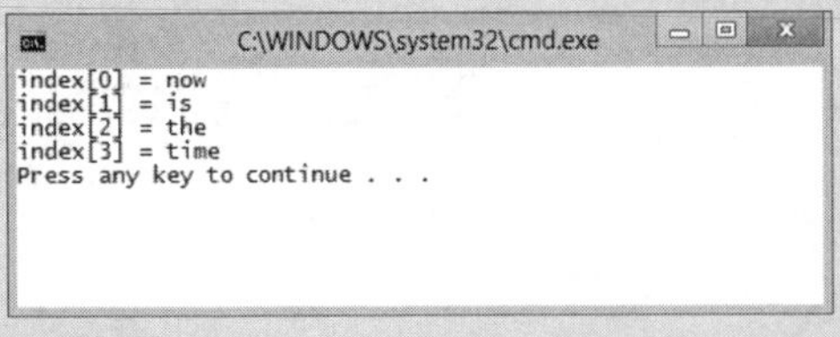

FIGURE 10.2
Results of using a custom indexer.

6. Now, declare a new variable of type `IndexerExample` named `example2` and write a `for` statement that sets the values of `example2` to those of `example1` in reverse order. This `for` statement should look like:

```
for (int i = example1.Length - 1, j = 0; i >= 0; i--, j++)
{
    example2[j] = example1[i];
}
```

7. Copy the `for` statement you wrote in step 4 below the code you just wrote, and change it to print the values of `example2`. You might want to print a blank line before the `for` statement starts.

8. Run the application using Ctrl+F5, and observe that the output matches what is shown in Figure 10.3.

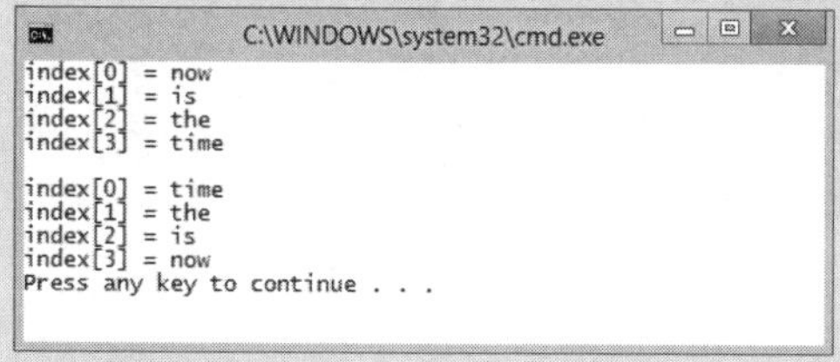

FIGURE 10.3
Results of using a custom indexer over two instances.

Generic Collections

Although arrays are the only built-in data structure in C# that supports the concept of a collection of objects, the base class library provides a rich set of collection and collection-related types to supplement them, which provide much more flexibility and enable you to derive custom collections for your own data types.

GO TO ▶ HOUR 12, "UNDERSTANDING GENERICS," for more information on generic types.

These types are separated into classes and interfaces, and are further separated into nongeneric and generic collections. The nongeneric collections are not type safe because they work only with the `object` type, and are available for backward compatibility with older versions of the .NET Framework. The generic collections are preferred because they provide type safety and better performance than the nongeneric collections. There are almost twice as many generic collections as there are nongeneric collections.

TIP

Generic Collections and Backward Compatibility

The .NET for Windows Store apps and Silverlight versions of the .NET Framework remove the nongeneric collections because there was no legacy code to be compatible with.

Lists

Within the set of collection types, List<T> is the one that could be considered to be closest to an array and is probably the most commonly used collection. Like an array, it is a numerically indexed collection of objects. Unlike an array, a List<T> is dynamically sized as needed.

The default capacity for a list is 16 elements. When you add the 17th element, the size of the list is automatically doubled. If the number (or an approximate number) of elements the list contains is known ahead of time, it can be beneficial to set the initial capacity using one of the overloaded constructors or by setting the Capacity property before adding the first item.

Table 10.2 lists some of the commonly used properties and methods of List<T>. If you compare this with the common static methods of System.Array (refer to Table 10.1), you should see a great deal of similarity.

TABLE 10.2 Common Members of List<T>

Name	Description
Capacity	Gets or sets the total number of elements the list can contain without resizing
Count	Gets the total number of elements actually contained in the list
Add	Adds an object to the end of the list
AddRange	Adds a collection of objects to the end of the list
BinarySearch	Searches a sorted list for a value using a binary search algorithm
Clear	Removes all elements from the list
Contains	Determines whether an element is in the list
Exists	Determines whether the list contains elements that match the conditions specified
Find	Searches for an element that matches the conditions defined and returns the first occurrence within the entire list
FindAll	Retrieves all the elements that match the conditions defined
ForEach	Performs the specified action on each element in the list

Name	Description
Sort	Sorts the elements in the list
TrimExcess	Sets the capacity to the actual number of elements in the list
TrueForAll	Determines whether every element in the list matches the conditions defined

Related to List<T> is LinkedList<T>, which is a general-purpose doubly linked list and might be the better choice when elements will be most commonly added at specific locations in the list and access to the elements will always be sequential.

Working with List<T>

To see how List<T> works, follow these steps. Keep Visual Studio open at the end of this exercise because you will use this application later.

1. Create a new console application.

2. In the Main method of the Program.cs file, declare a new integer list named list using the following statement:

```
List<int> list = new List<int>();
```

3. Write a for statement that initializes 16 elements of the list to its index position times 2.

4. Write a foreach statement that prints the value of each element.

5. Now, print the value of the Capacity property.

6. Run the application using Ctrl+F5, and observe that the output matches what is shown in Figure 10.4.

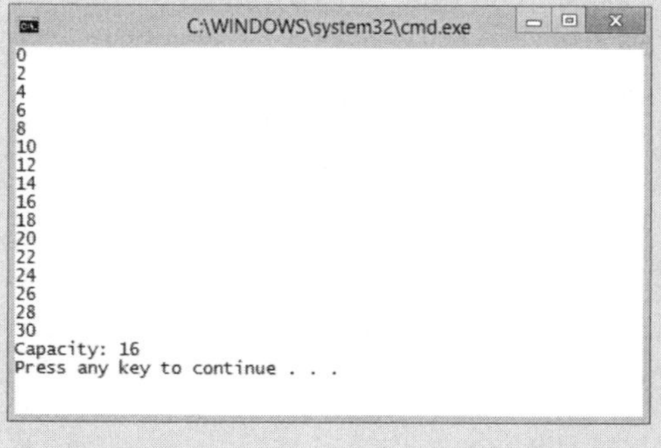

FIGURE 10.4
Results of working with List<T>.

7. Now, duplicate the code you wrote in steps 3 through 5.

8. Run the application again using Ctrl+F5, and observe that the output matches what is shown in Figure 10.5.

FIGURE 10.5
Results of `List<T>` showing an increased capacity.

Collections

Although `List<T>` is powerful, it has no virtual members and does not enable a way to prevent modification of the list. Because there are no virtual members, it is not easily extended, which can limit its usefulness as a base class for your own collections.

To create your own collections that can be accessed by a numeric index like an array, you can derive your collection from `Collection<T>`. It is also possible to use the `Collection<T>` class immediately by creating an instance and supplying the type of object to be contained in the collection. Table 10.3 shows some of the common members of `Collection<T>`.

TABLE 10.3 Common Members of `Collection<T>`

Name	Description
Count	Gets the number of elements actually contained in the collection
Add	Adds an object to the end of the collection
Clear	Removes all elements from the list
Contains	Determines whether an element is in the collection

Working with Collection<T>

By following these steps, you see how Collection<T> works. If you closed Visual Studio, repeat the previous exercise first. Be sure to keep Visual Studio open at the end of this exercise because you will use this application later.

1. Change the declaration of list from type List<int> to be of type Collection<int>. You might need to include the System.Collections.ObjectModel namespace.

2. Correct the two compiler errors by changing the Console.WriteLine statements to print the value of the Count property instead.

3. Run the application using Ctrl+F5, and observe that the output matches what is shown in Figure 10.6.

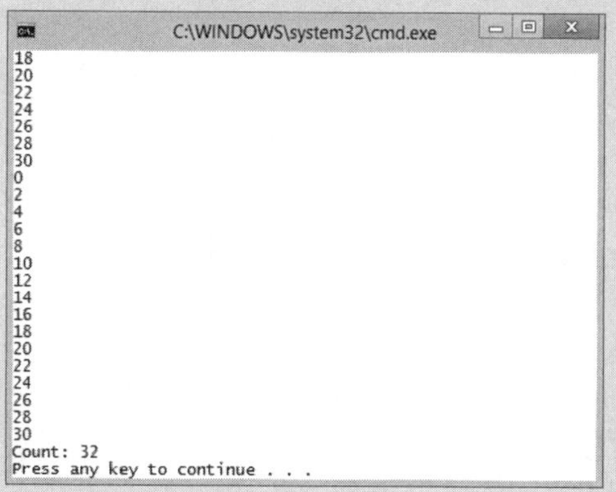

FIGURE 10.6
Results of working with Collection<T>.

To derive your own collection class, Collection<T> provides several protected virtual methods you can override to customize the behavior of the collection. These virtual methods are shown in Table 10.4.

TABLE 10.4   Protected Virtual Members of Collection<T>

Name	Description
ClearItems	Removes all elements from the collection. Can change the behavior of the Clear method.
InsertItem	Inserts an element into the collection at the specified index.

Name	Description
RemoveItem	Removes the element at the specified index.
SetItem	Replaces the element at the specified index.

▼ TRY IT YOURSELF

Deriving Your Own Collection

To derive a concrete (closed) integer collection, follow these steps. If you closed Visual Studio, repeat the previous exercise first.

1. Add a new class named `Int32Collection`, which derives from `Collection<int>` and overrides the `InsertItem` method. The body of the overridden `InsertItem` method should look like this:

```
protected override void InsertItem(int index, int item)
{
    Console.WriteLine("Inserting item {0} at position {1}", item, index);
    base.InsertItem(index, item);
}
```

2. Change the declaration of `list` from type `Collection<int>` to be of type `Int32Collection`.

3. Run the application using Ctrl+F5, and observe that the output matches what is shown in Figure 10.6. If you scroll the console window up, you should see the output from the overridden `InsertItem` method, as shown in Figure 10.7.

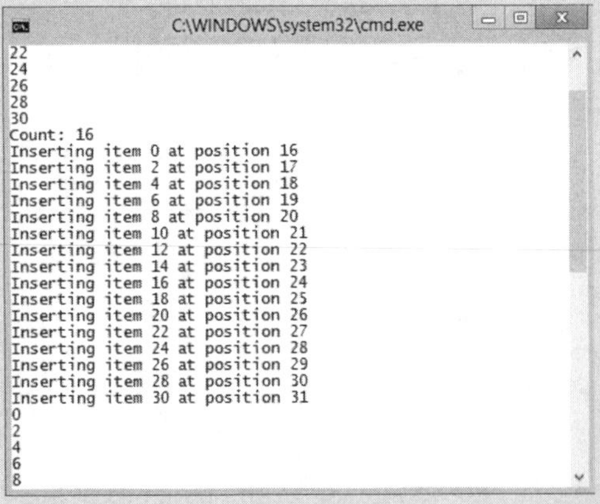

FIGURE 10.7
Results of a custom defined `Collection<int>`.

Related to Collection<T> is ReadOnlyCollection<T>, which can be used immediately just like Collection<T> or can be used to create your own read-only collections. It is also possible to create a read-only collection from an instance of a List<T>. The most commonly used members are shown in Table 10.5.

TIP

ReadOnlyCollection<T>

You can think of ReadOnlyCollection<T> as a wrapper around an existing mutable collection, which throws exceptions if you try to change it. The underlying collection is still mutable.

TABLE 10.5   Common Members of ReadOnlyCollection<T>

Name	Description
Count	Gets the number of elements actually contained in the collection
Contains	Determines whether an element is in the collection
IndexOf	Searches for the specified element and returns the index of the first occurrence

Dictionaries

List<T> and Collection<T> are useful for general-purpose collections, but sometimes it is necessary to have a collection that can provide a mapping between a set of keys and a set of values, not allowing duplicate keys.

The Dictionary<TKey, TValue> class provides such a mapping and enables access using the key rather than a numeric index. To add an element to a Dictionary<TKey, TValue> instance, you must provide both a key and a value. The key must be unique and cannot be null, but if TValue is a reference type, the value can be null. Table 10.6 shows the common members of the Dictionary<TKey, TValue> class.

TABLE 10.6   Common Members of Dictionary<TKey, TValue>

Name	Description
Count	Gets the number of key/value pairs contained in the dictionary
Keys	Gets a collection containing the keys in the dictionary
Values	Gets a collection containing the values in the dictionary
Add	Adds the specified key and value to the dictionary
Clear	Removes all keys and values from the dictionary

Name	Description
ContainsKey	Determines if the dictionary contains the specified key
ContainsValue	Determines if the dictionary contains a specific value
Remove	Removes the value with the specified key from the dictionary

Unlike List<T> and Collection<T> when the elements of a dictionary are enumerated, the dictionary returns a KeyValuePair<TKey, TValue> structure that represents a key and its associated value. Because of this, the var keyword is useful when using the foreach statement to iterate over the elements of a dictionary.

Normally, a dictionary does not provide any order to the elements it contains, and those elements are returned in an arbitrary order during enumeration. Although List<T> provides a Sort method to sort the elements of the list, dictionaries do not. If you need a collection that maintains sorting as you add or remove elements, you actually have two different choices: a SortedList<TKey, TValue> or a SortedDictionary<TKey, TValue>. The two classes are similar and provide the same performance when retrieving an element but are different in memory use and performance of element insertion and removal:

▶ SortedList<TKey, TValue> uses less memory.

▶ SortedDictionary<TKey, TValue> provides faster insertion and removal for unsorted data.

▶ SortedList<TKey, TValue> is faster when populating the list at one time from sorted data.

▶ SortedList<TKey, TValue> is more efficient for indexed retrieval of keys and values.

The common members of SortedList<TKey, TValue> and SortedDictionary<TKey, TValue> are shown in Table 10.7.

TABLE 10.7   Common Members of SortedList and SortedDictionary

Name	Description
Capacity	(Only available on SortedList<TKey, TValue>.) Gets or sets the number of elements that the list can contain.
Count	Gets the number of key/value pairs contained in the list.
Add	Adds the specified key and value to the list.
Clear	Removes all keys and values from the list.
ContainsKey	Determines if the list contains the specified key.

Name	Description
ContainsValue	Determines if the list contains a specific value.
Remove	Removes the value with the specified key from the list.
TrimExcess	Sets the capacity to the actual number of elements stored in the list, if that number is less than 90% of current capacity.
TryGetValue	Gets the value associated with the specified key.

TRY IT YOURSELF ▼

Working with Dictionaries

To use a `Dictionary<TKey, TValue>` and a `SortedDictionary<TKey, TValue>` for storing and retrieving data by an arbitrary key, follow these steps:

1. Create a new console application.

2. In the `Main` method of the `Program.cs` file, declare a new `Dictionary<string, double>` named `dictionary`.

3. Add the following lines to initialize the dictionary:

```
dictionary.Add("Speed Of Light", 2.997924580e+8F);
dictionary.Add("Gravitational Constant", 6.67428e-11F);
dictionary.Add("Planck's Constant", 6.62606896e-34F);
dictionary.Add("Atomic Mass Constant", 1.660538782e-27F);
dictionary.Add("Avogadro's number", 6.02214179e+23F);
dictionary.Add("Faraday Constant", 9.64853399e+4F);
dictionary.Add("Electron Volt", 1.602176487e-19F);
```

4. Write a `foreach` statement that prints the name of the key and its associated value. You can use either `var` or `KeyValuePair<string, double>` for the type of the iteration variable.

5. Run the application using Ctrl+F5, and observe that the output matches what is shown in Figure 10.8. Notice that the output is displayed in the same order the values were entered in the dictionary.

FIGURE 10.8
Result of using `Dictionary<TKey, TValue>`.

6. Change the declaration of `dictionary` to be a `SortedDictionary<string, Double>`.

7. Run the application using Ctrl+F5, and observe that the output matches what is shown in Figure 10.9. Notice that by simply changing the declaration, the output is displayed in alphabetically sorted order by key.

```
C:\WINDOWS\system32\cmd.exe
Atomic Mass Constant = 1.66053872398062E-27
Avogadro's number = 6.02214172441376E+23
Electron Volt = 1.60217646821162E-19
Faraday Constant = 96485.34375
Gravitational Constant = 6.67427987877112E-11
Planck's Constant = 6.6260688010433E-34
Speed Of Light = 299792448
Press any key to continue . . .
```

FIGURE 10.9
Result of using `SortedDictionary<TKey, TValue>`.

Sets

In mathematics, a set is a collection containing no duplicate elements that are stored and accessed in random order. In addition to standard insert and remove operations, sets support superset, subset, intersection, and union operations.

Sets in .NET are available through the `HashSet<T>` and `SortedSet<T>` classes. `HashSet<T>` is equivalent to a mathematical set, whereas `SortedSet<T>` maintains a sorted order through insertion and removal of elements without affecting performance. Both classes do not allow duplicate elements. These classes share an almost identical public interface, shown in Table 10.8.

TIP

Why `HashSet<T>`?

Unlike most of the other generic collections, `HashSet<T>` has a name that is based on its implementation details rather than its purpose. The reason is that `Set` is a reserved word in Visual Basic, so it could be used only by escaping it:

```
Dim s as [Set] of Int
```

Rather than requiring this syntax, the designers of the .NET Framework chose a name that would not conflict with any reserved words.

TABLE 10.8   Common Members of `HashSet<T>` and `SortedSet<T>`

Name	Description
Count	Gets the number of elements contained in the set.
Max	Gets the maximum value in the set. (`SortedSet<T>` only.)
Min	Gets the minimum value in the set. (`SortedSet<T>` only.)
Add	Adds the specified element to the set.
Clear	Removes all elements from the set.
Contains	Determines if the set contains the specified element.
ExceptWith	Removes all elements in the specified collection from the set.
IntersectWith	Modifies the current set to contain only elements that are present in the set and in the specified collection.
IsProperSubsetOf	Determines if the set is a proper subset of the specified collection.
IsProperSupersetOf	Determines if the set is a proper superset of the specified collection.
IsSubsetOf	Determines if the set is a subset of the specified collection.
IsSupersetOf	Determines if the set is a superset of the specified collection.
Overlaps	Determines if the set and a specified collection share common elements.
Remove	Removes the specified element from the set.
RemoveWhere	Removes all elements that match the specified conditions from the set.
Reverse	Returns an enumerator that iterates over the set in reverse order. (`SortedSet<T>` only.)
SetEquals	Determines if the set and a specified collection contain the same elements.
SymmetricExceptWith	Modifies the current set to contain only elements that are present either in the set or the specified collection, but not both.
TrimExcess	Sets the capacity of the set to the actual number of elements it contains, rounded up to a nearby value. (`HashSet<T>` only.)
UnionWith	Modifies the current set to contain all elements that are present in both the set and the specified collection.

▼ TRY IT YOURSELF

Working with Sets

By following these steps, you see how to work with `HashSet<T>` and `SortedSet<T>`:

1. Create a new console application.

2. In the `Main` method of the `Program.cs` file, declare two integer sets, as follows:

   ```
   HashSet<int> even = new HashSet<int>() { 0, 2, 4, 6, 8, 10, 12 };
   HashSet<int> odd = new HashSet<int>() { 1, 3, 5, 7, 9, 11 };
   ```

3. Print the result of performing a `SetEquals` call between `even` and `odd`.

4. Run the application using Ctrl+F5, and observe that the output is `False`.

5. Calculate the union between `even` and `odd` by executing the `UnionWith` method.

6. Print the contents of the `even` set using a `foreach` statement.

7. Run the application again using Ctrl+F5, and observe that the output contains the numbers from the original `even` set and the numbers from the `odd` set.

8. Calculate the intersection between `even` and `odd` by executing the `IntersectWith` method.

9. Repeat the line of code entered from step 3.

10. Run the application again using Ctrl+F5 and observe that the final output matches what is shown in Figure 10.10.

FIGURE 10.10
Result of using `HashSet<T>`.

11. Change the declarations of `even` and `odd` to use `SortedSet<int>`.

12. Run the application again using Ctrl+F5, and observe that the final output matches what is shown in Figure 10.11.

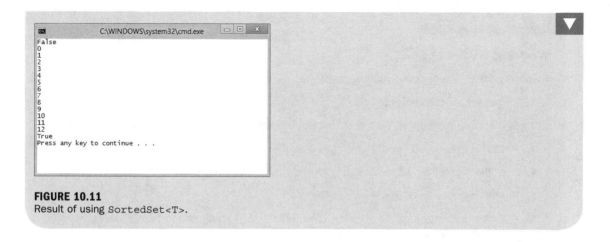

FIGURE 10.11
Result of using `SortedSet<T>`.

Stacks and Queues

Stacks and queues are relatively simple collections that represent either a last-in-first-out (LIFO) collection or first-in-first-out (FIFO) collection. Even though these are simple collections, they are nevertheless very useful as well. Queues are useful for storing data in the order received for sequential processing, whereas stacks are useful for operations such as statement parsing. In general, stacks and queues are used when operations should be restricted to either the beginning or end of the list.

The `Stack<T>` class provides a stack implemented as an array in which operations always occur at the end of that array and can contain duplicate elements and `null` elements. `Stack<T>` provides a simple public interface, shown in Table 10.9.

TABLE 10.9 Common Members of `Stack<T>`

Name	Description
Count	Gets the number of elements contained in the stack
Clear	Removes all elements from the stack
Contains	Determines if an element is in the stack
Peek	Returns the element at the top of the queue without removing it
Pop	Removes and returns the element at the top of the stack
Push	Inserts an element at the top of the stack
TrimExcess	Sets the capacity to the actual number of elements in the stack, if that number is less than 90% of the current capacity

▼ TRY IT YOURSELF

Working with Stack<T>

To implement an integer stack, follow these steps:

1. Create a new console application.

2. In the Main method of the Program.cs file, declare an integer stack named stack.

3. Push the values 0, 2, and 4 on to the stack.

4. Print the current top of the stack by calling the Peek() method.

5. Push the values 6, 8, and 10 on to the stack.

6. Print the current top of the stack by calling the Pop() method and then again by calling the Peek() method.

7. Run the application using Ctrl+F5, and observe that the output matches what is shown in Figure 10.12.

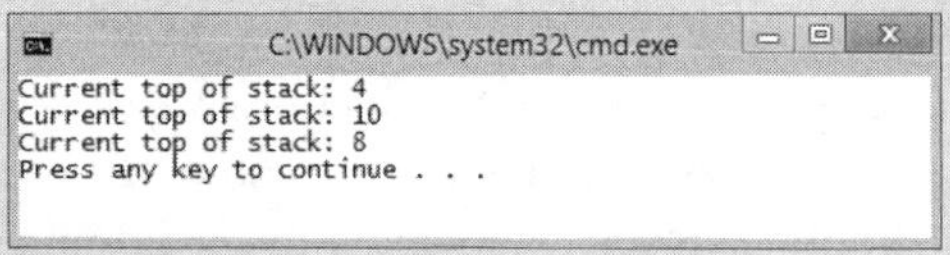

```
C:\WINDOWS\system32\cmd.exe
Current top of stack: 4
Current top of stack: 10
Current top of stack: 8
Press any key to continue . . .
```

FIGURE 10.12
Results of working with Stack<T>.

The Queue<T> class provides a queue implemented as an array in which insert operations always occur at one end of the array and remove operations occur at the other. Queue<T> also allows duplicate elements and null as an element. Queue<T> provides a simple public interface, as shown in Table 10.10.

TABLE 10.10 Common Members of Queue<T>

Name	Description
Count	Gets the number of elements contained in the queue
Clear	Removes all elements from the queue
Contains	Determines if an element is in the queue
Dequeue	Removes and returns the element at the beginning of the queue
Enqueue	Adds an element to the end of the queue

Name	Description
Peek	Returns the element at the beginning of the queue without removing it
TrimExcess	Sets the capacity to the actual number of elements in the queue, if that number is less than 90% of the current capacity

TRY IT YOURSELF ▼

Working with Queue<T>

By following these steps, you implement an integer queue:

1. Create a new console application.

2. In the Main method of the Program.cs file, declare an integer queue named queue.

3. Add the values 1, 3, and 5 to the end of the queue by calling the Enqueue() method.

4. Print the current beginning of the queue by calling the Peek() method.

5. Add the values 7, 9, and 11 to the queue.

6. Print the current beginning of the queue by calling the Dequeue() method and then again by calling the Peek() method.

7. Run the application using Ctrl+F5, and observe that the output matches what is shown in Figure 10.13.

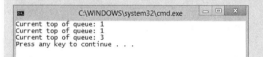

```
C:\WINDOWS\system32\cmd.exe
Current top of queue: 1
Current top of queue: 1
Current top of queue: 3
Press any key to continue . . .
```

FIGURE 10.13
Results of working with Queue<T>.

Collection Initializers

Just as arrays provide array initialization syntax and objects provide object initialization syntax, collections also provide collection initialization syntax, in the form of a **collection initializer**. If you look back through the exercises for this hour, you can notice the use of collection initializers already.

Collection initializers enable you to specify one or more element initializers, which enable you to initialize a collection that implements IEnumerable. Using a collection initializer enables you to omit multiple calls to the Add method of the collection, instead letting the compiler add the calls for you. An element initializer can be a value, an expression, or an object initializer.

CAUTION

Collection Initializers Work Only with Add Methods

Collection initializers can be used only with collections that contain an Add method. This means they cannot be used for collections such as Stack<T> and Queue<T>.

The syntax for a collection initializer is similar to an array initializer. You must still call the new operator but can then use the array initialization syntax to populate the collection. Listing 10.3 shows the same example as Listing 10.2, but uses List<int> and a collection initializer.

LISTING 10.3   Collection Initialization

```
class Program
{
    static void Main()
    {
        List<int> list = new List<int>() {0, 2, 4, 6, 8 };
    }
}
```

Collection initializers can also be more complex, enabling you to use object initializers for the element initializers, as shown in Listing 10.4.

LISTING 10.4   Complex Collection Initialization

```
class Program
{
    static void Main()
    {
        List<Contact> list = new List<Contact>()
        {
            new Contact() { FirstName = "Scott", LastName = "Dorman" },
            new Contact() { FirstName = "Jim", LastName = "Morrison" },
            new Contact() { FirstName = "Ray", LastName = "Manzarek" }
        };

        foreach(Contact c in list)
        {
```

```
        Console.WriteLine(c);
    }
  }
}
```

By enabling object initializers inside a collection initializer, it becomes possible to use collection initializers for any type of collection, including dictionaries, whose Add method takes multiple parameters.

Collection Interfaces

If you look back over the common members and properties for all the different collections, you should notice some similarities and consistency in their public interfaces. This consistency stems from a set of interfaces that these collection classes implement. Some classes implement more interfaces than others do, but all of them implement at least one interface.

The collection interfaces can be divided in to those that provide specific collection implementation contracts and those that provide supporting implementations, such as comparison and enumeration features. In the first group, those that provide specific collection behavior, there are just four interfaces:

▶ ICollection<T> defines the methods and properties for manipulating generic collections.

▶ IList<T> extends ICollection<T> to provide the methods and properties for manipulating generic collections whose elements can be individually accessed by index.

▶ IDictionary<TKey, TValue> extends ICollection<T> to provide the methods and properties for manipulating generic collections of key/value pairs in which each pair must have a unique key.

▶ ISet<T> extends ICollection<T> to provide the methods and properties for manipulating generic collections that have unique elements and provide set operations.

The second group also contains only four interfaces, as follows:

▶ IComparer<T> defines a method to compare two objects. This interface is used with the List<T>.Sort and List<T>.BinarySearch methods and provides a way to customize the sort order of a collection. The Comparer<T> class provides a default implementation of this interface and is usually sufficient for most requirements.

▶ IEnumerable<T> extends IEnumerable and provides support for simple iteration over a collection by exposing an enumerator. This interface is included for parity with the nongeneric collections, and by implementing this interface, a generic collection can be used any time an IEnumerable is expected.

▶ IEnumerator<T> also provides support for simple iteration over a collection.

▶ IEqualityComparer<T> provides a way for you to provide your own definition of equality for type T. The EqualityComparer<T> class provides a default implementation of this interface and is usually sufficient for most requirements.

Enumerable Objects and Iterators

If you look at the definitions given for IEnumerable<T> and IEnumerator<T>, you notice that they are similar. These interfaces (and their nongeneric counterparts) compose what is commonly referred to as the **iterator pattern**.

This pattern essentially enables you to ask an object that implements IEnumerable<T>, otherwise known as an **enumerable object**, for an enumerator (an object that implements IEnumerator<T>). When you have an IEnumerator<T>, you can then enumerate (or iterate) over the data one element at a time.

For example, the code in Listing 10.5 shows a typical foreach statement that iterates over the contents of an integer list, printing each value.

LISTING 10.5   A Simple foreach Statement

```
List<int> list = new List<int>() { 0, 2, 4, 6, 8 };
foreach(int i in list)
{
    Console.WriteLine(i);
}
```

This code is actually translated by the compiler into something that looks approximately like the code shown in Listing 10.6.

LISTING 10.6   The Compiler Expanded foreach Statement

```
List<int> list = new List<int>() { 0, 2, 4, 6, 8 };
IEnumerator<int> iterator = ((IEnumerable<int>)list).GetEnumerator();
while (iterator.MoveNext())
{
    Console.WriteLine(iterator.Current);
}
```

The GetEnumerator method is defined by the IEnumerable<T> interface (in fact, it's the only member defined by the interface) and simply provides a way for the enumerable object to expose an enumerator. It is the enumerator, through the MoveNext method and Current property (defined by the IEnumerator<T> and IEnumerator interfaces), that enables you to move forward through the data contained in the enumerable object.

NOTE

Why Two Interfaces?

By keeping a distinction between an enumerable object (IEnumerable<T>) and an enumerator over that object (IEnumerator<T>), you can perform multiple iterations over the same enumerable source. Obviously, you don't want the iterations interfering with each other as they move through the data, so you need two independent representations (enumerators) providing you the current data element and the mechanism to move to the next one.

Fortunately, all the generic collections (and the nongeneric ones as well) implement IEnumerable<T>, IEnumerable, IEnumerator<T>, and IEnumerator already, so you can use them without the extra complexity of writing the iterator mechanism yourself.

What happens if you want your own class to offer similar behavior? You can certainly make your class implement IEnumerable<T> and then write your own IEnumerator<T> derived class, but doing so isn't necessary if you use an iterator. This enables the compiler to do all the hard work for you.

An iterator is a method, property get accessor, or operator that returns an ordered sequence of values all of which are the same type. The yield keyword tells the compiler the block it appears in is an iterator block. A yield return statement returns each element, and a yield break statement ends the iteration. The body of such an iterator method, accessor, or operator has the following restrictions:

▶ Unsafe blocks are not permitted.

▶ Parameters cannot be ref or out parameters.

▶ A yield return statement cannot be located anywhere within a try-catch block. It can be located in a try block if it is followed by a finally block.

▶ A yield break statement can be located in either a try block or a catch block, but not a finally block.

▶ A yield statement cannot be in an anonymous method.

Listing 10.7 shows code that would produce the same output as that shown in Listing 10.6 using an iterator instead.

LISTING 10.7   A Simple Iterator

```
class Program
{
   static IEnumerable<int> GetEvenNumbers()
   {
      yield return 0;
      yield return 2;
      yield return 4;
      yield return 6;
      yield return 8;
   }

   static void Main()
   {
      foreach(int i in GetEvenNumbers())
      {
         Console.WriteLine(i);
      }
   }
}
```

Iterators can do much more than simply yield values. As long as you abide by the restrictions previously mentioned, iterators can have any degree of sophistication in how they determine the values to yield. Listing 10.8 produces the same output as that from Listing 10.7 but does so using a more complex iterator.

LISTING 10.8   A More Complex Iterator

```
class Program
{
   static IEnumerable<int> GetEvenNumbers()
   {
      for (int i = 0; i <= 9; i++)
      {
         if (i % 2 == 0)
         {
            yield return i;
         }
      }
   }

   static void Main()
   {
      foreach(int i in GetEvenNumbers())
```

```
        {
            Console.WriteLine(i);
        }
    }
}
```

Summary

In this hour, you have learned how to work with large amounts of data using arrays and collections. Arrays are the simplest type of collection and have direct language support, whereas the other collection types, such as List<T> and Stack<T>, offer more flexibility and enable you to create your own specialized collections. You also learned how indexers enable your own classes to provide the same type of index-based access that arrays and collections offer. Finally, you looked at the different collection interfaces available and saw how you can easily declare and initialize both arrays and collections using initializer syntax.

This completes your programming foundation. You now know the language syntax and fundamentals of creating your own classes, structs, enums, and collections, and how to manipulate string data and control program flow.

Q&A

Q. What is an array?

A. An array is a numerically indexed collection of objects that are all of the same compile-time type.

Q. Are arrays in C# zero-based or one-based?

A. Arrays in C# use a zero-based indexing scheme.

Q. Can arrays in C# be resized?

A. Arrays in C# can be indirectly resized using the Array.Resize static method, which creates a new array, if needed, and copying the values from the old array to the new one.

Q. What is an indexer?

A. An indexer is a special type of property that enables a class to be indexed like an array. Indexers are identified by signature rather than by name and must be an instance member.

Q. What is the List<T> collection?

A. The List<T> collection is the most commonly used collection and is similar to an array but is dynamically sized as needed.

Q. What is a dictionary?

A. A dictionary is a collection that does not enable duplicates that can provide a mapping between a set of keys and a set of values.

Q. What is the difference between `HashSet<T>` and `SortedSet<T>`?

A. `HashSet<T>` is equivalent to a mathematical set, whereas `SortedSet<T>` maintains a sorted order through insertion and removal of elements without affecting performance. Both classes do not allow duplicate elements.

Q. What is the `IEnumerable<T>` interface?

A. `IEnumerable<T>` extends `IEnumerable` and provides support for simple iteration over a collection by exposing an enumerator. This interface is included for parity with the nongeneric collections, and by implementing this interface, a generic collection can be used any time an `IEnumerable` is expected.

Q. What are an array initializer and a collection initializer?

A. An array initializer and a collection initializer are a special syntax that enables you to easily declare and initialize the contents of an array or collection. Array initializers enable you to omit the array type and simply provide the values for the array. Collection initializers enable you to omit multiple calls to the `Add` method of the collection by providing the values for each element in the initializer.

Workshop

Quiz

1. How is memory for an array allocated?

2. What modifiers are allowed for an indexer?

3. When would you use `Collection<T>` instead of `List<T>`?

4. What object is returned when the elements of a dictionary are enumerated?

5. What operations are available on `Stack<T>` that modify state?

6. What interface does `IDictionary<TKey, TValue>` extend?

7. What is the difference between `IComparer<T>` and `IEqualityComparer<T>`?

8. Can collection initializers be used with collections whose `Add` method takes more than one parameter?

Answers

1. Arrays are implicitly an instance of a `System.Array` object, so they are reference types, and the memory allocated to refer to the array itself is allocated on the managed heap. However, the elements of the array are allocated based on their own type.

2. The modifiers allowed for an indexer are `new`, `virtual`, `sealed`, `override`, `abstract`, and a valid combination of the four access modifiers.

3. `List<T>` is not designed to be easily extended because there are no virtual members that a derived class can override to modify behavior. `Collection<T>` does have virtual members that can be overridden, so `Collection<T>` is preferred when you need to customize behavior of the collection.

4. When the elements of a dictionary are enumerated, the dictionary returns a `KeyValuePair<TKey, TValue>` structure that represents a key and its associated value.

5. The `Stack<T>` class provides the `Clear`, `Pop`, and `Push` methods that remove all elements, remove the top element, or insert an element.

6. `IDictionary<TKey, TValue>` extends the `ICollection<T>` interface.

7. `IComparer<T>` defines a method to compare two objects, whereas `IEqualityComparer<T>` provides a way for you to provide your own definition of equality for type `T`.

8. Yes, collection initializers can be used with collections whose `Add` method takes more than one parameter.

Exercises

1. Add a new public class named `PhotoCollection` that derives from `ObservableCollection<IPhoto>` to the `PhotoViewer` project. This class should have a `string` field named `path`, a public constructor that accepts a `string` parameter and sets the field to the parameter value, and a public property named `Path` that gets or sets the value of the `directory` field.

2. Add a private `PhotoCollection` field named `photos` and a read-only property named `Photos` to the `MainWindow` class. In the constructor of the `MainWindow` class, add the following code after the `InitializeComponent()` method call:

```
var folder = Environment.GetFolderPath(Environment.SpecialFolder.MyPictures);
this.photos = new PhotoCollection(folder);
```

Handling Errors Using Exceptions

What You'll Learn in This Hour:

▶ Understanding exceptions
▶ `System.Exception`
▶ Throwing exceptions
▶ Handling exceptions
▶ Rethrowing caught exceptions
▶ Overflow and integer arithmetic
▶ Exceptions, code contracts, and parameter validation

As an application executes, it can encounter any number of possible error conditions. C# handles these error conditions using **exceptions**, which encapsulate the information about an error in a single class. Exceptions are intended to be used only for failure reporting, so they provide a consistent way to report and respond to those failures. Exceptions are not intended to provide a mechanism to control program flow, to report success conditions, or to be used as a feedback mechanism. They are for reporting failures that occur during execution.

In many languages, particularly non-object-oriented languages, the standard mechanism for reporting failures is to use a return code. However, in an object-oriented language, return codes aren't always possible, depending on the context in which the failure occurs. Return codes are also easily disregarded; when not, they introduce a lot of complexity to properly handle all the possible failure locations.

In this hour, you learn about the exception handling mechanisms provided by C#; you also learn how to throw and catch exceptions. You learn how to choose the right type of exception to throw, what exceptions are available to you, including how to create your own custom exceptions, and finish by looking at some performance considerations when using exceptions. Finally, you look at how exceptions and code contracts can be used for parameter validation.

Understanding Exceptions

Exceptions provide a clear, concise, and safe way to represent failures that occur during runtime and usually carry detailed information about the cause of the failure. Some of this information includes the call stack trace, which shows the execution path that would occur if the current block returned normally.

Exceptions are not meant to provide a way to handle anticipated errors, such as those that could come from user actions or input. In those cases, it is far better to prevent errors by validating the action or input for correctness. Exceptions are not protection against coding errors, either. They might be caused by coding errors, but those errors should be fixed rather than relying on exceptions.

An exception is handled when the application provides explicit code that is run when the exception occurs. Consequently, an unhandled exception occurs when no such code is found.

`System.Exception`

All exceptions derive from `System.Exception`. When managed code calls other unmanaged code or external services, such as Microsoft SQL Server, and an error condition occurs, the .NET runtime wraps that error condition in a `System.Exception` derived exception.

TIP

RuntimeWrappedException

Languages such as C++ enable you to throw exceptions of any type, not just ones derived from `System.Exception`. In those cases, the common language runtime wraps those exceptions in a `RuntimeWrappedException`. This maintains compatibility between languages.

`System.Exception` provides several properties that provide detailed information about the error that occurred:

▶ The most commonly used is the `Message` property, which provides the details about the cause of an exception in a user-readable description. Typically, the content of this property is a few sentences that describe the error in general terms.

▶ The `StackTrace` property contains the call stack trace, which can help determine where an error occurred. If debugging information is available during runtime, the stack trace includes the name of the source file and the line number where the error occurred.

▶ The `InnerException` property is typically used when one exception is wrapped in a new exception of a different type. The original exception is stored in the `InnerException` property so that error-handling code can examine the original information.

▶ The `HelpLink` property can contain a URL to a Help file containing additional detailed information about the exception.

▶ The `Data` property is an `IDictionary` (which is a nongeneric version of a dictionary) to hold arbitrary data in key/value pairs.

Using the Standard Exceptions

Although there are more than 200 public exception classes provided by the .NET Framework, approximately 15 of them are commonly used. The remaining exceptions generally derive from one of these standard exceptions.

The two primary base classes other than `Exception` are `SystemException`, which is the base class for almost all runtime-generated exceptions and `ExternalException`, which is for exceptions that occur in or are targeted at environments outside of the runtime.

The `Exception`, `SystemException`, and `ExternalException` classes should only be used as base classes for more specific derived exceptions, and you should avoid deriving your own exceptions directly from `SystemException`.

The remaining standard exceptions, shown in Table 11.1, make up a combination of exceptions thrown by the runtime, which your own code should not throw, and those that can, and should, be thrown from your own code.

TABLE 11.1 Standard Exceptions

Exception Type	Description
IndexOutOfRangeException	Thrown by the runtime only when an array or collection is indexed improperly
NullReferenceException	Thrown by the runtime only when a null reference is dereferenced
AccessViolationException	Thrown by the runtime only when invalid memory is accessed
InvalidOperationException	Thrown by members when in an invalid state
ArgumentException	Base class for all argument exceptions
ArgumentNullException	Thrown by methods that do not allow an argument to be null
ArgumentOutOfRangeException	Thrown by methods that verify that arguments are in a given range
COMException	Exception encapsulating COM HRESULT information

Exception Type	Description
SEHException	Exception encapsulating Win32 structured exception handling information
OutOfMemoryException	Thrown by the runtime when there is not enough memory to continue the execution of a program
StackOverflowException	Thrown by the runtime when the execution stack overflows because it contains too many nested method calls, usually occurring from deep or unbounded recursion
ExecutionEngineException	Thrown by the runtime when an internal error occurs in the execution engine of the common language runtime

If you are diligent about validating the parameters passed to your public methods, you should throw ArgumentException, or one of its subtypes, when bad arguments are passed.

You should use ArgumentNullException for those methods that receive a null argument when it is not expected; use ArgumentOutOfRangeException when the argument falls outside the acceptable range of values.

If a property or method call is not appropriate for the current state of the object, you can throw an InvalidOperationException. This is different from ArgumentException, which does not rely on object state to determine if it should be thrown.

NOTE
___

Validating Arguments

If it isn't straightforward for the caller to determine when an argument is valid, you should consider providing a method that allows it to check.
___

The remaining standard exceptions should be considered reserved exceptions. You should avoid throwing these from your own code and deriving your own exceptions from them.

You should perform argument checking to prevent an IndexOutOfRangeException or NullReferenceException from occurring.

Throwing Exceptions

You throw an exception using the throw keyword. Because Exception is a class, you must create an instance of it using the new keyword. The following code throws a new Exception object:

```
throw new System.Exception();
```

When an exception is thrown, program execution immediately halts while the exception propagates up the call stack, looking for an appropriate handler. If no handlers are found, one of three things happens:

- If the exception occurred within a destructor, that destructor is aborted, and if present, the destructor of the base class is called.

- If a static constructor or static field initializer is contained in the call stack, a `TypeInitializationException` is thrown containing the original exception in the `InnerException` property.

- If the start of the thread is reached, the thread is terminated. In most cases, this means that if the exception reaches all the way to the `Main()` method without finding a compatible handler, the application is terminated. This happens no matter which thread the exception originated from.

Knowing when an exception should be thrown requires understanding the difference between coding errors and execution errors. Coding errors can be avoided by changing your code, and there is no reason to handle these using exceptions. Coding errors can be fixed at compile time, and you can take steps to ensure they never occur at runtime.

TIP

`System.Environment.FailFast`

If your application encounters a situation in which it is unsafe to continue, you should consider calling `System.Environment.FailFast` instead of throwing an exception.

If continuing in such a situation causes a security risk, such as when a security impersonation cannot be reverted, you should also consider calling `FailFast`.

An exception is thrown when an unexpected error condition is encountered. This typically occurs when a class member cannot perform what it is designed to do. These execution errors cannot be completely avoided, no matter how many precautions you might take in the code. Program execution errors can be handled programmatically by your code. System execution errors are those that cannot be handled by your code.

Handling Exceptions

Handling exceptions uses exception objects and protected regions. Think of a **protected region** as a special block of code designed to enable you to work with exceptions. Almost any line of code can cause an exception, but most applications don't actually need to deal with these exceptions. You should handle an exception only if there is something meaningful you can do as a result.

In C#, you declare a protected region, also known as a **try block**, using the `try` keyword, with the statements being protected enclosed in braces. The associated handlers appear after the closing brace of the protected region. A protected region must have associated with it at least one of the following handlers:

- A **finally handler**, which executes whenever the protected region exits, even if an exception was encountered. A protected region can have at most one finally handler.

- A **catch handler** that is compatible with a specific exception or any one of its subclasses. A protected region can have multiple catch handlers, but a specific exception type can only be specified in a single handler.

When an exception occurs, the first protected region that contains the current instruction (the one that caused the exception) and has a matching catch handler block are located. If the current method does not contain a match, the calling method is searched, continuing until either a match is found or the top of the call stack is reached, in which case the application terminates. If a match is found, program execution returns to the point of the exception, executes any finally handlers, and then the catch handler is executed.

NOTE

General Catch Handlers

You can also specify a catch handler using just the `catch` keyword, commonly known as a general catch handler. Doing so, however, should be avoided.

In the .NET Framework 1.0 and 1.1 releases, situations existed in which unmanaged code would throw an exception that wasn't properly handled by the runtime. As a result, it wasn't wrapped in a `System.Exception` derived exception and couldn't be caught by anything other than an empty catch block.

This issue was corrected in .NET 2.0 and now these exceptions are wrapped in a `RuntimeWrappedException` (which inherits from `System.Exception`), so there is no longer a need for this empty catch block.

Protected regions can be broken down into three patterns, depending on the handlers they provide:

- **Try-Catch**—Provides one or more catch handlers only

- **Try-Finally**—Provides only a finally handler

- **Try-Catch-Finally**—Provides one or more catch handlers and a finally handler

When you specify a catch block, it is possible to provide only the exception type or the exception type and an identifier, called the **catch handler variable**. The catch handler variable defines a local variable within the scope of the catch handler, enabling you to reference the exception object inside the catch block. Because the catch handler variable is scoped to that specific catch handler, and only one catch handler will execute, the same identifier can be used by multiple catch handlers. However, you cannot use the same identifier as any of the method parameters or other local variables.

Listing 11.1 shows the most common way to write a catch handler and uses a catch handler variable.

LISTING 11.1   Declaring a Catch Handler

```
try
{
    int divisor = Convert.ToInt32(Console.ReadLine());
    int result = 3/divisor;
}
catch (DivideByZeroException ex)
{
    Console.WriteLine(ex.Message);
}
```

If you have multiple nested try blocks, each with a possibly matching catch handler, the order in which they are nested determines the order in which they execute. When a compatible catch handler has been found, no other catch handlers are executed. Listing 11.2 shows an example of catching multiple exceptions and shows how to write a catch handler that does not use a catch handler variable.

LISTING 11.2   Catching Multiple Exceptions

```
try
{
    int divisor = Convert.ToInt32(Console.ReadLine());
    int result = 3/divisor;
}
catch (DivideByZeroException)
{
    Console.WriteLine("Attempted to divide by zero");
}
catch (FormatException)
{
    Console.WriteLine("Input was not in the correct format");
}
```

```
catch (Exception)
{
    Console.WriteLine("General catch handler");
}
```

If the try block in Listing 11.2 resulted in a `DivideByZeroException`, the output would be "`Attempted to divide by zero`". If the try block resulted in a `FormatException`, the output would be "`Input was not in the correct format`". Any other exceptions would generate "`General catch handler`" as the output. However, if the catch blocks were rearranged so the general catch block came first, the program would fail to compile.

CAUTION

Swallowing Exceptions

It is common to write catch blocks that do nothing more than log the error. Although this is sometimes important, it can usually be done by the top-level caller and does not need to occur for every function.

This leads to a problem known as "swallowing exceptions," and occurs when you catch an exception and either do nothing with it or don't allow it to pass up the chain. This can also lead to problems because you are effectively hiding the exception and not doing anything with it, which can lead to intermittent problems that will be hard to track.

The best way to look at this situation is that you should catch an exception only if you have meaningful cleanup work that needs to be done as a result of the exception (such as closing files or database connections).

Remember, a catch handler executes only if an exception has occurred, so it should not be used for cleanup activities. If you do need to perform any type of cleanup activities, they should be done in a finally handler. This means that unless you can legitimately take some action because of an exception, you should use the try-finally pattern instead of the try-catch or try-catch-finally patterns.

▼ TRY IT YOURSELF

Working with Exceptions

To see how you can work with exceptions by throwing and catching several different exceptions, follow these steps:

1. Create a new console application.

2. In the `Program.cs` file, implement the following functions:

```
private static void ThrowsException()
{
    Console.WriteLine("About to throw an InvalidOperationException");
```

```
        throw new InvalidOperationException();
    }

    private static void PrintString(string message)
    {
        if (message == null)
        {
            throw new ArgumentNullException("message");
        }

        Console.WriteLine(message);
    }
```

3. In the `Main` method of the `Program.cs` file, call the `ThrowsException` method.

4. Run the application using Ctrl+F5. You see the console window initially, as shown in Figure 11.1.

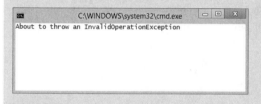

FIGURE 11.1
Console application just before throwing an exception.

If you run Windows Vista or later, you might see the dialog box shown in Figure 11.2.

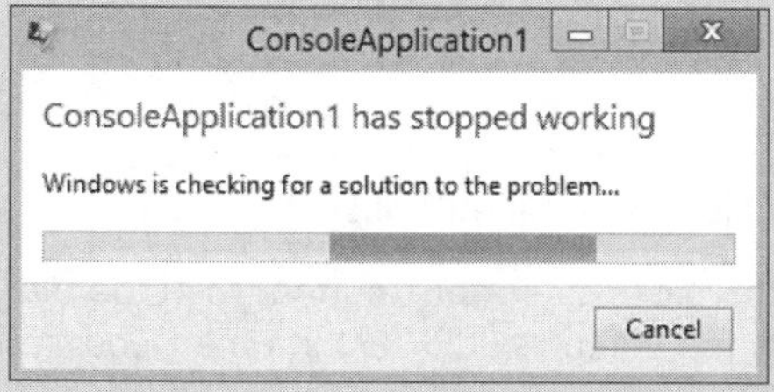

FIGURE 11.2
Windows application failure dialog box checking for solutions.

Express for Desktops does not support JIT Debugging, so after this dialog box completes, you see the exception information displayed, as shown in Figure 11.3.

```
                        C:\WINDOWS\system32\cmd.exe            [-][□][ X ]
About to throw an InvalidOperationException

Unhandled Exception: System.InvalidOperationException: Operation is not valid du
e to the current state of the object.
   at Chapter10.Program.ThrowsException() in c:\Users\Scott\SkyDrive\Documents\W
riting\Books\Sams Teach Yourself Visual C# 2012 in 24 Hours\Code\Hour 10\Try It
Yourself\Working with Exceptions\Steps 1 - 6\Program.cs:line 14
   at Chapter10.Program.Main(String[] args) in c:\Users\Scott\SkyDrive\Documents
\Writing\Books\Sams Teach Yourself Visual C# 2012 in 24 Hours\Code\Hour 10\Try I
t Yourself\Working with Exceptions\Steps 1 - 6\Program.cs:line 29
Press any key to continue . . .
```

FIGURE 11.3
Runtime exception generated from the lack of type safety.

The information displayed is the exception information and indicates that this was an unhandled exception of type `System.InvalidOperationException`. It also displays the stack trace information, which includes the method call stack, filename, and line numbers. This stack trace information helps you to identify the location in your code where the exception occurred.

If you have one of the Visual Studio with MSDN editions installed, you see a dialog box, as shown in Figure 11.4, enabling you to close or debug the application.

```
 ⚙              ConsoleApplication1   [—][ □ ][ X ]

   ConsoleApplication1 has stopped working

   A problem caused the program to stop working correctly.
   Windows will close the program and notify you if a solution is
   available.

                          [  Debug  ]  [ Close program ]
```

FIGURE 11.4
Windows application failure dialog box closing the application.

5. If you press the Close program button, the console window should look like Figure 11.3. If you press the Debug button, you see the Visual Studio Just-In-Time Debugger dialog box.

6. Run the application again using Ctrl+F5, but this time press the Debug button when the dialog box shown in Figure 11.3 appears. This displays the Visual Studio Just-In-Time Debugger dialog box, as shown in Figure 11.5.

If you press the Yes button, control returns to Visual Studio with the line containing the exception set to the current statement and the Exception Assistant dialog box displayed, as shown in Figure 11.6.

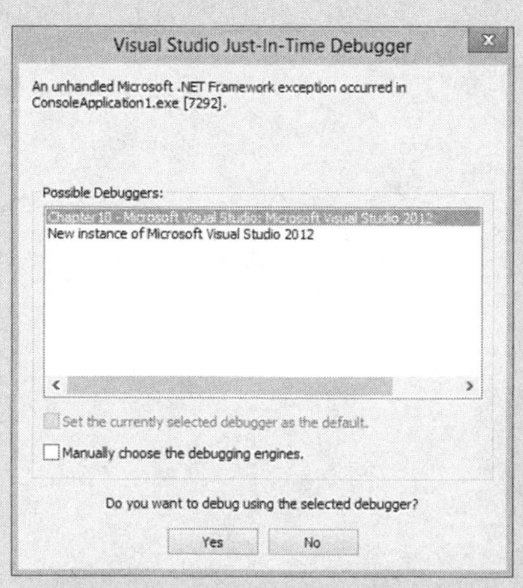

FIGURE 11.5
Visual Studio Just-In-Time Debugger dialog box.

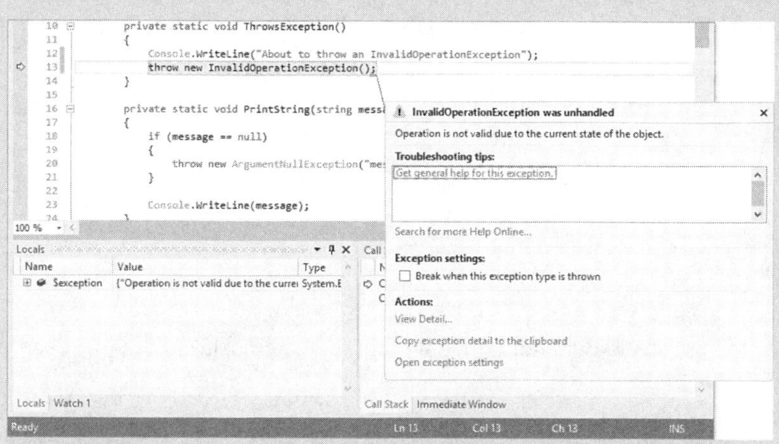

FIGURE 11.6
Exception Assistant.

By clicking the View Detail link under Actions, you can see the details of the exception, as shown in Figure 11.7.

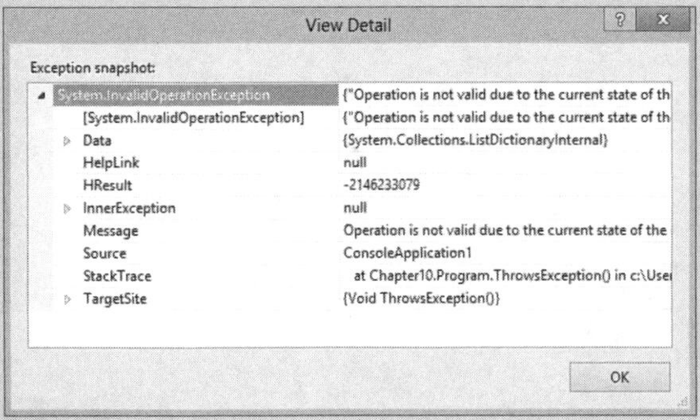

FIGURE 11.7
Exception details dialog box.

7. Enclose the call to `ThrowsException` in a try/catch block that specifically catches an `InvalidOperationException` assigning it to a catch handler variable named `ex`. In the body of the catch handler, print out the value of the `Message` property.

8. Run the application using Ctrl+F5. You see the console window shown in Figure 11.8.

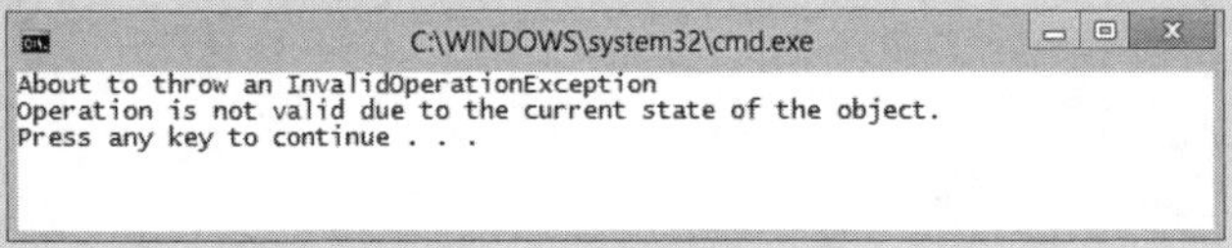

```
About to throw an InvalidOperationException
Operation is not valid due to the current state of the object.
Press any key to continue . . .
```

FIGURE 11.8
Handling the runtime exception.

Notice that this time, the application did not terminate, but instead displayed the message associated with the exception.

9. Change the body of `Main` to the following:

```
try
{
    PrintString(null);
}
catch (InvalidOperationException ex)
{
    Console.WriteLine(ex.GetType().Name);
    Console.WriteLine(ex.Message);
}
catch (ArgumentNullException ex)
{
```

```
        Console.WriteLine(ex.GetType().Name);
        Console.WriteLine(ex.Message);
    }
    catch (Exception ex)
    {
        Console.WriteLine(ex.GetType().Name);
        Console.WriteLine(ex.Message);
    }
```

10. Run the application using Ctrl+F5. You see the console window shown in Figure 11.9.

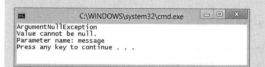

FIGURE 11.9
Multiple catch handlers.

11. Now change the order of the catch handlers so that the `catch(Exception)` handler is first. You should notice that you immediately see two compiler errors indicating that the additional two catch handlers will not be executed because a previous handler catches the base exception type, as shown in Figure 11.10.

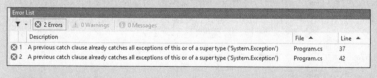

FIGURE 11.10
Multiple catch handlers in the wrong order.

In general, you should avoid catching nonspecific exceptions, such as `Exception`, `SystemException`, and `ExternalException`, in your code. You should also avoid catching critical system exceptions, such as `StackOverflowException` or `OutOfMemoryException`. With the exceptions of these types, usually little can be done in response that is meaningful and catching them can hide runtime problems and complicate debugging and troubleshooting processes.

NOTE

Corrupted State Exceptions

Corrupted state exceptions are those exceptions that occur in a context outside of your application, such as the OS kernel, and indicate that the integrity of the running process might be in question. There are approximately 12 corrupted state exceptions, which are different from regular exceptions.

The difference between a regular exception and a corrupted state exception is not the type of exception, but the context in which it was thrown. By default, you cannot catch a corrupted state exception using a catch block, even if you catch `Exception`.

Rethrowing Caught Exceptions

If you do catch an exception for the purposes of logging or some other activity that does not actually handle the exception condition, you should rethrow the exception. Rethrowing an exception allows it to continue following the call stack, looking for an appropriate catch handler.

Just as the `throw` keyword enables you to specify a new exception to be thrown (as you saw in the previous section), it is also used to rethrow an exception.

To preserve the stack trace information, you should rethrow an exception using just the `throw` keyword, even if your catch handler included a catch handler variable.

A subtle difference exists between the two rethrow approaches shown in Listing 11.3 that won't be apparent until you try to debug the problem. That difference is in the stack trace information sent with the exception.

LISTING 11.3   Rethrowing Exceptions

```
try
{
   // Some operation that results in an InvalidOperationException
}
catch (InvalidOperationException ex)
{
   Console.WriteLine("Invalid operation occurred");
   throw ex;
}
catch (Exception)
{
   Console.WriteLine("General catch handler");
   throw;
}
```

In the first approach, the catch handler for `InvalidOperationException` rethrows the exception using `throw ex`, which causes the stack trace to be truncated below the method that failed. This means that when you look at the stack trace, it looks as if the exception originated in your code. This isn't always the case, particularly if you are bubbling up a CLR-generated exception (such as a `SqlException`).

This is a problem known as "breaking the stack," because you no longer have the full stack trace information. This happens because, in essence, you are creating a new exception to throw.

By using `throw` by itself, as the catch handler for `Exception` does, you preserve the stack trace information. You can confirm this by looking at the IL generated for these two code blocks. This makes the difference obvious because in the first example, the IL instruction called is `throw`, whereas in the second, the instruction called is `rethrow`.

Wrapping Exceptions

You can also wrap a caught exception in a different exception and then throw that new exception. This is most commonly used when the actual exception provides no meaning or does not make sense in the context of a higher layer.

When you wrap an exception, you throw a new exception from your catch handler and should always include the original exception as the inner exception. Because the stack trace information is reset to the point of the new exception, including the inner exception is the only way to see the original stack trace and exception details. Listing 11.4 shows the correct way to throw a wrapped exception.

LISTING 11.4   Throwing a Wrapped Exception

```
try
{
    // Some operation that can fail
}
catch (Exception ex)
{
    throw new InvalidOperationException("The operation failed", ex);
}
```

Wrapping exceptions should be a rare occurrence, and should be carefully considered. If you have any doubt about whether an exception should be wrapped, don't wrap it. Wrapping exceptions can hide the method and location where the error actually occurred and can lead to a significant amount of time spent trying to debug the problem. It can also make it harder for the callers to handle the exception because now they not only have to handle the exception, but also your wrapped exception, and extract the real exception from it to handle it.

Overflow and Integer Arithmetic

In Hour 3, "Understanding C# Types," you learned that all the primitive numeric data types have a fixed range. The minimum and maximum values of that range can be accessed through the `MinValue` and `MaxValue` properties, respectively. As a result, what would happen if you attempted to add 1 to `int.MaxValue`?

The answer to that question depends on the compiler settings used. The C# compiler defaults to generating code that silently enables the overflow to occur, wrapping the value to the largest negative value possible. In many cases, this behavior is acceptable because the risk of it occurring is low.

The risk is so low compared with the high frequency of integer arithmetic operations that occur that the overhead of performing overflow checking on each operation would cause performance considerations.

If you need to safeguard against silently overflowing integer arithmetic operations, or otherwise want to control the overflow-checking behavior, you can use the `checked` and `unchecked` keywords. These keywords provide explicit control because they override any compiler settings specified.

CAUTION

Checked and Unchecked

In a checked context, statements resulting in arithmetic overflow raise an exception. In an unchecked context, the overflow is ignored and the result is truncated. Only certain numeric calculations are affected by a checked or unchecked context:

▶ Explicit conversions between integral types

▶ Expressions using the following operators: `++ -- -(unary) + - * /`

The `checked` or `unchecked` keywords can be applied to a statement block, in which all integer arithmetic directly inside the block is affected, as shown in Listing 11.5.

LISTING 11.5 Checked and Unchecked Blocks

```
int max = int.MaxValue;
checked
{
    int overflow = max++;
    Console.WriteLine("The integer arithmetic resulted in an OverflowException.");
}
```

```
unchecked
{
    int overflow = max++;
    Console.WriteLine("The integer arithmetic resulted in a silent overflow.");
}
```

The keywords can also be applied to integer expressions, in which case the contained expression is evaluated in either a checked or an unchecked context. The contained expression must be enclosed by parentheses.

In Listing 11.6, line 2 always results in an `OverflowException`, whereas line 3 never results in an `OverflowException`. Line 4, however, depends on the compiler settings in place when the program was compiled.

LISTING 11.6   Checked and Unchecked Expressions

```
1.   int x = int.MaxValue;
2.   int a = checked(x + 1);
3.   int b = unchecked(x + 1);
4.   int c = x + 1;
```

Exceptions, Code Contracts, and Parameter Validation

Whenever you write code, the implementation contains a set of assumptions about the inputs and outputs. Sometimes these assumptions are clearly defined by the business logic being implemented; however, they can also be implied, in which case they aren't documented at all. If you look back at the `PrintString` method you wrote in step 2 of the Working With Exceptions Try It Yourself exercise, you will see that the beginning of the method includes an `if` statement, which throws an exception if the `message` parameter is `null`. This statement is there to help ensure the correctness of the running application by not allowing invalid input.

If you look at the code shown in Listing 11.7, you will see several of these `if` statements, commonly called **guard statements**. These guard statements implement the following requirements:

▶ The divisor must be greater than 0.

▶ The dividend must be greater than 0.

▶ The divisor must be greater than the dividend.

LISTING 11.7   A Method Using Multiple Guard Statements

```
public int Calculate(int divisor, int dividend)
{
    if (divisor <= 0)
    {
        throw new ArgumentOutOfRangeException("divisor");
    }

    if (dividend <= 0)
    {
        throw new ArgumentOutOfRangeException("dividend");
    }

    if (divisor <= dividend)
    {
        throw new ArgumentException("divisor");
    }

    return dividend / divisor;
}
```

As you can see, there are more guard statements than actual implementation, making it difficult to read the intent of the code. In addition, a potentially more serious problem exists. The logic used by the guard statements is inverted from that described by the requirements.

To help solve these problems, the .NET Framework includes a set of code contract classes, available in the `System.Diagnostics.Contracts` namespace. The class you will use the most is the `Contract` class, which contains static methods that represent the code contract concepts of preconditions, postconditions, and invariants.

If you consider the guard statements to describe a set of assumptions about the input, it is reasonable to say that these assumptions describe a contract that the method satisfies. You could further say that these assumptions are actually preconditions that must be satisfied before the `Calculate` method will execute.

NOTE

Design by Contract

Specifying contracts is part of an idea called Design by Contract pioneered by the Eiffel programming language in late 1986. Code contracts operate on the belief that classes and methods should explicitly state what conditions they require (preconditions) and what they guarantee if those conditions are met (postconditions).

In effect, code contracts provide a way to document the contract of the method or class in a way that is not only easy to read but also usable by other development tools. It is these other development tools which can include contract specifications in generated documentation, perform static (compile-time) contract verification, or even perform runtime contract checking.

Although the name Design by Contract is commonly used in languages other than Eiffel, it is a registered trademark of Eiffel Software. As a result, it is also referred to as Programming by Contract, Contract Programming, Contract-First development, or Code Contracts.

Listing 11.8 shows the same `Calculate` method using code contracts rather than guard statements. The intent described by the contracts is much clearer than that described by the guard statements. In addition, the logic used by the code contract statements matches the way it is described in the business logic.

LISTING 11.8 A Method Using Code Contracts

```
public int Calculate(int divisor, int dividend)
{
    Contract.Requires(divisor > 0);
    Contract.Requires(divided > 0);
    Contract.Requires(divisor > dividend);

    return dividend / divisor;
}
```

Preconditions, Postconditions, and Invariants

Preconditions, such as the guard statements shown in Listing 11.8, help answer the question of what input is expected. They are contracts about the input when the method is invoked and are most commonly used to validate parameter values.

If you must throw a specific exception when a precondition fails, you can use the generic overload of Requires, as shown in Listing 11.9.

LISTING 11.9 Using `Contract.Requires<T>`

```
public int Calculate(int divisor, int dividend)
{
    Contract.Requires<ArgumentOutOfRangeException>(divisor > 0, "divisor");
    Contract.Requires<ArgumentOutOfRangeException>(dividend > 0, "dividend");
    Contract.Requires<ArgumentException>(divisor > dividend, "divisor");

    return dividend / divisor;
}
```

GO TO ▶ **HOUR 12, "UNDERSTANDING GENERICS,"** for more information on generic methods.

If preconditions help answer the question of what input is expected, postconditions help answer the question of what output is expected. They are contracts about the state of a method when it terminates and are checked just prior to exiting the method. Unlike preconditions, in which all members used in the precondition must be at least as accessible as the method itself, postconditions may reference members with less visibility.

Most postconditions will be specified using one of the `Contract.Ensures` overloads, as shown in Listing 11.10.

LISTING 11.10 Using Postconditions

```
public int Calculate(int divisor, int dividend)
{
   Contract.Requires<ArgumentOutOfRangeException>(divisor > 0, "divisor");
   Contract.Requires<ArgumentOutOfRangeException>(dividend > 0, "divisor");
   Contract.Requires<ArgumentException>(divisor > dividend, "divisor");
   Contract.Ensures(result != 0);

   int result = dividend / divisor;
   return result;
}
```

In order to write this postcondition, it was necessary to change the implementation so the result of the division was captured in a local variable. Because this isn't always practical, the code contracts library provides the `Contract.Result<T>` method to refer to the actual return value. Using `Contract.Result<T>` would allow the `Calculate` method to be written as shown in Listing 11.11.

CAUTION

`Contract.Result<T>` and `void` Methods

Methods that have a `void` return type cannot use `Contract.Result<T>` within their postconditions.

LISTING 11.11 Using Postconditions and `Contract.Result<T>`

```
public int Calculate(int divisor, int dividend)
{
   Contract.Requires<ArgumentOutOfRangeException>(divisor > 0, "divisor");
   Contract.Requires<ArgumentOutOfRangeException>(dividend > 0, "dividend");
   Contract.Requires<ArgumentException>(divisor > dividend, "divisor");
   Contract.Ensures(Contract.Result<int>() != 0);

   return dividend / divisor;
}
```

If you need to write a postcondition that references an out parameter, you must use the
Contract.ValueAtReturn<T> method instead of Contract.Result<T>.

Just as you can refer to method return values and out parameters, it is also possible to refer to
the original value of an expression from the precondition state using Contract.OldValue<T>.
There are, however, several restrictions:

▶ The old expression may only be used in a postcondition.

▶ An old expression cannot refer to another old expression.

▶ The old expression must refer to a value that existed in the method's prestate.

NOTE

Exceptional Postconditions

If you must ensure a particular postcondition when an exception occurs, you should use one of the
Contract.EnsuresOnThrow<T> overloads, which specify the condition that must be true whenever an exception of type T (or one of its subtypes) is thrown.

Because using Contract.EnsuresOnThrow<T> requires the method to guarantee the condition
when an exception is thrown, there are many exception types that make this difficult. For instance,
if you used the type Exception for T, the method would need to guarantee the condition even if a
stack overflow exception occurred. As a result, you should only use exceptional postconditions for
those exceptions a caller could expect as part of the application programming interface (API).

Sometimes, it is necessary to specify a condition that should be true on each instance of a class.
In other words, it defines a set of conditions that must be true both before and after an operation; therefore, invariants express the conditions that are required for the object to be in a
"good" state.

Specifying invariants is done using an invariant method, which is simply a method that
is marked with the ContractInvariantMethod attribute and contains only calls to the
Contract.Invariant method, as shown in Listing 11.12.

LISTING 11.12   Using Invariants

```
[ContractInvariantMethod]
private void ObjectInvariant()
{
    Contract.Invariant(this.result != 0);
}
```

While the name of the method is not meaningful, a best practice is to name it something meaningful like ObjectInvariants or just Invariants. It is also possible to specify more than one

method for the object invariants, although you should probably keep it to just one method for ease of maintenance.

NOTE

Conditions and Purity

In addition, the condition should be free of side effects. This applies to any methods that are called within a contract as well. Such side-effect-free methods are also called pure methods and must not update any preexisting state; they can, however, modify objects created after the pure method has begun executing.

Currently, the following are assumed to be pure:

▶ Methods marked with the `Pure` attribute. When a type is marked with the `Pure` attribute, all methods in that type are considered to also be marked with the `Pure` attribute.

▶ Property `get` accessors.

▶ Operators.

▶ Any method whose fully qualified name begins with `System.Diagnostics.Contracts.Contract`, `System.String`, `System.IO.Path`, or `System.Type`.

▶ Any invoked delegate if the delegate type itself is marked with the `Pure` attribute. The `System.Predicate<T>` and `System.Comparison<T>` delegates are considered pure.

GO TO ▶ **HOUR 21, "PROGRAMMING WITH ATTRIBUTES,"** for more information on attributes.

Summary

In this hour, you learned about exceptions and learned how to use them in your applications. Exceptions occur as the result of an unexpected error and can cause your application to crash if not handled correctly. It is important to catch exceptions only at a point where some meaningful action can be taken as a result. You saw how the C# compiler helps you to catch exceptions in the correct order, catching the most derived exceptions first. You then learned how to perform integer arithmetic in a checked and unchecked manner, which helps prevent integer overflow from occurring. Finally, you learned how exceptions, and specifically code contracts, can be used to perform parameter validation to help ensure your application executes correctly.

Q&A

Q. **When should you use exceptions?**

A. Exceptions provide a clear, concise, secure, and safe way to represent failures that occur during runtime and should be used when an unexpected error condition is encountered, typically when a class member cannot perform what it is designed to do.

Q. What is an unhandled exception?

A. An unhandled exception is one that occurs when the application has not provided explicit code to execute when that exception occurs.

Q. What is a try-catch block?

A. A try-catch block is a protected region that includes one or more exception handlers.

Q. What is a try-finally block?

A. A try-finally block is a protected region that includes no exception handlers and executes whenever the try block exits, even if an exception occurs.

Workshop

Quiz

1. What is the base class for all exceptions?

2. What is a `RuntimeWrappedException`?

3. Should `ArgumentException` (or any of its subclasses) or `InvalidOperationException` be handled programmatically?

4. What is a corrupted state exception?

5. What happens if an exception is thrown and a static constructor or static field initializer is contained in the call stack?

6. When should you handle exceptions?

Answers

1. The base class for all exceptions is `System.Exception`.

2. When another language, such as C++, throws an exception that does not derive from `System.Exception`, that exception is wrapped in a `RuntimeWrappedException` to maintain compatibility between languages.

3. Typically `ArgumentException`, any of its subclasses, and `InvalidOperationException` represent coding errors and are best corrected at compile time rather than handling them programmatically in your application.

4. A corrupted state exception is one that occurs in a context outside of your application and indicates that the integrity of the running process might be in question. By default, it is not possible to catch a corrupted state exception.

5. If a static constructor or static field initializer is contained in the call stack, a `TypeInitializationException` is thrown containing the original exception in the `InnerException` property.

6. In general, you should handle an exception only at the closest point to where you can perform some meaningful actions because of the exception. As a result, you should use the try-finally pattern more often than the try-catch or try-catch-finally patterns.

Exercises

1. Add the following code to the beginning of the `Photo(Uri)` constructor in the `Photo` class of the `PhotoViewer` project:

   ```
   System.Diagnostics.Contracts.Contract.Requires<ArgumentNullException>(path !=
   null);
   ```

   Wrap the existing `if` statement in a try-catch block. Use the following code for the `catch(InvalidOperationException)` handler:

   ```
   this.source = null;
   this.Refresh();
   ```

2. Modify the `ToString` method so that if `this.source` is `null`, an empty string is returned.

HOUR 12
Understanding Generics

What You'll Learn in This Hour:

▶ Why you should use generics
▶ Using generic methods
▶ Creating generic classes
▶ Combining generics and arrays
▶ Variance in generic interfaces
▶ Working with tuples

You have already seen how an object can refer to an instance of any class. This enables you to create classes that operate on any data type. Several significant problems can occur with this approach. By working only with `object`, there is no way for the class to restrict input to be only of a specific type. To perform meaningful operations on the data, it must be cast from `object` to a more well-defined type. This not only adds complexity, but also sacrifices type safety at compile time.

Generics in C# solve this problem by enabling generalization that is type safe at compile time by removing the need to cast or otherwise perform boxing and unboxing conversions. Generics combine type safety, reusability, and efficiency in ways nongeneric classes can't. The most common use for generics is with collections, which you saw in Hour 10, "Working with Arrays and Collections;" however, you can use generics to create your own custom generic types and methods.

In this hour, you learn how generics work and how to create your own generic types.

Why You Should Use Generics

In Hour 10, you saw how to create an array of integer values. Because you explicitly stated the data type for each element in the array was `int`, the compiler verified that you were assigning only integer values to each element. You also operated on each element using methods and operators defined for integer values. Imagine the code required to find the minimum value of an arbitrary array of integers (see Listing 12.1).

LISTING 12.1   Finding the Minimum Value

```
public int Min(int[] values)
{
   int min = values[0];
   foreach (int value in values)
   {
      if (value.CompareTo(min) < 0)
      {
         min = value;
      }
   }

   return min;
}
```

What would happen if you wanted this to work with any numeric type? Without generics, you would need to write a different version of Min for each numeric type with the only difference being the data type. Although that is certainly possible, it introduces a lot of redundancy in your code and makes it harder to maintain.

Knowing that the IComparable interface defines a CompareTo method, you could write this in a more generic way using objects. This would allow you to write the code once yet still use it for an array of any numeric type, as shown in Listing 12.2.

LISTING 12.2   Finding the Minimum Value Using Objects

```
public object Min(object[] values)
{
   IComparable min = (IComparable)values[0];
   foreach (object value in values)
   {
      if (((IComparable)value).CompareTo(min) < 0)
      {
         min = (IComparable)value;
      }
   }

   return min;
}
```

Unfortunately, although you now only have one method to maintain, you also lost any type safety. In addition, an array of integers is not convertible to an array of objects. Because this method works with objects, what happens when it is passed an array that was defined like the following?

```
object[] array = { 5, 3, "a", "hello" };
```

This is legal because the array holds elements of type `object` and any value is implicitly convertible to `object`.

Finding the Minimum Without Generics

By following these steps, you see how creating a generalized method without the use of generics prevents type safety yet still compiles correctly. Keep Visual Studio open at the end of this exercise because you will use this application later.

1. Create a new console application.

2. In the `Program.cs` file, implement the two functions shown in Listings 12.1 and 12.2. Make sure you declare these methods as static.

3. Change both versions of `Min` so that the first line of each has a `Console.WriteLine` to print out which method is executed.

4. In the `Main` method of the `Program.cs` file, declare and initialize an integer array named `array` of five elements followed by a `Console.WriteLine` statement to print the minimum value.

5. Run the application using Ctrl+F5, and make sure the output displays the correct minimum value for your array.

6. Change the declaration of `array` from `int` to `long`.

7. You should notice the call to `Min` has a red squiggly line, and two errors are reported in the error window. This happens because there is no implementation of `Min` that takes a `long[]` as a parameter.

8. Change the declaration of `array` from `long` to `object` to remove the compiler errors.

9. Run the application again using Ctrl+F5, and make sure the output displays the correct minimum value for your array. (This should be the same value as shown from step 4.)

10. Change the elements of `array` to the following:

    ```
    { 5, 3, "a", "hello", 1 };
    ```

11. Run the application using Ctrl+F5, and observe that the output matches what is shown in Figure 12.1.

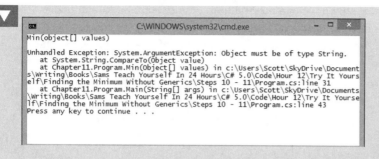

FIGURE 12.1
Runtime exception generated from the lack of type safety.

Not only have you lost type safety, but you are also performing *n+1* conversion operations, where *n* is the number of elements in the array. As you might guess, the larger the array, the more expensive this method becomes.

Using generics, this problem becomes simple. You gain the ability to write the code only once without losing type safety or incurring multiple conversion operations. Listing 12.3 shows the same Min method defined using generics. If you compare this with the method defined in Listing 12.1, you can see that they are almost identical.

NOTE

where T : IComparable<T>

This constraint might be a bit confusing because it looks like there is a circular dependency here. In fact, it's actually straightforward and means that T must be a type that can be compared with other Ts.

LISTING 12.3   Finding the Minimum Value Using Generics

```
public T Min<T>(T[] values) where T: IComparable<T>
{
    T min = values[0];
    foreach (T value in values)
    {
        if (value.CompareTo(min) < 0)
        {
            min = value;
        }
    }

    return min;
}
```

The biggest difference is that the generic version uses a generic type parameter T, specified by the <T> syntax, after the method name. The type parameter acts as a placeholder for a real type supplied at compile time. In this example, we know that any real type used in place of T must implement the IComparable<T> interface, where the T of the interface is the type parameter of the generic method. This constrains, or limits, the type parameter to be any type that implements the interface.

CAUTION

C# Generics, C++ Templates, and Java Generics

Although C# generics, Java generics, and C++ templates all provide support for parameterized types, several significant differences exist between them. The syntax for C# generics is similar to that of Java and simpler than C++ templates.

All the type substitutions for C# generics occur at runtime, thereby preserving the generic type information for instantiated objects. In Java, generics are a language-only construction implemented only in the compiler in a technique known as type erasure. As a result, the generic type information for instantiated objects is not available at runtime. This is different from C++ templates that are expanded at compile time, generating additional code for each template type.

C# generics do not provide the same amount of flexibility as C++ templates and Java generics in some cases. For example, C# generics do not support the idea of a wildcard for the type parameter like Java generics. It is also not possible to call arithmetic operators on a type parameter, as you can in C++ templates.

TRY IT YOURSELF ▼

Finding the Minimum with Generics

To modify the code written in the previous exercise to use a generic version of the Min function, follow these steps. If you closed Visual Studio, repeat the previous exercise first.

1. In the Program.cs file, implement the generic function shown in Listing 12.3. Make sure you declare this method as static and make the same change to add as the first line a call to Console.Write to print out the method name.

2. Change the declaration of array so that it is int[] and change the elements to be all numeric values again so that your program compiles and executes correctly.

3. Run the application using Ctrl+F5. Notice that you are still using the nongeneric strongly typed version of Min.

4. Change only the type of array so that it is long[].

5. Run the application again using Ctrl+F5. Notice that you are now using the generic version of Min.

6. Change only the elements of `array` to the following:

```
{ 5, 3, "a", "hello", 1 };
```

7. Run the application again. This time, instead of running and generating a runtime exception, you receive two compiler errors saying that you cannot implicitly convert type 'string' to 'long', as shown in Figure 12.2.

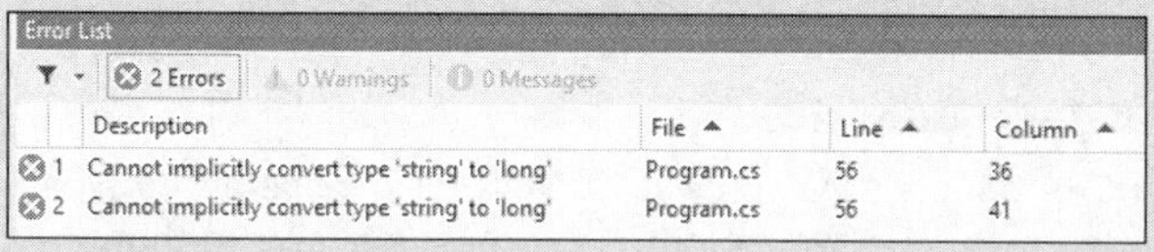

FIGURE 12.2
Compiler errors generated by enforcing type safety.

Understanding Generic Type Parameters

Just as methods have parameters and the values of those parameters at runtime are arguments, generic types and methods also have type parameters and type arguments. Type parameters act as placeholders for a type argument supplied at compile time.

This is more than simple text replacement of the type parameter with the supplied type. When a generic type or method is compiled, the Common Intermediate Language (CIL) contains metadata identifying it as having type parameters. At runtime, the Just-In-Time (JIT) compiler creates a constructed type with the supplied type parameter substituted in the appropriate locations.

A generic type or method can have multiple type parameters separated by a comma (,) in the type parameter specification. Several of the generic collection classes, such as `Dictionary<TKey, TValue>` and `KeyValuePair<TKey, TValue>`, use more than one type parameter. The `Tuple` class, which we discuss a bit later, is also generic and has up to eight type parameters.

Constraints

Constraints enable you to apply restrictions on the types used for the type arguments at compile time. These restrictions are specified using the `where` keyword, as you saw in Listing 12.3. When you constrain a type parameter, the number of allowable operations and methods increase to those supported by the constrained type and all types in its inheritance chain.

There are six possible constraints, as shown in Table 12.1.

TABLE 12.1 Generic Type Parameter Constraints

Constraint	Description
where T : struct	The type argument must be a value type, except a nullable value type.
where T : class	The type argument must be a reference type. This applies to any class, interface, delegate, or array type.
where T : new()	The type argument must have a public parameterless constructor and be a concrete type. If used with other constraints, the new() constraint must be specified last.
where T : <base class name>	The type argument must be or derive from the specified base class.
where T : <interface name>	There must be an identity or implicit reference conversion from the type argument to the stated type. The constraining interface can be generic and multiple interface constraints can be specified.
where T : U	The type argument must be, or derive from, the argument supplied for U, which is another generic type parameter.

Constraints guarantee to the compiler that any operator or method called on a type parameter will be supported. Type parameters that have no constraints are **unconstrained type parameters** and support only simple assignment and calling methods supported by System.Object. In addition, the != and == operators cannot be used with unconstrained type parameters because the compiler has no guarantee that they are supported.

A single type parameter can have multiple constraints, and you can apply constraints to multiple parameters:

```
CustomDictionary<TKey, TValue>
    where TKey : IComparable
    where TValue : class, new()
```

NOTE

Testing for Value Equality with Generics

Even if you apply the where T : class constraint, you should still avoid using the == and != operators on the type parameter. These operators test for reference identity, not value equality.

This happens even if those operators are overloaded in the type because the compiler knows only that T is a reference type. As a result, it can use only the default operators defined on System.Object that are valid for all reference types.

The recommended way to test for value equality is to apply the `where T : IComparable<T>` constraint and ensure that interface is implemented in any class that will be used to construct the generic class. By applying this constraint, you can use the `CompareTo` method to perform value equality, as you saw in Listing 12.3.

A **type parameter constraint** is a generic type parameter used as a constraint for another type parameter. Type parameter constraints are most commonly found when a generic method has to constrain its type parameter to the type parameter of the containing type, as shown in Listing 12.4. In this example, T is a type parameter constraint for the Add method that means Add accepts a List<U>, where any type substituted for U must be or derive from T.

LISTING 12.4   Type Parameter Constraints on a Method

```
public class List<T>
{
    public void Add<U>(List<U> items) where U : T
    {
    }
}
```

Type parameter constraints can also be used with generic classes when you want to enforce a relationship between two type parameters, as shown in Listing 12.5. In this example, you state that Example has three type parameters (T, U, and V) such that any type substituted for T must be, or derive from V, and that U and V are unconstrained.

LISTING 12.5   Type Parameter Constraints on a Class

```
public class Example<T, U, V> where T : V
{
}
```

Default Values for Generic Types

Remember, C# is a strongly typed language that requires definite assignment of a variable before it can be used. To help simplify this requirement, every type has a default value. Obviously, it isn't possible for you to know ahead of time whether the default value should be null, 0, or a zero-initialized struct. How then do you specify the default value for a type T that can represent any type?

C# provides the `default` keyword, which represents the appropriate default value for a type parameter based on the actual type specified. That means it returns null for reference types and zero for all numeric value types. If the type argument is a struct, each member of the struct is initialized to `null` or zero, as appropriate for the member type. For nullable value types, it returns `null`.

Using Generic Methods

Generic methods are no different from their nongeneric relatives but are defined using a set of generic type parameters rather than concrete types. A generic method is a blueprint for a method generated at runtime. If you look back at Listing 12.3, you have already used a generic method.

NOTE

Generic Methods in Nongeneric Classes

Generic methods are not restricted to only generic classes. It is perfectly valid, and fairly common, for a nongeneric class to include generic methods.

It is also possible for generic classes to include nongeneric methods, which have full access to the type parameters of the generic class.

By using constraints on a generic method, you can make use of more specialized operations the constraint guarantees will be available. The type parameters defined by a generic class are available to both generic and nongeneric methods. Because of this, if a generic method defines the same type parameter as the containing class, the argument supplied for the inner `T` hides the one supplied for the outer `T` and generates a compiler warning. If you need a method that uses different type arguments than provided when the class was instantiated, you should provide a different identifier for the type parameter, as shown in Listing 12.6.

LISTING 12.6   Type Parameter Hiding

```
class GenericClass<T>
{
    void GenerateWarning<T>()
    {
    }

    void NoWarning<U>()
    {
    }
}
```

When you call a generic method, you must provide a real data type for the type arguments defined by that method. Listing 12.7 shows one way to call the `Min<T>` method defined in Listing 12.3.

LISTING 12.7 Calling a Generic Method

```
public static class Program
{
   static void Main()
   {
      int[] array = {3, 5, 7, 0, 2, 4, 6 };
      Console.WriteLine(Min<int>(array));
   }
}
```

Although this is acceptable, it isn't necessary in the majority of calls, thanks to **type inference**. When you omit the type argument, the compiler attempts to discover, or infer, the type based on the method arguments. Listing 12.8 shows the same call using type inference.

LISTING 12.8 Calling a Generic Method Using Type Inference

```
public static class Program
{
   static void Main()
   {
      int[] array = {3, 5, 7, 0, 2, 4, 6 };
      Console.WriteLine(Min(array));
   }
}
```

Because type inference relies on the method arguments, it cannot infer the type only from a constraint or return value. This means you can't use it with methods that have no parameters.

For generic methods, the type parameters are part of the method signature. This enables a generic method to be overloaded by declaring multiple generic methods with the same formal parameter list but which differ by type parameter.

TIP

Type Inference and Overload Resolution

Type inference occurs at compile time and before the compiler tries to resolve overloaded method signatures. When type substitution occurs, it is possible for a nongeneric method and a generic method to have identical signatures. In such a case, the most specific method will be used, which is always the nongeneric method.

Creating Generic Classes

You have already seen generic classes in action when you looked at the different collection types. Generic classes are most commonly used with collections because the behavior of the collection is the same for any data type stored. Just as a generic method is a blueprint for a method generated at runtime, a generic class is a blueprint for a class constructed at runtime.

Not only are generic classes used within the .NET Framework, you can create your own generic classes as well. This is no different from creating a nongeneric class, except that you provide a type parameter rather than an actual data type.

Keep in mind a few important questions when you create your own generic types:

▶ **What types should be type parameters?** Generally, the more types you parameterize, the more flexibility your type has. There are practical limits on how many type parameters should be used, however, because the readability of your code can decrease as the number of type parameters increases.

▶ **What constraints should be applied?** There are multiple ways to determine this. One is to apply as many constraints as possible that will still allow you to work with the types you are expecting. Another is to apply as few constraints as possible so that the generic type is maximally flexible. Both approaches are valid, but you can also take a more pragmatic approach of applying just the constraints necessary to limit the class to implementing its defined purpose. For example, if you know your generic class should work only with reference types, you would apply the class constraint. This prevents your class from being used with value types but enables you to use the as operator and check for null values.

▶ **Should behavior be provided in base classes and subclasses?** Generic classes can be used as base classes, just like nongeneric classes. As a result, the same design choices apply here as they do with nongeneric classes.

▶ **Should generic interfaces be implemented?** Depending on the type of generic class you are designing, you might have to implement, and possibly create, one or more generic interfaces. How your class will be used also determines which interfaces, if any, are implemented.

Just as nongeneric classes can inherit from either concrete or abstract nongeneric base classes, generic classes can also inherit from a nongeneric concrete or abstract base class. However, generic classes can also inherit from other generic classes.

NOTE

Generic Structs and Interfaces

Structs can be generic as well and use the same syntax and type constraints as classes. The only differences between a generic struct and a generic class are the same differences for nongeneric classes and structs.

Generic interfaces use the same type parameter syntax and constraints as generic classes and follow the same rules as nongeneric interface declarations. The one notable exception is that the interfaces implemented by a generic type remain unique for all possible constructed types. What this actually means is that if, after type parameter substitution, two generic interfaces implemented by the same generic class would be identical, the declaration of that generic class is invalid.

Although generic classes can inherit from nongeneric interfaces, a generic interface is the preferred choice for use with generic classes.

To understand inheritance with generic classes, you first need to understand the difference between an open and closed type. An **open type** is one that involves type parameters. More specifically, it is a generic type that has not been supplied any type arguments for its type parameters. A **closed type**, also called a **constructed type**, is a generic type that is not open. (That is, it has been supplied a type argument for all its type parameters.)

Generic classes can inherit from either an open type or a closed type. A derived class can provide type arguments for all the type parameters on its base class, in which case it is a constructed type. If the derived class provides no type arguments, it is an open type. Although generic classes can inherit from closed or open types, nongeneric classes can inherit only from closed types; otherwise, there is no way for the compiler to know what type argument should be used.

Some examples of inheriting from open and closed types are shown in Listing 12.9.

LISTING 12.9   Inheritance with Generics

```
abstract class Element { }

class Element<T> : Element { }

class BasicElement<T> : Element<T> { }

class Int32Element : BasicElement<int> { }
```

In this example, `Element<T>` derives from `Element` and is an open type. `BasicElement<T>` derives from `Element<T>` and is an open type. `Int32Element` is a constructed type because it derives from the constructed type `BasicElement<int>`.

However, a derived class can provide type arguments for some of the type parameters on its base class, in which case it is an **open constructed type**. Think of an open constructed type as being somewhere in between an open type and a closed type; that is, it has provided arguments for at least one type parameter, but also has at least one type parameter for which an argument must still be provided before it is a constructed type.

Expanding on the example in Listing 12.9 to create an open type `Element` with two type parameters `T` and `K`, the different possibilities for creating open constructed types are shown in Listing 12.10.

LISTING 12.10   Inheriting from an Open Constructed Class

```
class Element<T, K> { }

class Element1<T> : Element<T, int> { }

class Element2<K> : Element<string, K> { }
```

If the open constructed type specifies constraints, the derived type is required to provide type arguments that meet those constraints. This can be done by specifying constraints itself. The constraints on the subclass can be the same constraints applied to the base class, or they can be a superset of those constraints. Listing 12.11 shows an example of inheriting from an open constructed class with constraints.

LISTING 12.11   Inheriting from an Open Constructed Class with Constraints

```
class ConstrainedElement<T>
    where T : IComparable<T>, new()

class ConstrainedElement1<T> : ConstrainedElement<T>
    where T : IComparable<T>, new()
```

Finally, if a generic class implements an interface, all instances of that class can be cast to the interface.

Combining Generics and Arrays

In Hour 10, you learned that all single-dimensional arrays that have a lower bound of zero automatically implement `IList<T>`. As a result, you can create a generic method that iterates over the contents of an `IList<T>` that will work for any of the collection types (because they all implement `IList<T>`) and any single-dimensional array.

Listing 12.12 shows an example of such a generic method.

LISTING 12.12   Printing the Items of a Collection or Array with a Generic Method

```
public static class Program
{
    public static void PrintCollection<T>(IList<T> collection)
    {
        StringBuilder builder = new StringBuilder();
        foreach(var item in collection)
        {
            builder.AppendFormat("{0} ", item);
        }

        Console.WriteLine(builder.ToString());
    }

    public static void Main()
    {
        int[] array = {0, 2, 4, 6, 8};
        List<int> list = new List<int>() { 1, 3, 5, 7, 9 };
        PrintCollection(array);
        PrintCollection(list);

        string[] array2 = { "hello", "world" };
        List<string> list2 = new List<string>() { "now", "is", "the", "time" };
        PrintCollection(array2);
        PrintCollection(list2);
    }
}
```

Variance in Generic Interfaces

Type variance refers to the ability to use a type other than the one originally specified. **Covariance** enables you to use a more-derived type than the one specified, whereas **contravariance** enables you to use a less-derived type. C# supports covariance for return types and contravariance for parameters.

The generic collections in C# are **invariant**, meaning you must use an exact match of the formal type specified. As a result, it is not possible to substitute a collection containing a more-derived type where a less-derived type is expected. For example, if you have a collection of cars, you can't treat it as a collection of police cars because it might contain a car that is not a police car. Similarly, you can't treat it as a collection of vehicles because you could put a truck (which is clearly not a car) into a collection of vehicles but not into a collection of cars.

NOTE

Classes Implementing Generic Variant Interfaces

Classes implementing generic variant interfaces are always invariant.

The real problem here is that the collections are mutable. If you could restrict the collection to a read-only subset of behavior, you can make it covariant, allowing a sequence of cars to be treated as a sequence of vehicles with no problem.

In C#, an interface is **variant** if its type parameters are declared covariant or contravariant. Covariance and contravariance apply only when there is a reference conversion between the two types. This means you can't use variance with value types. You also can't use variance with ref or out parameters.

Several of the generic collection interfaces, shown in Table 12.2, support variance.

TABLE 12.2   Generic Interfaces Supporting Variance

Interface	Variance
IEnumerable<T>	T is covariant.
IEnumerator<T>	T is covariant.
IQueryable<T>	T is covariant.
IGrouping<TKey, TElement>	TKey and TElement are covariant.
IComparer<T>	T is contravariant.
IEqualityComparer<T>	T is contravariant.
IComparable<T>	T is contravariant.

TRY IT YOURSELF ▼

Exploring Variance

By following these steps, you explore how variance works by modifying the code shown in Listing 12.12.

1. Create a new console application and modify the content of Program.cs to look as shown in Listing 12.12.

2. Run the application using Ctrl+F5, and observe that the output matches what is shown in Figure 12.3.

3. Change PrintCollection<T> so that it is no longer a generic method and that the type of collection is IEnumerable<object>.

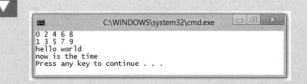

FIGURE 12.3
Printing the contents of an array.

4. You should immediately see the compiler errors shown in Figure 12.4.

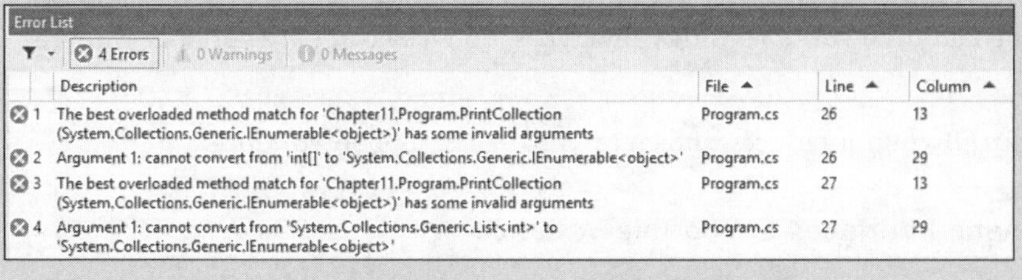

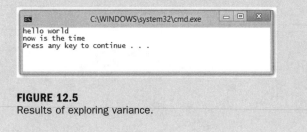

FIGURE 12.4
Compiler errors.

5. Correct the two errors by commenting out the invalid lines of code. Remember, variance doesn't work for value types, which is the reason for the compiler errors.

6. Run the application again and observe that the output matches what is shown in Figure 12.5.

```
C:\WINDOWS\system32\cmd.exe
hello world
now is the time
Press any key to continue . . .
```

FIGURE 12.5
Results of exploring variance.

Extending Variant Generic Interfaces

The compiler does not infer variance from the inherited interface, which requires that you explicitly specify if the derived interface supports variance, as shown in Listing 12.13.

LISTING 12.13 Extending a Generic Variant Interface

```
interface ICovariant<out T>
{
}

interface IInvariant<T> : ICovariant<T>
{
}

interface IExtendedCovariant<out T> : ICovariant<T>
{
}
```

Even though the `IInvariant<T>` interface and the `IExtendedCovariant<out T>` interface both extend the same covariant interface, only `IExtendedCovariant<out T>` is also covariant. You can extend contravariant interfaces in the same manner.

You can also extend both a covariant and a contravariant interface in the same derived interface if it is invariant, as shown in Listing 12.14.

LISTING 12.14 Extending Both a Covariant and Contravariant Interface

```
interface ICovariant<out T>
{
}

interface IContravariant<in T>
{
}

interface IInvariant<T> : IContravariant<T>, ICovariant<T>
{
}
```

However, you cannot extend a contravariant interface with a covariant interface, or the other way around, if the base interface is open, as shown in Listing 12.15.

NOTE

Creating Your Own Variant Generic Interfaces

Just as you can define your own generic interfaces, you can define your own variant generic interfaces using the `in` and `out` keywords with the generic type parameters. These keywords appear only in the interface declaration and are not part of the implementing code.

The out keyword declares a generic type parameter as covariant, whereas the in keyword declares a generic type parameter as contravariant. An interface can also support both covariance and contravariance for different type parameters.

LISTING 12.15   **Extending Both a Covariant and Contravariant Interface**

```
// Generates a compiler error.
interface IInvalidVariance<in T> : ICovariant<T>
{
}
```

Working with Tuples

A tuple is commonly used to represent a set of data in a single data structure. Typically, tuples are used to:

▶ Represent a single set of data.

▶ Provide easy access and manipulation of a set of data.

▶ Return multiple values from a method.

▶ Pass multiple values to a method in a single parameter.

For example, to store a person's name and date of birth together in a single data structure, you would use a 2-tuple (a tuple with two elements), as shown in the following code:

```
var t2 = Tuple.Create("Jim Morrison", new DateTime(1943, 12, 8));
Console.WriteLine("{0} was born on {1}.", t2.Item1, t2.Item2);
```

Although tuples are most frequently found in functional programming languages such as F#, Ruby, or Python, the .NET Framework provides several Tuple classes representing tuples containing from one to seven values. There is also an n-tuple class, where n is any value greater than or equal to eight. This n-tuple class is slightly different from the one-to-seven-tuple classes in that the eighth component of the tuple is another Tuple object that defines the rest of the remaining components.

Working with Tuples

To create a new `Tuple<T1, T2>` instance and access the values of that tuple, follow these steps:

1. Create a new console application.

2. Create a new method in the `Program.cs` file that returns a `Tuple<int, string>`:

```
public static Tuple<int, string> GenerateTuple()
{
    return Tuple.Create(1, "hello, world");
}
```

3. In the `Main` method, enter the following code:

```
var t = GenerateTuple();
Console.WriteLine(t.GetType());
Console.WriteLine("{0}:{1}", t.Item1, t.Item2);
```

4. Run the application by pressing Ctrl+F5; you should see what is displayed in Figure 12.6.

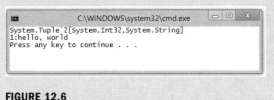

FIGURE 12.6
Results of working with tuples.

Summary

In this hour, you learned why generic programming is important and how it enables you to solve problems in a way that is reusable no matter what data type is used. You learned how type parameters work and how to constrain those type parameters to provide restrictions on the allowable types.

You learned how to create your own generic classes, interfaces, and methods, including the ability to create generic methods in nongeneric classes. Finally, you learned how to explicitly specify the variance of a type parameter for a generic interface.

Generic programming, both by creating your own generic types and using the existing generic collections, is a flexible and powerful concept that enables you to still have type safety while only having to write a single implementation.

Q&A

Q. What is the most common use of generics?

A. Generics are most commonly used in the collection classes and interfaces, although you can use them for your own classes as well.

Q. What problems do using generics prevent?

A. Using generics enables you to write a single implementation that is type safe and does not require boxing or unboxing operations.

Q. Are C# generics like Java generics or C++ templates?

A. Although the syntax is similar to both, the implementations are different. Java generics are a language-only construction, and the generic type information is not known at runtime. C++ templates are expanded at compile time, which generates additional code for each template type.

Q. What are type constraints?

A. Constraints enable you to apply restrictions on the types that can be used for the type arguments at compile time and guarantee to the compiler that any operator or method called on a type parameter will be supported.

Q. Can a nongeneric class contain a generic method?

A. Yes, a generic method can be defined within either a generic or nongeneric class.

Q. What is co- and contravariance for generic interfaces?

A. Variance is defined as the capability for two generic types to be made assignment-compatible based solely on the known assignment compatibility of their type arguments. Covariance enables interface methods to have more derived return types than originally specified by the type parameters. Contravariance enables interface methods to have argument types that are less derived than originally specified by the type parameters.

Workshop

Quiz

1. What is the correct way to test for value equality with generics?

2. What is a type parameter constraint?

3. What is a closed and open type?

Answers

1. The correct way to test for value equality using generics is to apply the `where T :
ICompparable<T>` and use the `CompareTo` method to perform value equality.

2. A type parameter constraint is when a generic parameter is used as the constraint for
another generic parameter.

3. An open type is a generic type that has not been supplied any type arguments for its type
parameters. A closed type is a generic type that is not open (that is, it has been supplied a
type argument for all its type parameters).

Exercises

1. Replace the implementation of the `QueryMetadata<T>` method in the `ExifMetadata`
struct of the `PhotoViewer` project with the following:

```
Nullable<T> result = new Nullable<T>();

if (metadata.ContainsQuery(query))
{
    try
    {
        object queryResult = metadata.GetQuery(query);
        if (queryResult.GetType() == typeof(T))
        {
            result = (T)queryResult;
        }
        else
        {
            try
            {
                result = (T)Convert.ChangeType(queryResult, typeof(T));
            }
            catch (InvalidCastException)
            {
                result = null;
            }
            catch (FormatException)
            {
                result = null;
            }
            catch (OverflowException)
            {
                result = null;
            }
        }
```

```
        }
        catch
        {
            result = null;
        }
    }

    return result;
```

Understanding Query Expressions

What You'll Learn in This Hour:

▶ Introducing LINQ
▶ Using LINQ to manipulate data
▶ Standard query operator methods
▶ Deferred execution

In Hour 10, "Working with Arrays and Collections," you learned how applications could work with data stored in collections. Applications also need to work with data stored in other data sources, such as SQL databases or XML files, or even accessed through a web service. Traditionally, queries against these different data sources required different syntax and performed no type checking at compile time.

For example, consider a collection of customers. How would you search that collection for all customers with a specific job title? Using what you have learned so far, you would need to write code that iterates over each item in the collection, examining the appropriate field and returning those items that match the job title for which you are searching. What would happen if the source of your customer data were to change and no longer be an in-memory collection but an XML file or data retrieved from a web service call? You would most likely need to rewrite your search logic to accommodate this new data source.

In this hour, you learn about Language Integrated Query (LINQ) and query expression expressions, which enable you to write a single query that works correctly for any supported data source.

Introducing LINQ

Query expressions in the .NET Framework are part of a set of technologies called LINQ, which integrate query capabilities directly into the C# language. LINQ eliminates the language mismatch commonly found between working with data and working with objects by providing the same query language for the following data sources:

- ▶ SQL databases

- ▶ XML documents

- ▶ Web services

- ▶ ADO.NET Datasets

- ▶ Any collections that support the `IEnumerable` or `IEnumerable<T>` interfaces.

This enables a query to be a first-class language construct, just like arithmetic operations and control flow statements are first-class concepts in C#.

Using LINQ to Manipulate Data

Query expressions in LINQ can query and transform data from any supported data source in a consistent fashion by working with the common operations performed rather than focusing on the structure. You can freely change the structure of the underlying data being queried without needing to change the query itself.

Listing 13.1 shows a query against a collection of `Contact` objects. Assume for the moment that the list has been populated as a result of calling `GetContacts`.

LISTING 13.1 A LINQ Query

```
class Contact
{
    public int Id { get; set; }
    public string Company { get; set; }
    public string LastName { get; set; }
    public string FirstName { get; set; }
    public string Address { get; set; }
    public string City { get; set; }
    public string StateProvince { get; set; }
}

IEnumerable<Contact> contacts = GetContacts();

var result =
    from contact in contacts
    select contact.FirstName;

foreach(var name in result)
{
    Console.WriteLine(name);
}
```

This simple query illustrates the **declarative syntax**, also called the **query comprehension syntax**, supported by the C# language. This syntax enables you to write queries using Structured Query Language (SQL)-like query syntax, providing a great deal of flexibility and expressiveness. Although all the variables in a query expression are strongly typed, in most cases you don't need to provide the type explicitly because the compiler can infer it.

NOTE
_____

Query Comprehension Syntax

If you are familiar with SQL, the query comprehension syntax used by LINQ will be familiar since it uses some of the same keywords and offers many of the same advantages. The most noticeable difference is that the `from` operator occurs before the `select` operator, rather than after it as it does in SQL. Although SQL is designed to handle relational data only, LINQ actually supports far more data structures.

_____

Selecting Data

Although the code shown in Listing 13.1 might look simple, a lot is actually going on. The first thing you should notice is the use of an implicitly typed variable named `result`, which is actually of type `IEnumerable<string>`. The result of the query expression (the code on the right side of the assignment operator) is actually a query, not the result of the query. The `select` clause returns an object that represents the operation of projecting a result (the `contact.FirstName` values) from a sequence (the `contacts` list). Because the results are strings, `result` must be an enumerable collection of strings. It does not actually retrieve the data at this time; rather, it simply returns an enumerable collection that will fetch the data later.

This query literally says "select the `FirstName` field from each element, called `contact`, in the data source specified by `contacts`." You can think of the `contact` variable specified in the `from` clause as being similar to the iteration variable of a `foreach` statement. It corresponds to a read-only local variable scoped only to the query expression. The `in` clause specifies the data source containing the elements to be queried, and the `select` clause says to select only the `contact.FirstName` field for each element during the iteration.

Although this syntax works well for selecting a single field, it is common to select multiple fields or even to transform the data in some way, such as combining fields. Fortunately, LINQ enables these scenarios as well, using similar syntax. You actually have several options for performing these types of selections.

The first is simply to concatenate the fields in the `select` statement, thereby still returning a single field, as shown in Listing 13.2.

LISTING 13.2   A LINQ Query Concatenating Data

```
var result =
   from contact in contacts
   select contact.FirstName + " " + contact.LastName;

foreach(var name in result)
{
   Console.WriteLine(name);
}
```

Obviously, this form of selection works only in a limited number of cases. A more flexible approach is to return multiple fields, essentially returning a subset of data, as shown in Listing 13.3.

LISTING 13.3   A LINQ Query Returning an Anonymous Type

```
var result =
   from contact in contacts
   select new
   {
      Name = contact.LastName + ", " + contact.FirstName,
      DateOfBirth = contact.DateOfBirth
   };

foreach(var contact in result)
{
   Console.WriteLine("{0} born on {1}", contact.Name, contact.DateOfBirth);
}
```

In this case, you are still returning an `IEnumerable`, but what is its type? If you look at the `select` clause in Listing 13.3, you should notice it is returning a new type containing the values from the `contact.FirstName` and `contact.LastName` fields. This new type is actually an **anonymous type** containing properties named `Name` and `DateOfBirth`. The type is anonymous because it doesn't have a name. You did not explicitly declare a new type that corresponds to the returned value; the compiler generated it for you.

NOTE

Anonymous Types

The ability to create anonymous types in this manner is central to the way LINQ works and would not be possible without the type inference provided by `var`.

Selecting Data

To select data using `select` query statements, follow these steps. Keep Visual Studio open at the end of this exercise because you will use this application later.

1. Open the `ConsoleApplication1` project in Visual Studio. This project can be found in the Hour 13\Try It Yourself\Selecting Data\Starting folder of the book downloads.

2. Open `Program.cs` and add a query that selects the `LastName` property for each `contact` in the `contacts` collection.

3. Write a `foreach` statement that prints the results of the query.

4. Run the application by pressing Ctrl+F5. The output should look similar to Figure 13.1.

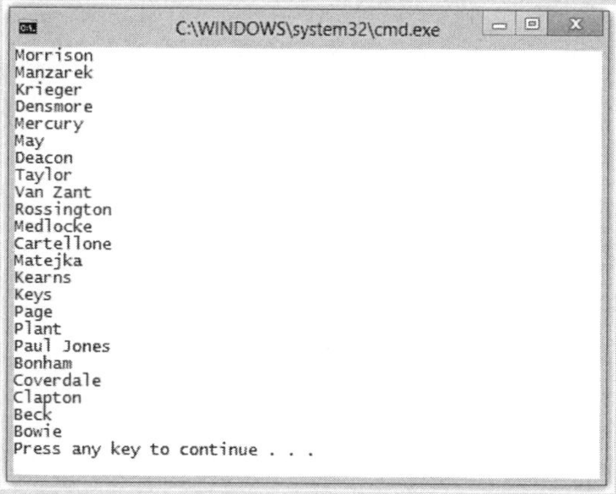

```
C:\WINDOWS\system32\cmd.exe
Morrison
Manzarek
Krieger
Densmore
Mercury
May
Deacon
Taylor
Van Zant
Rossington
Medlocke
Cartellone
Matejka
Kearns
Keys
Page
Plant
Paul Jones
Bonham
Coverdale
Clapton
Beck
Bowie
Press any key to continue . . .
```

FIGURE 13.1
Selecting data.

5. Write an additional query that selects the concatenation of `LastName, FirstName` in to the `Name` property of a new anonymous type.

6. Write a `foreach` statement that prints the results of the query.

7. Run the application by pressing Ctrl+F5. The output should look similar to Figure 13.2.

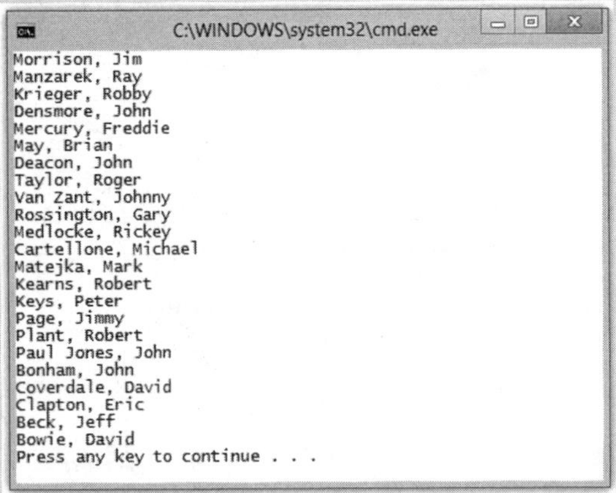

FIGURE 13.2
Selecting data using anonymous types.

Filtering Data

Selecting data is important, but selecting data in this way provides no option to restrict what data is returned. Just as SQL provides a where clause, LINQ provides a where clause that returns an enumerable collection containing elements that match the specified criteria. Listing 13.4 applies a where clause to the query in Listing 13.3, restricting the results to only those contacts where the value of StateProvince is equal to "FL".

LISTING 13.4 A Filtered LINQ Query

```
var result =
    from contact in contacts
    where contact.StateProvince == "FL"
    select new { customer.FirstName, customer.LastName };

foreach(var name in result)
{
    Console.WriteLine(name.FirstName + " " + name.LastName);
}
```

The where clause is applied first, resulting in an enumerable collection to which the select clause is applied, resulting in an anonymous type containing the FirstName and LastName properties.

Filtering Data

By following these steps, you learn how to write query statements that filter the resulting data. If you closed Visual Studio, repeat the previous exercise first. Be sure to keep Visual Studio open at the end of this exercise because you will use this application later.

1. Modify both of the queries you previously wrote to include a `where` clause that filters the resultset to just contacts whose last name starts with "M."

2. Run the application by pressing Ctrl+F5. The output should look similar to Figure 13.3.

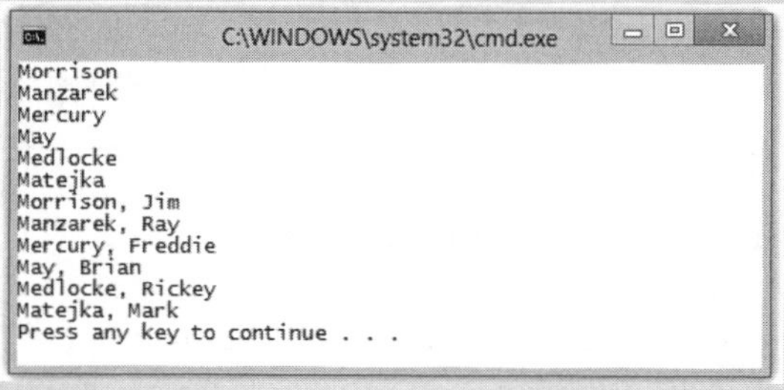

```
C:\WINDOWS\system32\cmd.exe
Morrison
Manzarek
Mercury
May
Medlocke
Matejka
Morrison, Jim
Manzarek, Ray
Mercury, Freddie
May, Brian
Medlocke, Rickey
Matejka, Mark
Press any key to continue . . .
```

FIGURE 13.3
Filtering data.

Grouping and Ordering Data

To support more complex scenarios, such as ordering or grouping the returned data, LINQ provides the `orderby` and `group` clauses. You can order data in either ascending (smallest to largest) or descending (largest to smallest) order. Because ascending is the default, you don't need to specify it. Listing 13.5 shows the query from Listing 13.1 ordered by the `LastName` field.

LISTING 13.5 A LINQ Query Using `OrderBy`

```
var result =
    from contact in contacts
    orderby contact.LastName
    select contact.FirstName;

foreach(var name in result)
{
    Console.WriteLine(name);
}
```

You can order by multiple fields and can mix ascending and descending to create rather sophisticated `orderby` statements, as shown in Listing 13.6.

LISTING 13.6   A LINQ Query Using a Complex `OrderBy`

```
var result =
    from contact in contacts
    orderby
        contact.LastName ascending,
        contact.FirstName descending
    select customer.FirstName;

foreach(var name in result)
{
    Console.WriteLine(name);
}
```

Grouping data follows a similar pattern, but the `group` clause takes the place of the `select` clause. The difference when grouping data is that the result returned is an `IEnumerable` of `IGrouping<TKey, TElement>` objects, which you can think of as a list of lists. This requires two nested `foreach` statements to access the results.

Listing 13.7 shows the same query as in Listing 13.1, but this time groups by the first character of the last name.

LISTING 13.7   A LINQ Query Using `Group`

```
var result =
    from contact in contacts
    group contact by contact.LastName[0];

foreach(var group in result)
{
    Console.WriteLine("Last names starting with {0}", group.Key);
    foreach(var name in group)
    {
        Console.WriteLine(name);
    }

    Console.WriteLine();
}
```

If you need to refer to the result of a grouping operation, you can create an identifier that can be queried further using the `into` keyword. This form of composability is a query **continuation**.

Listing 13.8 performs the same query as Listing 13.7 but returns only those groups that have more than two entries.

LISTING 13.8   A LINQ Query Using Group and Into

```
var result =
    from contact in contacts
    group contact by contact.LastName[0] into namesGroup
    where namesGroup.Count() > 2
    select namesGroup;

foreach(var group in result)
{
    Console.WriteLine("Last names starting with {0}", group.Key);
    foreach(var name in group)
    {
        Console.WriteLine(name);
    }

    Console.WriteLine();
}
```

TRY IT YOURSELF ▼

Grouping and Ordering Data

To write query statements that perform grouping, ordering, and other aggregating functions, follow these steps. If you closed Visual Studio, repeat the previous exercise first. Be sure to keep Visual Studio open at the end of this exercise because you will use this application later.

1. Write a new query that groups the contacts collection by the first character of the last name.

2. Write a `foreach` statement that prints the grouping key and includes a nested `foreach` statement that prints the last name of each contact in the group.

3. Run the application by pressing Ctrl+F5. The output should look similar to Figure 13.4.

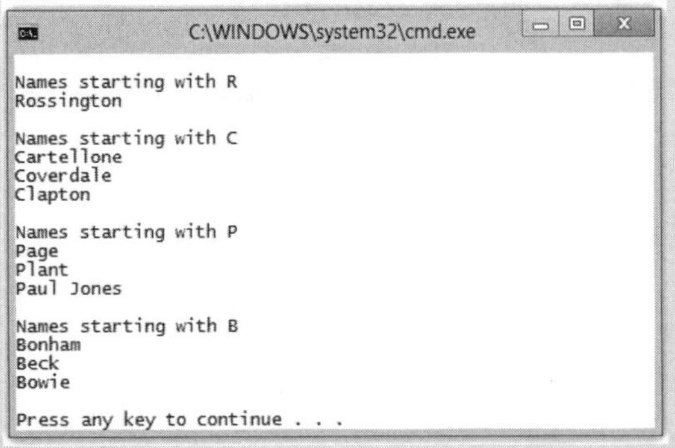

FIGURE 13.4
Grouping data.

Joining Data

LINQ also enables you to combine multiple data sources by joining them together on one or more common fields. Joining data is important for queries against data sources where their relationship cannot be followed directly. Unlike SQL, which supports joins using many different operators, join operations in LINQ are based on the equality of their keys.

Expanding on the earlier examples that used only the Contact class, you need at least two classes to perform join operations. The Contact class is shown again in Listing 13.9, along with a new JournalEntry class. Continue the assumption that the contacts list has been populated as a result of calling GetContacts and that the journal list has been populated as a result of calling GetJournalEntries.

Listing 13.9 The Contact and JournalEntry Classes

```
class Contact
{
    public int Id { get; set; }
    public string Company { get; set; }
    public string LastName { get; set; }
    public string FirstName { get; set; }
    public string Address { get; set; }
    public string City { get; set; }
    public string StateProvince { get; set; }
}

class JournalEntry
{
    public int Id { get; set; }
```

```
    public int ContactId { get; set; }
    public string Description { get; set; }
    public string EntryType { get; set; }
    public DateTime Date { get; set; }
}


IEnumerable<Contact> contacts = GetContacts();
IEnumerable<JournalEntry> journal = GetJournalEntries();
```

The simplest `join` query in LINQ is the functional equivalent of an inner join in SQL and uses the `join` clause. Unlike `joins` in SQL, which can use many different operators, `joins` in LINQ can use only an equality operator and are called **equijoins**.

Listing 13.10 shows a query against a list of `Contact` objects joined to a list of `JournalEntry` objects using the `Contact.ID` and `JournalEntry.ContactId` fields as the keys for the join.

LISTING 13.10   A LINQ Query Using `Join`

```
var result =
    from contact in contacts
    join journalEntry in journal
    on contact.Id equals journalEntry.ContactId
    select new
    {
        contact.FirstName,
        contact.LastName,
        journalEntry.Date,
        journalEntry.EntryType,
        journalEntry.Description
    };
```

The `join` clause in Listing 13.10 creates a **range variable** named `journalEntry`, which is of type `JournalEntry`, and then uses the `equals` operator to join the two data sources.

LINQ also has the concept of a group join, which has no corresponding SQL query. A group join uses the `into` keyword and creates results that have a hierarchical structure. Just as you did with the `group` clause, you need nested `foreach` statements to access the results.

CAUTION

Order Is Important

When working with LINQ joins, order is important. The data source to be joined must be on the left side of the `equals` operator and the joining data source must be on the right. In this example, `contacts` is the data source to be joined and `journal` is the joining data source.

Fortunately, the compiler can catch these types of errors and generate a compiler error. If you were to swap the parameters in the `join` clause, you would get the following compiler error:

```
The name 'journalentry' is not in scope on the left side of 'equals'. Consider
swapping the expressions on either side of 'equals'.
```

Another important thing to watch out for is that the `join` clause uses the `equals` operator, which is not the same as the equality (`==`) operator.

Listing 13.11 shows a query that joins `contacts` and `journal` and returns a result grouped by contact name. Each entry in the group has an enumerable collection of journal entries, represented by the `JournalEntries` property in the returned anonymous type.

Listing 13.11   A LINQ Query Using a Group Join

```
var result =
    from contact in contacts
    join journalEntry in journal
    on contact.Id equals journalEntry.ContactId
    into journalGroups
    select new
    {
        Name = contact.LastName + ", " + contact.FirstName,
        JournalEntries = journalGroups
    };
```

Flattening Data

Although selecting and joining data often return results in the right shape, that hierarchical shape can sometimes be cumbersome to work with. LINQ enables you to create queries that instead return the flattened data, much the same way you would when querying a SQL data source.

Suppose you were to change the `Contact` and `JournalEntry` classes so that a `List<JournalEntries>` field named `Journal` is added to the `Contact` class and the `ContactId` property is removed from the `JournalEntry` class, as shown in Listing 13.12.

LISTING 13.12   Revised `Contact` and `JournalEntry` Classes

```
class Contact
{
    public int Id { get; set; }
    public string Company { get; set; }
    public string LastName { get; set; }
    public string FirstName { get; set; }
    public string Address { get; set; }
```

```
    public string City { get; set; }
    public string StateProvince { get; set; }
    public List<JournalEntries> Journal;
}

class JournalEntry
{
    public int Id { get; set; }
    public string Description { get; set; }
    public string EntryType { get; set; }
    public DateTime Date { get; set; }
}

IEnumerable<Contact> contacts = GetContacts ();
```

You could then query the contacts collection using the following query to retrieve the list of journal entries for a specific contact, as shown in Listing 13.13.

LISTING 13.13   A LINQ Query Selecting an Enumerable Collection

```
var result =
    from contact in contacts
    where contact.Id == 1
    select contact.Journal;

foreach(var item in result)
{
    foreach(var journalEntry in item)
    {
        Console.WriteLine(journalEntry);
    }
}
```

Although this works and returns the results, it still requires nested `foreach` statements to generate the proper results. Fortunately, LINQ provides a query syntax that enables the data to be returned in a flattened manner by supporting a `select` from more than one data source. The code in Listing 13.14 shows how this query would be written so that only a single `foreach` statement is required by using multiple `from` clauses.

LISTING 13.14   A LINQ Query Selecting Flattened Data

```
var result =
    from contact in contacts
    from journalEntry in contact.Journal
    where contact.Id == 1
```

```
    select journalEntry;

foreach(var journalEntry in result)
{
    Console.WriteLine(journalEntry);
}
```

Standard Query Operator Methods

All the queries you have just seen use declarative query syntax; however, they could have also been written using standard query operator method calls, which are actually extension methods for the Enumerable class defined in the System.Linq namespace. The compiler converts query expressions using the declarative syntax to the equivalent query operator method calls.

As long as you include the System.Linq namespace with a using statement, you can see the standard query operator methods on any classes that implement the IEnumerable<T> interface, as shown in Figure 13.5.

FIGURE 13.5
LINQ extension methods in IntelliSense.

Although the declarative query syntax supports almost all query operations, there are some, such as Count or Max, which have no equivalent query syntax and must be expressed as a method call. Because each method call returns an IEnumerable, you can compose complex queries by chaining the method calls together. This is what the compiler does on your behalf when it compiles your declarative query expressions.

Listing 13.15 shows the same query from Listing 13.4 using method syntax rather than declarative syntax, and the output from both will be identical. The Where method corresponds to the where clause, whereas the Select method corresponds to the select clause.

Declarative or Method Syntax

The choice of using the declarative syntax or the method syntax is entirely personal and depends on which one you find easier to read. No matter which one you choose, the result of executing the query will be the same.

LISTING 13.15   A LINQ Query Using Method Syntax

```
var result = contacts.
    Where(contact => contact.StateProvince == "FL").
    Select(contact => new { contact.FirstName, contact.LastName });

foreach(var name in result)
{
    Console.WriteLine(name.FirstName + " " + name.LastName);
}
```

Lambdas

In Listing 13.15, you might have noticed that the arguments passed to the `Where` and `Select` methods look different from what you have used before. These arguments actually contain code rather than data types. In Hour 7, "Events and Event Handling," you learned about delegates, which enable a method to be passed as an argument to other methods, and about anonymous methods, which enable you to write an unnamed inline statement block that can be executed in a delegate invocation.

The combination of these concepts is a **lambda**, which is an anonymous function that can contain expressions and statements. Lambdas enable you to write code normally written using an anonymous method or generic delegate in a more convenient and compact way.

Lambdas and Delegates

Because lambdas are a more compact way to write a delegate, you can use them anywhere you would ordinarily have used a delegate. As a result, the lambda formal parameter types must match the corresponding delegate type exactly. The return type must also be implicitly convertible to the delegate's return type.

Although lambdas have no type, they are implicitly convertible to any compatible delegate type. That implicit conversion is what enables you to pass them without explicit assignment.

Lambdas in C# use the lambda operator (=>). If you think about a lambda in the context of a method, the left side of the operator specifies the formal parameter list, and the right side of the operator contains the method body. All the restrictions that apply to anonymous methods also apply to lambdas.

The argument to the `Where` method shown in Listing 13.15, `contact => contact.StateProvince == "FL"`, is read as "contact goes to contact.StateProvince equals FL."

TIP

Captured and Defined Variables

Lambdas also have the capability to "capture" variables, which can be local variables or parameters of the containing method. This enables the body of the lambda to access the captured variable by name. If the captured variable is a local variable, it must be definitely assigned before it can be used in the lambda. Captured parameters cannot be `ref` or `out` parameters.

Be careful, however, because variables that are captured by lambdas will not be eligible for garbage collection until the delegate that references it goes out of scope.

Any variables introduced within the lambda are not visible in the outer containing method. This also applies to the input parameter names, so you can use the same identifiers for multiple lambdas.

Expression Lambdas

When a lambda contains an expression on the right side of the operator, it is an **expression lambda** and returns the result of that expression. The basic form of an expression lambda is as follows:

```
(input parameters) => expressions
```

If there is only one input parameter, the parentheses are optional. If you have any other number of input parameters, including none, the parentheses are required.

Just as generic methods can infer the type of their type parameter, lambdas can infer the type for their input parameters. If the compiler cannot infer the type, you can specify the type explicitly. Listing 13.16 shows different forms of expression lambdas.

LISTING 13.16   Sample Expression Lambdas

```
x => Math.Pow(x, 2)

(x, y) => Math.Pow(x, y)

() => Math.Pow(2, 2)

(int x, string s) => s.Length < x
```

If you consider the expression portion of an expression lambda as the body of a method, an expression lambda contains an implicit `return` statement that returns the result of the expression.

CAUTION

Expression Lambdas Containing Method Calls

Although most of the examples in Listing 13.16 used methods on the right side of the operator, if you create lambdas that will be used in another domain, such as SQL Server, you should not use method calls because they have no meaning outside the boundary of the .NET Framework common language runtime.

TRY IT YOURSELF ▼

Working with Expression Lambdas

By following these steps, you learn how to use expression lambdas with the LINQ query methods. If you closed Visual Studio, repeat the previous exercise first.

1. Modify the declarative query expressions you wrote in the previous exercises to use the corresponding standard query method.

2. Run the application by pressing Ctrl+F5. The output should match the output from the previous exercises.

Statement Lambdas

A lambda that has one or more statements enclosed by curly braces on the right side is a **statement lambda**. The basic form of a statement lambda is as follows:

```
(input parameters) => { statement; }
```

Like expression lambdas, if there is only one input parameter, the parentheses are optional; otherwise, they are required. Statement lambdas also follow the same rules of type inference.

Although expression lambdas contain an implicit `return` statement, statement lambdas do not. You must explicitly specify the `return` statement from a statement lambda. The `return` statement causes only the implicit method represented by the lambda to return, not the enclosing method. Listing 13.17 shows different forms of statement lambdas.

LISTING 13.17 Sample Statement Lambdas

```
(x) => { return x++; };

CheckBox cb = new CheckBox();
cb.CheckedChanged += (sender, e) =>
{
   MessageBox.Show(cb.Checked.ToString());
};

Action<string> myDel = n =>
{
   string s = n + " " + "World";
   Console.WriteLine(s);
};

myDel("Hello");
```

A statement lambda cannot contain a `goto`, `break`, or `continue` statement whose target is outside the scope of the lambda itself. Similarly, normal scoping rules prevent a branch into a nested lambda from an outer lambda.

Predefined Delegates

Although lambdas are an integral component of LINQ, they can be used anywhere you can use a delegate. As a result, the .NET Framework provides many predefined delegates that can be used to represent a method that can be passed as a parameter without requiring you to first declare an explicit delegate type.

Because delegates that return a `Boolean` value are common, the .NET Framework defines a `Predicate<in T>` delegate, which is used by many of the methods in the `Array` and `List<T>` classes.

Although `Predicate<T>` defines a delegate that always returns a `Boolean` value, the `Func` family of delegates encapsulates a method that has the specified return value and 0 to 16 input parameters.

Because `Predicate<T>` and the `Func` delegates all have a return type, the family of `Action` delegates represents a method that has a `void` return type. Just like the `Func` delegates, the `Action` delegates also accept from 0 to 16 input parameters.

Deferred Execution

Unlike many traditional data query techniques, a LINQ query is not evaluated until you actually iterate over it. One advantage of this approach, called **lazy evaluation**, is that it enables the data in the original collection to change between when the query is executed and the data identified by the query is retrieved. Ultimately, this means you will always have the most up-to-date data.

Even though LINQ prefers to use lazy evaluation, any queries that use any of the aggregation functions must first iterate over all the elements. These functions, such as `Count`, `Max`, `Average`, and `First`, return a single value and execute without using an explicit `foreach` statement.

TIP

Deferred Execution and Chained Queries

Another advantage of deferred execution is that it enables queries to be efficiently chained together. Because query objects represent queries, not the results of those queries, they can easily be chained together or reused without causing potentially expensive data fetching operations.

You can also force immediate evaluation, sometimes called **greedy evaluation**, by placing the `foreach` statement immediately after the query expression or by calling the `ToList` or `ToArray` methods. You can also use either `ToList` or `ToArray` to cache the data in a single collection object.

Summary

LINQ takes the best ideas from functional languages such as Haskell and other research languages and brings them together to introduce a way to query data in a consistent manner, no matter what the original data source might be, using a simple declarative or method-based syntax. By enabling queries to be written in a source-agnostic fashion, LINQ enables access to a wide variety of data sources, including databases, XML files, and in-memory collections.

Using syntax similar to that used by SQL queries, the declarative syntax of LINQ enables a query to be a first-class language construct, just like arithmetic operations and control flow statements. LINQ is actually implemented as a set of extension methods on the `IEnumerable<T>` interface, which accept lambdas as a parameter. Lambdas, in the form of expression or statement lambdas, are a compact way to write anonymous delegates. When you first start with LINQ, you don't need to use lambdas extensively, but as you become more familiar with them, you will find that they are extremely powerful.

Q&A

Q. What is LINQ?

A. LINQ is a set of technologies that integrates query capabilities directly into the C# language and eliminates the language mismatch commonly found between working with data and working with objects by providing the same query language for each supported data source.

Q. What is a lambda expression?

A. A lambda expression represents a compact and concise way to write an anonymous delegate and can be used anywhere a traditional delegate can be used.

Workshop

Quiz

1. Is there a difference between the declarative and method syntax for LINQ?

2. When is a LINQ query executed?

3. What is the underlying delegate type for lambda expressions?

Answers

1. The choice of using the declarative syntax or the method syntax is entirely personal and depends on which one you find easier to read. No matter which one you choose, the result of executing the query will be the same.

2. By default, LINQ utilizes deferred execution of queries. This means that the query is not actually executed until the result is iterated over using a `foreach` statement.

3. Lambda expressions are inherently typeless, so they have no underlying type; however, they can be implicitly converted to any compatible delegate type.

Exercises

There are no exercises for this hour.

Using Files and Streams

What You'll Learn in This Hour:

▶ Files and directories
▶ Reading and writing data

In Hour 10, "Working with Arrays and Collections," and Hour 13, "Understanding Query Expressions," you learned how applications could work with data stored in collections and how to query and manipulate that data. Although these are common activities, many applications need to store or retrieve data from files on a disk.

The .NET Framework treats files as a stream of data. A **stream** is a sequential flow of packets of data, represented as bytes. Data streams have an underlying storage medium, typically called a **backing store**, which provides a source for the stream. Fortunately, the .NET Framework makes working with files and directories easier by the `File`, `Directory`, and `Path` classes provided by the .NET Framework.

The `System.IO` namespace contains all the classes you need to work with both buffered and unbuffered streams. Buffered streams enable the operating system to create its own internal buffer that it uses to read and write data in whatever increments are most efficient.

In this hour, you learn how to work with files, using the `File`, `Directory`, and `Path` classes to explore and manage the file system and for reading and writing files. You also learn how you can use the `Stream` class, or any of its derived classes, to perform more complex read and write operations.

Files and Directories

You can think of a file as a sequence of bytes having a well-defined name and a persistent backing store. Files are manipulated through directory paths, disk storage, and file and directory names. The .NET Framework provides several classes in the `System.IO` namespace that make working with files easy.

Working with Paths

A path is a string that provides the location of a file or directory, and can contain either absolute or relative location information. An **absolute path** fully specifies a location, whereas a **relative path** specifies a partial location. When using relative paths, the current location is the starting point when locating the file specified.

NOTE

Current Location

Every process has a processwide "current location," which is usually, but not always, the location where the process executable was loaded.

The `Path` class provides static methods that perform operations on path strings in a cross-platform manner. Although most `Path` class members don't interact with the file system, they do validate that the specified path string contains valid characters. Table 14.1 shows the commonly used methods.

TABLE 14.1 Commonly Used Methods of the `Path` Class

Method	Description
ChangeExtension	Changes the extension
Combine	Combines strings into a path
GetDirectoryName	Gets the directory name of the specified path
GetExtension	Gets the extension of the specified path
GetFileName	Gets the filename and extension of the specified path
GetFileNameWithoutExtension	Gets the filename without the extension of the specified path
GetPathRoot	Gets the root directory of the specified path
GetRandomFileName	Gets a random name
GetTempFileName	Creates a unique randomly named temporary file and returns the full path to that file
GetTempPath	Gets the path to the temporary folder

Interacting with the Windows Special Directories

The Windows operating system includes many "special" folders frequently used by applications. Typically, the operating system sets these folders; however, a user can also explicitly set them when installing a version of Windows. As a result, many might not have the same location or name on any given machine.

These special directories are listed in the `Environment.SpecialFolder` enumeration. Some of the common folders are shown in Table 14.2.

TABLE 14.2 Common `Environment.SpecialFolder` Values

Member	Description
ApplicationData	The directory that serves as a common repository for application-specific data for the current roaming user.
CommonApplicationData	The directory that serves as a common repository for application-specific data that is used by all users.
LocalApplicationData	The directory that serves as a common repository for application-specific data that is used by the current, nonroaming user.
CommonDocuments	The file system directory that contains documents common to all users. This special folder is valid for Windows NT systems, Windows 95, and Windows 98 systems with shfolder.dll installed.
Desktop	The logical Desktop rather than the physical file system location.
DesktopDirectory	The directory used to physically store file objects on the desktop. Do not confuse this directory with the desktop folder itself, which is a virtual folder.
MyDocuments	The My Documents folder. This member is equivalent to Personal.
Personal	The directory that serves as a common repository for documents.
System	The System directory.
Windows	The Windows directory or SYSROOT. This corresponds to the %windir% or %SYSTEMROOT% environment variables.

The enumeration simply provides a consistent way to reference these folders; to get the actual folder path for a given folder you should use the `Environment.GetFolderPath` method. For example, to find the path to the user's Documents directory, use the following code:

```
string path = Environment.GetFolderPath(Environment.SpecialFolder.MyDocuments);
```

The DirectoryInfo and FileInfo Classes

The DirectoryInfo and FileInfo classes both derive from the FileSystemInfo class, which contains the methods common to file and directory manipulation and can represent either a file or a directory. When a FileSystemInfo is instantiated, the directory or file information is cached, so you must refresh it using the Refresh method to ensure current information.

The DirectoryInfo class contains instance members that provide a number of properties and methods for performing common operations such as copying, moving, creating, and enumerating directories. The commonly used methods and properties of the DirectoryInfo class are listed in Table 14.3.

TABLE 14.3 Commonly Used DirectoryInfo Members

Member	Description
Create	Creates a directory
CreateSubdirectory	Creates a subdirectory on the specified path
Delete	Deletes the current directory, optionally deleting all files and subdirectories
EnumerateDirectories	Gets an enumerable collection of directory information in the current directory
EnumerateFiles	Gets an enumerable collection of file information in the current directory
EnumerateFileSystemInfos	Gets an enumerable collection of file and directory information in the current directory
Exists	Indicates if the current directory exists on disk
FullName	Gets the full path of the current directory
MoveTo	Moves the current directory, including all files and subdirectories, to a new location
Name	Gets the name of the current directory
Parent	Gets the parent directory for the current directory
Refresh	Refreshes the cached directory information
Root	Gets the root portion of the path

Listing 14.1 shows how the `DirectoryInfo` class might perform some common operations.

LISTING 14.1   Using the `DirectoryInfo` Class

```
public class DirectoryInfoExample
{
   public static void Main()
   {
      string tempPath = Path.GetTempFileName();

      DirectoryInfo directoryInfo = new DirectoryInfo(tempPath);
      try
      {
         if (directoryInfo.Exists)
         {
            Console.WriteLine("The directory already exists.");
         }
         else
         {
            directoryInfo.Create();
            Console.WriteLine("The directory was successfully created.");
            directoryInfo.Delete();
            Console.WriteLine("The directory was deleted.");
         }
      }
      catch (IOException e)
      {
         Console.WriteLine("An error occurred: {0}", e.Message);
      }
   }
}
```

The `FileInfo` class contains instance members that provide a number of properties and methods for performing common file operations such as copying, moving, creating, and opening files. The commonly used methods and properties are listed in Table 14.4.

TABLE 14.4   Commonly Used `FileInfo` Members

Member	Description
AppendText	Creates a `StreamWriter` for appending text to the current file
Attributes	Gets or sets the attributes of the current file
CopyTo	Copies the current file to a new file
Create	Creates a file
CreateText	Creates or opens a file for writing text

Member	Description
Delete	Deletes the current file
Directory	Gets the parent directory
DirectoryName	Gets the name of the parent directory
Exists	Determines if the current file exists on disk
Extension	The extension of the current file
FullName	Gets the full path of the current file
IsReadOnly	Gets or sets a value that determines if the current file is read only
Length	The size of the current file
MoveTo	Moves the current file to a new location
Name	Gets the name of the current file
Open	Opens a file
OpenRead	Opens an existing file for reading
OpenText	Opens an existing text file for reading
OpenWrite	Opens an existing file for writing
Refresh	Refreshes the cached file information
Replace	Replaces the contents of the specified file with the contents of the current file

Listing 14.2 shows how the `FileInfo` class might perform some common operations.

LISTING 14.2   Using the `FileInfo` Class

```
public class FileInfoExample
{
   public static void Main()
   {
      string tempFile = Path.GetTempFileName();

      FileInfo fileInfo = new FileInfo(tempFile);
      try
      {
         if (!fileInfo.Exists)
         {
            using (StreamWriter writer = fileInfo.CreateText())
            {
               writer.WriteLine("Line 1");
               writer.WriteLine("Line 2");
```

```
            }
        }

        fileInfo.CopyTo(Path.GetTempFileName());
        fileInfo.Delete();
    }
    catch (IOException e)
    {
        Console.WriteLine("An error occurred: {0}", e.Message);
    }
    }
}
```

NOTE

Streams Are Disposable

You should be sure to dispose of the stream when you finish using it by calling the `Close` method. You can also wrap the streams in a `using` statement, which is the preferred way to ensure the stream is closed correctly.

TRY IT YOURSELF ▼

Working with the `DirectoryInfo` and `FileInfo` Classes

To see how the `DirectoryInfo` and `FileInfo` classes can be used, follow these steps. Keep Visual Studio open at the end of this exercise because you will use this application later.

1. Create a new console application.

2. In the `Main` method of the `Program.cs` file, create a new variable of type `string` named `path` whose value is the result of the following code:

```
Path.Combine(
    Environment.GetFolderPath(Environment.SpecialFolder.Windows),
    "Web",
    "Wallpaper")
```

3. Create a new `DirectoryInfo` instance over the `path` variable you just declared.

4. In a `try-catch` statement, enumerate the directories using the `EnumerateDirectories` method and display the full name of each directory using a `foreach` statement only if the directory exists. The `catch` handler should catch an `UnauthorizedAccessException` and print the `Message` of the exception.

5. Run the application using Ctrl+F5. The output should look similar to what is shown in Figure 14.1. (This is what you should see if you run on Windows 8. Earlier versions of Windows might provide different results.)

C:\WINDOWS\system32\cmd.exe
C:\WINDOWS\Web\Wallpaper\Theme1
C:\WINDOWS\Web\Wallpaper\Windows
Press any key to continue . . .

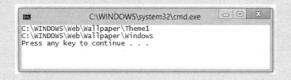

FIGURE 14.1
Results of working with `DirectoryInfo`.

6. Modify the `foreach` statement from step 4 to enumerate all the files matching the pattern "*.jpg" and print both the filename and the creation date using a nested `foreach` statement. The completed `foreach` statement should look like:

```
foreach (var d in directoryInfo.EnumerateDirectories())
{
   Console.WriteLine(d.FullName);
   foreach (var f in d.EnumerateFiles("*.jpg",SearchOption.AllDirectories))
   {
      Console.WriteLine("{0} {1}", f.Name, f.CreationTime);
   }
}
```

7. Run the application again using Ctrl+F5. The output should look similar to what is shown in Figure 14.2. (Again, this is what you should see if you run Windows 8. Earlier versions of Windows might provide different results.)

C:\WINDOWS\system32\cmd.exe
C:\WINDOWS\Web\Wallpaper\Theme1
img1.jpg 5/19/2012 5:11:53 AM
img2.jpg 5/19/2012 5:11:53 AM
img3.jpg 5/19/2012 5:11:53 AM
img4.jpg 5/19/2012 5:11:53 AM
img5.jpg 5/19/2012 5:11:53 AM
img6.jpg 5/19/2012 5:11:53 AM
C:\WINDOWS\Web\Wallpaper\Windows
img0.jpg 5/19/2012 5:33:41 AM
Press any key to continue . . .

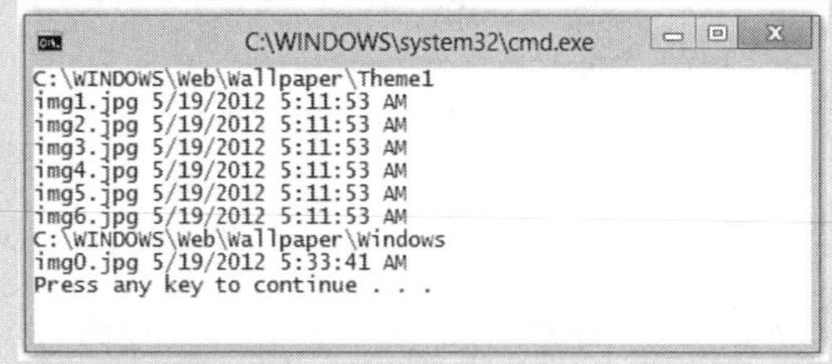

FIGURE 14.2
Results of working with `FileInfo`.

The Directory and File Classes

If you don't want to create an instance of a DirectoryInfo or FileInfo class, you can use the Directory or File class instead. These classes provide only static methods for performing the same directory and file operations provided by the DirectoryInfo and FileInfo classes.

The commonly used methods of the Directory class are shown in Table 14.5.

TABLE 14.5 Commonly Used Methods of the Directory Class

Method	Description
CreateDirectory	Creates all the directories in the specified path
Delete	Deletes the specified directory
EnumerateDirectories	Gets an enumerable collection of directory names in the specified path
EnumerateFiles	Gets an enumerable collection of filenames in the specified path
EnumerateFileSystemEntries	Gets an enumerable collection of the names of all files and subdirectories in the specified path
Exists	Indicates if the specified path exists on disk
GetCurrentDirectory	Gets the current working directory
GetDirectoryRoot	Gets the volume information, root information, or both, for the specified path
GetLogicalDrives	Gets the names of the logical drives on the current computer
GetParent	Gets the parent directory of the specified path
Move	Moves a file or a directory, including all files and subdirectories, to a new location

Listing 14.3 shows the same operations from Listing 14.1, but using the Directory class instead of the DirectoryInfo class.

LISTING 14.3 Using the Directory Class

```
public class DirectoryInfoExample
{
    public static void Main()
    {
        string tempPath = Path.GetTempFileName();
```

```
    try
    {
      if (Directory.Exists(tempPath))
      {
        Console.WriteLine("The directory already exists.");
      }
      else
      {
        Directory.CreateDirectory(path);
        Console.WriteLine("The directory was successfully created.");
        Directory.Delete(path);
        Console.WriteLine("The directory was deleted.");
      }
    }
    catch (IOException e)
    {
      Console.WriteLine("An error occurred: {0}", e.Message);
    }
  }
}
```

One significant difference between the `Directory` and `DirectoryInfo` classes is the `EnumerateFiles, EnumerateDirectories,` and `EnumerateFileSystemEntries` methods. In the `Directory` class, these methods return an `IEnumerable<string>` of just directory and filenames, whereas in the `DirectoryInfo` class, they return `IEnumerable<FileInfo>`, `IEnumerable<DirectoryInfo>`, and `IEnumerable<FileSystemInfo>`, respectively.

The commonly used methods of the `File` class are shown in Table 14.6, and Listing 14.4 shows the same operations used in Listing 14.2, but using the `File` class instead of the `FileInfo` class.

TABLE 14.6 Commonly Used Methods of the `File` Class

Method	Description
AppendAllLines	Appends lines to a file and then closes the file
AppendAllText	Appends the specified strings to a file, creating the file if it doesn't already exist
AppendText	Creates a `StreamWriter` for appending text to the current file
Copy	Copies an existing file to a new file
Create	Creates a file
CreateText	Creates or opens a file for writing text
Delete	Deletes the specified file
Exists	Determines if the specified file exists on disk

Method	Description
GetAttributes	Gets the attributes of the specified file
Move	Moves the specified file to a new location
OpenRead	Opens an existing file for reading
OpenText	Opens an existing text file for reading
OpenWrite	Opens an existing file for writing
ReadAllBytes	Opens a binary file, reads the contents into a byte array, and then closes the file
ReadAllLines	Opens a text file, reads all the lines into a string array, and then closes the file
ReadAllText	Opens a test file, reads all the lines into a string, and then closes the file
ReadLines	Reads the lines of a file
Replace	Replaces the contents of the specified file with the contents of another file
SetAttributes	Sets the attributes of the specified file
WriteAllBytes	Writes the specified bytes to a new file and then closes the file
WriteAllLines	Writes one or more strings to a new text file and then closes the file
WriteAllText	Writes a string to a new file and then closes the file

LISTING 14.4   Using the `File` Class

```
public class FileExample
{
   public static void Main()
   {
      string tempFile = Path.GetTempFileName();

      try
      {
         if (!File.Exists(tempFile))
         {
            using (StreamWriter writer = File.CreateText(tempFile))
            {
               writer.WriteLine("Line 1");
               writer.WriteLine("Line 2");
            }
         }
      }
```

```
        File.Copy(tempFile, Path.GetTempFileName());
        File.Delete(tempFile);
    }
    catch (IOException e)
    {
        Console.WriteLine("An error occurred: {0}", e.Message);
    }
  }
}
```

▼ TRY IT YOURSELF

Working with the Directory and File Classes

By following these steps, you learn how to work with the Directory and File classes. If you closed Visual Studio, repeat the previous exercise first. Be sure to keep Visual Studio open at the end of this exercise because you will use this application later.

1. Modify the code so that it calls the Exists and EnumerateDirectories methods on Directory rather than using the methods of the DirectoryInfo instance.

2. Modify the nested foreach statement to call Directory.EnumerateFiles. Because this returns a path string rather than a FileInfo, you also need to modify the statement that prints the filename and creation time to get the filename from the resulting path string and use the appropriate static method on the File class to retrieve the creation date and time.

3. Run the application using Ctrl+F5. The output should match the output generated from step 6 of the previous exercise.

Reading and Writing Data

Working with the data contained in files (by either reading or writing) uses streams, represented by the Stream class. All stream-based classes provided by the .NET Framework derive from this class. The commonly used members of the Stream class are shown in Table 14.7.

TABLE 14.7 Commonly Used Members of the Stream Class

Member	Description
CanRead	Indicates if the current stream supports reading
CanWrite	Indicates if the current stream supports writing
Close	Closes the current stream

Member	Description
CopyTo	Copies the contents of the current stream into another stream
Flush	Clears all buffers and writes any buffered data to the backing store
Read	Reads a sequence of bytes from the current stream
Write	Writes a sequence of bytes to the current stream

Binary Files

When you aren't certain about the content of a file, it is usually best to treat it as a **binary file**, which is simply a stream of bytes. To read data from a binary file, you use the static `OpenRead` method of the `File` class, which returns a `FileStream`:

```
FileStream input = File.OpenRead(Path.GetTempFileName());
```

You can then use the `Read` method on the resulting `FileStream` to read data into a buffer that you provide. A **buffer** is simply an array of bytes that holds the data returned by the `Read` method. You pass the buffer, the number of bytes to read, and an offset into the buffer at which data then will be stored. The `Read` method reads the number of bytes specified from the backing store into the buffer and returns the total number of bytes actually read:

```
byte[] buffer = new byte[1024];
int bytesRead = input.Read(buffer, 0, 1024);
```

Of course, reading from a stream isn't the only operation you can perform. Writing binary data to a stream is also a common activity and is accomplished in a similar manner. You first open a binary file for writing using the `OpenWrite` method of the `File` class and then use the `Write` method on the resulting `FileStream` to write a buffer of data to the backing store. The `Write` method is passed the buffer containing the data to write, the offset into the buffer at which to start reading, and the number of bytes to write:

```
FileStream output = File.OpenWrite(Path.GetTempFileName());
output.Write(buffer, 0, bytesRead);
```

Listing 14.5 shows a complete example of reading data from one binary file and writing it to another. This example continues to read and write bytes until the `Read` method indicates that it has read no more bytes by returning 0.

LISTING 14.5   Binary Reads and Writes

```
public class BinaryReaderWriter
{
   const int BufferSize = 1024;

   public static void Main()
   {
      string tempPath = Path.GetTempFileName();
      string tempPath2 = Path.GetTempFileName();

      if (File.Exists(tempPath))
      {
         using (FileStream input = File.OpenRead(tempPath))
         {
            byte[] buffer = new byte[BufferSize];
            int bytesRead;

            using (FileStream output = File.OpenWrite(tempPath2))
            {
               while ((bytesRead = input.Read(buffer, 0, BufferSize)) > 0)
               {
                  output.Write(buffer, 0, bytesRead);
               }
            }
         }
      }
   }
}
```

▼ TRY IT YOURSELF

Binary Reads and Writes

To perform binary reads and writes using the `File` and `FileStream` classes, follow these
steps.

1. Open the `BinaryReadWrite` project in Visual Studio.

2. Open `Program.cs` by double-clicking the file.

3. The `Main` method already contains some code, including an `if` statement similar to the
   one shown in Listing 14.5. Modify the statement block of the `if` statement to read from
   the file indicated in the `fileName` field and write to a temporary file. Use the code shown
   in Listing 14.5 as a guide.

4. Modify the `while` statement to increment the `bufferCounter` field after each `Write`.

5. Run the application using Ctrl+F5. The output should look similar to what is shown in Figure 14.3.

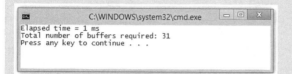

FIGURE 14.3
Results of performing binary reads and writes.

6. Modify the value of `BufferSize` and run the application again using Ctrl+F5. Observe how different values of `BufferSize` change the total number of buffers required.

Buffered Streams

Using the basic `FileStream` from the previous example, you needed to provide the buffer used for reading and the size of that buffer. In many cases, it might be more efficient for you to let the operating system determine the number of bytes to read.

The `BufferedStream` class enables the operating system to create its own internal buffer and fill it using whatever increments it thinks are most efficient. It still fills a buffer you provide in the increment you provide, but that buffer is filled from the internal buffer not directly from the backing store. To create a buffered stream, you construct a new `BufferedStream` instance from another `Stream`, as shown in Listing 14.6, which shows the code from the previous example using `BufferedStream` instances for the input and output streams.

LISTING 14.6   Buffered Reads and Writes

```
public class BufferedReaderWriter
{
    const int BufferSize = 1024;

    public static void Main()
    {
        string tempPath = Path.GetTempFileName();
        string tempPath2 = Path.GetTempFileName();

        if (File.Exists(tempPath))
        {
            using (BufferedStream input = new
                BufferedStream(File.OpenRead(tempPath)))
```

```
        {
            byte[] buffer = new byte[BufferSize];
            int bytesRead;

            using (BufferedStream output = new
                BufferedStream(File.OpenWrite(tempPath2)))
            {
                while ((bytesRead = input.Read(buffer, 0, BufferSize)) > 0)
                {
                    output.Write(buffer, 0, bytesRead);
                }
            }
        }
    }
}
```

Text Files

Using the Read and Write methods on the Stream class works not only for binary files but also for **text files**, which are files containing nothing but text data. The problem is that you read and write a byte array rather than strings, which isn't convenient. To make working with text files easier, the .NET Framework provides the StreamReader and StreamWriter classes.

Although StreamReader provides a Read method that reads one character at a time from the backing store, it also provides a ReadLine method that reads a line of characters as a string. A line is defined as a sequence of characters followed by a line feed ("\n"), a carriage return ("\r"), or a carriage return-line feed ("\r\n"). If the end of the input stream is reached, ReadLine returns null; otherwise, it returns the line of characters, excluding the terminating characters. To write text data, you can use the WriteLine method of the StreamWriter class.

Listing 14.7 shows an example of reading and writing text data.

LISTING 14.7   Reading and Writing Text Data

```
public class TextReaderWriter
{
    public static void Main()
    {
        string tempPath = Path.GetTempFileName();
        string tempPath2 = Path.GetTempFileName();

        if (File.Exists(tempPath))
        {
```

```
        using (StreamReader reader = File.OpenText(tempPath))
        {
            string buffer = null;
            using (StreamWriter writer = new StreamWriter(tempPath2))
            {
                while ((buffer = reader.ReadLine()) != null)
                {
                    writer.WriteLine(buffer);
                }
            }
        }
    }
  }
}
```

TRY IT YOURSELF ▼

Buffered Reads and Writes

To perform text reads and writes using the `File`, `StreamReader`, and `StreamWriter` classes, follow these steps:

1. Open the `TextReadWrite` project in Visual Studio.

2. Open `Program.cs` by double-clicking the file.

3. The `Main` method already contains some code, including an `if` statement similar to the one shown in Listing 14.3. Modify the statement block of the `if` statement to read and write to the file indicated in the `fileName` field. Use the code shown in Listing 14.7 as a guide.

4. Modify the `while` statement to increment the `bufferCounter` field after each `Write`.

5. Run the application using Ctrl+F5. The output should look similar to what is shown in Figure 14.4.

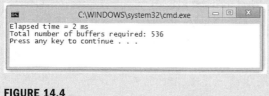

FIGURE 14.4
Results of performing buffered reads and writes.

Reading and Writing Data Using the File Class

Because reading and writing data, whether it is text or binary, from files is a common task, the File class provides several methods that make this even more convenient than working directly with streams.

To read or write binary data, you can use the ReadAllBytes and WriteAllBytes methods, respectively. These methods open the file, read or write the bytes, and then close the file. The code shown in Listing 14.8 performs the same actions as Listing 14.5 using the ReadAllBytes and WriteAllBytes methods.

LISTING 14.8 Binary Reads and Writes Using the File Class

```
public class BinaryReaderWriterFile
{
    public static void Main()
    {
        string tempPath = Path.GetTempFileName();
        string tempPath2 = Path.GetTempFileName();

        if (File.Exists(tempPath))
        {
            byte[] data = File.ReadAllBytes(tempPath);
            File.WriteAllBytes(tempPath2, data);
        }
    }
}
```

Reading and writing text data is just as easy using the ReadAllLines and ReadAllText methods for reading and the WriteAllLines and WriteAllText methods for writing. The ReadAllLines method reads all the lines from the file into a string array, where each line is a new element in the array, whereas the ReadAllText reads all the lines into a single string.

The WriteAllLines method writes each element of a string array to a file, whereas the WriteAllText method writes the contents of a string to the file. Both of these create a new file or overwrite the file if it already exists. To append text to an existing file, you can use the AppendAllLines or AppendAllText methods. If you need to open a stream, you can use the AppendText method.

The code shown in Listing 14.9 performs the same actions as Listing 14.7 using the ReadAllLines and WriteAllLines methods.

LISTING 14.9 Text Reads and Writes Using `ReadAllLines` and `WriteAllLines`

```
public class TextReaderWriterFile
{
   public static void Main()
   {
      string tempPath = Path.GetTempFileName();
      string tempPath2 = Path.GetTempFileName();

      if (File.Exists(tempPath))
      {
         string[] data = File.ReadAllLines(tempPath);
         File.WriteAllLines(tempPath2, data);
      }
   }
}
```

The one drawback to using `ReadAllLines`, or even `ReadAllText`, is that the entire file must first be read into memory. To resolve this issue and return an `IEnumerable<string>` collection, you can use the `ReadLines` method. Because this method returns an `IEnumerable<string>`, you can start to enumerate the returned collection immediately, before the whole collection is returned. The code shown in Listing 14.10 performs the same actions as Listing 14.9 using the `File.ReadLines` method.

LISTING 14.10 Text Reads and Writes Using `WriteAllLines` and `ReadLines`

```
public class TextReaderWriterFile
{
   public static void Main()
   {
      string tempPath = Path.GetTempFileName();
      string tempPath2 = Path.GetTempFileName();

      if (File.Exists(tempPath))
      {
         File.WriteAllLines(tempPath, File.ReadLines(tempPath2));
      }
   }
}
```

Summary

In this hour, you learned how to work with streams to read and write text and binary files. Although you focused only on using the `FileStream` and `StreamWriter` classes, the mechanisms used for reading and writing using `FileStream` is essentially the same for any `Stream` derived class.

You also learned how the .NET Framework makes working with files, directories, and string paths simple through the `File`, `Directory`, `FileInfo`, `DirectoryInfo`, and `Path` classes.

Q&A

Q. **What is a stream?**

A. A stream is a sequential flow of packets of data represented as bytes. Data streams have an underlying storage medium, typically called a backing store, which provides a source for the stream.

Q. **What is the difference between a relative path and an absolute path?**

A. An absolute path fully specifies a location, whereas a relative path specifies a partial location. When using relative paths, the current location is the starting point when locating the file specified.

Q. **What is the `FileSystemInfo` class used for?**

A. The `FileSystemInfo` class contains methods common to file and directory manipulation and can represent either a file or directory. It is the base class for the `DirectoryInfo` and `FileInfo` classes.

Q. **How is the `Directory` class different from the `DirectoryInfo` class?**

A. The `Directory` class provides only static methods, whereas the `DirectoryInfo` class provides only instance methods and caches the information retrieved for the specified directory.

Q. **What is the difference between a binary file and a text file?**

A. A binary file is simply a stream of bytes, whereas a text file is known to contain only text data.

Workshop

Quiz

1. How do the `Path` class members interact directly with the file system?

2. What method should be used on a `FileSystemInfo` instance to update the cached information it contains?

3. What is the difference between the `EnumerateDirectories` method on the `DirectoryInfo` and `Directory` classes?

4. What is the return type of the `File.OpenRead` method?

5. What is the return type of the `File.OpenText` method?

6. What is the difference between the `File.ReadAllLines` method and the `File.ReadLines` method?

Answers

1. Most `Path` class members don't interact with the file system; they do, however, validate that the specified path string contains valid characters.

2. The `FileSystemInfo` class contains a `Refresh` method that should be used to update the cached file or directory information.

3. The `DirectoryInfo.EnumerateDirectories` returns an `IEnumerable<DirectoryInfo>`, whereas `Directory.EnumerateDirectories` returns an `IEnumerable<string>`.

4. The `File.OpenRead` method returns a `FileStream` opened to the specified file for reading only.

5. The `File.OpenText` method returns a `StreamReader` opened to the specified text file.

6. `File.ReadAllLines` must read the entire file into memory and returns a string array containing the lines whereas `File.ReadLines` returns an `IEnumerable<string>` enabling you to start enumerating the collection before the entire file is read.

Exercises

1. Modify the `PhotoCollection` class of the `PhotoViewer` project by changing the data type of the `path` field to be a `DirectoryInfo`. Change the `Path` property so that the `get` accessor returns the value of the `FullName` property and the `set` accessor creates a new `DirectoryInfo` instance from `value` after validating that `value` is not `null` or an empty string. Also change the constructor so that it uses the `set` accessor rather than setting the backing field directly.

2. Add a private method named Update to the PhotoCollection class and call it from the constructor right after the Path property is set. This method should perform the following actions:

   a. Clear the collection.

   b. If path.Exists is true, enumerate over all files in the directory whose extension is ".jpg" and add a new Photo instance to the collection. This code should be in a try-catch block that catches a DirectoryNotFoundException. The catch handler should contain the following code:

   ```
   System.Windows.MessageBox.Show("No Such Directory");
   ```

HOUR 15
Working with XML

What You'll Learn in This Hour:

▶ Understanding the XML DOM

▶ Using LINQ to XML

▶ Selecting and querying XML

▶ Modifying XML

Although working with text files is common and made easier through the classes provided by the System.IO namespace, these classes do not enable you to easily work with and manipulate structured text in the form of XML. XML, which stands for Extensible Markup Language, is a simple and flexible text format that enables the exchange of data in a platform-independent manner.

The use of XML as a data exchange format is prevalent not just in the .NET Framework, but in other Microsoft products as well. The .NET Framework uses it for web services through Simple Object Access Protocol (SOAP) and Windows Communication Foundation (WCF), as the file format for Windows Presentation Foundation (WPF) and Silverlight Extensible Application Markup Language (XAML) files, the file format for Windows Workflow Foundation (WF) files, and as part of ADO.NET.

Even though XML is text-based and readable by humans, there must be a way to programmatically manipulate the XML. This is accomplished using an XML parser. The .NET Framework provides two XML parsers. One is a stream-based parser that reads the XML stream as it goes; the other is a tree-based parser that must read the entire stream into memory before constructing the tree.

In this hour, you learn about the different XML classes provided by the .NET Framework and how to use them to create and manipulate XML files.

Understanding the XML DOM

For you to programmatically read and manipulate an XML document, it must be represented in memory through the XML Document Object Model (DOM). The DOM provides a common and structured way XML data is represented in memory and is most commonly used for reading XML data into memory to change its structure, add or remove elements, or modify the data contained in an element.

A sample XML document is shown in Listing 15.1 and the corresponding DOM structure is shown in Figure 15.1.

LISTING 15.1   XML Data

```
<books>
   <book>
      <title>Sams Teach Yourself C# 5.0 in 24 Hours</title>
      <isbn-10>0-672-33684-7</isbn-10>
      <author>Dorman</author>
      <price currency="US">34.99</price>
      <publisher>
         <name>Sams Publishing</name>
         <state>IN</state>
      </publisher>
   </book>
</books>
```

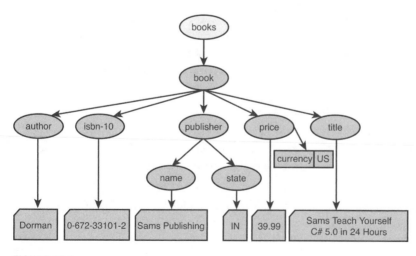

FIGURE 15.1
XML DOM representation.

In Figure 15.1, each circle represents an element in the XML data. The lighter circle represents the **document root**, or starting, element. The document root node is the top-level node containing the document itself. All nodes except the document root have a single parent node, which is the node directly above them. When nodes have the same parent node, such as the author, isbn-10, publisher, price, and title nodes, they are **child nodes**, or **descendent nodes**, of that parent. Nodes all at the same level are **sibling nodes**.

Using LINQ to XML

LINQ to XML exposes the XML DOM through LINQ extension methods that enable you to manipulate and query XML documents that have been loaded into memory. All the classes needed to create and manipulate XML documents using LINQ to XML are contained in the System.Xml.Linq namespace. The most commonly used classes are shown in Figure 15.2.

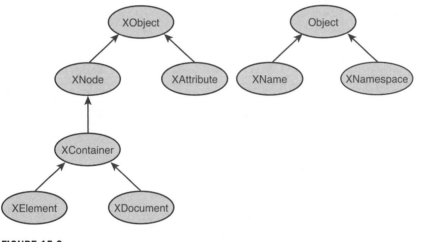

FIGURE 15.2
LINQ to XML object model.

XDocument

The XDocument class represents an XML document instance. Unless you need to specify document type declarations, processing instructions (used by the XML parser), or top-level comments, you rarely interact with an XDocument instance. Instead, you should use the XElement class.

XElement **and** XAttribute

The XElement class, which represents an XML element, is one of the most commonly used classes and provides many useful methods and properties used for creating, modifying, and querying the XML data. An XML attribute is a name-value pair associated with an XML element, represented by the XAttribute class. Unlike elements, they are not nodes in the XML tree. Because attributes are simply name-value pairs associated with an element, they must have a name that is unique only to that element.

The XElement class contains a list of the attributes for that element. The most commonly used properties of the XAttribute class are NextAttribute and PreviousAttribute, which are useful for browsing the sequence of attributes on an element.

The code to create the XML from Listing 15.1 using XElement instances is shown in Listing 15.2.

LISTING 15.2 Creating XML Using LINQ to XML

```
XElement document = new XElement("books",
   new XElement("book",
      new XElement("title", "Sams Teach Yourself C# 5.0 in 24 Hours"),
      new XElement("isbn-10", "0-672-33684-7"),
      new XElement("author", "Dorman"),
      new XElement("price", new XAttribute("currency", "US"), 34.99M),
      new XElement("publisher",
         new XElement("name", "Sams Publishing"),
         new XElement("state", "IN")))));
```

In contrast, using the standard DOM approach, supported by the classes in the System.Xml namespace, is shown in Listing 15.3.

LISTING 15.3 Creating XML Using XML DOM

```
XmlDocument document = new XmlDocument();

XmlElement booksElement = document.CreateElement("books");
   XmlElement bookElement = document.CreateElement("book");
      XmlElement titleElement = document.CreateElement("title");
      titleElement.InnerText = "Sams Teach Yourself C# 5.0 in 24 Hours";
      XmlElement isbn10Element = document.CreateElement("isbn-10");
      isbn10Element.InnerText = "0-672-33684-7";
      XmlElement authorElement = document.CreateElement("author");
      authorElement.InnerText = "Dorman";
      XmlElement priceElement = document.CreateElement("price");
      priceElement.InnerText = "34.99";
         XmlAttribute currencyAttribute = document.CreateAttribute("currency");
         currencyAttribute.Value = "US";
      priceElement.Attributes.Append(currencyAttribute);

   XmlElement publisherElement = document.CreateElement("publisher");
      XmlElement publisherNameElement = document.CreateElement("name");
      publisherNameElement.InnerText = "Sams Publishing";
```

```
        XmlElement publisherStateElement = document.CreateElement("state");
        publisherStateElement.InnerText = "IN";

booksElement.AppendChild(bookElement);
bookElement.AppendChild(titleElement);
bookElement.AppendChild(isbn10Element);
bookElement.AppendChild(authorElement);
bookElement.AppendChild(priceElement);
bookElement.AppendChild(publisherElement);

publisherElement.AppendChild(publisherNameElement);
publisherElement.AppendChild(publisherStateElement);

document.AppendChild(booksElement);
```

As you can see, the code in Listing 15.3 is almost three times as long and is much more difficult to read and understand. In addition, if you look at the declaration of the price element in Listing 15.2, you can set the value as a decimal directly, whereas the same code in Listing 15.3 must set the value as a string. This difference becomes important when you retrieve the value. Both the XElement and XAttribute classes enable you to read their contents using a direct cast to the desired type. If the conversion specified by the direct cast fails, it throws a FormatException.

Listing 15.4 shows two ways you could retrieve the value of the price element.

LISTING 15.4   Retrieving the Value of an **XElement** Using a Direct Cast

```
decimal price = (Decimal)(document.Element("book").Element("price"));
price = (Decimal)document.XPathSelectElement("//price");
```

NOTE

XML Character Encoding

The XElement and XAttribute classes automatically handle encoding and decoding text that contains invalid XML characters. Given the following statement

```
XElement comments = new XElement("comments",
"This line contains special characters <node> & </node>");
```

the result is automatically encoded as follows:

```
<comments>This line contains special characters &lt;node&gt; &amp; &lt;/node&gt;</
comments>
```

When the value is retrieved, it is automatically decoded.

▼ TRY IT YOURSELF

Creating XML Documents

By following these steps, you see how to use the LINQ to XML classes to create XML documents. Keep Visual Studio open at the end of this exercise because you will use this application later.

1. Create a new console application.

2. In the `Main` method of the `Program.cs` file, implement the code in Listing 15.2.

3. Write a statement that will print the content of the `XElement` created in step 2.

4. Run the application using Ctrl+F5. The output should look like Figure 15.3.

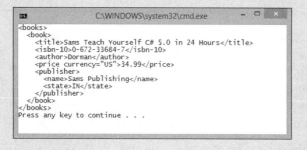

FIGURE 15.3
Creating XML documents.

NOTE

SetElementValue and SetAttributeValue

Using the constructor syntax shown in Listing 15.2 is not the only way to create XML. You can also use the `SetElementValue` and `SetAttributeValue` methods provided by the `XElement` class.

These methods make it easy to maintain a list of name-value pairs as a set of children elements or attributes, allowing you to add, modify, or delete pairs. If the name provided does not already exist as a child element or attribute, it will be created for you; otherwise, its value will be changed to the value you specified. If the value is `null`, the element or attribute is removed. When modifying or removing child elements or attributes, the first one with the specified name is modified or removed.

The following code shows how to create the same XML as produced in Listing 15.2, but uses the `SetElementValue` and `SetAttributeValue` methods:

```
XElement document = new XElement("books",
    new XElement("book",
        new XElement("publisher")));

XElement bookElement = document.Element("book");
XElement publisherElement = document.Element("publisher");
```

```
bookElement.SetElementValue("title",
    "Sams Teach Yourself C# 5.0 in 24 Hours");
bookElement.SetElementValue("isbn-10", "0-672-33684-7");
bookElement.SetElementValue("author", "Dorman");
bookElement.SetElementValue("price", 34.99M);
bookElement.Element("price").
    SetAttributeValue("currency", "US");

publisherElement.SetElementValue("name", "Sams Publishing");
publisherElement.SetElementValue("state", "IN");
```

XName **and** XNamespace

An XML name represents the name of an element or attribute in an XML document and consists of two parts: an XML namespace and a local name. An XML namespace enables you to uniquely qualify the names of elements and attributes to help avoid conflicts between different parts of an XML document. When you have declared an XML namespace, you can select a local name that is unique only within that namespace.

When using XML namespaces, you make use of XML prefixes, allowing you to create a shortcut for an XML namespace. Although XML prefixes can make the XML document more readable, they add complexity because they depend on their context to have meaning. The .NET Framework provides the XNamespace class to represent XML namespaces.

The XName class represents the local name. Throughout LINQ to XML, wherever an XML name is required, an XName is used. Fortunately, XName contains an implicit conversion from string, so you rarely work directly with an XName. Every XName contains an XNamespace. If the element is not in a namespace, the XNamespace is XNamespace.None.

NOTE

XML Namespaces

XML namespace declarations have the same syntax as XML attributes, so it is common to think of them as attributes even though they are not. LINQ to XML represents namespaces in the XML tree as attributes to simplify the programming interface. If you need to determine if an attribute is actually a namespace declaration, you can use the IsNamespaceDeclaration property.

The code in Listing 15.5 shows creating the same XML from Listing 15.2 using a namespace.

LISTING 15.5   Creating XML with a Namespace Using LINQ to XML

```
XNamespace ns = "http://www.w3.org/1999/xhtml";
XElement document = new XElement(ns + "books",
    new XElement(ns + "book",
```

```
    new XElement(ns + "title", "Sams Teach Yourself C# 5.0 in 24 Hours"),
    new XElement(ns + "isbn-10", "0-672-33684-7"),
    new XElement(ns + "author", "Dorman"),
    new XElement(ns + "price", new XAttribute("currency", "US"), 34.99M),
    new XElement(ns + "publisher",
        new XElement(ns + "name", "Sams Publishing"),
        new XElement(ns + "state", "IN"))));
```

This produces the XML shown in Listing 15.6.

LISTING 15.6   XML Data

```xml
<books xmlns="http://www.w3.org/1999/xhtml">
    <book>
        <title>Sams Teach Yourself C# 5.0 in 24 Hours</title>
        <isbn-10>0-672-33684-7</isbn-10>
        <author>Dorman</author>
        <price currency="US">34.99</price>
        <publisher>
            <name>Sams Publishing</name>
            <state>IN</state>
        </publisher>
    </book>
</books>
```

Even though the LINQ to XML classes automatically handle namespace declarations, it might be necessary to control how the namespace is represented in the XML data by providing a namespace prefix. This can be accomplished by explicitly defining the prefix to use for the namespace by including an xmlns attribute, as shown in Listing 15.7.

LISTING 15.7   Creating XML with a Namespace Prefix Using LINQ to XML

```csharp
XNamespace ns = "http://www.w3.org/1999/xhtml";
XElement document = new XElement(ns + "books",
    new XAttribute(XNamespace.Xmlns + "ns", ns),
    new XElement(ns + "book",
        new XElement(ns + "title", "Sams Teach Yourself C# 5.0 in 24 Hours"),
        new XElement(ns + "isbn-10", "0-672-33684-7"),
        new XElement(ns + "author", "Dorman"),
        new XElement(ns + "price", new XAttribute("currency", "US"), 34.99M),
        new XElement(ns + "publisher",
            new XElement(ns + "name", "Sams Publishing"),
            new XElement(ns + "state", "IN"))));
```

This produces the XML shown in Listing 15.8.

LISTING 15.8   XML Data with a `Namespace` Prefix

```
<ns:books xmlns:ns="http://www.w3.org/1999/xhtml">
    <ns:book>
        <ns:title>Sams Teach Yourself C# 5.0 in 24 Hours</ns:title>
        <ns:isbn-10>0-672-33684-7</ns:isbn-10>
        <ns:author>Dorman</ns:author>
        <ns:price currency="US">34.99</ns:price>
        <ns:publisher>
            <ns:name>Sams Publishing</ns:name>
            <ns:state>IN</ns:state>
        </ns:publisher>
    </ns:book>
</ns:books>
```

When you work with a document that uses namespaces, you usually access the namespaces through the URI and not through the namespace prefix. This allows you to work with the fully qualified name, also called the **expanded name**, which has the following form:

```
{namespacename}name
```

For example, the expanded name for the title element from Listing 15.6 is as follows:

```
{http://www.w3.org/1999/xhtml}title
```

NOTE

Atomization

`XNamespace` objects are **atomized**, which means that if two objects have exactly the same URI, they will share the same instance. Although it is possible to use the expanded name when creating an `XElement` or `XAttribute` instance, doing so has potential performance implications. Each time a string containing an expanded name is encountered, the string must be parsed to find the atomized namespace and name.

TRY IT YOURSELF ▼

Working with XML Namespaces

To modify the code you wrote in the previous exercise to work with an XML namespace, follow these steps. If you closed Visual Studio, repeat the previous exercise first. Be sure to keep Visual Studio open at the end of this exercise because you will use this application later.

1. Add a new statement that declares an `XNamespace` instance that defines a namespace of `http://www.w3.org/TR/html4`.

2. Modify the statements you previously wrote to include the namespace you just declared with a namespace prefix of `ns` and include the namespace as part of the element names.

3. Run the application using Ctrl+F5. The output should look like Figure 15.4.

FIGURE 15.4
Creating XML documents with namespaces.

Selecting and Querying XML

When you have an XML document represented in memory through an `XElement` instance, you almost always need to select or query information. All classes that derive from `XNode` provide methods and properties for navigating directly to specific nodes in the XML tree.

The `FirstNode` and `LastNode` properties return the first and last child node, respectively, whereas the `NextNode` and `PreviousNode` properties enable you to move forward and backward through the collection of nodes. The `Parent` property enables you to navigate directly to the parent node.

Listing 15.9 shows an example of using these navigation properties with a simplified version of the XML presented in Listing 15.1.

LISTING 15.9 Using the Navigation Properties of `XElement`

```
XElement document = new XElement("book",
   new XElement("title", "Sams Teach Yourself C# 5.0 in 24 Hours"),
   new XElement("isbn-10", "0-672-33684-7"),
   new XElement("author", "Dorman"),
   new XElement("price", new XAttribute("currency", "US"), 34.99M));

Console.WriteLine(document.LastNode);
Console.WriteLine(document.FirstNode);
```

```
Console.WriteLine(document.LastNode.Parent);
Console.WriteLine(document.LastNode.PreviousNode);
Console.WriteLine(document.FirstNode.NextNode);
```

XElement also provides the FirstAttribute and LastAttribute properties, which return the first and last attribute associated with the XElement they are invoked from. If the element contains no attributes, both of these properties will return null; if the element contains only one attribute they both return the same value. When you have retrieved the first or last attribute, you can use the NextAttribute and PreviousAttribute properties to move forward and backward through the collection of attributes.

Although these properties are convenient, they do not offer much flexibility. If you think of every node in the XML tree being a sequence of nodes, it would be possible to use the same LINQ queries you used in Hour 13, "Understanding Query Expressions." This is entirely possible because each collection of nodes is an IEnumerable<T> instance.

Listing 15.10 shows how to perform a simple LINQ query against the XElement created from Listing 15.2.

LISTING 15.10   A LINQ Query over an XElement

```
foreach (var o in document.Elements().
   Where(e => (string)e.Element("author") == "Dorman"))
{
   Console.WriteLine(o);
}
```

The code shown in Listing 15.10 makes use of the Elements method to return an IEnumerable<XElement> sequence of all child elements of the current XElement. In this case, all the child elements are returned; however, if a name were provided as an argument, only those child elements with the same name would be returned.

NOTE

LINQ to XML and XPath Queries

When using the traditional XML DOM classes provided in System.XML, you must use XPath queries to select node collections or single nodes. In LINQ to XML, this is no longer necessary but is supported through a set of extension methods provided by the System.Xml.XPath namespace.

These extension methods are as follows:

▶ **CreateNavigator**—Creates an XPathNavigator for an XNode

▶ **XPathEvaluate**—Evaluates an XPath expression, returning an object containing the result of the expression

▶ **XPathSelectElement**—Selects an `XElement` using an XPath expression

▶ **XPathSelectElements**—Selects a collection of elements using an XPath expression

The lambda expression provided to the `Where` method restricts the resulting sequence to those containing an author element whose value is equal to the string "Dorman". The `Element` method is used to return the first `XElement` whose name corresponds to the name provided.

Selecting attributes is just as easy through the `Attributes` and `Attribute` method. The `Attribute` method returns the single attribute whose name corresponds to the name provided, or `null` if no matching attribute is found. The `Attributes` method returns an `IEnumerable<XAttribute>` sequence of attributes for the current `XElement`. Although the `Attributes` method can accept a name as an argument, it always returns either an empty collection if a matching attribute is not found or a collection of one because attributes must be uniquely named within each element.

▼ TRY IT YOURSELF

Selecting XML

By following these steps, you see how to select specific elements using LINQ to XML. If you closed Visual Studio, repeat the previous exercise first. Be sure to keep Visual Studio open at the end of this exercise because you will use this application later.

1. Replace the statement that prints the content of the `XElement` instance from the previous exercise with the code shown in Listing 15.10. Be sure to change the name of the element you are querying to include the `XNamespace`.

2. Run the application using Ctrl+F5. The output should look like Figure 15.5.

FIGURE 15.5
Selecting XML using a LINQ query.

3. Add a new XML file named `books.xml` that contains the XML shown in Listing 15.11.

4. Modify the `XElement` instance to load data, using the `Load` method, from the file named `books.xml`.

5. Modify the `foreach` statement to print only the `title` for all `book` elements.

6. Run the application again using Ctrl+F5. The output should look like Figure 15.6.

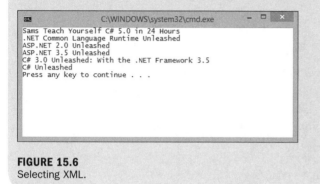

```
C:\WINDOWS\system32\cmd.exe
Sams Teach Yourself C# 5.0 in 24 Hours
.NET Common Language Runtime Unleashed
ASP.NET 2.0 Unleashed
ASP.NET 3.5 Unleashed
C# 3.0 Unleashed: With the .NET Framework 3.5
C# Unleashed
Press any key to continue . . .
```

FIGURE 15.6
Selecting XML.

Putting all this together, it becomes possible to perform rather complex queries that can return XML that has been **reshaped**, or converted from one structural representation to another.

For example, the XML shown in Listing 15.11 can be reshaped to what is shown in Listing 15.12.

LISTING 15.11   Source XML

```
<books>
  <book title="Sams Teach Yourself C# 5.0 in 24 Hours" author="Dorman" />
  <book title=".NET Common Language Runtime Unleashed" author="Burton" />
  <book title="ASP.NET 2.0 Unleashed" author="Walther" />
  <book title="ASP.NET 3.5 Unleashed" author="Walther" />
  <book title="C# 3.0 Unleashed: With the .NET Framework 3.5" author="Mayo" />
  <book title="C# Unleashed" author="Mayo" />
</books>
```

LISTING 15.12   Destination XML

```
<books>
  <author name="Dorman">
    <book title="Sams Teach Yourself C# 5.0 in 24 Hours"/>
  </author>
  <author name="Burton">
    <book title=".NET Common Language Runtime Unleashed" />
  </author>
  <author name="Walther">
    <book title="ASP.NET 2.0 Unleashed" />
```

```
    <book title="ASP.NET 3.5 Unleashed" />
  </author>
  <author name="Mayo">
    <book title="C# 3.0 Unleashed: With the .NET Framework 3.5" />
    <book title="C# Unleashed" />
  </author>
</books>
```

When using the LINQ to XML query shown in Listing 15.13, assume it has already been loaded into an XElement named books.

LISTING 15.13   Transforming the Source XML Using a LINQ Query

```
XElement booksByAuthor = new XElement("books",
    from book in books.Elements("book")
    group book by (string)book.Attribute("author") into author
    select new XElement("author", new XAttribute("name", (string)author.Key),
        from book in author
        select new XElement("book",
            new XAttribute("title", (string)book.Attribute("title")))));
```

Modifying XML

Although creating and selecting XML is important, it is equally important to modify that XML. This can be accomplished quite easily using methods provided by XNode and its derived classes. When modifying XML, the technique used to navigate to the node being changed influences when the modification occurs. When using the properties shown in the beginning of the previous section (such as FirstNode or LastNode), the result occurs at the time you invoke it. If you remove or replace a node, the action is taken immediately within the XML tree held in memory. When using queries over XML, the modification methods are applied to the query expression result at the time the query is enumerated. This follows the default LINQ behavior of deferred query execution.

Earlier you saw how the SetElementValue and SetAttributeValue methods can be used to add a new element or attribute, remove an element or attribute, or change the value of an existing element or attribute. You can also use the SetValue method to change the value of the current element or attribute. The code shown in Listing 15.14 uses SetValue to change the content of the price element.

LISTING 15.14   Using `SetValue`

```
XElement books = XElement.Load("books.xml");
XElement book = books.Elements("book").
   FirstOrDefault(b => (string)b.Element("author") == "Dorman");
book.Element("price").SetValue(30.99);
```

Replacing data is just as simple and uses the `ReplaceAll`, `ReplaceAttributes`, `ReplaceNodes`, or `ReplaceWith` methods. The `ReplaceAll` method replaces all children nodes and attributes of the current element, whereas the `ReplaceAttributes` and `ReplaceNodes` methods replace all the attributes and all the children nodes, respectively.

CAUTION

`ReplaceWith` and Children Nodes

The `ReplaceWith` method will replace only the current element with the new element. If the element you are replacing has any children, those children will not automatically be included as children of the new element.

The `ReplaceWith` method replaces only the current element with the element specified. The code shown in Listing 15.15 completely replaces the `price` element with a new one using the `ReplaceWith` method.

LISTING 15.15   Using `ReplaceWith`

```
XElement books = XElement.Load("books.xml");
XElement book = books.Elements("book").
   FirstOrDefault(b => (string)b.Element("author") == "Dorman");
book.Element("price"). ReplaceWith(new XElement("price", 30.99));
```

To remove the current element or attribute, use the `Remove` method. To remove all attributes associated with the current element, use the `RemoveAttributes` method. To remove all children nodes, use the `RemoveNodes` method. To remove both children nodes and attributes from the current element, use the `RemoveAll` method. The code shown in Listing 15.16 removes the `book` element that contains an `author` element whose value is equal to "Dorman".

LISTING 15.16   Using Remove

```
XElement books = XElement.Load("books.xml");
books.Elements("book").
   FirstOrDefault(b => (string)b.Element("author") == "Dorman").
   Remove();
```

Finally, adding new elements uses the Add, AddAfterSelf, AddBeforeSelf, or AddFirst methods. The Add method adds the provided content as child nodes to the current element, whereas AddFirst adds the content as the first child. The AddAfterSelf and AddBeforeSelf methods add the content as a sibling node after or before the current node, respectively. The code shown in Listing 15.17 adds a new child element to the book element.

LISTING 15.17   Using Add

```
XElement books = XElement.Load("books.xml");
XElement book = books.Elements("book").
   FirstOrDefault(b => (string)b.Element("author") == "Dorman");
book.Add(new XElement("summary", ""));
```

▼ TRY IT YOURSELF

Modifying XML

To modify the XML from the previous exercise using LINQ to XML, follow these steps. In this exercise, you explore how to modify XML. If you closed Visual Studio, repeat the previous exercise first.

1. After the foreach statement you wrote in step 5 of the previous exercise, add a new foreach statement that inserts an empty summary child element as the first element of each book element.

2. Add a new child element of books named publisher, which includes the following children elements:

   ▶ <name>Sams Publishing</name>

   ▶ <state>IN</state>

3. Move the book elements from the root books element to a books child element of publisher.

4. Run the application using Ctrl+F5. The output should look like Figure 15.7.

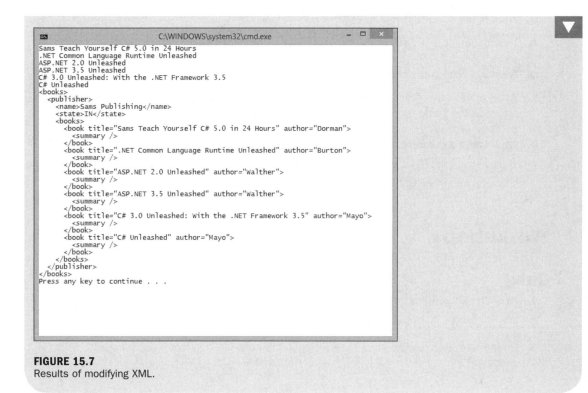

FIGURE 15.7
Results of modifying XML.

Summary

In this hour, you learned how to work with XML data using LINQ to XML. You learned how the
XElement class enables you to create XML documents and how the XNamespace class simplifies working with XML namespaces. Next, you learned how to select and query XML using both
properties and methods provided by the XNode derived classes and using the declarative LINQ
query syntax. Finally, you learned how to modify XML by removing, replacing, and creating new
elements and attributes.

Q&A

Q. What is the XML Document Object Model (DOM)?

A. The DOM provides a common and structured way XML data is represented in memory and
is most commonly used for reading XML data into memory to change its structure, add or
remove elements, or modify the data contained in an element.

Q. What is the document root node?

A. The document root node is the top-level node containing the document itself.

Q. What are child and sibling nodes?

A. When nodes have the same parent node, they are child nodes of that parent. Nodes that are all at the same level are sibling nodes.

Q. What is the `XElement` class?

A. The `XElement` class represents an XML element and is the most commonly used because it can represent an entire document or an element within a document.

Workshop

Quiz

1. What three operations can `SetElementValue` perform?

2. Is it possible to explicitly define a namespace prefix for an XML namespace?

3. Do the `XElement` and `XAttribute` classes handle XML character encoding and decoding?

Answers

1. The `SetElementValue` method enables you to add a new child element, change the value of an existing child element, or delete a child element. If the name provided does not already exist as a child element, it will be created for you; otherwise, the value of the child element will be changed to the value you specified. If the value is null, the child element is removed. When modifying or removing child elements or attributes, the first one with the specified name is modified or removed.

2. Yes, a namespace prefix can be specified by including an `xmlns` attribute.

3. Yes, the `XElement` and `XAttribute` classes automatically handle encoding and decoding text that contains invalid XML characters.

Exercises

1. Create a new console application that transforms the XML shown in Listing 15.11 to that shown in Listing 15.12. The implementation necessary is shown in Listing 15.13.

Working with Databases

What You'll Learn in This Hour:

▶ Prerequisites

▶ Understanding ADO.NET

▶ Understanding LINQ to ADO.NET

Interacting with a database is something that many applications need to do. A **database** is simply a repository of data, much like a text file or an XML file. As you might imagine, using files in this manner to store data isn't always the best approach. As a result, most applications make use of a **relational database**, which organizes data into tables, rows, and records. Each table is organized into rows, and each row represents a single record. Rows are further organized into columns, and each row in a table has the same column structure.

The .NET Framework provides a rich set of classes for database interaction through ADO.NET, which is a library of objects specifically designed to simplify writing applications that use databases, and LINQ to ADO.NET.

In this hour, you briefly learn ADO.NET and LINQ to ADO.NET.

Prerequisites

All the examples and exercises in this hour require you to have SQL Server or SQL Server Express (2005 or higher) installed. If you don't already have SQL Server or SQL Server Express installed, you can download it from http://www.microsoft.com/sqlserver.

You will also need to install the AdventureWorks sample database. These examples use the AdventureWorksLT 2012 version of the OLTP database, which can be directly downloaded from http://msftdbprodsamples.codeplex.com/downloads/get/354847. Once the data file has been downloaded, you will need to attach the database by following these steps:

1. Display the Database Explorer window, shown in Figure 16.1. This is available through the VIEW|Other Windows menu.

FIGURE 16.1
Database Explorer.

2. Add a new Data Connection by right-clicking Data Connections and selecting Add Connection.

3. When the Choose Data Source dialog box, shown in Figure 16.2, displays, select Microsoft SQL Server Database File as the data source.

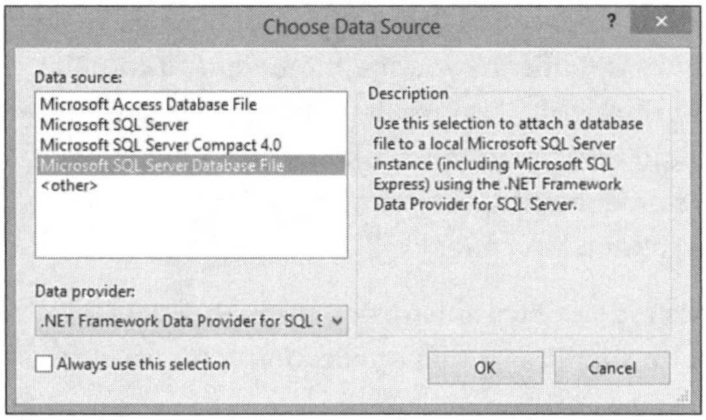

FIGURE 16.2
Choose Data Source dialog box.

4. When you click Continue, the Add Connection dialog box is displayed, as shown in Figure 16.3. Browse to the AdventureWorksLT2012_Data file you previously downloaded and click the OK button.

NOTE

Upgrading the Database File

At this point, you may see a dialog box, similar to the one shown in Figure 16.4, letting you know that the database file is not compatible with the current instance of SQL Server. If that's the case, go ahead and click Yes to upgrade the file.

FIGURE 16.3
Add Connection dialog box.

FIGURE 16.4
Database conversion required dialog box.

5. Expand the connection that was just added to view the available tables, as shown in Figure 16.5.

6. At this point, the database name is AdventureWorksLT2012_Data.mdf. You should rename it to be just AdventureWorksLT2012 by right-clicking the database and selecting the Rename menu command, as shown in Figure 16.6.

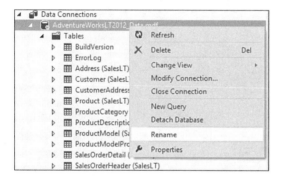

FIGURE 16.5
An expanded data connection.

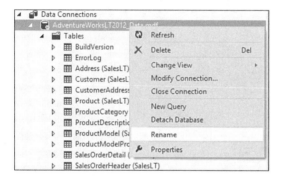

FIGURE 16.6
Renaming the database.

Understanding ADO.NET

The ADO.NET library is a rich framework enabling you to build applications that can retrieve and update information in relational databases. In keeping with the ideals of language and platform independence, ADO.NET is built upon the idea of data providers. Each database system that ADO.NET supports (such as SQL Server, Oracle, and DB2) has a data provider that implements the mechanisms for connecting to a database, executing queries, and updating data. Because each provider implements the same interfaces, you can write code that is independent of the underlying database.

One of the primary classes in ADO.NET is the `DataSet`, which represents a portion of the database. A `DataSet` does not require a continuous connection to the database, enabling you to work in a disconnected manner. To update the database and the `DataSet`, you periodically reconnect the `DataSet` to its parent database and perform any updates required.

NOTE

ADO.NET Data Providers

An ADO.NET data provider encapsulates the logic needed for connecting to a database, executing commands and retrieving results. It provides a lightweight layer between the underlying data source and your application code.

The .NET Framework currently ships with five data providers, each in their own namespace:

▶ Data Provider for SQL Server (`System.Data.SqlClient`)

▶ Data Provider for OLE DB (`System.Data.OleDb`)

▶ Data Provider for ODBC (`System.Data.Odbc`)

▶ Data Provider for Oracle (`System.Data.OracleClient`)

▶ EntityClient Provider (`System.Data.EntityClient`)

Even though SQL Server and Oracle both support OLE DB, you should use the specific SQL Server or Oracle providers because they are optimized for those database systems.

To accomplish all this, the `DataSet` must represent database tables and the relationships between those tables. The collection of database tables is available through the `Tables` property, with each table represented as a `DataTable` instance. The `Relations` property is a collection of `DataRelation` instances, with each `DataRelation` representing a relationship between two tables.

A `DataTable` is most commonly created as a result of a query against the database and represents an actual table in that database. Each column in the database table is represented as a `DataColumn`, exposed through the `Columns` property of `DataTable`. The `DataTable` also contains a `Rows` property, which returns a `DataRow` object for each actual row of the database table.

If you think of a `DataSet` as an abstraction of the database, you need a way to bridge the gap between the `DataSet` and the underlying database. This is done with a `DataAdapter`, which is used to exchange data between a data source and a `DataSet`, primarily through the `Fill` and `Update` methods. The benefit this provides is that a `DataSet` can represent tables from multiple databases.

NOTE

Read-Only Access Using a Data Reader

Both a `DataSet` and a `DataAdapter` enable two-way interaction with the database, allowing you to both read and write data. If you only need to read data, which is common, you can create a `DbDataReader`, or one of its derived classes like `SqlDataReader`, instead. The simplest way to create a `DataReader` is to use the `ExecuteReader` method available from `DbCommand`.

A `DbDataReader` provides connected, forward-only, read-only access to a collection of tables, often referred to as a **fire hose cursor**. (The name "fire hose cursor" is due to the similarities of accessing data in a fast, forward-only, continuous stream of data and the fast, forward-only, continuous stream of water through a fire hose.)

As a result, they are lightweight objects and are ideally suited for filling controls with data and then breaking the database connection.

Finally, you need to represent a connection to the data source through a DbConnection and a database command (such as a SQL statement or stored procedure) through a DbCommand. After a DbConnection is created, it can be shared with many different DbCommand instances.

Each data provider typically provides customized subclasses of DbConnection and DbCommand specific to that database system. For example, the Data Provider for SQL Server provides the SqlConnection and SqlCommand classes.

CAUTION

Required References

To use ADO.NET, you need to ensure that the project has a reference to the System.Data assembly and that the correct namespace for the data provider you use is included.

Listing 16.1 shows how to execute a query using ADO.NET and the classes provided by the Data Provider for SQL Server.

LISTING 16.1   A Simple ADO.NET Query

```
using (SqlConnection connection = new SqlConnection())
{
    connection.ConnectionString = @"Integrated Security=SSPI;
        database=AdventureWorksLT2012;server=(local)\SQLEXPRESS";

    try
    {
        using (SqlCommand command = new SqlCommand())
        {
            command.Connection = connection;
            command.CommandText = @"SELECT *
                FROM [AdventureWorksLT2012].[SalesLT].[Customer]
                WHERE [CompanyName] = 'A Bike Store'";

            connection.Open();
            SqlDataReader reader = command.ExecuteReader();
            while (reader.Read())
            {
                // Retrieve the second, third, and fifth columns
                // explicitly as a string value.
```

```
        Console.WriteLine("{0} {1} {2}",
            reader.GetString(2),
            reader.GetString(3),
            reader.GetString(5));
    }

    connection.Close();
    }
}
catch (SqlException e)
{
    Console.WriteLine("An error occurred: {0}", e.Message);
}
}
```

To ensure that the database command and connection instances are disposed of properly and that the connection is closed, it is best to place them in a `using` statement.

NOTE

Connection Pooling

Most of the data providers also provide support for connection pooling. You can think of the connection pool as a set of available database connections. When an application requires a connection, the provider extracts the next available connection from the pool. When the application closes the connection, it is returned to the pool, ready for the next application that needs a connection.

As a result, you should not keep a connection longer than you need to. Instead, open a connection when you need it and then close it as soon as you finish using it.

TRY IT YOURSELF ▼

Working with ADO.NET

To use the ADO.NET Data Provider for SQL Server to insert a record and then query a table, use the following steps:

1. Create a new console application.

2. Include the `System.Data.SqlClient` namespace with a `using` directive.

3. In the `Main` method of the `Program.cs` file, implement the code shown in Listing 16.1.

4. Just before the second `using` statement (that declares a `SqlCommand` instance), write a `using` statement that creates a `SqlCommand` to insert a record into the database. Instead of calling the `ExecuteReader` method on command, use the `ExecuteNonQuery` method because the SQL statement does not return any data. Use the following text for the `CommandText` property:

```
@"INSERT INTO [AdventureWorksLT2012].[SalesLT].[Customer]
(NameStyle, Title, FirstName, LastName, CompanyName, PasswordHash,
PasswordSalt, ModifiedDate)
VALUES (0, 'Mr.', 'Scott', 'Dorman', 'A Bike Store', 'aaaaa', 'aaa',
'" + DateTime.Now.ToString("G") + "')";
```

5. Run the application using Ctrl+F5. The output should look like what is shown in Figure 16.7.

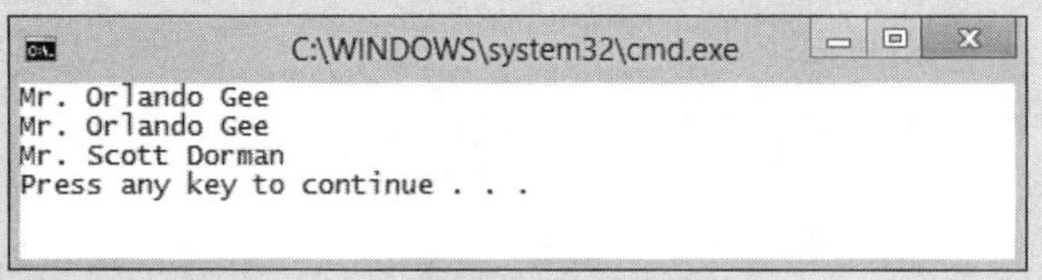

FIGURE 16.7
Results of working with ADO.NET.

CAUTION
_____

SQL Injection Attacks

The code you wrote in the "Working with ADO.NET" Try It Yourself explicitly passed text values to the insert statement. In production quality code, you should avoid this whenever possible because it introduces the possibility of someone injecting malicious SQL text as the values. Instead, you should use parameters, as shown in the following:

```
command.CommandText = @"INSERT INTO [AdventureWorksLT2012].[SalesLT].[Customer]
(NameStyle, Title, FirstName, LastName, CompanyName, PasswordHash,
PasswordSalt, ModifiedDate)
VALUES (@NameStyle, @Title, @FirstName, @LastName, @CompanyName, @PasswordHash,
@PasswordSalt, @ModifiedDate)";

command.Parameters.Add(new SqlParameter("@NameStyle", 0));
command.Parameters.Add(new SqlParameter("@Title", "Mr"));
command.Parameters.Add(new SqlParameter("@FirstName", "Scott"));
command.Parameters.Add(new SqlParameter("@LastName", "Dorman"));
command.Parameters.Add(new SqlParameter("@CompanyName", "A Bike Store"));
command.Parameters.Add(new SqlParameter("@PasswordHash", "aaaaa"));
command.Parameters.Add(new SqlParameter("@PasswordSalt", "aaa"));
command.Parameters.Add(new SqlParameter("@ModifiedDate",
  DateTime.Now.ToString("G")));
```

Understanding LINQ to ADO.NET

LINQ to ADO.NET is actually three separate technologies that enable you to interact with relational databases. Figure 16.8 shows how the LINQ to ADO.NET technologies relate to each other, the other LINQ-enabled data sources, and the higher-level programming languages such as C#.

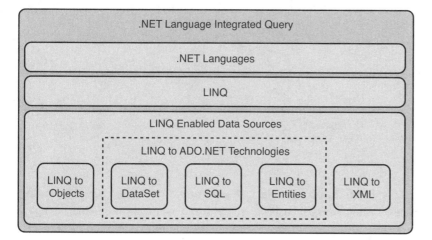

FIGURE 16.8
LINQ to ADO.NET.

Working with LINQ to DataSet

LINQ to DataSet builds upon the existing ADO.NET architecture and enables you to build queries over data stored in a `DataSet` easily and quickly. It is not meant to replace ADO.NET in an application but to enable you to write queries using the LINQ syntax and fills the void left by the limited query capabilities of the `DataSet`.

To use LINQ to DataSet, you must first populate the `DataSet`. After data has been loaded, you can begin querying it using the same techniques you have already learned with LINQ to Objects (Hour 13, "Understanding Query Expressions") and LINQ to XML (Hour 15, "Working with XML"). These queries can be performed against a single table in the `DataSet` or against multiple tables using the `Join` and `GroupJoin` query operators.

Listing 16.2 is functionally equivalent to the query shown in Listing 16.1 using a LINQ to DataSet query instead. This code first creates a `SqlDataAdapter` and then fills the `DataSet` instance with data. This code is necessary with both ADO.NET and LINQ to DataSet. However, by using the `AsEnumerable` extension method on the `DataTable`, you can execute standard LINQ queries against the data.

LISTING 16.2   A Simple LINQ to DataSet Query

```
string connectionString = @"Integrated Security=SSPI;
   database= AdventureWorksLT2012;server=(local)\SQLEXPRESS";

string selectSQL = @"SELECT * FROM [AdventureWorksLT2012].[SalesLT].[Customer]";

SqlDataAdapter adapter = new SqlDataAdapter(selectSQL, connectionString);
DataSet ds = new DataSet();
adapter.Fill(ds);
foreach (var customer in ds.Tables[0].AsEnumerable().
   Where(row => row.Field<string>("CompanyName") == "A Bike Store"))
{
   Console.WriteLine("{0} {1} {2}",
   customer.Field<string>("Title"),
   customer.Field<string>("FirstName"),
   customer.Field<string>("LastName"));
}
```

Just as LINQ to XML added XML-specific extensions, LINQ to DataSet also adds several DataSet specific extensions. These extensions make it easier to query over a set of DataRow objects, enabling you to compare sequences of rows or directly access the column values of a DataRow.

CAUTION

Required References

To use LINQ to DataSet, you need to ensure that the project has references to the following assemblies:

- ▶ System.Core
- ▶ System.Data
- ▶ System.Data.DataSetExtensions
- ▶ System.Data.Common or System.Data.SqlClient, depending on how you connect to the database

You also need to include the System.Linq and System.Data namespaces.

Working with LINQ to SQL

LINQ to SQL enables you to write queries directly against SQL databases using the same query syntax you use for an in-memory collection or any other LINQ data source. Although ADO.NET maps the database to a conceptual data model, represented by a DataSet, LINQ to SQL maps directly to an object model in your application code. When your application executes, the LINQ syntax queries are translated by LINQ to SQL into SQL language queries that are then sent to the database to be executed. When the results are returned, LINQ to SQL translates them back to data model objects.

To use LINQ to SQL, you must first create the object model that represents the database. There are two ways to do this, as follows:

▶ The Object Relational Designer (O/R Designer), which is part of Visual Studio 2012, provides a rich user interface for creating the object model from an existing database. The O/R Designer supports only SQL Server Express or SQL Server 2000 (and higher) databases.

▶ The SQLMetal command-line tool, which should be used for large databases, or databases that the O/R Designer does not support.

When you decide how you will generate the object model, you need to decide what type of code you want to generate. Using the O/R Designer, you can generate C# source code that provides attribute-based mapping. If you use the SQLMetal command-line tool, you can also generate an external XML file containing the mapping metadata.

NOTE

Creating the Object Model

There is actually a third way to create the object model, in which you use the code editor to write the object model by hand. This is not recommended because it can be error-prone, especially when creating the object model to represent an existing database.

You can use the code editor to modify or refine the code generated by the Object Relational Designer or the SQLMetal command-line tool.

When you have the object model created, you can then use it in your applications by writing LINQ queries. The code in Listing 16.3 shows a complete example from defining the `DataContext` to executing the query and observing the results, and produces the same result as the code shown in Listing 16.1 and Listing 16.2.

LISTING 16.3   A Simple LINQ to SQL Query

```
DataContext dataContext = new DataContext(@"Integrated Security=SSPI;
   database=AdventureWorksLT2012;server=(local)\SQLEXPRESS");

Table<Customer> customers = dataContext.GetTable<Customer>();
IQueryable<Customer> query =
   from customer in customers
   where customer.CompanyName == "A Bike Store"
   select customer;
```

```
foreach(Customer customer in query)
{
    Console.WriteLine("{0} {1} {2}",
        customer.Title,
        customer.FirstName,
        customer.LastName);
}
```

CAUTION

Required Namespaces

To use LINQ to SQL, you need to include the `System.Linq` and `System.Data.Linq` namespaces.

You must first establish the connection between your object model and the database, done through a `DataContext`. You then create a `Table<T>` class that acts as the table you will query. Although not actually the case, you can think of the `DataContext` as being similar to a `DBConnection` and `Table<T>` as being similar to a `DataTable`. You then define and subsequently execute your query.

▼ TRY IT YOURSELF

Working with LINQ to SQL

By following these steps, you use the O/R Designer and LINQ to SQL to insert a record and then query a table:

1. Create a new console application.

2. Include the `System.Data.Linq` namespace with a `using` directive.

3. Use the O/R Designer to create the object model. To do this, add a new item to your project by selecting LINQ to SQL Classes, as shown in Figure 16.9. Name the file **AdventureWorksLT**.

4. In the resulting editor, a portion of which is shown in Figure 16.10, click the Database Explorer link to display the Visual Studio Database Explorer tool window.

5. Expand the AdventureWorksLT2012 connection to view the available tables, select the Customer table and drag it on to the `AdventureWorksLT.dbml` editor window, as shown in Figure 16.11. This creates the entity class that represents the `Customer` table.

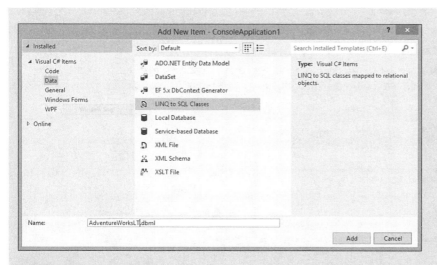

FIGURE 16.9
Add New Item dialog box.

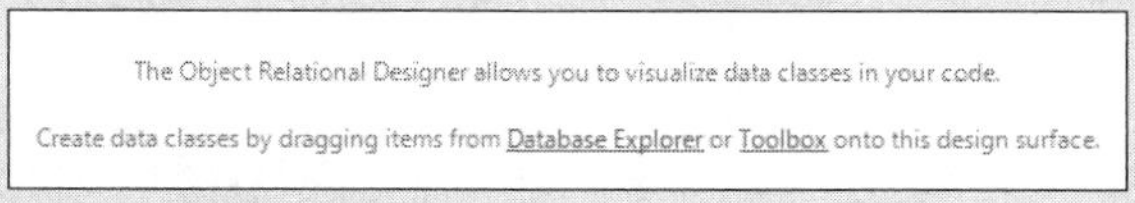

The Object Relational Designer allows you to visualize data classes in your code.

Create data classes by dragging items from Database Explorer or Toolbox onto this design surface.

FIGURE 16.10
O/R Designer.

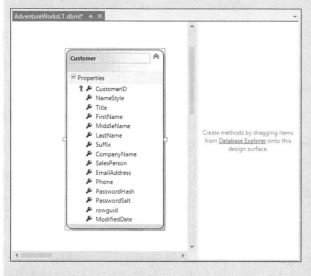

FIGURE 16.11
O/R Designer displaying a table.

> **NOTE**
>
> ## Copying the Database File to Your Project
>
> If you see a dialog box, similar to the one shown in Figure 16.12, saying that the connection is using a local data file that isn't in the project and asking if you want to copy the file to your project, be sure to say No.
>
>
>
> **FIGURE 16.12**
> Copy database file to your project dialog box.

6. In the `Main` method of the `Program.cs` file, implement the code shown in Listing 16.3.

7. Run the application using Ctrl+F5. The output should look like what is shown in Figure 16.13.

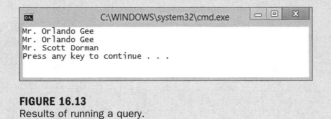

FIGURE 16.13
Results of running a query.

Selecting data, also known as **projection**, is accomplished simply by writing a LINQ query and then executing it. LINQ to SQL also enables you to add, modify, or delete data in the database. Whenever you make changes using LINQ to SQL, you are modifying only the local cache. The changes you have made are not sent to the database until you call the `SubmitChanges` method on the `DataContext` instance.

To add a new record to the database, you simply create a new instance of the appropriate data model object, calling the `InsertOnSubmit` method of the `Table<T>` instance. The code in

Listing 16.4 shows an example of adding a new `Customer` record to the `Customers` table, and is equivalent to the code you wrote earlier to insert a new record using ADO.NET.

LISTING 16.4   Adding a New Record

```
DataContext dataContext = new DataContext(@"Integrated Security=SSPI;
   database= AdventureWorksLT2012;server=(local)\SQLEXPRESS");

Table<Customer> customers = dataContext.GetTable<Customer>();

Customer customer = new Customer();
customer.NameStyle = true;
customer.Title = "Mr."
customer.FirstName = "Scott";
customer.LastName = "Dorman";
customer.PasswordHash = "aaaaa";
customer.PasswordSalt = "aaaa";
customer.ModifiedDate = DateTime.Now;
customers.InsertOnSubmit(customer);

dataContext.SubmitChanges();
```

Updating an existing entity simply requires you to retrieve the specific object from the database using a LINQ to SQL query and then modifying its properties, as shown in Listing 16.5.

LISTING 16.5   Updating a Record

```
DataContext dataContext = new DataContext(@"Integrated Security=SSPI;
   database= AdventureWorksLT2012;server=(local)\SQLEXPRESS");

Table<Customer> customers = dataContext.GetTable<Customer>();

Customer customer =
   (from customer in customers
    where customer.LastName == "Dorman"
    select customer).First();

customer.Title = "Mr.";

dataContext.SubmitChanges();
```

Deleting an item is also just as simple because you remove the item from its containing collection using the `DeleteOnSubmit` method and then call `SubmitChanges`. Listing 16.6 shows an example of deleting a record from the database.

LISTING 16.6　Deleting a Record

```
DataContext dataContext = new DataContext(@"Integrated Security=SSPI;
   database= AdventureWorksLT2012;server=(local)\SQLEXPRESS");

Table<Customer> customers = dataContext.GetTable<Customer>();

IQueryable<Customer> query =
   from customer in customers
   where customer.LastName == "Dorman"
   select customer;

if (query.Count() > 0)
{
   customers.DeleteOnSubmit(query.First());
}

dataContext.SubmitChanges();
```

Defining a Custom `DataContext`

In all the preceding examples, you used the `DataContext` class provided by LINQ to SQL. The `GetTable` method enables you to instantiate any entity class even if that table is not contained in the underlying database the `DataContext` is connected to. It is only while your program is executing that you can discover this problem. As a result, it is recommended that you create specialized `DataContext` classes specific to the database you will use.

To create a derived `DataContext` class, you simply inherit from `DataContext` and then provide the various `Table<T>` collections as public members. Listing 16.7 shows a strongly typed `DataContext` class for the AdventureWorksLT database and how it would be used in a simple query.

LISTING 16.7　A Custom `DataContext`

```
public partial class AdventureWorksLT : DataContext
{
   public Table<Customer> Customers;
   public Table<Order> Orders;

   public AdventureWorksLT (string connection) : base(connection) { }
}

AdventureWorksLT dataContext = new AdventureWorksLT(@"Integrated Security=SSPI;
   database= AdventureWorksLT2012;server=(local)\SQLEXPRESS");

IQueryable<Customer> query =
   from customer in dataContext.Customers
```

```
    customer.CompanyName == "A Bike Store"
    select customer;

foreach(Customer customer in query)
{
    Console.WriteLine("{0} {1} {2}",
        customer.Title,
        customer.FirstName,
        customer.LastName);
}
```

Working with LINQ to Entities

Earlier you learned about ADO.NET and how LINQ to SQL can be used to develop applications that interact with databases. The Entity Framework extends the basic capabilities of ADO.NET to support developing data-centric applications.

Traditionally, when developing data-centric applications, not only must you model the database tables, relations, and business logic, but also you must work directly with the database to store and retrieve data. Although LINQ to SQL helps solve some of these problems, the Entity Framework enables you to work at a higher level of abstraction by creating a **domain model** that defines the entities and relationship being modeled.

The Entity Framework then translates this domain model, commonly called a conceptual model, to data source–specific commands. This approach enables you to develop your application without being concerned about dependencies on a particular data source.

When the domain model has been defined, the Entity Framework then maps relational tables, columns, and foreign key constraints to classes in the logical model. This approach enables a great deal of flexibility to define and optimize the logical model. The classes generated are partial classes, enabling you to extend them easily.

To access or modify data through the Entity Framework, you execute queries against the conceptual model to return objects through one of the following methods:

▶ LINQ to Entities provides LINQ support for querying directly against the conceptual model. Both the Entity Framework and LINQ can then use the objects returned from a LINQ to Entities query.

▶ Entity SQL, which is a data source-independent version of SQL that works directly with the conceptual model.

▶ Query builder methods, which enable you to create Entity SQL queries using a similar syntax to the LINQ extension methods.

To make creating entity models easier, Visual Studio 2012 includes the Entity Data Model Designer, shown in Figure 16.14.

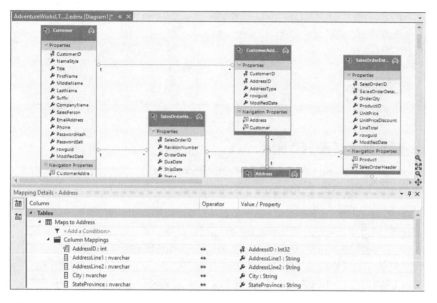

FIGURE 16.14
Entity data model designer. (Image not meant to be read in detail.)

NOTE

EntityClient Data Provider

Because the Entity Framework is built on top of the traditional ADO.NET services, it includes the EntityClient data provider that is responsible for translating the entity queries into their data source–specific versions and translating entity data into their object equivalents.

It is also possible to use the EntityClient provider like any other ADO.NET data provider, enabling you to execute Entity SQL queries that return the data using a data reader.

This designer enables you to visually create and modify the entities, mappings, associations, and inheritance of your models.

It is divided into the following components:

▶ The visual design surface

▶ The mapping details window, which enables you to view and edit mappings

▶ The model browser window, which displays the conceptual and logical models in a tree view

The easiest way to get started using the Entity Framework is to add a new ADO.NET Entity Data Model item to your project. This starts the Entity Data Model Wizard, which enables you to generate an entity data model from an existing database or by creating an empty data model.

When the data model has been created, you can then easily perform queries against the data context using LINQ to Entities, as shown in Listing 16.8. This query selects the first 10 records from the Products table and displays the product name. The Entity Data Model Wizard created the `AdventureWorksLT2012_DataEntities` and `Product` classes.

LISTING 16.8 A Custom `DataContext`

```
using (AdventureWorksLT2012_DataEntities context =
    new AdventureWorksLT2012_DataEntities())
{
    IQueryable<Product> productsQuery = (from product in context.Products
                                         select product).Take(10);

    Console.WriteLine("Product Names:");
    foreach (var prod in productsQuery)
    {
        Console.WriteLine(prod.Name);
    }
}
```

The results of running this query are shown in Figure 16.15.

FIGURE 16.15
Selecting the top 10 products.

Summary

In this hour, you learned how ADO.NET and the LINQ to ADO.NET technologies make it easy to work with databases. You learned the basics of working with ADO.NET and then built upon that to see how LINQ to DataSets enable you to add complex queries over the data in a `DataSet`.

You then learned how LINQ to SQL enables you to create an object model that represents your database, enabling you to easily query, add, update, and remove data from the database. Finally, you saw how easy it is to create custom data contexts for use with LINQ to SQL.

Q&A

Q. What is a relational database?

A. A relational database is simply a repository of data that is organized into tables, rows, and records.

Q. What is ADO.NET?

A. The ADO.NET library is a rich framework enabling you to easily build applications that can retrieve and update information in relational databases.

Q. Does ADO.NET require a constant connection to the database?

A. No, most of the ADO.NET classes are designed so that they do not require a continuous connection to the database, enabling you to work in a disconnected manner. The `DataReader` class and any derived classes do require a constant connection to the database.

Q. What is LINQ to ADO.NET?

A. LINQ to ADO.NET is actually three separate technologies that enable you to interact with relational databases: LINQ to DataSet, LINQ to SQL, and LINQ to Entities.

Q. What is a LINQ to SQL object model?

A. A LINQ to SQL object model directly represents, or maps, objects in your application to objects (tables) in the underlying database.

Q. Can LINQ to SQL be used to update data?

A. Yes, LINQ to SQL can be used to update data. It can also be used to add new data or delete existing data.

Workshop

Quiz

1. What are the ADO.NET data providers that ship with the .NET Framework?

2. What references are required to use LINQ to DataSet?

3. What references are required to use LINQ to SQL?

4. What is the benefit to creating a custom `DataContext` class?

Answers

1. The .NET Framework currently ships with five data providers, which support SQL Server, Oracle, any OLE DB-compliant database, any ODBC-compliant database, and the Entity Data Model (which is part of the Entity Framework).

2. LINQ to DataSet requires references to the following assemblies:

- ► `System.Core`

- ► `System.Data`

- ► `System.Data.DataSetExtensions`

- ► `System.Data.Common` or `System.Data.SqlClient`

3. LINQ to DataSet requires references to the following assemblies:

- ► `System.Core`

- ► `System.Data.Linq`

4. Creating a custom `DataContext` helps to ensure that you can only access tables defined by the underlying database by providing the various `Table<T>` collections as public members.

Exercises

There are no exercises for this hour.

Building a Windows Application

What You'll Learn in This Hour:

▶ Understanding WPF
▶ Creating a WPF application
▶ Styling the layout

Now that you have completed the first three parts of this book, you should be familiar with the .NET Framework and C# language. You have learned the fundamental differences between reference and value types, including how to create your own types. You learned about language features, such as extension methods, automatic properties, lambdas, events, and exceptions. You now know how to create and query collections of data and work with files and directories in the file system, XML, and databases. In short, you should now have all the essential language skills necessary to create complex applications that take advantage of the user interface libraries provided by the .NET Framework.

Although the .NET Framework provides two different class libraries for developing Windows applications, the Windows Forms and Windows Presentation Foundation (WPF) libraries, WPF provides a much more complete and unified model for building rich Windows applications. In this hour, you learn how to build a basic WPF application. You see how to do this visually using the visual design tools and through Extensible Application Markup Language (XAML). Finally, you learn about styling your application using WPF visual styles to build an application that can be easily customized.

Understanding WPF

Windows Presentation Foundation (WPF) provides a unified programming model enabling you to build Windows applications that incorporate user interface elements, media, and documents. WPF, however, goes beyond just user interfaces. It is a next-generation presentation system enabling you to create a wide range of visually rich standalone and browser-hosted applications. At the center of WPF is a resolution-independent, vector-based rendering engine designed to take advantage of modern graphics hardware. WPF is part of the .NET Framework and most of the types you need are located in the `System.Windows` namespace.

Working with Markup and Code-Behind

If you have previously developed ASP.NET applications, the idea of markup and code-behind should already be familiar. In a WPF application, you use a markup language to implement the appearance of the application; you implement the behavior using a programming language, such as C#, "behind" the markup. This enables a clean separation between appearance and behavior, providing the following benefits:

▶ Development and maintenance costs are reduced.

▶ Development is more efficient, allowing the application's appearance to be created simultaneously with other developers who are implementing the application's behavior.

▶ Multiple design tools can create and share the markup.

Introducing the Extensible Application Markup Language

WPF uses Extensible Application Markup Language (XAML), which is an XML-based compositional markup language. Because XAML is XML based, the user interface (UI) you compose with it is assembled in an element tree, which is a hierarchy of nested elements. The element tree provides a logical way to create and manage the user interface.

Figure 17.1 shows a simple WPF application written completely in XAML. Specifically, the XAML defines a window and a button using the `Window` and `Button` elements, respectively, and then sets various attributes to specify the text, sizes, and so on.

FIGURE 17.1
"Hello World" in WPF.

Listing 17.1 shows the XAML necessary to produce the application shown in Figure 17.1.

LISTING 17.1   Simple XAML

```
<Window x:Class="WpfApplication1.MainWindow"
    xmlns="http://schemas.microsoft.com/winfx/2006/xaml/presentation"
    xmlns:x="http://schemas.microsoft.com/winfx/2006/xaml"
    Title="Hello World" Height="162" Width="328">

    <Grid Height="111" Width="303">
        <Button Content="Hello, world from WPF!"
            Margin="82,37,93,32"
            Name="button1"
            Height="42"
            HorizontalAlignment="Center"
            VerticalAlignment="Center" />
    </Grid>
</Window>
```

CAUTION

The x:Class Attribute

The x:Class attribute specifies the name of the class, not the name of the file that contains the class. If you rename the class using the built-in refactoring support, Visual Studio updates the XAML, but it won't change the actual filename. If you rename the file, Visual Studio will not automatically rename the class. To help avoid confusion, your filenames and class names should always match.

Code-Behind

Although this simple application contains a button, it isn't very functional. The application provides no behavior that responds to user interactions, such as responding to events, calling business logic, or accessing data. This behavior is generally implemented in code associated with the markup, known as code-behind.

You can respond to the Click event of the button by adding the following attribute to the Button element:

```
Click="button1_Click"
```

This simply creates the association in the markup between the event and a method in the code-behind file. The actual code-behind required is shown in Listing 17.2. In this example, the code-behind implements a class named MainWindow that derives from the Window class. The x:Class attribute in the markup associates the markup with its code-behind class. A default public constructor that calls InitializeComponent is also automatically generated for you. The button1_Click method implements the event handler for the button's Click event.

NOTE

Routed Events

A routed event is one that can invoke handlers on multiple listeners in an element tree, not just on the element that raised the event. Because of the compositional nature of WPF and WPF enabling users to interact with more than just traditional user interface elements, many events in WPF are routed events. Following are three different strategies used to route events:

▶ Bubbling, in which event handlers on the event source are invoked. The event then routes to successive parent elements until the root of the tree is reached.

▶ Direct, in which only event handlers on the event source are invoked. This is analogous to the way events in Windows Forms applications behave.

▶ Tunneling, in which event handlers on the event source are invoked. The event then routes to successive parent elements until the root of the tree is reached or one of the elements specifically indicates the event has been handled and no other event handlers should respond to the event.

LISTING 17.2   Code-Behind Class

```
public partial class MainWindow : Window
{
    public MainWindow()
    {
        InitializeComponent();
    }

    private void button1_Click(object sender, RoutedEventArgs e)
    {
        MessageBox.Show("You clicked the button!");
    }
}
```

Figure 17.2 shows the result when the button is clicked.

Applications

The types and services required for packaging your XAML-based content and delivering it to users as an application are part of what WPF calls the **application model**. Through the application model, you can create both standalone and browser-hosted applications.

FIGURE 17.2
Handling the button's Click event.

Because standalone applications and browser-hosted applications are often complex and require application-scoped services, such as shared properties and startup management, WPF provides the Application class. Just like other WPF-based resources, the Application class is made up of markup and code-behind. Listing 17.3 shows the XAML that makes up the Application markup for the simple application from Listing 17.1.

LISTING 17.3 Application XAML

```
<Application x:Class="WpfApplication1.App"
            xmlns="http://schemas.microsoft.com/winfx/2006/xaml/presentation"
            xmlns:x="http://schemas.microsoft.com/winfx/2006/xaml"
            StartupUri="MainWindow.xaml">
    <Application.Resources>

    </Application.Resources>
</Application>
```

You already saw an example of a standalone application in the previous section. These applications use the Window class to create windows and dialog boxes that are accessed through menus, toolbars, and other UI elements. The primary purpose of a window is to host and display content, such as media, XAML pages, web pages, and documents.

Browser-hosted applications, also known as XAML browser applications (XBAPs), use pages (from the Page class) and page functions (from the PageFunction<T> class). With XBAPs, you can navigate between pages using hyperlinks. Because XBAPs are hosted in a browser (Internet Explorer 6 or later), they use a partial-trust security sandbox to enforce restrictions similar to those imposed on HTML-based applications. XBAPs can run under a full-trust sandbox, but users are prompted with a security warning dialog box, enabling them to decide if they want to run the application.

Understanding WPF Layouts

Creating a user interface requires you to arrange controls by location and size, forming a layout that must adapt to changes in window size and display settings. WPF provides a robust layout and rendering system that handles these complexities for you. The layout system is based on relative positioning rather than fixed positioning and manages the interactions between controls to determine the layout. WPF provides several layout controls for you, and you can extend the layout system with your own customized layout controls. The default layout controls follow:

- ▶ **Canvas**—You can think of a Canvas layout as an artist's canvas. All child controls of a Canvas must provide their own layout. Canvas should be used with caution because it provides no inherent layout characteristics and uses exact positioning. The layout system provided by a Canvas is similar to that of Windows Forms or other layout systems that use exact x and y coordinates to position controls.

- ▶ **DockPanel**—The child controls are aligned to the edges of the panel. By default, the last control of a DockPanel fills the remaining space.

- ▶ **Grid**—The child controls are positioned by rows and columns, much like a table.

- ▶ **StackPanel**—The child controls are stacked either vertically or horizontally.

- ▶ **WrapPanel**—The child controls are arranged in a left-to-right order and wrapped to the next line when there are more controls than will display in the space provided. A WrapPanel also supports a top-to-bottom order, in which controls are wrapped to the next column when there are more controls than will display in the available space.

Figure 17.3 shows an example of using a DockPanel. The XAML for this layout is shown in Listing 17.4.

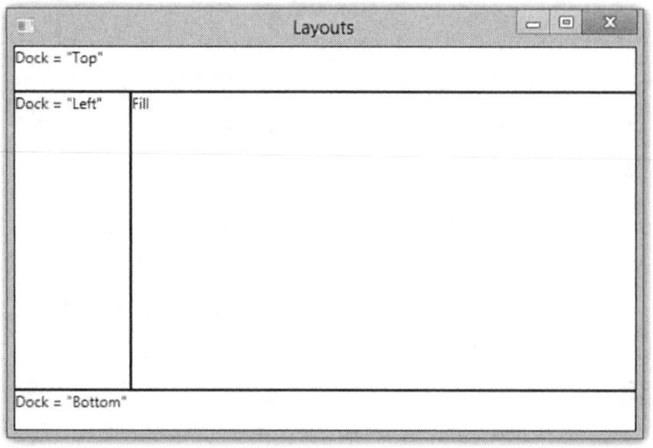

FIGURE 17.3
A DockPanel layout.

LISTING 17.4   XAML Creating a Layout Using `DockPanel`

```
<Window x:Class="WpfApplication1.Layouts"
        xmlns="http://schemas.microsoft.com/winfx/2006/xaml/presentation"
        xmlns:x="http://schemas.microsoft.com/winfx/2006/xaml"
        Title="Layouts" Height="182" Width="272">
    <Grid>
        <DockPanel>
            <Border DockPanel.Dock="Top" BorderThickness="1" BorderBrush="Black">
                <TextBlock Height="35">Dock = "Top"</TextBlock>
            </Border>
            <Border DockPanel.Dock="Bottom" BorderThickness="1" BorderBrush="Black">
                <TextBlock Height="31" >Dock = "Bottom"</TextBlock>
            </Border>
            <Border DockPanel.Dock="Left" BorderThickness="1" BorderBrush="Black">
                <TextBlock Width="93" >Dock = "Left"</TextBlock>
            </Border>
            <Border BorderThickness="1" BorderBrush="Black">
                <TextBlock>Fill</TextBlock>
            </Border>
        </DockPanel>
    </Grid>
</Window>
```

Like all WPF elements, layouts can be nested inside each other, allowing you to create complex layouts.

Using Graphics, Animation, and Media

WPF provides a flexible and rich graphics environment featuring resolution- and device-independent graphics, improved precision, advanced graphics and animation support, and support for hardware acceleration. All graphics measurements in WPF use pixels (1/96th of an inch), no matter what the actual screen resolution might be.

WPF provides support for the following:

▶ 2D shapes, like rectangles and ellipses

▶ 2D geometries to create custom shapes

▶ 2D effects, such as gradients, painting with videos, rotation, and scaling

▶ 3D rendering, which integrates with 2D graphics, enabling you to show 2D images rendered onto 3D shapes

In addition to the 2D and 3D graphics capabilities, WPF also provides animation support. This enables you to make controls grow, shake, spin, or fade, creating unique and interesting transition effects.

WPF directly supports using media, such as images, video, and audio, to convey information. Many controls, including an `Image` control, implicitly know how to display images. Audio and video are both supported through the `MediaElement` control, which is powerful enough to be the basis for a custom media player.

Understanding Text, Typography, and Documents

High-quality text rendering and manipulation are supported through OpenType font support and ClearType enhancements. WPF also has intrinsic support for working with flow documents, fixed documents, and XML Paper Specification (XPS) documents.

Flow documents optimize viewing and readability by dynamically reflowing content as the window size and display settings change. Fixed documents can be used when a precise presentation is required, such as in desktop publishing applications. XPS is an open, cross-platform document format, and support for XPS documents in WPF is built on the support for fixed documents.

Data Binding

Data binding in WPF is handled through a sophisticated and flexible binding engine that enables you to bind a control (the target) to data (the source). This binding engine provides a simple and consistent way to present and interact with data. Many controls have built-in support for displaying single data items or collections of data items, and controls can be bound to a variety of data sources, including .NET objects and XML. The data binding support in WPF is so powerful that many things that were previously only possible in code are now possible directly in XAML.

Creating a WPF Application

In the rest of this hour, you work with a Visual Studio project that has been provided as part of the book downloads, which serves as a starting point for the Desktop photo viewer application you will work on. This is the same project that you have modified during some of the previous hours. However, if you want to create a new Windows application, you would use the New Project dialog box, as shown in Figure 17.4, and choose the WPF Application template.

Just as it does with console applications, Visual Studio creates a solution and project for you. In this case, both the XAML file layout file and the generated C# code-behind file are opened for you, as shown in Figure 17.5.

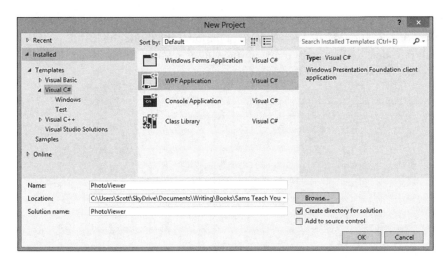

FIGURE 17.4
New Project dialog box.

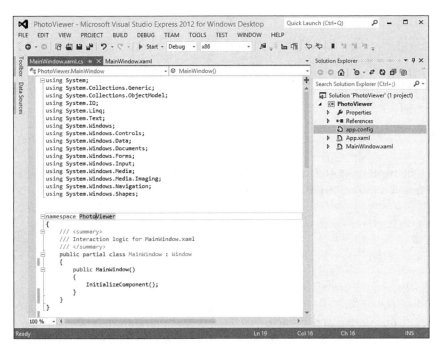

FIGURE 17.5
Visual Studio after creating a WPF application.

The visual designer for XAML-based user interfaces is split into two sections. By default, the top half shows the visual representation of the layout and the bottom half shows the XAML. You can make changes in both portions, and changes made in one will be reflected in the other. Figure 17.6 shows a more detailed view of the XAML designer.

FIGURE 17.6
Detailed view of the XAML editing surface.

You can easily switch between the XAML and Design panes, including swapping them, using the tabs and the Swap Panes button (shown circled), as shown in Figure 17.7.

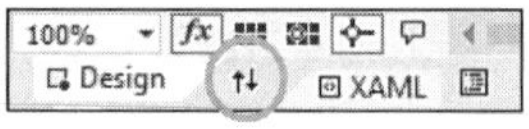

FIGURE 17.7
Design and XAML tabs.

You can also change the orientation of the panes, switching between a horizontal (which is the default) or vertical layout, and collapse the XAML pane entirely using the buttons on the right side of the Design and XAML tabs, as shown in Figure 17.8.

FIGURE 17.8
XAML pane Orientation buttons.

The button to the right of the XAML tab displays the Document Outline tool window, shown in Figure 17.9, which is a tree-oriented view showing all of the visual elements in the window and their relationships to each other. In this example, the Document Outline is not interesting because the window has no other elements. However, when you start adding controls and creating complex layouts, the Document Outline and selected element outline both become helpful for navigating through your layout.

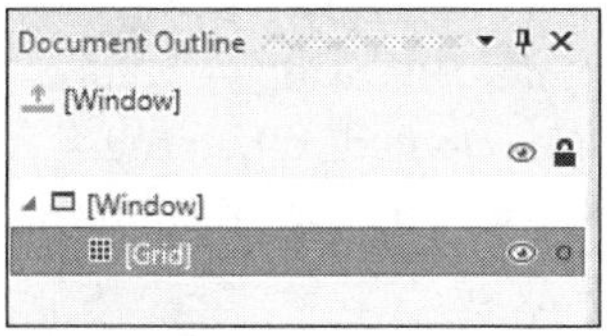

FIGURE 17.9
Document Outline.

If you look at the XAML generated by Visual Studio, the x:Class attribute specifies the fully qualified name of the class that implements the window. In this case, the class is MainWindow in the PhotoViewer namespace. The window Title, Width, and Height are also specified. These can be changed directly in the XAML or by using the Properties window, as shown in Figure 17.10.

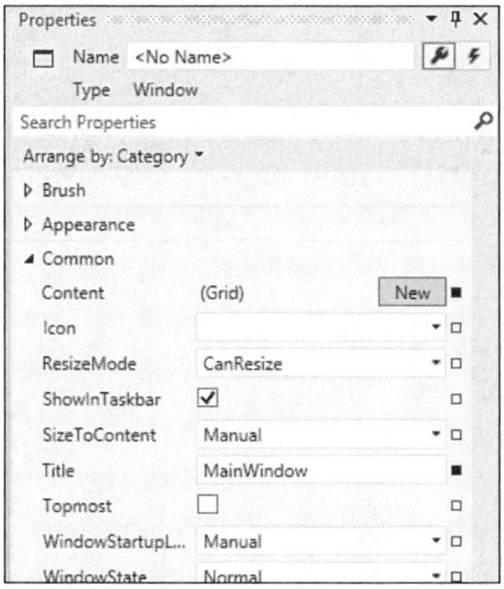

FIGURE 17.10
Properties window.

The xmlns namespace attributes define the schemas used by WPF. These schemas include definitions for all the controls and other items you can incorporate into a WPF application.

Creating the Layout

You are now ready to start creating the layout for the photo viewer application. If you look at the XAML again, you notice that the Window already includes a child element named Grid. In this case, the Grid doesn't explicitly define any rows or columns, so it is a 1×1 table. For the photo viewer application, you need a grid structure containing one row and two columns.

If you click on the large area of whitespace in the Design tab, click on the blank line between the Grid element in the XAML, or click the Grid in the Document Outline, the Grid becomes the selected element. You can visually design the table structure using the mouse by moving the mouse cursor over the blue-shaded edge of the grid in the Design pane. This displays a light orange guideline across the grid showing where the row or column will be created. When the guideline is in the correct place, you can click the left mouse button to create the row or column. An example of what this would look like is shown in Figure 17.11.

FIGURE 17.11
Creating a row visually.

You can also edit the structure using the ColumnDefinitions and RowDefinitions properties of the Grid through the Properties window, as shown in Figure 17.12. These properties are available when you show the advanced Layout properties.

FIGURE 17.12
ColumnDefinitions property.

This displays a Collection Editor dialog box, shown in Figure 17.13, enabling you to easily add rows and columns and configure their properties at the same time. Using the Collection Editor is generally the easiest way to add or edit rows and columns, particularly if you are adding a lot of rows or columns. In fact, if you need to change anything about an existing row or column, you must do so using either the Collection Editor or directly in the XAML.

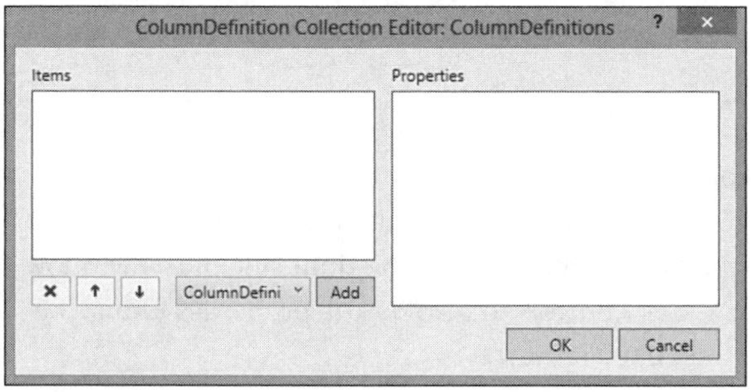

FIGURE 17.13
Collection Editor.

No matter if you visually create the row and column definitions or use the Collection Editor, both methods make changes to the XAML. This means that you can also edit the XAML directly to create the row and column definitions. If you have already created your rows and columns, make sure the generated XAML looks like that shown in Listing 17.5. Otherwise, add the row and column definitions shown in that listing inside the `Grid` element tags in the XAML.

LISTING 17.5   Grid Row and Column Definitions

```
<Grid.RowDefinitions>
    <RowDefinition Height="*" />
</Grid.RowDefinitions>
<Grid.ColumnDefinitions>
    <ColumnDefinition />
    <ColumnDefinition Width="350" />
</Grid.ColumnDefinitions>
```

NOTE

Height and Width Sizing

Everything in WPF is rendered in a resolution-independent manner using pixels as the unit of measurement. Although width and height are normally thought of as just numeric values, WPF has some special values it understands as well.

By providing an actual numeric value, you are telling WPF that the width or height should be exactly that size. However, if you want WPF to automatically distribute space evenly based on content, you should enter a value of `Auto`.

To distribute rows or columns proportionally (using the remaining space if there are also fixed or auto-sized rows or columns), you can use what is called star sizing. To use star sizing, you specify the asterisk symbol (*) as the value. When using star sizing, you can indicate a weighting value that controls how much of the available space is given to that element. For example, a row using * for height would receive one times the available space, and a row using 2* would receive two times the available space.

Now that you have the frame of the layout constructed, you need to start adding controls to it. The left side of the window contains a ListBox control that displays the photos and a Slider control, enabling you to resize the images displayed in the list box. The right side of the window contains a Grid consisting of a series of TextBlock controls to display the properties about the selected photo. The completed layout should look like Figure 17.14.

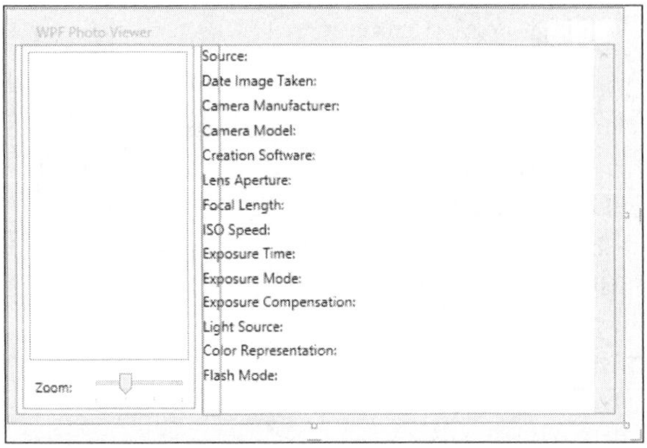

FIGURE 17.14
The completed MainWindow.xaml.

The XAML required for this is shown in Listing 17.6 and would be added to the Grid control, just after the row and column definitions.

CAUTION

WPF and Windows Runtime Controls

Although you don't learn about the Windows Runtime and Windows Store apps until Hour 19, "Building Windows Store Apps," not all of the WPF controls are available in the Windows Runtime. For example, the DockPanel and Label controls are not supported.

If there is a possibility of porting your Desktop application to a Windows Store app, you should choose the WPF controls so that as many as possible are supported by both environments to minimize the amount of redesign that will be required.

LISTING 17.6 XAML for the Photo Viewer Layout

```
<DockPanel Grid.Row="0" Grid.Column="0" Margin="5,0,7,5">
   <DockPanel DockPanel.Dock="Bottom" Margin="5">
      <TextBlock DockPanel.Dock="Left">Zoom:</TextBlock>
      <Slider Name="ZoomSlider" Margin="10,0,0,0" Orientation="Horizontal"
         Minimum="80" Maximum="320" Value="160" TickFrequency="80"
         TickPlacement="BottomRight" SmallChange="5" LargeChange="20" />
   </DockPanel>

   <ScrollViewer VerticalScrollBarVisibility="Auto"
      HorizontalScrollBarVisibility="Disabled">
      <ListBox IsSynchronizedWithCurrentItem="True" x:Name="photosListBox"
         Margin="5" SelectionMode="Extended" SelectedIndex="0" />
   </ScrollViewer>
</DockPanel>

<GridSplitter Grid.Column="1" Grid.RowSpan="2" HorizontalAlignment="Left"
   VerticalAlignment="Stretch" Width="15" Background="Transparent"
   ShowsPreview="True" />

<ScrollViewer Grid.Row="1" Grid.Column="1">
   <Grid x:Name="metadataPanel">
      <Grid.RowDefinitions>
         <RowDefinition />
         <RowDefinition />
         <RowDefinition />
         <RowDefinition />
         <RowDefinition />
         <RowDefinition />
         <RowDefinition />
         <RowDefinition />
         <RowDefinition />
         <RowDefinition />
         <RowDefinition />
         <RowDefinition />
         <RowDefinition />
         <RowDefinition />
         <RowDefinition />
      </Grid.RowDefinitions>
      <Grid.ColumnDefinitions>
         <ColumnDefinition />
         <ColumnDefinition />
      </Grid.ColumnDefinitions>

      <TextBlock Grid.Row="0" Grid.Column="0">Source:</TextBlock>
      <TextBlock Grid.Row="1" Grid.Column="0">Date Image Taken:</TextBlock>
```

```
    <TextBlock Grid.Row="2" Grid.Column="0">Camera Manufacturer:</TextBlock>
    <TextBlock Grid.Row="3" Grid.Column="0">Camera Model:</TextBlock>
    <TextBlock Grid.Row="4" Grid.Column="0">Creation Software:</TextBlock>
    <TextBlock Grid.Row="5" Grid.Column="0">Lens Aperture:</TextBlock>
    <TextBlock Grid.Row="6" Grid.Column="0">Focal Length:</TextBlock>
    <TextBlock Grid.Row="7" Grid.Column="0">ISO Speed:</TextBlock>
    <TextBlock Grid.Row="8" Grid.Column="0">Exposure Time:</TextBlock>
    <TextBlock Grid.Row="9" Grid.Column="0">Exposure Mode:</TextBlock>
    <TextBlock Grid.Row="10" Grid.Column="0">Exposure Compensation:</TextBlock>
    <TextBlock Grid.Row="11" Grid.Column="0">Light Source:</TextBlock>
    <TextBlock Grid.Row="12" Grid.Column="0">Color Representation:</TextBlock>
    <TextBlock Grid.Row="13" Grid.Column="0">Flash Mode:</TextBlock>

    <TextBlock Grid.Row="0" Grid.Column="1" />
    <TextBlock Grid.Row="1" Grid.Column="1" />
    <TextBlock Grid.Row="2" Grid.Column="1" />
    <TextBlock Grid.Row="3" Grid.Column="1" />
    <TextBlock Grid.Row="4" Grid.Column="1" />
    <TextBlock Grid.Row="5" Grid.Column="1" />
    <TextBlock Grid.Row="6" Grid.Column="1" />
    <TextBlock Grid.Row="7" Grid.Column="1" />
    <TextBlock Grid.Row="8" Grid.Column="1" />
    <TextBlock Grid.Row="9" Grid.Column="1" />
    <TextBlock Grid.Row="10" Grid.Column="1" />
    <TextBlock Grid.Row="11" Grid.Column="1" />
    <TextBlock Grid.Row="12" Grid.Column="1" />
    <TextBlock Grid.Row="13" Grid.Column="1" />
  </Grid>
</ScrollViewer>
```

Although this might seem like a lot of work to create a user interface that isn't very functional at the moment, it has several significant advantages over more traditional user interface development. The simplest, yet probably most significant, is that you can deliver the XAML file to a graphics-oriented person who can apply styles and other visual resources to make the application stand out while you can continue developing the core functionality of the application. As long as the underlying user interface controls aren't changed, the designer and the developer can both continue working without impacting the other.

TIP

The `Name` Attribute in XAML

If you look at the `ListBox` and `Grid` definitions in Listing 17.6, you should notice an `x:Name` attribute. By including this attribute, the compiler actually generates a field representing that control, allowing you to reference it directly in the code-behind.

Styling the Layout

Styling a layout can actually mean a variety of different things, each with varying degrees of complexity. On one end of the spectrum is simply applying colors, background images, and various other visual elements directly to the controls. On the other end is creating complete style sheets (similar to Cascading Style Sheets [CSS] for web development) and data templates that can transform controls with an entirely new look.

Every WPF `Window` and `Application` can contain resources that define the style and data templates. Resources defined in a `Window` are placed in a `Window.Resources` element and are local only to that window. If you need resources available to the entire application, they can be placed in the `Application.Resources` element in your `App.xaml` file.

Because style and data templates can become rather large, WPF also supports the idea of resource dictionaries. A resource dictionary is simply a XAML file containing style and data templates within a `ResourceDictionary` element. To include a resource dictionary, you simply add a `ResourceDictionary` element to either `Window.Resources` or `Application.Resources` and provide it the XAML file containing the resources.

Add a new Resource Dictionary item to the project named `Resources.xaml` and include it in the `Application.Resources` element of the `App.xaml` file, as shown in Listing 17.7.

LISTING 17.7 `App.xaml` with a Resource Dictionary

```
<Application x:Class="PhotoViewer.App"
            xmlns="http://schemas.microsoft.com/winfx/2006/xaml/presentation"
            xmlns:x="http://schemas.microsoft.com/winfx/2006/xaml"
            StartupUri="MainWindow.xaml">
    <Application.Resources>
        <ResourceDictionary Source="Resources.xaml"/>
    </Application.Resources>
</Application>
```

The complete resource dictionary definition is shown in Listing 17.8. The `x:Key` attribute defines the name of the style. You use this name when applying it to user interface elements in your XAML files. The `TargetType` defines the type name of the class the style will be applied to.

LISTING 17.8 `Resources.xaml` Resource Dictionary

```
<ResourceDictionary
        xmlns="http://schemas.microsoft.com/winfx/2006/xaml/presentation"
        xmlns:x="http://schemas.microsoft.com/winfx/2006/xaml">

    <Style x:Key="BasicTextStyle" TargetType="TextBlock">
        <Setter Property="TextTrimming" Value="WordEllipsis"/>
```

```
        <Setter Property="TextWrapping" Value="Wrap"/>
        <Setter Property="Typography.StylisticSet20" Value="True"/>
        <Setter Property="Typography.DiscretionaryLigatures" Value="True"/>
        <Setter Property="Typography.CaseSensitiveForms" Value="True"/>
    </Style>

    <Style x:Key="BaselineTextStyle" TargetType="TextBlock"
        BasedOn="{StaticResource BasicTextStyle}">
        <Setter Property="LineHeight" Value="20"/>
        <Setter Property="LineStackingStrategy" Value="BlockLineHeight"/>
        <Setter Property="RenderTransform">
            <Setter.Value>
                <TranslateTransform X="-1" Y="4"/>
            </Setter.Value>
        </Setter>
    </Style>

    <Style x:Key="BodyTextStyle" TargetType="TextBlock"
        BasedOn="{StaticResource BaselineTextStyle}">
        <Setter Property="FontWeight" Value="Light"/>
    </Style>

    <Style TargetType="{x:Type ListBox}" x:Key="PhotoListBoxStyle">
        <Setter Property="Foreground" Value="White" />
        <Setter Property="Template">
            <Setter.Value>
                <ControlTemplate TargetType="{x:Type ListBox}" >
                    <WrapPanel Margin="5" IsItemsHost="True"
                        Orientation="Horizontal"
                        ItemHeight="{Binding ElementName=ZoomSlider, Path='Value'}"
                        ItemWidth="{Binding ElementName=ZoomSlider, Path='Value'}"
                        VerticalAlignment="Top" HorizontalAlignment="Stretch" />
                </ControlTemplate>
            </Setter.Value>
        </Setter>
    </Style>
</ResourceDictionary>
```

Apply the `BodyTextStyle` style to each of the `TextBlock` controls, by adding the following attribute:

```
Style="{StaticResource BodyTextStyle}"
```

Similarly, add the `PhotoListBoxStyle` to the `ListBox` control as well.

If you run the application again, you should see the new styles, as shown in Figure 17.15.

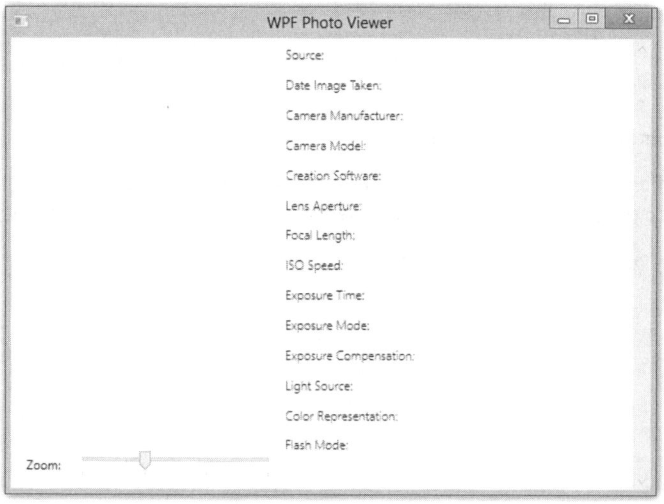

FIGURE 17.15
The restyled application.

Summary

In this hour, you had a quick overview of Windows Presentation Foundation and what it enables you to do. You created a simple WPF application and added code to respond to user events. Finally, you learned how to create styles for your application, completely changing the look with relative ease.

At this point, the application works and looks good but doesn't actually do anything yet. You learn how to put the remaining pieces together in the next hour when you learn about the data-binding capabilities provided by WPF in more detail.

Q&A

Q. What is Windows Presentation Foundation?

A. Windows Presentation Foundation (WPF) is a presentation technology that provides a unified programming model enabling you to build Windows applications that incorporate user interface elements, media, and documents.

Q. What is the benefit to developing with the markup and code-behind style?

A. This enables a clean separation between appearance and behavior, providing the following benefits:

a. Development and maintenance costs are reduced.

b. Development is more efficient, allowing the application's appearance to be created simultaneously with other developers who are implementing the application's behavior.

c. Multiple design tools can be used to create and share the markup.

Workshop

Quiz

1. What is star sizing for rows and columns in a `Grid`?

2. What is a routed event?

Answers

1. To distribute rows or columns proportionally (using the remaining space if there are also fixed or auto-sized rows or columns), you can use what is called star sizing. To use star sizing, you specify the asterisk symbol (*) as the value. When using star sizing, you can indicate a weighting value that controls how much of the available space is given to that element. For example, a row using * for height would receive one times the available space, and a row using 2* would receive two times the available space.

2. A routed event is one that can invoke handlers on multiple listeners in an element tree, not just on the element that raised the event.

Exercises

1. If you haven't already modified the `PhotoViewer` project to include the resource dictionary shown in Listing 17.8, applied the appropriate styles to the `ListBox` and `TextBlock` controls, and modified the `MainWindow.xaml` so that it implements the layout defined in Listing 17.5 and Listing 17.6, do so now.

Using Data Binding and Validation

What You'll Learn in This Hour:

▶ Understanding data binding

▶ Converting data

▶ Validating data

▶ Working with data templates

In the previous hour, you learned how to create a Windows Presentation Foundation (WPF) application and saw how WPF enables you to cleanly separate the user interface portion of an application from the business logic. You learned how to handle events raised by the user interface so that your application does something other than look nice. Although controlling user input can be accomplished through careful user interface design, it is also common to validate that input to ensure the information entered is correct. In addition to accepting and validating user input, applications typically need to display data to the user—for either informational purposes or so the user can modify the data. In WPF applications, this is most easily accomplished using data binding.

In this hour, you learn more about how to use the data-binding capabilities of WPF and how to validate user-entered data to ensure it matches the business rules specified by the application requirements.

Understanding Data Binding

The data-binding capabilities in WPF enable applications to present and interact with data in a simple and consistent manner. You can bind elements to data from a variety of sources, including common language runtime (CLR) objects and Extensible Markup Language (XML). Data binding enables you to establish a connection between user interface controls and business logic. If the data provides the necessary notifications and the binding has the necessary settings, when the data changes the user interface elements bound to it will automatically reflect those changes. In addition, data binding also enables the underlying data source to be automatically updated to reflect changes made to it through the user interface.

As shown in Figure 18.1, you can think of data binding as the bridge between a binding target and a binding source. Most bindings have the following four components:

▶ Binding target object

▶ Target property

▶ Binding source object

▶ Path to the value in the binding source object to use

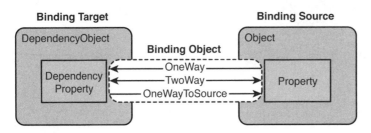

FIGURE 18.1
Data binding conceptual diagram.

The binding target must always be a DependencyObject, which represents an object that participates in the dependency property system. All the user interface objects provided by WPF are derived from UIElement, which, in turn, is derived from DependencyObject. The target property must also be a dependency property, which is a property backed by a DependencyProperty object. Fortunately, most UIElement properties are dependency properties and, other than read-only ones, support data binding by default.

Looking again at Figure 18.1, you can see that a binding can go from the source to the target (OneWay), the target to the source (OneWayToSource), or both (TwoWay):

▶ In OneWay binding, changes to the source property automatically update the target and are typically used when the control bound is implicitly read-only.

▶ In TwoWay binding, changes to either the source or the target property update the other and are typically used in editable forms or other fully interactive interfaces. Most properties default to OneWay binding; however, some (such as properties of user-editable controls, such as the Text property of a TextBox) default to TwoWay binding.

▶ In OneWayToSource, changes to the target property automatically update the source. You can think of this as the reverse of OneWay binding.

▶ There is also a OneTime binding mode, which causes the source property only to initialize the target. When this occurs, subsequent changes do not update the target.

For bindings that are TwoWay or OneWaytoSource to update the source property, they listen for changes in the target property. To know when the source should be updated, bindings use the UpdateSourceTrigger property. When the UpdateSourceTrigger value is PropertyChanged, the source property is updated as soon as the target property changes. If the value is LostFocus, the source property is updated only when the target property loses focus in the user interface. For most dependency properties, the default value for the UpdateSourceTrigger property is PropertyChanged. Some, such as the Text property of a TextBox, default to LostFocus.

Creating a Binding

In the previous hour, you wrote a photo viewer application that didn't display any information, which isn't actually useful. Clearly, more work is needed. If you look again at the Extensible Application Markup Language (XAML) from Listing 17.6, you will notice a group of TextBlock controls that don't display any text. You could programmatically respond to the SelectionChanged event of the ListBox and set the Text property of each TextBlock, but that would be a lot of boilerplate code. A better option would to use the data-binding capabilities of WPF so that each TextBlock can be "told" in the XAML declaration what data to display. This is done by adding a binding for the Text property, as shown:

```
{Binding Path=Source}
```

The Path property of the binding identifies the property of the source object to be displayed. Go ahead and add the appropriate bindings to each of the TextBlock controls, as shown in Listing 18.1.

LISTING 18.1 Creating a Binding

```
<TextBlock Grid.Row="0" Grid.Column="1" Text="{Binding Path=Source}" />
<TextBlock Grid.Row="1" Grid.Column="1" Text="{Binding Path=DateTaken}" />
<TextBlock Grid.Row="2" Grid.Column="1" Text="{Binding Path=EquipmentManufacturer}" />
<TextBlock Grid.Row="3" Grid.Column="1" Text="{Binding Path=CameraModel}" />
<TextBlock Grid.Row="4" Grid.Column="1" Text="{Binding Path=CreationSoftware}" />
<TextBlock Grid.Row="5" Grid.Column="1" Text="{Binding Path=LensAperature}" />
<TextBlock Grid.Row="6" Grid.Column="1" Text="{Binding Path=FocalLength}" />
<TextBlock Grid.Row="7" Grid.Column="1" Text="{Binding Path=IsoSpeed}" />
<TextBlock Grid.Row="8" Grid.Column="1" Text="{Binding Path=ExposureTime}" />
<TextBlock Grid.Row="9" Grid.Column="1" Text="{Binding Path=ExposureMode}" />
<TextBlock Grid.Row="10" Grid.Column="1" Text="{Binding Path=ExposureCompensation}" />
<TextBlock Grid.Row="11" Grid.Column="1" Text="{Binding Path=LightSource}" />
<TextBlock Grid.Row="12" Grid.Column="1" Text="{Binding Path=ColorRepresentation}" />
<TextBlock Grid.Row="13" Grid.Column="1" Text="{Binding Path=FlashMode}" />
```

Up until now, you have been working with bindings to single objects. Typically, you would use an `ItemsControl` (such as a `ListBox`, `ListView`, or `TreeView`) to display collections, binding the `ItemsSource` property to the collection instance. By default, the `ItemsSource` property supports `OneWay` binding. In the `PhotoViewer` application, you are using a `ListBox` that needs to show the instance of the `PhotoCollection` you created in the `MainWindow` class in Hour 10, "Working with Arrays and Collections."

Listing 18.2 shows the XAML you could use to bind the `ItemsSource` property of the `ListBox` control and uses the empty binding syntax `{Binding}`, meaning that the source object has not been specified. Because this is one of the four required components of a binding, how does this work? When the binding engine encounters a binding that has not specified a source, it looks upward through the hierarchy of visual elements looking for a `DataContext`. When it finds a `DataContext`, it uses that as the binding source.

LISTING 18.2   Binding the `ItemsSource` Property of an `ItemsControl`

```
<ListBox Name="photosListBox"
    SelectionMode="Extended" SelectedIndex="0" IsSynchronizedWithCurrentItem="True"
    ItemsSource="{Binding}" />
```

Although it appears as if you are binding the `ListBox` control to a collection, you are actually binding it to an implicit `CollectionViewSource` instance that WPF creates for you. This default view is shared by all bindings to the same collection. If you need access in the code-behind file to the default view, you can use the static `CollectionViewSource.GetDefaultView()` method.

NOTE

Creating a `CollectionViewSource`

You can also create a view directly in XAML using the `CollectionViewSource`, which is an XAML proxy of a class that inherits from `CollectionView`, as shown here:

```
<Window.Resources>
    <CollectionViewSource x:Key="view"
        Source="{Binding Source={x:Static Application.Current},
            Path=Contacts}" />
</Window.Resources>.
```

This creates a new resource named `view`, which is bound to the `Contacts` property of the current application object.

A collection view is a layer over the binding source collection and enables you to navigate and display data based on sort, filter, or group queries without changing the underlying collection. Because views don't change the underlying collection, you can create multiple views that refer to the same source, enabling you to display the same data in different ways.

The default views created for the different source collection types are shown in Table 18.1.

TABLE 18.1   Default Views

Source Collection Type	Collection View Type
IEnumerable	An internal type based on CollectionView
IList	ListCollectionView
IBindingList	BindingListCollectionView

CAUTION

The Default Collection View for IEnumerable

The default collection view created when the source collection type is an IEnumerable does not support grouping items.

The code in Listing 18.3 shows how to add sorting to a collection view.

LISTING 18.3   Changing the Sort Order on a View

```
// Clear any existing SortDescriptions that may have been added. You only need to
// do this if you are changing the sorting.
view.SortDescriptions.Clear();

// Add a new sort which will sort the LastName property ascending.
var sortDescription = new SortDescription("LastName", ListSortDirection.Ascending);
view.SortDescriptions.Add(sortDescription);
```

NOTE

The SortDescription **Structure**

The propertyName parameter of the SortDescription structure supports referencing nested properties through a "dot" notation. For example, to create a SortDescription for a Contact. PhoneNumber.Extension property, you would use the string PhoneNumber.Extension for the propertyName parameter value.

When you are sorting on a property whose data type is an enumeration, the order of the items is the same as in the enumeration declaration.

All collection views, except for the internal class used for viewing IEnumerable collections, support grouping capabilities, enabling the user to partition the data into logical groups. Groups can be explicit, in which case they are determined by the user, or implicit, in which case they are generated dynamically based on the data. The code in Listing 18.4 shows how to add grouping to a collection view.

LISTING 18.4   Adding Grouping to a View

```
// Clear any existing GroupDescriptions that may have been added.
view.GroupDescriptions.Clear();

var groupDescription = new PropertyGroupDescription("LastName");
view.GroupDescriptions.Add(groupDescription);
```

Filtering changes the data displayed by the view without changing the underlying collection. Think of filtering as generating subsets of data. Filtering involves the use of a delegate to perform the actual filtering. For example, the delegate needed to filter a collection of Contact instances to display only those contacts whose last name starts with the letter *D* is shown in Listing 18.5.

LISTING 18.5   Method Used for Filtering

```
private void NameFilter(object sender, FilterEventArgs e)
{
    Contact contact = e.Item as Contact;
    if (contact != null)
    {
        e.Accepted = contact.LastName.StartsWith("D");
    }
    else
    {
        e.Accepted = false;
    }
}
```

If you use one of the `CollectionView` classes directly, you would set the callback using the `Filter` property. However, if you use a `CollectionViewSource`, you need to add the event handler, as shown here:

```
view.Filter += new FilterEventHandler(NameFilter);
```

NOTE

Implementing Collections

If you want a collection to be usable by the data-binding engine so that insertions or deletions automatically update the UI elements, the collection must implement the `System.Collections.Specialized.INotifyCollectionChanged` interface. This interface defines the `CollectionChanged` event that should be raised whenever the collection changes.

To fully support transferring values, each object in the collection that supports bindable properties must also implement the INotifyPropertyChanged interface, which defines a single public event: the PropertyChanged event. Any property that should notify when its value has changed would raise the OnPropertyChanged method.

The .NET Framework provides the ObservableCollection<T> class, which already implements both the INotifyCollectionChanged and the INotifyPropertyChanged interfaces. Unless you have an advanced scenario and want to implement your own collection for use in data binding, you should consider using ObservableCollection<T>.

At this point, you have created bindings for all of the TextBlock controls to display the selected image's information, but you still need to provide a binding that will set the DataContext of the metadataPanel Grid. To do this, you need to modify the Grid definition so that it looks like the following:

```
<Grid x:Name="metadataPanel" DataContext="{Binding Items.CurrentItem,
ElementName=photosListBox, Mode=OneWay}">
```

If you haven't already added the binding shown in Listing 18.2, go ahead and add it now. Because this binding uses the empty binding syntax, you will need to programmatically set DataContext to an object that has already been instantiated. You can do this by modifying the App.xaml file so that it looks like the code shown in Listing 18.6.

LISTING 18.6   Application XAML

```
<Application x:Class="PhotoViewer.App"
             xmlns="http://schemas.microsoft.com/winfx/2006/xaml/presentation"
             xmlns:x="http://schemas.microsoft.com/winfx/2006/xaml"
             Startup="OnApplicationStartup">
    <Application.Resources>
    </Application.Resources>
</Application>
```

Then, in the App.xaml.cs, add the event handler method, as shown in Listing 18.7.

LISTING 18.7   The OnApplicationStartup Event Handler

```
void OnApplicationStartup(object sender, StartupEventArgs args)
{
    MainWindow mainWindow = new MainWindow();
    mainWindow.Show();
    this.MainWindow.DataContext = mainWindow.Photos;
}
```

NOTE

Current Item Pointers

Because WPF always binds to a collection using a view, all bindings to collections have a current item pointer. This is true whether you use the collection's default view or you specify your own view. Sorting operations preserve the current item pointer on the last item selected, but the collection view is restructured around it.

For example, if the selected item were at the beginning of the list before sorting, it might be somewhere in the middle of the list afterward. If a filter is applied and the selected item remains in the view after the filtering has occurred, it continues to be the selected item; otherwise, the first item of the filtered view becomes the current item. The slash (/) character in a `Path` value indicates the current item of the view. Some sample bindings, which assume the data context is a collection view, are shown here:

```
<!-- Bind to the entire collection. -->
<Label Content="{Binding}" />

<!-- Bind to the current item. -->
<Label Content="{Binding Path=/}" />

<!-- Bind to the LastName property of the current item. -->
<Label Content="{Binding Path=/LastName}" />
```

When elements, such as a `Label`, that do not support an `ItemsSource` property are bound to a collection view, they automatically bind to the current item of that view. `CollectionViewSource` objects automatically synchronize the currently selected item, but if the `ItemsControl` were not bound to a `CollectionViewSource`, you would need to set the `IsSynchronizedWithCurrentItem` property to `true` for this to work.

As you might imagine, the current item pointer is also useful for creating master-detail style bindings in which one section of the user interface shows the entire collection, perhaps in a summary or condensed manner, and another shows the full details of the current item.

Converting Data

If you run the application, you may notice that some of the photo details do not look as user friendly as they could. For example, the exposure time displays as a decimal value and any of the metadata details backed by enumerations simply show the named value. The data-binding capabilities in WPF enable you to change, or convert, the value from one side of the binding to something the other side of the binding can accept. Figure 18.2 shows how data conversion fits into the binding picture.

Although WPF provides many standard default converters (for example, to convert between a `Color` and a `Brush`), there are times when it is necessary to create your own converter:

▶ The data needs to be displayed differently based on culture, such as currency or calendar date/time values.

▶ The data needs to be displayed differently than it is stored to make it more readable, such as displaying decimal values as fractions.

▶ The data is bound to multiple controls or multiple properties of controls and each needs to display the data in a different way.

▶ The data used is intended to change some other value, such as an image source or text style.

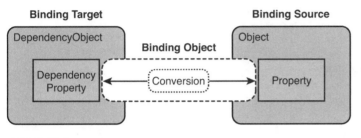

FIGURE 18.2
Data conversion conceptual diagram.

To create your own converter, you implement the IValueConverter interface. The Convert method performs data conversion from source to target, whereas the ConvertBack method performs data conversion from target to source.

Listing 18.8 shows a custom converter for the exposure time that converts between a decimal value and a string value showing the decimal represented as a fraction.

LISTING 18.8   Exposure Time Converter

```
public class ExposureTimeConverter : IValueConverter
{
    public object Convert(object value, Type targetType, object parameter,
      CultureInfo culture)
    {
        object result = DependencyProperty.UnsetValue;

        if (value != null)
        {
            decimal exposure = (decimal)value;
            if (exposure > 0)
            {
                exposure = Math.Round(1 / exposure);
                result = String.Format("1/{0} sec.", exposure.ToString());
            }
        }
```

```
        return result;
    }

    public object ConvertBack(object value, Type targetTypes, object parameter,
        CultureInfo culture)
    {
        object result = DependencyProperty.UnsetValue;

        if (value != null)
        {
            string temp = ((string)value).Substring(2);
            decimal exposure = Decimal.Parse(temp);
            if (exposure > 0)
            {
                result = (1 / exposure);
            }
        }

        return result;
    }
}
```

When you have created the converter, you can add it as a resource in the XAML file, as shown here. This assumes an XML namespace local that maps to the CLR namespace in which ExposureTimeConverter is defined:

```
<local:ExposureTimeConverter x:Key="exposureTimeConverter" />
```

Finally, you can use the converter in your own bindings by adding it to the binding in the XAML. The following shows the binding for the exposure time Label using the new converter:

```
{Binding Path=ExposureTime, Converter={StaticResource exposureTimeConverter }}
```

A converter that implements IValueConverter can convert only a single value. Although this is sufficient for many converters, it is sometimes necessary to produce a final value from multiple source properties, or even multiple source objects. For example, if you wanted to display the x and y coordinates of a point in the standard mathematical representation of (x, y) you would need to use a multivalue converter. Listing 18.9 shows an example of a multivalue converter. In a production application, you should ensure that the conversions are robust in the face of exceptions. To keep the example simple, this exception handling code has been omitted.

LISTING 18.9   Size Multivalue Converter

```
public class CoordinatesConverter : IMultiValueConverter
{
    public object Convert(object[] values, Type targetType, object parameter,
```

```
      CultureInfo culture)
   {
      if (values[0] == null || values[1] == null)
      {
         return String.Empty;
      }
      else if (values[0] == DependencyProperty.UnsetValue ||
               values[1] == DependencyProperty.UnsetValue)
      {
         return String.Empty;
      }
      else
      {
         return String.Format("({0},{1})", values[0], values[1]);
      }
   }

   public object[] ConvertBack(object value, Type[] targetTypes, object parameter,
      CultureInfo culture)
   {
      string temp = value as String;
      if (String.IsNullOrWhiteSpace(temp))
      {
         return new object[2];
      }
      else
      {
         temp = temp.Replace("(", "").Replace(")", "");
         string[] sSize = new string[2];
         sSize = ((string)value).Split(',');

         object[] size = new object[2];
         size[0] = UInt32.Parse(sSize[0]);
         size[1] = UInt32.Parse(sSize[1]);
         return size;
      }
   }
}
```

Adding a multivalue converter as a resource in XAML is done the same way as for a single-value converter; however, using it as part of a binding is different. Rather than using a simple binding, as you have been doing, you need to use a MultiBinding instead. A MultiBinding enables you to bind a property of the target to a list of source properties and get back a single value. Because a MultiBinding is made up of individual Binding elements, each binding can have its own converters if necessary.

Listing 18.10 shows how to use the `CoordinatesConverter` in XAML.

LISTING 18.10   Using a Multivalue Converter

```
<TextBlock>
    <TextBlock.Text>
        <MultiBinding Converter="{StaticResource coordinatesConverter}">
            <Binding Path="xValue"/>
            <Binding Path="yValue"/>
        </MultiBinding>
    </TextBlock.Text>
</TextBlock>
```

The order in which the individual `Binding` elements appear in the `MultiBinding` is the order those values are stored in the array passed to the `Convert` method.

Converters, whether they are single or multivalue, are culture aware. The `Convert` and `ConvertBack` methods both have a `culture` parameter that can be used to change the conversion based on cultural information.

The `Convert` and `ConvertBack` methods also have a parameter named `parameter`, which can be used to change the conversion. This parameter enables the flexibility of using a single converter that can produce different formats based on the value of the converter `parameter` argument.

CAUTION

The `ConverterParameter` Property

The `ConverterParameter` property of a `MultiBinding` is not a `DependencyProperty`, so you can't bind it. If you need an `IMultiValueConverter` to behave differently based on the value of some other source property, you need to find an alternative way of providing that value. One simple option is to include that value as the last binding element in the list.

Validating Data

If your application accepts user input, and most do, you probably have a need to validate that input against business rules to ensure the user entered the expected information. These validation checks can be based on type, range, format, or some other application-specific requirements and are part of the data-binding engine.

To add validation checks, you need to add one or more validation rules to the `ValidationRules` collection of the `Binding`, as shown in Listing 18.11.

LISTING 18.11 Associating `ValidationRules` with a Binding

```
<TextBox Name="PhoneNumber">
   <TextBox.Text>
      <Binding Path="LastName" UpdateSourceTrigger="PropertyChanged">
         <Binding.ValidationRules>
            <ExceptionValidationRule />
         </Binding.ValidationRules>
      </Binding>
   </TextBox.Text>
</TextBox>
```

As you can see, the `ValidationRules` property takes a collection of `ValidationRule` objects. The `ExceptionValidationRule` is a built-in validation rule that checks for exceptions thrown during the update of the binding source. If the source object implements the `IDataError` interface, you can use the built-in `DataErrorValidationRule` to check for errors raised by the `IDataError` implementation.

NOTE

`ValidatesOnException` **and** `ValidatesOnDataErrors`

As an alternative to explicitly including the `ExceptionValidationRule`, you can set the `ValidatesOnExceptions` property to `true`. Similarly, you can set the `ValidatesOnDataErrors` property to `true` rather than explicitly including the `DataErrorValidationRule`.

To provide your own application-specific validation rules, you derive a new class from the `ValidationRule` class and implement the `Validate` method. Listing 18.12 shows a validation rule for the `AddressBook` application that can validate phone numbers.

LISTING 18.12 A Custom `ValidationRule`

```
class PhoneNumberValidationRule : ValidationRule
{
   public override ValidationResult Validate(object value, CultureInfo cultureInfo)
   {
      string stringValue = value.ToString();
      string pattern = @"^[2-9]\d{2}-\d{3}-\d{4}$";

      if (String.IsNullOrWhiteSpace(stringValue) ||
          Regex.IsMatch(stringValue, pattern))
      {
         return ValidationResult.ValidResult;
      }
      else
```

```
    {
        return new ValidationResult(false, "Value is not a valid phone number.");
    }
  }
}
```

CAUTION

The `UpdateSourceTrigger` Property

When the `UpdateSourceTrigger` value is `PropertyChanged`, as it is in Listing 18.12, the binding engine updates the source value on every keystroke. This also means that every rule in the `ValidationRules` collection will be checked on every keystroke.

Although determining that the user has entered an invalid value is the primary use for data validation, you can also provide visual feedback that the value is invalid. To do this, you should first define a `ControlTemplate`, which defines the visual and structural appearance of the control. For example, Listing 18.13 defines a `ControlTemplate` that places a reddish-colored asterisk symbol in front of the control containing the error.

LISTING 18.13   A Custom `ControlTemplate`

```
<ControlTemplate x:Key="validationTemplate">
    <DockPanel>
        <TextBlock Foreground="FireBrick" FontSize="18">*</TextBlock>
        <AdornedElementPlaceholder />
    </DockPanel>
</ControlTemplate>
```

The `AdornedElementPlaceholder` element indicates where the actual control containing the error will be placed.

To use this `ControlTemplate`, you set the `Validation.ErrorTemplate` property of the `UIElement` to a custom `ControlTemplate`, as shown in Listing 18.14.

LISTING 18.14   Setting the `Validation.ErrorTemplate` Property

```
<TextBox Name="PhoneNumber"
    Validation.ErrorTemplate="{StaticResource validationTemplate}">
    <TextBox.Text>
        <Binding Path="PhoneNumber"
            UpdateSourceTrigger="PropertyChanged">
            <Binding.ValidationRules>
                <ExceptionValidationRule />
                <local:PhoneNumberValidationRule />
```

```
        </Binding.ValidationRules>
      </Binding>
    </TextBox.Text>
</TextBox>
```

If you don't specify an `ErrorTemplate`, a default template will be used. This default template defines a red border around the adorned control.

Working with Data Templates

At the end of the last hour, you learned how to style your application by completely changing how a control looks. These visual styles change only the appearance of the control; they do not specify how that control visualizes data. To change how data is visualized by a control, you use a `DataTemplate`. This is particularly useful when binding an `ItemsControl`, such as a `ListBox`, to a collection.

Without a `DataTemplate`, the `ItemsControl` calls `ToString` when trying to display the objects in the collection. Although you could override `ToString` to provide a meaningful string representation, that isn't always the best approach (or might not be possible). The solution is to define a `DataTemplate`, which enables you to change the visual structure used by the `ItemsControl` to display the data.

Listing 18.15 shows the `DataTemplate` used by the `PhotoViewer` application so that the `ListBox` control displays a thumbnail of the image instead of the filename.

LISTING 18.15   Defining a `DataTemplate`

```
<DataTemplate DataType="{x:Type local:Photo}">
    <Grid Width="190" Height="130">
        <Border Width="190" Height="130">
            <Image Source="{Binding Image}" Stretch="None" Width="190" Height="130" />
        </Border>
    </Grid>
</DataTemplate>
```

In this case, the `DataTemplate` specified a value for the `DataType` property. This is similar to the `TargetType` property of a `Style` and indicates that the `DataTemplate` should be used by any control displaying an object of that type.

You could also have specified the `x:Key` property, in which case you would need to explicitly associate the template with the control. Listing 18.16 shows such an association, assuming the `DataTemplate` has an `x:Key` property whose value is `photoTemplate`.

LISTING 18.16   Associating a `DataTemplate`

```
<ListBox
    ItemsSource="{Binding}"
    ItemTemplate="{StaticResource photoTemplate}" />
```

Summary

In this hour, you learned about data binding in WPF and added bindings to the `PhotoViewer` application to make it more complete. As part of this, you learned how collection views enable you to sort, group, or filter your data without affecting the underlying collection. From there, you learned how data converters can change the value from one side of the binding to something the other side of the binding will accept. You learned how validation works with data binding by using a custom validation rule. Finally, you learned that data templates enable you to change the structural representation of how a control displays data, which is particularly useful when binding to collections.

Q&A

Q. What are the four components of a binding?

A. A binding is made up of a binding target object, a target property, a binding source object, and a path to the value in the binding source object.

Q. What is a `OneWayToSource` binding?

A. A OneWayToSource binding changes the source property automatically whenever the target property changes.

Q. What is a data converter?

A. A data converter is a class that implements either `IValueConverter` or `IMultiValueConverter` and enables you to convert a value between different values going in either direction through a binding.

Q. Why are collection views useful?

A. Collection views enable you to create multiple independent views over the same source collection, which can be filtered, grouped, or sorted without affecting the underlying collection.

Q. What is a data template used for?

A. A data template enables you to change how data is displayed by a control.

Q. Does WPF provide any built-in validation rules?

A. Yes, WPF provides the `ExceptionValidationRule`, which checks for exceptions thrown during the update of the binding source, and the `DataErrorValidationRule` to check for errors raised by a control that implements the `IDataError` interface.

Workshop

Quiz

1. What happens when the binding engine encounters a binding that has not specified a source?

2. Can the `ConverterParameter` property of a `MultiBinding` get its value from another binding?

3. Does WPF bind directly to collections?

4. What class do you inherit from to provide custom validation rules?

5. What is the `AdornedElementPlaceholder` element in a control template?

Answers

1. When the binding engine encounters a binding that has not specified a source, it looks upward through the hierarchy of visual elements looking for a `DataContext`. When it finds a `DataContext`, it uses that as the binding source.

2. Because the `ConverterParameter` property of a `MultiBinding` is not a `DependencyProperty`, you can't bind it.

3. Even though you might specify a binding directly to a collection, WPF actually binds to the default `CollectionView` for that collection.

4. To provide a custom validation rule, you must derive from `ValidationRule`.

5. The `AdornedElementPlaceholder` element in a control template indicates where the control being adorned will be placed.

Exercises

1. Modify the bindings for the lens aperture, focal length, exposure time, and exposure mode to include the appropriate converters. To do this, you will need to add the converters as resources to the `Resources.xaml` file and then update the bindings appropriately. If you haven't already added the other bindings shown in Listing 18.1, do so now as well. In addition, if you haven't already done so, modify the `ListBox` control to include the binding shown in Listing 18.2, add a binding to set the `DataContext` of the `metadataPanel`

Grid, and implement the OnApplicationStartup event, as shown in Listings 18.6 and 18.7. Finally, add the data template shown in Listing 18.15 to the Resources.xaml file.

2. Create a new WPF application and add a class that implements the custom validation rule shown in Listing 18.12. Modify the MainWindow.xaml to replace the Grid control with the following StackPanel control:

```
<StackPanel>
    <TextBlock Text="Enter a phone number:" />
    <TextBox x:Name="phoneNumber">
      <TextBox.Text>
        <Binding Path="PhoneNumber" UpdateSourceTrigger="PropertyChanged">
          <Binding.ValidationRules>
            <local:PhoneNumberValidationRule />
          </Binding.ValidationRules>
        </Binding>
      </TextBox.Text>
    </TextBox>
</StackPanel>
```

Add a new class named DataSource that implements a simple string auto property named PhoneNumber and assign an instance of that class to the DataContext of the MainWindow. You can do this in the MainWindow constructor with the following code:

```
this.DataContext = new DataSource();
```

HOUR 19
Building Windows Store Apps

What You'll Learn in This Hour:

- ▶ Understanding the Windows Runtime
- ▶ What's a Windows Store app?
- ▶ Working asynchronously
- ▶ Building an app

Similar to Windows Phone, apps are at the center of the Windows 8 user experience. Although Windows 8 can run traditional desktop style applications (like the one you developed in Hour 17, "Building a Windows Application"), the real app potential lies in the new Windows Store apps. These apps immerse the user in a full-screen experience where they can concentrate on the content rather than on the operating system.

Visual Studio 2012 allows you to use your existing development skills to create Windows Store apps. If you prefer web development, you can continue to use your HTML5, CSS3, and JavaScript skills. For desktop developers who are familiar with the .NET Framework or Silverlight, you can continue to use your Extensible Application Markup Language (XAML), C#, and Visual Basic skills. You can also leverage the power of DirectX 11 for games and other graphics-intensive apps.

CAUTION

Visual Studio Express for Windows 8

If you use Visual Studio Express for Windows Desktop or Visual Studio Express for Web, you cannot build Windows Store apps. Instead, you need to install Visual Studio Express for Windows 8. If you use one of the paid editions of Visual Studio, you already have everything you need to build Windows Store apps.

In this hour, you learn what a Windows Store app is and how to build a basic app using XAML and C#. As part of this, you will be introduced to the Windows Runtime and the async pattern available in C#.

Understanding the Windows Runtime

The Windows Runtime is a set of application programming interfaces (APIs) used to build Windows Store apps and is available to all of the supported programming languages. To build a Windows Store app, you can only use the Windows Runtime APIs; however, if you are building a traditional desktop application, you can access a subset of the Windows Runtime API in addition to the standard Win32 and .NET APIs.

Even though the .NET Framework is already a sandboxed API, you can think of Windows Runtime as being an even smaller sandbox. The APIs were designed specifically to help you create Windows Store apps that focus on content rather than chrome; they are power conscious because most Windows Store apps will be running on a laptop, slate, or tablet. To support these considerations, Windows Runtime presents a simple programming model and only provides access to certain parts of the underlying operating system. In addition to the sandboxing provided by Windows Runtime, all of the APIs are designed to be asynchronous. This was done to help ensure that an app isn't able to drain battery power by waiting for a long-running task to complete and that the app always stays responsive to user input.

It is important to understand that Windows Runtime and the .NET Framework are not synonymous with each other and one is not replacing the other. When you build a Windows Store app using C# and the .NET Framework, you are using a subset of managed types called .NET for Windows Store apps. This subset allows you to create Windows Store apps in C# without needing to jump through a lot of hoops to get the job done. Any of the .NET Framework types that aren't related to developing a Windows Store app are not exposed as part of that subset. Because the .NET APIs for Windows Store apps was designed with the sole focus of developing Windows Store apps, the following are not exposed:

▶ Types and members that aren't related to developing Windows Store apps (such as the `Console` class and the ASP.NET types)

▶ Obsolete and legacy types

▶ Types that overlap with those provided by the Windows Runtime

▶ Types and members that wrap operating system capabilities (such as `System.Diagnostics.EventLog`)

▶ Members that tend to be confusing

Ordinarily you shouldn't notice any difference when using a .NET Framework type or a Windows Runtime type except for the namespace. The .NET Framework types are in namespaces that all start with `System`, whereas the Windows Runtime types are in namespaces that start with

`Windows`. The Windows Runtime together with .NET for Windows Store apps provide the complete set of types and members required for developing Windows Store apps.

What's a Windows Store App?

Put simply, a Windows Store app has a single chromeless window that fills the entire screen, as seen in Figure 19.1. Although these types of apps are common on mobile devices (just look at any Windows Phone), they are new for Windows. By keeping the user's focus on the content, there are no distractions for the user.

FIGURE 19.1
A Windows Store app.

Windows Store apps can also support either Portrait or Landscape views as well as a smaller "Snap" view, as shown in Figure 19.2.

FIGURE 19.2
A Windows Store app in Snap view.

These apps are designed to work with touch, pen, mouse, and keyboard input and the Windows Runtime provides a single set of events that works for all of the different input sources.

To help make it easier to create a great user experience, Windows Store apps provide several new controls, including the app bar and charms, as shown in Figure 19.3. The app bar provides the primary command area for your app and can be used to present navigation, commands, and tools to the user. Normally hidden, it appears when the user swipes a finger from the top or bottom edge of the screen. Charms provide a consistent set of buttons available in every app that allows the user to do the following:

- ▶ Search in your app or in another app, including the ability to search your app's content from another app.
- ▶ Share content from your app.
- ▶ Go to the Start screen.
- ▶ Connect to devices to send content, stream media, and print.
- ▶ Access settings to configure your app.

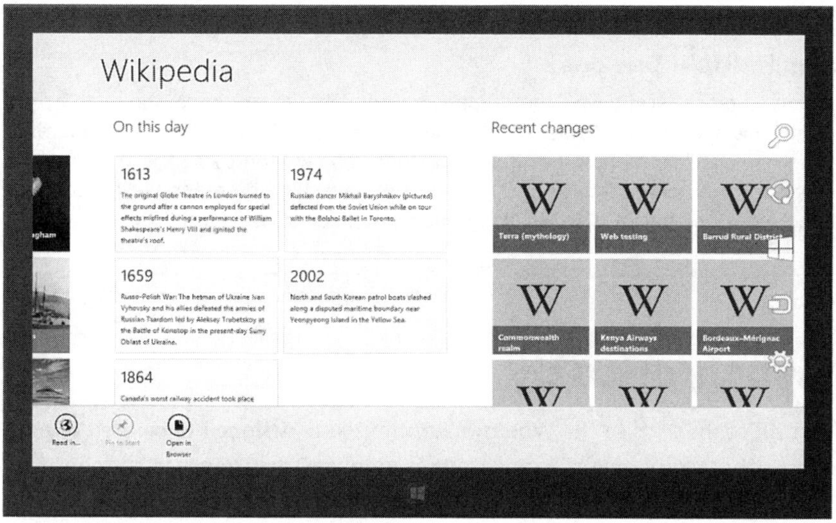

FIGURE 19.3
The app bar and charms.

Searching and sharing make use of app contracts, allowing you to not worry (or know anything) about the target app other than its support for the target contract.

Unlike traditional desktop applications that can be obtained from virtually anywhere, Windows Store apps can only be obtained through the Windows Store. This means that any Windows Store app you create must be submitted to the Store where it is reviewed and certified by Microsoft before being made available.

NOTE

Enterprise Access to Windows Store

To fully support enterprises, it is possible to control access to the Windows Store and allow applications to be deployed directly to the computers they manage without going through the Windows Store infrastructure. This process is commonly called **sideloading**.

This model is similar to the Marketplace used by Windows Phone. By limiting distribution to the Windows Store, users have a single, trusted location to find apps and Microsoft certifies that those apps will run both on Intel-based Windows 8 Pro devices and ARM-based Windows RT devices.

TIP

Write Once, Run on Multiple Devices?

At the time this book went to press, Windows Store apps were only able to run on Windows 8 Pro and Windows RT devices. However, the next release of Windows Phone will share the same operating system kernel as Windows 8. This means that it is likely that apps written using the Windows Runtime will be easily ported to Windows Phone 8. If you want an app that can reach the broadest possible audience on the most number of devices, you should consider building it as a Windows Store app.

Working Asynchronously

You learned earlier that all of the APIs in the Windows Runtime were designed to be used asynchronously, but what does that really mean? Asynchrony is a natural occurrence in humans and is what allows us to process input from multiple sources simultaneously while still being responsive to the world around us. As a result, we expect apps to behave the same way. Using asynchronous programming, you can indicate areas of your code where potentially long-running tasks are suspended while other parts of your program continue, thereby avoiding potential bottlenecks and enhancing the overall responsiveness of your application.

This ability is important for activities such as accessing the web. If such an activity is blocked within a synchronous process, the entire program is blocked; however, in an asynchronous process, the program can continue making progress in other areas while waiting for the blocking task to finish. It is even more important for providing a fast and fluid user interface. Typically, all user interface–related activity shares a single thread; if one process is blocked, all are blocked and your user interface will appear to "freeze."

TIP

Asynchrony and Threads

Asynchronous methods are intended to be nonblocking operations, meaning that they don't block the current thread while it is running. Because an asynchronous method doesn't run on its own thread, it doesn't require multithreading. Instead, the method runs on the current synchronization context, using time on the thread only when it's active.

Although asynchronous programming has always been possible, it has been difficult to get right and, as a result, was typically avoided. The code shown in Listing 19.1 is very straightforward. The logic and intent are clear: This is a method that downloads a set of uniform resource locators (URLs) to total their size and displays progress messages as it works.

LISTING 19.1 **A Simple Synchronous Method**

```
private int TotalPageSizes(IList<Uri> collection)
{
   int total = 0;
   foreach(var uri in collection)
   {
      statusText.Text = String.Format("Found {0} bytes ...", total);
      using (var content = new MemoryStream())
      {
         var request = WebRequest.CreateHttp(uri);
         using (var response = request.GetResponse())
         {
            response.GetResponseStream().CopyTo(content);
         }
         total += content.ToArray().Length;
      }
   }
   statusText.Text = String.Format("Found {0} total bytes.", total);
   return total;
}
```

To make this code asynchronous using traditional methods, you would need code that looks similar to that shown in Listing 19.2.

LISTING 19.2 **A Traditional Asynchronous Method**

```
private void TotalPageSizesAsync(IList<Uri> collection,
  Action<int, Exception> callback)
{
   TotalPageSizeAsyncHelper(collection.GetEnumerator(), 0, callback);
}

private void TotalPageSizeAsyncHelper(IEnumerator<Uri> enumerator, int total,
   Action<int, Exception> callback)
{
   try
   {
      if (enumerator.MoveNext())
      {
         statusText.Text = String.Format("Found {0} bytes ...", total);
         using (var content = new MemoryStream())
         {
            var request = WebRequest.CreateHttp(enumerator.Current);
            using (var response = request.GetResponse())
            {
               response.GetResponseStream().CopyTo(content);
            }
```

```
                total += content.ToArray().Length;
            }
        }
        else
        {
            statusText.Text = String.Format("Found {0} total bytes.", total);
            enumerator.Dispose();
            callback(total, null);
        }
    }
    catch (Exception ex)
    {
        enumerator.Dispose();
        callback(0, ex);
    }
}
```

Although the code shown in Listing 19.2 is functionally equivalent to that of Listing 19.1, it required a lot of changes to expand the `foreach` statement and propagate all of the exception. In fact, it's unlikely that we got everything correct and we have lost the ability to quickly look at the code and easily understand what it does.

NOTE

The Async Pattern Isn't Just for Windows Store Apps

Although the async pattern will be most frequently used in Windows Store apps, it is actually defined in the C# language and supported by the compiler. This means that you can, and should, also use this pattern in your traditional desktop applications to ensure that they are responsive as well.

To help simplify the task of creating and consuming asynchronous methods, a new, simplified approach was introduced using the `async` and `await` keywords. This approach makes it easier to write, understand, and maintain asynchronous code. The difficult work (that you used to do) is now done by the compiler. You can now write asynchronous code in much the same way as you would write synchronous code.

The `async` modifier lets the compiler know that the method, lambda expression, or anonymous method it modifies is asynchronous and that suspension (or await) points can be designated with the `await` operator. To suspend execution of the method (commonly called an async method), you apply an `await` operator to a particular task. Execution control is then returned to the caller of the async method while the task completes its work. This is accomplished without exiting from the async method, which also means that no `finally` blocks are executed. Although async methods typically contain one or more `await` operators, they don't have to. In such a case, the method operates as if it were a synchronous method, although the compiler will issue a warning.

NOTE

Asynchronous Naming Convention

Numerous asynchronous methods are available in the .NET Framework and the Windows Runtime. By convention, the suffix `"Async"` is added to the names of these methods to distinguish them from their synchronous counterparts (if available) but to make it clear that it is an asynchronous method.

If an event, base class, or interface suggests a different name, you can make exceptions to this naming convention. For example, renaming an event handler for a button click wouldn't necessarily make sense.

The async version of this method is shown in Listing 19.3 and is almost identical to the original synchronous method.

LISTING 19.3   A Simple Async Method

```
private async Task<int> TotalPageSizesAsync(IList<Uri> collection)
{
    int total = 0;
    foreach (var uri in collection)
    {
        statusText.Text = String.Format("Found {0} bytes ...", total);
        using (var content = new MemoryStream())
        {
            var request = WebRequest.CreateHttp(uri);
            using (var response = await request.GetResponseAsync())
            {
                await response.GetResponseStream().CopyToAsync(content);
            }

            total += content.ToArray().Length;
        }
    }

    statusText.Text = String.Format("Found {0} total bytes.", total);
    return total;
}
```

In fact, the changes are simple enough to list:

- ▶ Add the `async` modifier to the method signature and change the return type to `Task<int>`.

- ▶ Add the `"Async"` suffix to the method name.

- ▶ Replace the call to `GetResponse` with `GetResponseAsync` and apply the `await` operator.

- ▶ Replace the call to `CopyTo` with `CopyToAsync` and apply the `await` operator.

Probably the most significant change made was to the return type. An async method always has a return type of void, Task, or Task<T>. A void return type is primarily used to define event handlers and such a method cannot be awaited. Similarly, if no meaningful value is returned when the method completes, you should use Task as the return type. In effect, you are saying that the method returns a Task, but when that task is completed, any awaiting expression evaluates to void. If the return type is Task<T>, you should think of this as indicating that the method is promising to return a type T when any awaiting expressions are evaluated.

Building an App

Although the concepts presented in Hour 17 focused on building a traditional desktop application using Windows Presentation Foundation (WPF), almost everything you learned about working with markup and code-behind, how the WPF layout system works, and how to create data-bound applications, also applies to a Windows Store app. In fact, even though Windows Store apps don't use WPF, they do still use XAML for the user interface definition. This allows you to use many of the same UI types; those types are located in the Windows.UI.Xaml namespaces instead of the System.Windows namespaces. In the rest of this hour, you create a Windows Store photo viewer application that is similar to the one you created in Hour 17.

Just as for Hour 17, a Visual Studio project is provided in the book downloads that will serve as the starting point for the Windows Store photo viewer application. However, if you want to create a new Windows Store project, you would use the New Project dialog box, as shown in Figure 19.4.

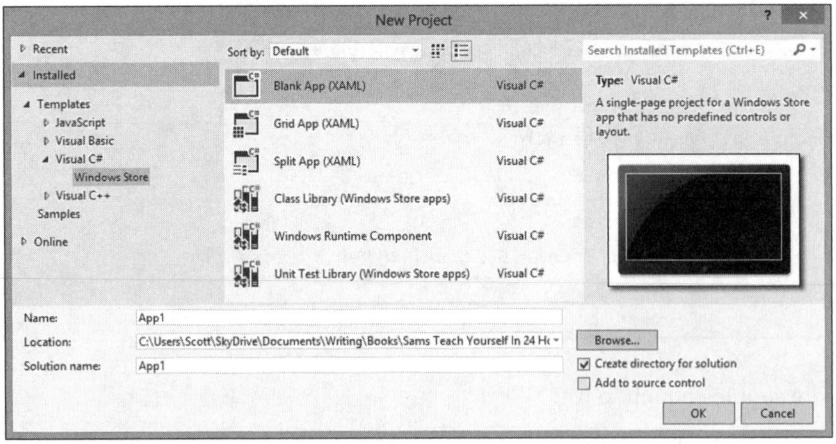

FIGURE 19.4
New Project dialog box.

If you compare the initial code for the MainPage.xaml.cs for this project with that of the starting project for Hour 17, you will see that there are only minor differences.

Creating the Layout

You are now ready to start creating the layout for the photo viewer application. Although Windows applications and Windows Store applications both use XAML, there are some differences in the user interface controls available to you. These differences alone will most likely prevent you from simply reusing the XAML from a WPF application. Even if you were able to reuse the XAML, you may want to consider changing the user interface interactions because Windows Store apps are designed to be touchcentric and many actions the user would perform in a desktop application may not make sense (or be very cumbersome) in a touchcentric tablet.

NOTE

User Interface Considerations for Windows Store Apps

Developing a Windows Store app is actually very similar to developing a Windows Phone app, and not just because they both use the Windows 8 design language. The same usability concerns that need to be addressed when developing a Windows Phone app should also be addressed when developing a Windows Store app.

The completed Windows Store photo viewer app is shown in Figure 19.5. As you can see, the majority of the layout between the desktop application and the Windows Store application is the same. Because the desktop application UI controls were chosen so that much of the XAML would be reusable, it can serve as a starting point for the Windows Store app as well.

FIGURE 19.5
The Windows Store Photo Viewer app.

CAUTION

Porting a Desktop Application to a Windows Store App

Although an XAML-based desktop application and a Windows Store app can share much of the same XAML definitions for the user interface components, due to the differences between the .NET Framework and .NET for Windows Store apps it will not always be possible to reuse the same back-end code for the business logic.

To start creating the Windows Store photo viewer app, copy the `Grid` content from the `MainPage.xaml` file in the desktop project and paste it as the `Grid` content for the Windows 8 project's `MainPage.xaml`. Although a lot of the XAML can be reused, there are still a few changes to make before the layout is complete and the project will compile:

1. Add a new `RowDefinition` whose `Height` is 140. Make sure this new row is the first row of the `Grid`.

2. Add a new `TextBlock` control using the following XAML:

```
<TextBlock x:Name="pageTitle" Grid.Row="0" Grid.Column="0" Grid.ColumnSpan="2"
    Text="{StaticResource AppName}"
    Style="{StaticResource PageHeaderTextStyle}"
    Margin="0,-4,0,0" Padding="116,0,40,46"/>
```

3. Because `DockPanel` and `GridSplitter` are not supported by the Windows Runtime, you will need to replace them with the following `GridView` control:

```
<GridView
    x:Name="itemGridView"
    AutomationProperties.AutomationId="ItemGridView"
    AutomationProperties.Name="Items"
    Grid.Row="1"
    Grid.Column="0"
    Margin="0,-4,40,0"
    Padding="116,0,40,46"
    ItemTemplate="{Binding Source={StaticResource FileTemplate}}"
    ItemsSource="{Binding Source={StaticResource itemsViewSource}}"
    SelectionMode="None"/>
```

Now you are ready to write the code necessary to display pictures from your Pictures library. Add the code shown in Listing 19.4 to the `MainPage` class in `MainPage.xaml.cs` file and add a call to it in the `OnNavigatedTo` method.

LISTING 19.4   The `PopulatePicturesGrid` Method

```
private void PopulatePicturesGrid()
{
    var folder = Windows.Storage.KnownFolders.PicturesLibrary;
    var queryOptions = new Windows.Storage.Search.QueryOptions()
    {
```

```
    FolderDepth = Windows.Storage.Search.FolderDepth.Deep,
    IndexerOption = Windows.Storage.Search.IndexerOption.UseIndexerWhenAvailable
  };

  var fileQuery = folder.CreateFileQueryWithOptions(queryOptions);

  var fif = new Windows.Storage.BulkAccess.FileInformationFactory(
    fileQuery,
    Windows.Storage.FileProperties.ThumbnailMode.PicturesView,
    190,
    Windows.Storage.FileProperties.ThumbnailOptions.UseCurrentScale,
    false
    );

  this.itemsViewSource.Source = fif.GetVirtualizedFilesVector();
}
```

The first line of the method shown Listing 19.4 creates a `StorageFolder` variable that points to the Pictures Library. A `StorageFolder` is a Windows Runtime class that provides information about a folder and allows you to manipulate that folder and its contents; however, it isn't something that can be bound to the UI. To bind the results of a file system query to a UI, you need to use the `GetVirtualizedFilesVector` method of a `FileInformationFactory` instance.

Now that the app is displaying pictures, you need to respond to the user selecting a picture. To do this, add an event handler for the `Tapped` event on the `GridView`, which looks like the code shown in Listing 19.5.

LISTING 19.5   The `GridView.Tapped` Event Handler

```
private async void itemGridView_Tapped(object sender, TappedRoutedEventArgs e)
{
  var item = e.OriginalSource as Image;
  if (item != null)
  {
    var fileInformation = item.DataContext as FileInformation;
    if (fileInformation != null)
    {
      var photo = await ExifMetadata.Create(fileInformation);
      this.metadataPanel.DataContext = photo;
    }
  }
}
```

If you were to run the app now, it would throw an exception, as shown in Figure 19.6.

FIGURE 19.6
Exception from incorrect capabilities.

To display the pictures from your Pictures library, you must first enable the Pictures Library Access capability. Capabilities define the system features or devices your app can use; without being set correctly, your app may not function and will not pass Store certification. To enable the correct capability, double-click on the `Package.appxmanifest` file in the Solution Explorer to display the App Manifest Designer, as shown in Figure 19.7. Click the Capabilities tab, select Pictures Library Access, and save the file.

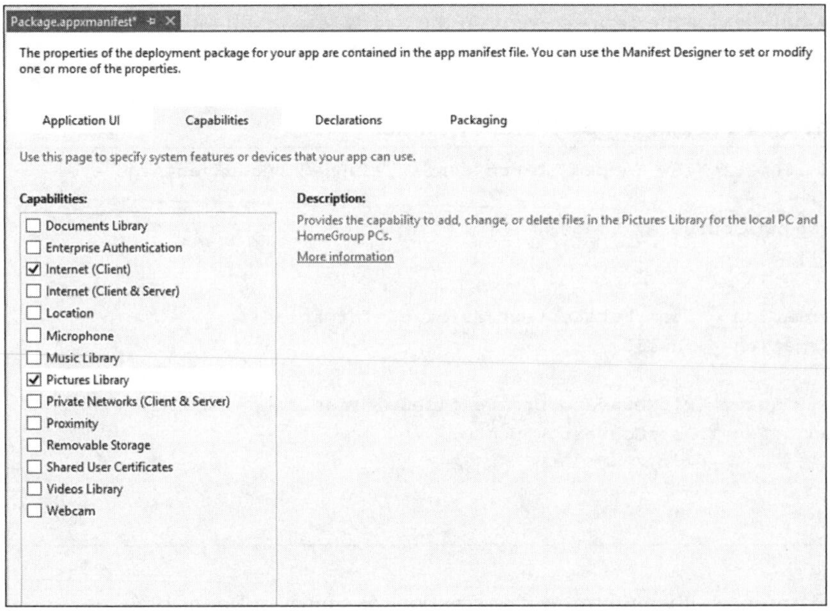

FIGURE 19.7
The App Manifest Designer.

If you run the application, it should look similar to Figure 19.5. Tapping (or clicking) on an image should display the image details.

Summary

In this hour, you had a quick overview of a Windows Store app and what it enables you to do. You created a simple Windows Store app by reusing some of the layout and logic contained in a desktop app.

Q&A

Q. What is a Windows Store app?

A. A Windows Store app has a single chromeless window that fills the entire screen.

Q. What is the Windows Runtime?

A. The Windows Runtime is a set of APIs used to build Windows Store apps and is available to all of the supported programming languages.

Q. Can the async pattern be used with desktop applications?

A. Because this pattern is actually defined in the C# language and supported by the compiler, it can be used in desktop applications just as easily as it can be used for Windows Store apps.

Workshop

Quiz

1. What namespaces are used for the UI types for Windows Store apps?

2. What are app capabilities?

Answers

1. All of the UI types used by Windows Store apps are found in the `Windows.UI.Xaml` namespaces.

2. Capabilities define the system features or devices your app can use; without being set correctly, your app may not function and will not pass Store certification.

Exercises

There are no exercises for this hour.

Building a Web Application

What You'll Learn in This Hour:

- ▶ Understanding web application architecture
- ▶ Working with ASP.NET
- ▶ Creating a web application
- ▶ Understanding data validation

Up until now, you have focused on building applications that run on the desktop. These applications enable you to use the full richness of the Windows platform in your applications. They also pose potential deployment concerns because these applications typically must be installed on the end user's computer. Although technologies such as ClickOnce ease these issues, there are times when building such an application is not the most appropriate choice.

CAUTION

Visual Studio Express for Web

If you use Visual Studio Express for Windows 8 or Visual Studio Express for Windows Desktop, you cannot build web applications. Instead, you need to install Visual Studio Express for Web. If you use one of the paid editions of Visual Studio, you already have everything you need to build web applications.

In this hour, you learn about an alternative to creating rich desktop applications using web applications and the ASP.NET Framework. You explore the different classes provided by the .NET Framework that enable you to create web applications and see how the architecture of a web application is different from that of traditional desktop applications.

Understanding Web Application Architecture

Web applications reside on web servers and are accessed through a web browser, such as Internet Explorer. These applications can be highly distributed, such that the application and database reside in one physical location but are accessed worldwide over the Internet or a corporate wide area network. Even today, despite the advances in computer hardware, network bandwidth is still a scarce resource that should be consumed sparingly.

Running an application distributed over any network can suffer when network performance degrades. Ultimately, you are dependent upon any number of network switches, servers, and routers sending requests from a web browser to your web application.

Communication between a web browser and a web application uses Hypertext Transfer Protocol (HTTP). Typically, a web server, such as Internet Information Services (IIS), understands how to read HTTP requests. When that request has been received and processed, the server sends an HTTP response back to the client. Most HTTP responses consist of a Hypertext Markup Language (HTML) page that the web browser knows how to translate, or render, into a visual representation.

Due to the request/response nature of HTTP communication, it is commonly referred to as a connectionless protocol. A connection is established only long enough to send a response or receive a request; other than that, there is no active connection between the browser and the server.

Working with ASP.NET

To help make building web applications easier, and in keeping with the overall theme of "making the simple things easier and the difficult things possible," Microsoft developed the ASP.NET web application framework. This is the successor to Microsoft's Active Server Pages (ASP) technology and is built on the common language runtime (CLR), enabling you to write ASP.NET applications using any programming language that targets the .NET Framework.

Applications built using ASP.NET can use the more traditional ASP.NET Web Forms or the Model View Controller (MVC) Framework. The ASP.NET MVC Framework is an application framework that utilizes the model-view-controller pattern. This hour provides an overview of building applications using the traditional web forms model.

An application built using Web Forms uses one or more pages that are contained in ASPX files. These ASPX files describe the user interface using HTML and other markup defining server-side web controls and user controls. The application logic, written using C#, is contained in a code-behind file. This code-behind file typically has the same name as the ASPX file with a `.cs` extension. This arrangement should sound familiar because it is similar to the model used by Windows Presentation Foundation (WPF).

A simple ASP.NET page is shown in Listing 20.1, which is the web application equivalent to the "Hello, world" application you wrote in Hour 1, "The .NET Framework and C#."

LISTING 20.1 `HelloWorld.aspx`

```
<%@ Page
   Title="Hello, world"
   CodeFile="HelloWorld.aspx.cs"
   Inherits="HelloWorldWeb.HelloWorld"
%>

<html>
   <body>
      <form id="form1" runat="server">
      </form>
   </body>
</html>
```

As you can see, the page in Listing 20.1 is not very exciting. It contains a `Page` directive that specifies the following:

▶ Code-behind file (`CodeFile`)

▶ Class from which the page derives (`Inherits`)

▶ Page title displayed by the web browser (`Title`)

All ASP.NET pages must include an HTML form element that specifies `runat="server"` that is included within `<html>` and `<body>` tags.

The accompanying code-behind file is shown in Listing 20.2.

LISTING 20.2 `HelloWorld.aspx.cs`

```
namespace HelloWorldWeb
{
   public partial class HelloWorld : System.Web.UI.Page
   {
      protected void Page_Load(object sender, EventArgs e)
      {
         Response.Write("Hello, world from the Web.");
      }
   }
}
```

The output of this simple web application is shown in Figure 20.1.

FIGURE 20.1
Hello, world from the Web.

The Page class supports several events that you can handle, the most common of which are shown in Table 20.1.

NOTE

Developing Web Applications Without IIS

You do not need to have Internet Information Services (IIS) installed to develop and test web applications. All editions of Visual Studio include a built-in web server that will be used when you run the application. For hosting product web applications, you should still use IIS.

TABLE 20.1   Common Page Event Handlers

Event Handler Method Name	Description
Page_Load	Occurs when the server control is loaded into the page object
Page_LoadComplete	Occurs at the end of the load stage
Page_PreInit	Occurs at the beginning of page initialization
Page_PreLoad	Occurs before the page Load event
Page_PreRender	Occurs after the page is loaded but prior to rendering
Page_PreRenderComplete	Occurs before the page content is rendered
Page_Unload	Occurs when the server control is unloaded from memory

Just as WPF provides the `App.xaml` for application-level events and code, ASP.NET applications provide a `Global.asax`. Table 20.2 shows the common events handled by `Global.asax`.

TABLE 20.2   Common `Global.asax` Event Handlers

Event Handler Method Name	Description
`Application_Start`	Used to set up the application environment and is only called when the application first starts
`Session_Start`	Occurs when any new user accesses the website
`Application_BeginRequest`	Occurs as the first event in the HTTP execution chain when responding to a request
`Application_AuthenticateRequest`	Occurs when a security module has established the identity of the user
`Application_Error`	Occurs when an unhandled exception is thrown
`Session_End`	Occurs when a user's session ends or times out; the default timeout is 20 minutes after the user leaves the site
`Application_End`	Used to clean up the application environment when the application ends

Creating a Web Application

In the rest of this hour, you create a web-based photo viewer application by creating a new project, laying out the form, and adding controls.

First, create a new ASP.NET Web Forms Application project using the New Project dialog box, as shown in Figure 20.2. In the Name field, enter **PhotoViewerWeb**.

Just as it does with desktop applications, Visual Studio creates a solution and project for you. This time, instead of displaying the generated C# class file or Extensible Application Markup Language (XAML) designer, Visual Studio displays the code editor for the application's `default.aspx` page and the Properties window. Figure 20.3 shows what Visual Studio should look like after having just created the project.

The editor for ASPX pages can show you the source markup, the visual representation of the layout, or a split view showing both. By default, the editor shows the source markup. You can make changes in either view, and changes made in one will be reflected in the other. Figure 20.4 shows a more detailed view of the ASPX editor.

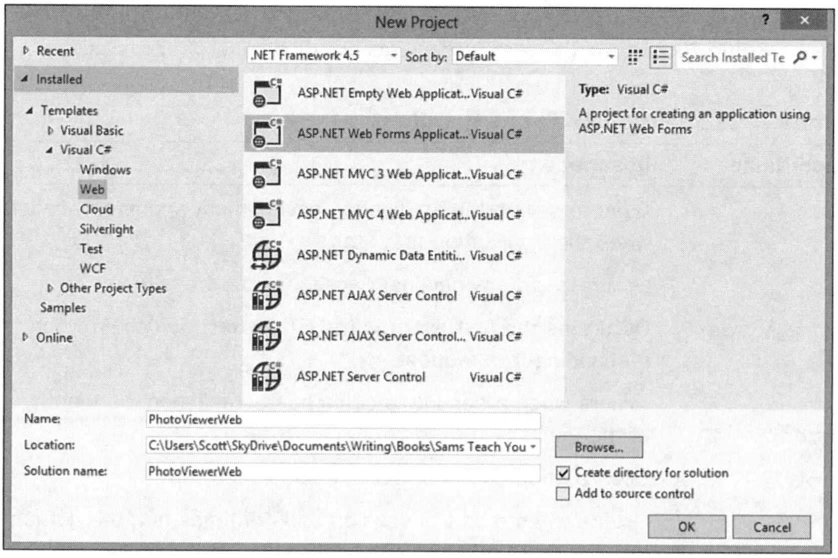

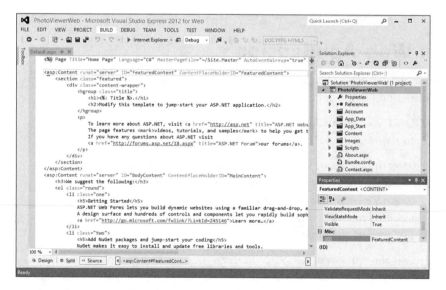

FIGURE 20.2
New Project dialog box.

FIGURE 20.3
Visual Studio after creating a web application.

```
Default.aspx  ⊕ ✕
    <%@ Page Title="Home Page" Language="C#" MasterPageFile="~/Site.Master" AutoEvent┃ ✛
<asp:Content runat="server" ID="FeaturedContent" ContentPlaceHolderID="FeaturedCon
    <section class="featured">
        <div class="content-wrapper">
            <hgroup class="title">
                <h1><%: Title %>.</h1>
                <h2>Modify this template to jump-start your ASP.NET application.</
            </hgroup>
            <p>
                To learn more about ASP.NET, visit <a href="http://asp.net" title=
                The page features <mark>videos, tutorials, and samples</mark> to h
                If you have any questions about ASP.NET visit
                <a href="http://forums.asp.net/18.aspx" title="ASP.NET Forum">our
            </p>
        </div>
    </section>
</asp:Content>
<asp:Content runat="server" ID="BodyContent" ContentPlaceHolderID="MainContent">
    <h3>We suggest the following:</h3>
    <ol class="round">
        <li class="one">
            <h5>Getting Started</h5>
            ASP.NET Web Forms lets you build dynamic websites using a familiar dra
            A design surface and hundreds of controls and components let you rapid
            <a href="http://go.microsoft.com/fwlink/?LinkId=245146">Learn more</a
        </li>
        <li class="two">
            <h5>Add NuGet packages and jump-start your coding</h5>
            NuGet makes it easy to install and update free libraries and tools.
```
```
100 % ▾ ◂                                                                      ▸
ⓖ Design │ ⊞ Split │ ◂▸ Source │ ◂ <asp:Content#FeaturedCont...>              ▸
```

FIGURE 20.4
Detailed view of the ASPX editing surface.

You can easily switch between the ASPX and Design panes, including the Split view, using the tabs, as shown in Figure 20.5.

FIGURE 20.5
Design and Source tabs.

At the bottom of the editing window is the selected element outline, as shown in Figure 20.6. This shows you visually what element you have selected and the path of visual elements that contain the currently selected element.

```
◂ <asp:Content#BodyContent> │ <ol.round> │ <li.two> │ <h5>          ▸
```

FIGURE 20.6
Selected element outline.

If you look at the ASPX generated by Visual Studio, the Page directive specifies the code-behind file and the class that implements the web form. In this case, the code file is named Default.aspx.cs and the class is PhotoViewerWeb._Default. The page Title is also specified. Any of the attributes defined by the Page directive, HTML elements, or ASP.NET controls can be changed directly in the ASPX or using the Properties window, shown in Figure 20.7.

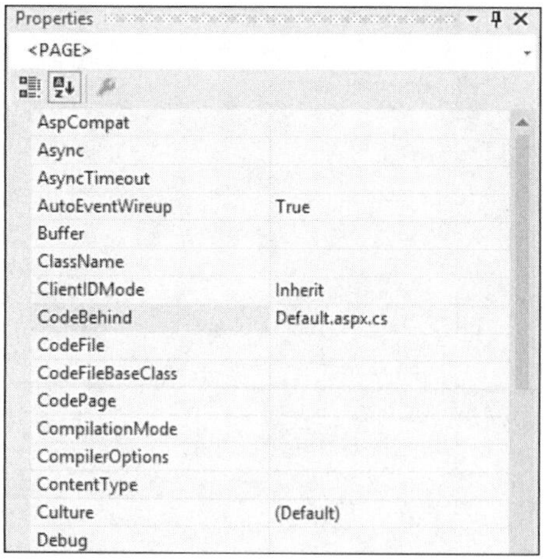

FIGURE 20.7
Properties window.

Change the page title to **Photo Web Viewer**, either through the Properties window or directly in the ASPX.

Creating the Layout

You are now ready to start creating the layout for the application. If you look at the ASPX again, you notice that the page already includes two content controls. These content controls are part of a template engine provided by ASP.NET. This template engine utilizes the idea of master pages, which define a structure and layout that can be used throughout the site. Master pages have placeholder controls, identified by an `<asp:ContentPlaceHolder>` element, which denote where dynamic content can be placed. A web application can make use of multiple master pages, and master pages can also be nested.

NOTE

Master Pages

You can think of the concept behind master pages as being similar to the mail merge capability in many word processing applications. The child page uses the `ContentPlaceHolder` controls mapped to the placeholders defined in the master page, which defines the rest of the page. When a request is made, ASP.NET merges the output of the child page with that of the master page and sends the merged content to the user.

Figure 20.8 shows the project structure in more detail, showing a master page named Site.Master that has been created for you.

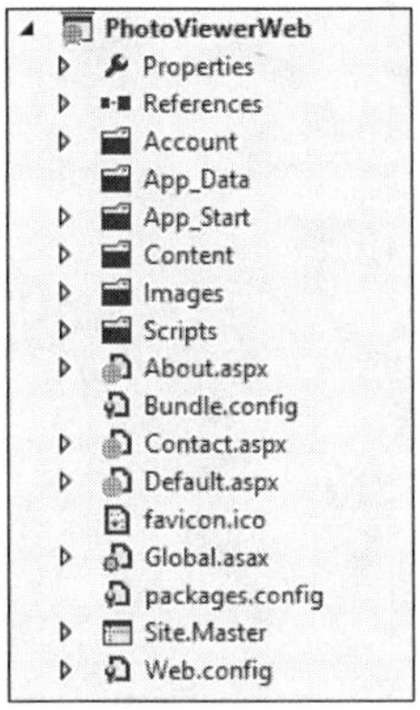

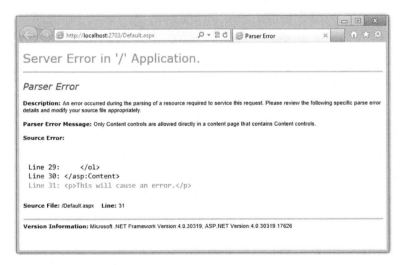

FIGURE 20.8
Web application project structure.

If you look again at the Page directive shown in Figure 20.4, you see that it defines the associated master page. Web forms do not need to be associated with a master page, but if they are, content can be placed only within the content controls mapped to the content placeholders of the master page. If you were to try to add text outside one of those content controls, the web application generates an error at runtime, as shown in Figure 20.9.

FIGURE 20.9
Parser error.

The default page for the application should display a list of photo albums, as shown in Figure 20.10.

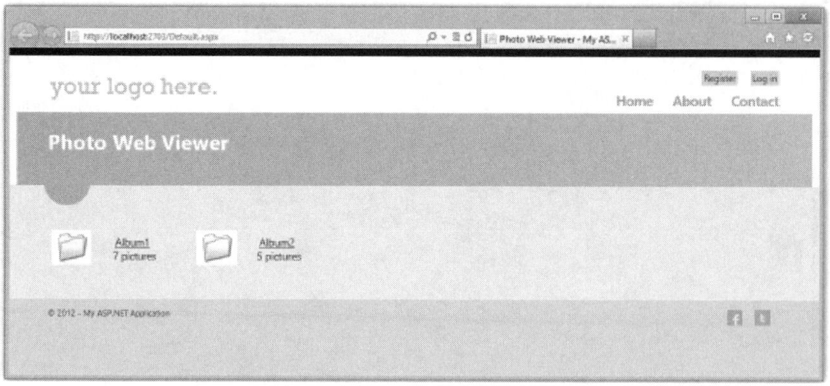

FIGURE 20.10
Photo Web Viewer default page.

The necessary HTML, which would be included in the MainContent placeholder, is shown in Listing 20.3.

LISTING 20.3 Markup for the **MainContent** Layout

```
<asp:DataList ID="albums" runat="server" RepeatDirection="Horizontal"
    RepeatColumns="3" CssClass="groupbox" Height="100%">
    <ItemTemplate>
        <table>
            <tr>
                <td>
                    <img src="Images/folder.png">
                </td>
                <td>
                    <asp:HyperLink runat="server" ID="albumLink" />
                    <br>
                    <asp:Label runat="server" ID="albumCount" />
                </td>
            </tr>
        </table>
    </ItemTemplate>
</asp:DataList>
```

Styling the Layout

Styling a layout can be accomplished using a Cascading Style Sheets (CSS) file, called a style sheet, or through inline styles declared directly on each element. Inline styles have the benefit of being declared along with the element but cannot be easily shared. CSS files enable you to define styles globally that can be shared by multiple pages.

When styling an element using inline styles, you add a `style` attribute to each element that contains the CSS properties and values you set. For example, to style the first table cell (the `td` element) of the second table row (the `tr` element) so that it has a border, you can use the following:

```
<td style="border: thick solid #E5EBD8;">
```

This defines an inline style that sets the border width to "thick," the border style to "solid," and the border color to "#E5EBD8."

If you look at Figure 20.8 again, you will see a Content folder. By default, when you create a new web application project, the Site.Master page already includes a style sheet named `site.css`, found in that folder. You can modify this style sheet, replace it with one of your own, or add an additional style sheet by providing another style sheet link in the Site.Master ASPX, as shown in Listing 20.4.

LISTING 20.4   Including a Style Sheet Link in a Master Page

```
<head runat="server">
   <link href="~Content/PhotoViewer.css" rel="stylesheet" type="text/css" />
</head>
```

You could also include additional style sheets only for a specific child page by including it in the `HeadContent ContentControl`, as shown in Listing 20.5.

LISTING 20.5   Including a Style Sheet Link in a Child Page

```
<asp:Content ID="HeaderContent" runat="server" ContentPlaceHolderID="HeadContent>
   <link href="Styles/PhotoViewer.css" rel="stylesheet" type="text/css" />
</asp:Content >
```

CSS style sheets enable you to define styles that will be applied to any element. These styles are the broadest type of style you can define and use element selectors. You can also define classes that apply to specifically named elements using ID selectors. Applying styles to an element using element or ID selectors is automatic.

NOTE

Use Style Sheets Instead of Inline Styles

Even though you can use inline styles instead of defining your CSS in a separate file (and can even mix them), you should use style sheets as much as possible.

Inline styles are somewhat limited because you cannot easily build up styles, apply the same style to all instances of a certain element or to any element, or apply a style to an element with a specific name.

CSS style sheets help to make your web application markup more maintainable and enable you to easily modify styles, even swapping style sheets entirely to completely change the look of your web application.

Listing 20.6 shows a portion of the `site.css` style sheet. The first two declarations apply a style to the specific HTML elements listed, which occurs automatically. The next declaration, starting with a dot (.), is a CSS class definition, which is applied only to elements that specifically include the class through their `class` attribute. The benefit to CSS classes is that you can provide multiple classes (separated by a space) to the `class` attribute. If you want to apply a CSS class to an ASP.NET web control, use the `CssClass` attribute instead. Finally, the last declaration is an ID selector definition, which is automatically applied to any element whose ID is `body`.

LISTING 20.6   Part of the `site.css` Style Sheet

```
html
{
    background-color: #e2e2e2;
    margin: 0;
    padding: 0;
}

header, footer, hgroup, nav, section
{
    display: block;
}

.float-left
{
    float: left;
}

#body
{
    background-color: #efeeef;
    clear: both;
    padding-bottom: 35px;
}
```

Understanding Data Binding

ASP.NET supports both one-way and two-way data binding in a way that is similar, although more limited, to that of WPF. The data-binding expressions are contained within `<%#` and `%>` delimiters and use either the `Eval` (one-way) or `Bind` (two-way) function. These expressions are resolved when the `DataBind` method of a control or `Page` class is called.

To make the page shown in Listing 20.3 useful, you need to provide text for the `Label` control and both text and a navigation URL for the `HyperLink` control. This can easily be accomplished through data binding. The default page represents an album viewer and needs to be bound to an album collection. In the `Page_Load` method of `Default.aspx.cs`, add the code shown in Listing 20.7.

LISTING 20.7   `Page_Load` Method of `Default.aspx.cs`

```
albums.DataSource = new AlbumCollection(
    Path.Combine(Request.PhysicalApplicationPath, "Albums"));
albums.DataBind();
```

The first line creates a new `AlbumCollection` instance. The `Request.PhysicalApplicationPath` property represents the physical path on the web server that contains the web application. The second line tells the ASP.NET runtime engine to actually perform the binding. Now you need to add the binding expressions to the user interface controls, as shown in Listing 20.8.

LISTING 20.8   Adding Binding Expressions

```
<asp:HyperLink runat="server" ID="hlItem"
    NavigateUrl='<%# Eval("Name", "viewalbum.aspx?id={0}") %>'
    Text='<%# Eval("Name") %>' />
<br>
<asp:Label runat="server" ID="lbItem"
    Text='<%# Eval("Count", "{0} pictures") %>' />
```

The `Eval` method takes the name of a data field in the current data item and, optionally, a formatting string used to display the data. This formatting string uses the same formatting syntax as the `String.Format` method. Notice that you don't specify the container (or data context) of the binding. That's because the `Eval` method uses the naming container, which is generally the smallest part of the data-bound control that contains a whole record. As a result, you can use only `Eval` for binding expressions inside templates of a data-bound control like a `DataList`.

Embedded ASP.NET Code Blocks

The `<% %>` tags indicate embedded code blocks, which is server code that executes during the page's render stage. If the `Page` directive includes the `Language` attribute, the embedded code must be written using the indicated language. The common types of embedded code block follow:

- ► `<% %>`—The simplest form of embedded code block that can contain any code
- ► `<%@ %>`—Directives
- ► `<%# %>`—Data-binding expressions
- ► `<%= %>`—Used to write text data to the page, the equivalent of `<% Response.Write() %>`
- ► `<%-- %>`—Server-side comments

If you need to use data binding in another control, you can still do so by using the `DataBinder.Eval` method directly. In fact, the binding expressions you just saw internally call `DataBinder.Eval` and pass `Container.DataItem`, which refers to the current data item of the current data container, as the first parameter.

You could rewrite the binding expression for the `Label` control as shown here:

```
<%# DataBinder.Eval(Container.DataItem, "Count", "{0} pictures") %>
```

Using the `Bind` method is similar and uses the same syntax as the `Eval` method. The difference is that `Bind` establishes a two-way binding, enabling you to also update the source control.

Understanding Data Validation

Just as desktop applications enable you to validate user input, web applications do as well. However, to perform data validation for web applications, you have a choice of where that validation occurs—either at the server or at the client. Server-side validation is best used when the validation logic is complex or can be performed only on the server, such as validating data against a database.

Performing server-side validation is similar to the way you perform validation in a desktop application. You add event handlers to the necessary events, such as the `TextChanged` event of a `TextBox` control, to perform any required validation. However, for server-side validation to execute, the page (and all its data) must be sent to the server, validated, and then a response sent back to the client.

Server-Side Validation and Security

If there is a possibility of a security impact with the input data, it is important to perform server-side validation even if you are also performing client-side validation.

You should not trust the client to always pass well-formed data because a potential attacker might have written his or her own client that bypasses your client-side validation.

Client-side validation involves the use of validation controls that intelligently generate client-side JavaScript and Dynamic HTML (DHTML) code (for older browsers, the validator controls generate server-side code). ASP.NET provides the following validation controls:

▶ `RequiredFieldValidator`, which can be used to ensure the user has entered data into the control.

▶ `CompareValidator`, which compares the data entered with a constant value, the value of a property of another control, or a value retrieved from a database.

▶ `RangeValidator`, which checks the data entered to ensure that it falls either inside or outside of a given range of values.

▶ `RegularExpressionValidator`, which determines if the entered data matches a specified regular expression. If the data entered is empty, validation always succeeds.

▶ `CustomValidator`, which enables you to define your own custom validation logic.

Each validation control performs only a single, well-defined validation, but you can combine multiple validation controls to perform validations that are more complicated. When a validation control determines that a control contains invalid data, it displays the supplied error message next to the control.

You can also use a `ValidationSummary` control, allowing you to summarize the error messages from all validation controls on a page in a list, bulleted list, or single paragraph.

The commonly used properties of validation controls are shown in Table 20.3.

TABLE 20.3   Common Validation Control Properties

Name	Description
ControlToValidate	The ID of the input control that the validation control will evaluate.
Display	The display behavior for the validation control. The accepted values are as follows:
	▶ None—Validation control is never displayed (most commonly used in combination with a `ValidationSummary` control).
	▶ Static—Validation control displays an error message if validation fails and space is allocated for the error message even if the control passes validation.
	▶ Dynamic—Validation control displays an error message if validation fails and space is allocated for the error message only if the control passes validation.

Name	Description
ErrorMessage	The message to display in the ValidationSummary control if valida- tion fails. If the Text property is not also set, this text is also displayed in the validation control when validation fails.
Text	The message to display in the validation control when validation fails. If this is not set, the ErrorMessage value is used.

Listing 20.9 shows a simple ASPX page that uses some of the validation controls.

LISTING 20.9   Associating Validation Rules with a Binding

```
<%@ Page Language="C#" AutoEventWireup="True" %>
<!DOCTYPE html PUBLIC "-//W3C//DTD XHTML 1.0 Transitional//EN"
    "http://www.w3.org/TR/xhtml1/DTD/xhtml1-transitional.dtd">
<html>
    <head>
        <title>Validation Controls</title>
    </head>
    <body>
        <form id="Form1" runat="server">
            <h3>Validator Example</h3>
            Enter a number from 1 to 30:
            <asp:TextBox ID="TextBox1" runat="server" /><br />
            <asp:RequiredFieldValidator
                ID="RequiredFieldValidator1"
                ControlToValidate="TextBox1"
                Display="None" ErrorMessage="You must enter a value."
                runat="server" />
            <asp:RegularExpressionValidator
                ID="RegularExpressionValidator1"
                ControlToValidate="TextBox1"
                Display="None" ValidationExpression="\d+"
                ErrorMessage="You must enter a numeric value."
                runat="server" />
            <asp:RangeValidator
                ID="Range1"
                ControlToValidate="TextBox1"
                Display="None"
                MinimumValue="1"
                MaximumValue="30"
                Type="Integer"
                ErrorMessage="The value must be from 1 to 30"
```

```
             runat="server" />
        <p />
        <asp:ValidationSummary runat="server" />
        <p />
        <asp:Button ID="Button1" Text="Submit" runat="server" />
      </form>
   </body>
</html>
```

Figure 20.11 shows this simple validator example after having entered invalid data.

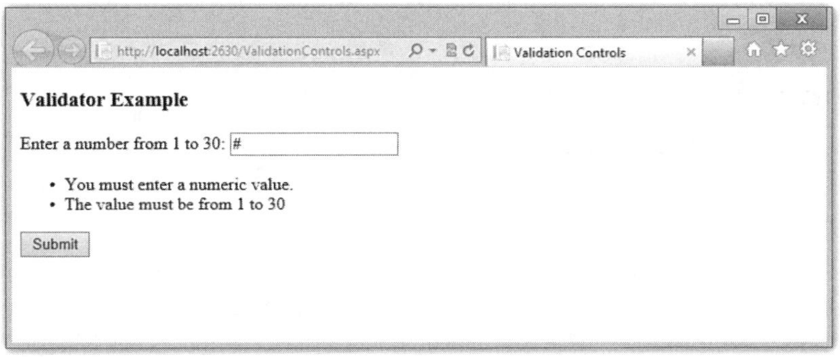

FIGURE 20.11
Validator example.

Summary

In this hour, you learned about building web applications, including how to apply styles, data binding, and validation. As you can see, although there are many similarities between building web applications and WPF desktop applications, there are also many differences. Although many developers are familiar with both types of applications, most tend to specialize in one or the other.

Q&A

Q. What is a web form?

A. A web form is an ASPX page that describes the user interface markup using HTML and, typically, a code-behind file.

Q. What is the `Global.asax` file used for?

A. The `Global.asax` file provides application-level events and code for web applications, much the same way the `App.xaml` file does for WPF applications.

Q. How are web applications styled?

A. Web applications can be styled using Cascading Style Sheets (CSS).

Workshop

Quiz

1. What is a master page?

2. Do web forms always need to be associated with a master page?

3. How do you specify data-binding expressions in a web form?

Answers

1. You can think of the concept behind master pages as being similar to the mail merge capability in many word processing applications. The child page uses the `ContentPlaceHolder` controls mapped to the placeholders defined in the master page, which defines the rest of the page. When a request is made, ASP.NET merges the output of the child page with that of the master page and sends the merged content to the user.

2. No, web forms can be created that are not associated with a master page.

3. Data-binding expressions are contained within `<%#` and `%>` delimiters and use either the `Eval` (one-way) or `Bind` (two-way) functions. These expressions are resolved when the `DataBind` method of a control or `Page` class is called.

Exercises

There are no exercises for this hour.

Programming with Attributes

What You'll Learn in This Hour:

▶ Understanding attributes
▶ Using the caller info attributes
▶ Working with the common attributes
▶ Using custom attributes
▶ Accessing attributes at runtime

In Hour 1, "The .NET Framework and C#," you learned that C# supports component-oriented programming by enabling you to create assemblies that are self-contained, self-documenting, redistributable units of code. Metadata specifies how the types, properties, events, methods, and other code elements relate to one another. Attributes enable you to add additional metadata to an assembly, providing a way of associating declarative information with your code. Attributes are compiled and stored in the resulting common intermediate language (CIL) and can be accessed at runtime.

The .NET Framework provides and uses attributes for many different purposes. You saw one example of attributes in Hour 6, "Creating Enumerated Types and Structures," when you learned about flags enumerations. Attributes also describe security, describe how to serialize data, limit optimizations by the Just-In-Time (JIT) compiler, and control the visibility of properties and methods during application development, among many other things. To add your own custom metadata, you use custom attributes that you create.

In this hour, you learn more about attributes—how to use them, how to create your own custom attributes, and how to access them at runtime.

Understanding Attributes

Although attributes can be added to almost any code declaration, including assemblies, classes, methods, properties, and fields, many are valid only on certain code declarations. For example, some attributes are valid only on methods, whereas others are valid only on type declarations.

Attribute Names

Although it is considered a best practice for all attribute names to end with the word *Attribute* so that they can be easily distinguished from other types, you don't need to specify the *Attribute* suffix when using them in code. For example, [Flags] is equivalent to [FlagsAttribute]. The actual class name for the attribute is FlagsAttribute.

To place an attribute on a code declaration, you place the name of the attribute enclosed in square brackets ([ ]) immediately before the declaration to which it is applied. For example, the System.IO.FileShare enumeration shown in Listing 21.1 has the FlagsAttribute applied.

LISTING 21.1   Using the FlagsAttribute

```
[Flags]
public enum FileShare
{
    None = 0,
    Read = 0x001,
    Write = 0x002,
    ReadWrite = 0x003,
    Delete = 0x004,
    Inheritable = 0x010,
}
```

A code declaration can have multiple attributes, and some attributes can be specified more than once for the same declaration, as shown in Listing 21.2.

LISTING 21.2   Additional Attribute Usage

```
[Conditional("DEBUG"), Conditional("EXAMPLE")]
void Method() { }

void TestMethod([In][Out] string value) { }
void TestMethod2([In, Out] string value) { }
```

When you apply an attribute to a code declaration, you, in effect, are calling one of the constructors of the attribute class. This means that you can provide parameters to the attribute, as shown by the ConditionalAttribute from Listing 21.2.

NOTE

Named Attribute Parameters

The named parameters used by attributes are not the same as the named parameters you learned about in Hour 4, "Understanding Classes and Objects the C# Way." When used with attributes, they are really more like object initializers (which you also learned about in Hour 4); they actually correspond to public read-write properties of the attribute, easily allowing you to set the property value.

Parameters defined by a constructor are called positional parameters because they must be specified in a defined order and cannot be omitted. Attributes also make use of named parameters, which are optional and can be specified in any order. Positional parameters must always be specified first. For example, the attributes shown in Listing 21.3 are all equivalent.

LISTING 21.3   Attribute Parameters

```
[DllImport("kernel32.dll")]
[DllImport("kernel32.dll", SetLastError = false, ExactSpelling = true)]
[DllImport("kernel32.dll", ExactSpelling = true, SetLastError = false)]
```

The type of code declaration to which an attribute is applied is called the target. Table 21.1 shows the possible target values.

TABLE 21.1   Attribute Targets

Target	Applies To
assembly	Entire assembly
module	Current assembly module
field	Class field
event	Event
method	Method, property get accessor, or property set accessor
param	Method or property set accessor parameter
property	Property
return	Return value of a method, indexer property, or property get accessor
type	Struct, class, interface, or enum

Although an attribute normally applies to the element it precedes, you can also explicitly identify the target to which it applies. For example, you can identify whether an attribute applies to a method, its parameter, or its return value, as shown in Listing 21.4.

LISTING 21.4   Attribute Parameters

```
[CustomAttribute]
string Method()
{
    return String.Empty;
}


[method: CustomAttribute]
string Method()
{
    return String.Empty;
}


[return: CustomAttribute]
string Method()
{
    return String.Empty;
}
```

Using the Caller Info Attributes

The Caller Info attributes allow you to obtain information about the caller to a method, such as the path to the source file, the line number where the method was called, and the name of the caller. The Caller Info attributes are shown in Table 21.2.

TABLE 21.2   Caller Info Attributes

Attribute	Description
CallerFilePathAttribute	The full path (at compile time) of the source file containing the caller
CallerLineNumberAttribute	The line number in the source file where the method is called
CallerMemberNameAttribute	The method or property name of the caller

These attributes are applied to optional parameters and change the default value that's passed in when the argument is omitted. Listing 21.5 shows an example of how to use the Caller Info attributes. Because these attributes are defined in the System.Runtime.CompilerServices namespace, you should add a using statement to include this namespace in your code file.

LISTING 21.5   Using the Caller Info Attributes

```
public void DoSomething()
{
   Log("Performing some action.");
}

public void Log(string message,
   [System.Runtime.CompilerServices.CallerMemberName] string memberName = "",
   [System.Runtime.CompilerServices.CallerFilePath] string filePath = "",
   [System.Runtime.CompilerServices.CallerLineNumber] int lineNumber = 0)
{
   System.Diagnostics.Debug.WriteLine("message: {0}", memberName);
   System.Diagnostics.Debug.WriteLine("filePath: {0}", filePath);
   System.Diagnostics.Debug.WriteLine("lineNumber: {0}", lineNumber);
}
```

The most common use for the Caller Info attributes is to specify the name of the caller for tracing and diagnostic methods or for implementing data-binding interfaces, such as INotifyPropertyChanged. An example of how to use the CallerMemberNameAttribute is shown in Listing 21.6.

LISTING 21.6   `INotifyPropertyChanged` Using `CallerMemberNameAttribute`

```
public class Contact : INotifyPropertyChanged
{
   public event PropertyChangedEventHandler PropertyChanged;

   private string firstName;
   private string lastName;
   public string FirstName
   {
      get
      {
         return this.firstName;
      }

      set
      {
         this.firstName = value;
         NotifyPropertyChanged();
      }
   }

   public string LastName
   {
```

```
   get
   {
      return this.lastName;
   }

   set
   {
      this.lastName = value;
      NotifyPropertyChanged();
   }
}

private void NotifyPropertyChanged([CallerMemberName] string propertyName = "")
{
   var handler = PropertyChanged;
   if (handler != null)
   {
      handler(this, new PropertyChangedEventArgs(propertyName));
   }
}
}
```

Table 21.3 shows the member name values returned when using the CallerMemberNameAttribute.

TABLE 21.3 `CallerMemberNameAttribute` Results

Occurs Within	Result
Method, property, event	The name of the method, property, or event
Constructor	The string ".ctor"
Static constructor	The string ".cctor"
Destructor	The string "Finalize"
User-defined conversions or operators	The generated member name (for example, "op_Addition")
Attribute constructor	The name of the member to which the attribute is applied
No containing member	The default value of the optional parameter

Working with the Common Attributes

The .NET Framework defines many attributes that you can use in your own applications. The most common ones are the Obsolete attribute, the Conditional attribute, and the set of global attributes.

The Obsolete **Attribute**

The Obsolete attribute indicates that a code declaration should no longer be used and causes the compiler to generate a warning or error, depending on how the attribute is configured. This attribute can be used with no parameters, but it is recommended to supply an explanation and indicate if a compiler warning or error should be generated. Listing 21.7 shows an example of using the Obsolete attribute.

LISTING 21.7   Obsolete Attribute

```
public class Example
{
    [Obsolete("Consider using OtherMethod instead.", false)]
    public string Method()
    {
        return String.Empty;
    }

    public string OtherMethod()
    {
        return "Test";
    }
}
```

The Conditional **Attribute**

The Conditional attribute indicates that a code declaration is dependent on a preprocessor conditional compilation symbol, such as DEBUG, and can be applied to a class or a method. The compiler uses this attribute to determine if the call is included or left out. If the conditional symbol is present during compilation, the call is included; otherwise, it is not. If the Conditional attribute is applied to a method, the method must not have a return value. Listing 21.8 shows an example of using the Conditional attribute.

LISTING 21.8   Conditional Attribute

```
public class Example
{
    [Conditional("DEBUG")]
    public void DisplayDiagnostics()
    {
        Console.WriteLine("Diagnostic information.");
    }
```

```
   public string Method()
   {
      return "Test";
   }
}
```

The `Conditional` attribute can also be applied to custom attributes, in which case the attribute adds metadata information only if the compilation symbol is defined.

NOTE

The `#if` and `#endif` Preprocessor Symbols

Using the `Conditional` attribute is similar to using the `#if` and `#endif` preprocessor symbols but can provide a cleaner alternative that leads to fewer bugs. The class shown in Listing 21.8 using `#if`/`#endif` instead of the `Conditional` attribute is shown here.

```
   public class Example
   {
#if DEBUG
      public void DisplayDiagnostics()
      {
         Console.WriteLine("Diagnostic information.");
      }
#endif

      public string Method()
      {
         return "Test";
      }
   }
```

Although you can mix the `Conditional` attribute and the `#if`/`#endif` preprocessor symbols, you need to be very careful if you do so. Removing code using `#if`/`#endif` occurs earlier in the compilation process and may cause the compiler to be unable to compile the `Conditional` method.

The Global Attributes

Although most attributes apply to specific code declarations, some apply to an entire assembly or module. These attributes appear in the source code after any `using` directives but before any code declarations (such as class or namespace declarations).

NOTE

Assembly Manifest

The assembly manifest contains the data that describes how the elements in the assembly are related, including version and security information. The manifest is typically included with the compiled file.

Typically, global attributes are placed in an `AssemblyInfo.cs` file, but they can appear in multiple files if those files are compiled in a single compilation pass. The common global attributes are shown in Table 21.4.

TABLE 21.4   Global Attributes

Attribute	Purpose
Assembly Identity Attributes	
AssemblyName	Full name of the assembly
AssemblyVersion	Version of the assembly
AssemblyCulture	Culture the assembly supports
AssemblyFlags	Indicates if multiple copies of the assembly can coexist
Informational Attributes	
AssemblyProduct	Specifies a product name for the assembly
AssemblyTrademark	Specifies a trademark for the assembly
AssemblyInformationalVersion	Specifies an information version for the assembly
AssemblyCompany	Specifies a company name for the assembly
AssemblyCopyright	Specifies a copyright for the assembly
AssemblyFileVersion	Specifies a version number for the Windows file version resource
CLSCompliant	Indicates if the assembly is CLS-compliant
Assembly Manifest Attributes	
AssemblyTitle	Specifies a title for the assembly manifest
AssemblyDescription	Specifies a description for the assembly manifest
AssemblyConfiguration	Specifies the configuration for the assembly manifest
AssemblyDefaultAlias	Specifies a friendly default alias for the assembly manifest

Using Custom Attributes

If you need to provide custom metadata for your own applications, you can create custom attributes by defining an attribute class that derives from `Attribute`, either directly or indirectly.

For example, you can define a custom attribute that contains the Team Foundation Server Work Item number associated with a code change, as shown in Listing 21.9.

LISTING 21.9   Creating a Custom Attribute

```
[AttributeUsage(AttributeTargets.All, Inherited = false, AllowMultiple = true)]
public sealed class WorkItemAttribute : System.Attribute
{
   private int workItemId;

   public WorkItemAttribute(int workItemId)
   {
      this.workItemId = workItemId;
   }

   public int WorkItemId
   {
      get
      {
         return this.workItemId;
      }
   }

   public string Comment
   {
      get;
      set;
   }
}
```

The custom attribute has a single public constructor whose parameters form the attribute's positional parameters. Any public read-write fields or properties—in this case, the `Comment` property—become named parameters. Finally, the `AttributeUsage` attribute indicates that the `WorkItem` attribute is valid on any declaration, that it can be applied more than once, and that it is not automatically applied to derived types.

You can then use this attribute as shown in Listing 21.10.

LISTING 21.10 Applying a Custom Attribute

```
[WorkItem(1234, Comment = "Created class showing attributes being used.")]
public class Test
{
   [WorkItem(5678, Comment = "Changed property to use auto-property syntax.")]
   public int P
   {
      get;
      set;
   }
}
```

Accessing Attributes at Runtime

Adding metadata to your application through attributes doesn't do much if you can't access that information at runtime. The .NET Framework provides access to the runtime type information, including metadata provided by attributes, through a process called reflection. Because attributes provide metadata, the code associated with an attribute is not actually executed until the attributes are queried.

Retrieving custom attributes is easy using the `Attribute.GetCustomAttribute` method. Listing 21.11 shows an example of accessing the custom attribute defined in Listing 21.9 and the simple class defined in Listing 21.10 at runtime. Figure 21.1 shows the output of Listing 21.11.

LISTING 21.11 Accessing a Single Attribute at Runtime

```
public class Program
{
   public static void Main(string[] args)
   {
      WorkItemAttribute attribute =
         Attribute.GetCustomAttribute(typeof(Test), typeof(WorkItemAttribute))
         as WorkItemAttribute;

      if (attribute != null)
      {
         Console.WriteLine("{0}: {1}", attribute.WorkItemId, attribute.Comment);
      }
   }
}
```

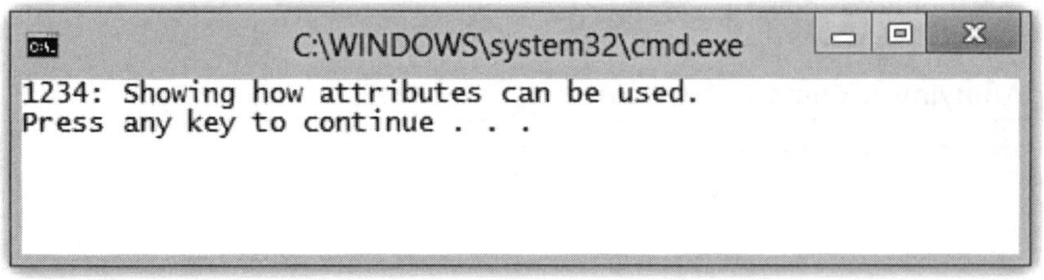

FIGURE 21.1
Output of retrieving a single attribute at runtime.

`Attribute.GetCustomAttribute` returns a single attribute. If multiple attributes of the same type defined on the code element exist or you need to work with multiple attributes of different types, you can use the `Attribute.GetCustomAttributes` method to return an array of custom attributes. You can then enumerate the resulting array, examining and extracting information from the array elements, as shown in Listing 21.12.

LISTING 21.12 Accessing Multiple Attributes at Runtime

```
public class Program
{
    public static void Main(string[] args)
    {
        var workItems = from attribute in
                        Attribute.GetCustomAttributes(typeof(Test)).
                        OfType<WorkItemAttribute>()
                        select attribute;

        foreach (var attribute in workItems)
        {
            Console.WriteLine("{0}: {1}", attribute.WorkItemId, attribute.Comment);
        }
    }
}
```

Summary

Attributes provide a simple yet powerful way to add metadata to your applications. They are used throughout the .NET Framework for calling unmanaged code; describing component object model (COM) properties for classes, methods, and interfaces; describing which class members should be serialized for persistence; specifying security requirements; and controlling JIT compiler optimizations, just to name a few.

In this hour, you learned about attributes, including some of the common attributes provided by the .NET Framework. You then created your own custom attribute and learned how to retrieve that attribute and access its values at runtime.

Q&A

Q. What is an attribute?

A. An attribute is a class that is used to add metadata to a code element.

Q. What are positional attribute parameters?

A. Positional attribute parameters are parameters required by the attribute and must be provided in a specific order. They are defined by the attribute's constructor parameters.

Q. How do you define a custom attribute?

A. A custom attribute is defined by creating a class that derives from `Attribute`.

Workshop

Quiz

1. Can the `Obsolete` attribute generate compiler errors?
2. Does the `Conditional` attribute affect compilation?
3. What are two methods that can retrieve custom attributes at runtime?

Answers

1. Yes, the `Obsolete` attribute can generate a compiler error if the second positional parameter is set to `true`.
2. Yes, the `Conditional` attribute can affect compilation. If the conditional symbol specified in the attribute parameters is not present, the call to the method is not included.
3. Two methods to retrieve custom attributes at runtime are `Attribute.GetCustomAttribute` and `Attribute.GetCustomAttributes`.

Exercises

There are no exercises for this hour.

HOUR 22

Dynamic Types and Language Interoperability

What You'll Learn in This Hour:

▶ Using dynamic types
▶ Understanding the DLR
▶ Interoperating with COM
▶ Reflection interoperability

In Hour 1, "The .NET Framework and C#," you learned that the fourth primary component of the .NET Framework is the dynamic language runtime, or DLR. The DLR is built on top of the common language runtime (CLR) and provides the language services for dynamic languages such as IronRuby and IronPython. Although the C# language has always allowed you to write code that would interact with dynamic languages—for example, calling a method defined in a JavaScript object—the syntax necessary to do so was far from simple. That syntax also changed depending on the particular dynamic language you were targeting.

With the help of the DLR, C# can provide simple and consistent language syntax for interacting with dynamic languages. In this hour, you learn about `dynamic` types and learn how you can use them to interoperate with dynamic languages.

Using Dynamic Types

A `dynamic` type, indicated by the `dynamic` keyword, is one whose operations bypass the compile-time type checking provided by the C# compiler. Instead, these operations are resolved at runtime. Bypassing the static type checking simplifies access to component object model (COM) application programming interfaces (APIs), such as the Office API, and to dynamic languages, such as IronPython and JavaScript.

The `dynamic` keyword indicates the type of a property, field, indexer, parameter, return value, or local variable. It can also be the destination type of an explicit conversion or as the argument to the `typeof` operator.

NOTE

Dynamic Types

Even though the term *dynamic types* is used throughout this hour, there is actually only a single "dynamic" type, just as there is a single "object" type. When used in this hour, *dynamic types* refers to different types that are treated as being of type `dynamic`.

Although it might seem contradictory, a variable of `dynamic` type is statically typed at compile time to be of type `dynamic` and, in most situations, behaves as if it were an `object`. When the compiler encounters a `dynamic` type, it assumes it can support any operation. If the code isn't valid, the errors will be caught only at runtime.

▼ TRY IT YOURSELF

Exploring Dynamic Types

To see how dynamic types behave at compile time and runtime, follow these steps:

1. Create a new console application in Visual Studio.

2. Add a new class named `SimulatedDynamic` that looks as shown here:

```
class SimulatedDynamic
{
    public SimulatedDynamic() { }
    public void Method1(string s)
    {
        Console.WriteLine(s);
    }
}
```

3. Modify the `Main` method of the `Program` class by adding the statements shown here:

```
SimulatedDynamic c1 = new SimulatedDynamic();
c1.Method1(3);
```

4. Try to compile the application. You should receive the compiler errors shown in Figure 22.1.

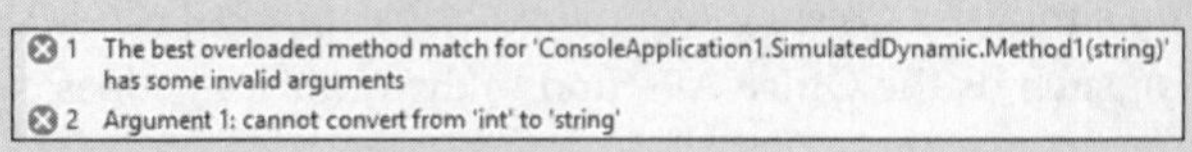

```
⊗ 1  The best overloaded method match for 'ConsoleApplication1.SimulatedDynamic.Method1(string)'
      has some invalid arguments
⊗ 2  Argument 1: cannot convert from 'int' to 'string'
```

FIGURE 22.1
Error messages.

5. Change the first statement you entered in step 3 so that `c1` is typed to be `dynamic`.

6. Run the application by pressing F5 (you want to run this under the debugger for this step). You should notice that the application now compiles but throws a runtime exception, as shown in Figure 22.2.

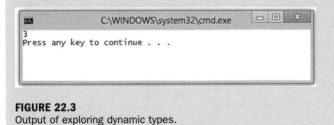

> **!** **RuntimeBinderException was unhandled**   ✕
>
> The best overloaded method match for
> 'ConsoleApplication1.SimulatedDynamic.Method1(string)' has some invalid
> arguments
>
> **Troubleshooting tips:**
>
> Get general help for exceptions.
>
> Search for more Help Online...
>
> **Exception settings:**
> ☐ Break when this exception type is thrown
>
> **Actions:**
> View Detail...
>
> Copy exception detail to the clipboard
>
> Open exception settings

FIGURE 22.2
RuntimeBinderException.

7. Change the second statement so that the argument passed is the string "3" rather than the integer value 3.

8. Run the application again by pressing Ctrl+F5 and observe that the output matches what is shown in Figure 22.3.

```
C:\WINDOWS\system32\cmd.exe
3
Press any key to continue . . .
```

FIGURE 22.3
Output of exploring dynamic types.

When you first tried to compile the application you just wrote, the compiler determined that the method you were attempting to execute did not exist because `c1` was statically typed to be of type `SimulatedDynamic`. However, when you changed its static type to be of type `dynamic`, the compiler no longer performed the type checking, causing the runtime exception to occur.

NOTE

Determining Dynamic Types at Runtime

At compile time, a `dynamic` variable is compiled as an `object` type, and the compiler ensures that metadata about what each statement is attempting to do is stored. At runtime, this information is examined, and any statement that is not valid causes a runtime exception.

When the runtime encounters a "dynamic" type (which is actually just an `object` type with the additional metadata indicating it should be evaluated dynamically), it uses the runtime type of the object to determine what the actual type should be. In step 6 of the previous exercise, the runtime type of the method argument is `System.Int32`. This caused the runtime to attempt to resolve a method with the following signature:

```
void Method1(int)
```

Because such a method does not exist in the type `SimulatedDynamic`, a runtime exception is thrown. However, in step 8, the runtime attempts to resolve a method with the signature

```
void Method1(string)
```

that does exist.

Conversions

The result of most dynamic operations is another dynamic object. However, conversions exist between dynamic objects and other types, easily enabling you to switch between dynamic and nondynamic behavior.

An implicit conversion exists between all the predefined data types and `dynamic`, which means that all the following statements shown in Listing 22.1 are valid.

LISTING 22.1 Implicit Conversion with Dynamic Types

```
dynamic d1 = 42;
dynamic d2 = "The quick brown fox";
dynamic d3 = DateTime.Now;

int s1 = d1;
string s2 = d2;
DateTime s3 = d3;
```

CAUTION

Dynamic Conversions

The implicit conversions that exist are dynamic conversions that, like all dynamic operations, are resolved at runtime. You should be careful and not mix dynamic and nondynamic conversions. For example, trying to assign `d3` to `s1` would result in a runtime exception.

Dynamic Overload Resolution

Because the actual type of a value of `dynamic` type is not known until runtime, if one or more method parameters are specified to be `dynamic`, the method might not be resolved until runtime. The compiler first attempts normal overload resolution, and, if an exact match is found, that is the overload that is used. This means that if more than one method resolves to match the same runtime types and the runtime cannot determine how to resolve that ambiguity, the method resolution fails with an ambiguous match exception.

Consider the code shown in Listing 22.2.

LISTING 22.2 A Class with Dynamic Methods

```
class MethodResolution
{
    public void M(int i) { }
    public void M(int i, dynamic d) { }
    public void M(dynamic d, int i) { }
    public void M(dynamic d1, dynamic d2) { }
}
```

The following code will fail at runtime, as shown in Figure 22.4.

```
dynamic m = new MethodResolution();
m.M(42, 7);
```

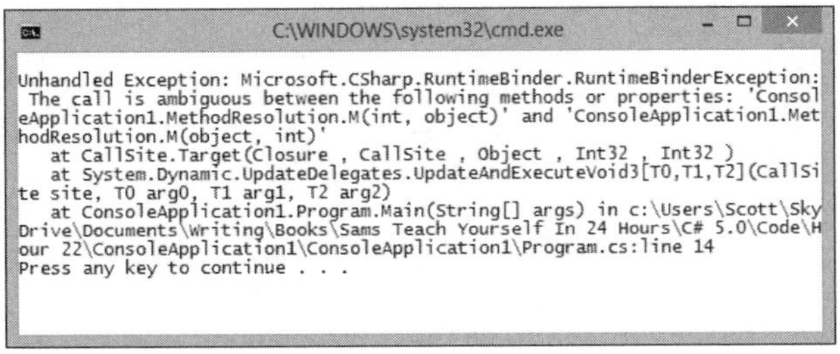

FIGURE 22.4
Ambiguous method call exception at runtime.

This method call is ambiguous because both arguments have a runtime type of `System.Int32`. When the runtime attempts to resolve method `M`, it sees these methods as if they were defined as shown in Listing 22.3.

LISTING 22.3   Dynamic Method Definitions for Method Resolution

```
class MethodResolution
{
    public void M(int i) { }
    public void M(int i, object d) { }
    public void M(object d, int i) { }
    public void M(object d1, object d2) { }
}
```

Given that list of overloads, none of them are the best match because each matches better on one argument than the other. Because the method cannot be resolved, a runtime error is thrown.

Understanding the DLR

For C# to work with dynamic types, it makes use of the DLR, which is a runtime environment that sits on top of the CLR and provides language services and support for dynamic languages. This enables dynamic languages the same level of language interoperability enjoyed by the statically typed languages and introduces dynamic objects to those languages. Figure 22.5 shows the basic architecture of the DLR and shows how it fits with the rest of the .NET Framework.

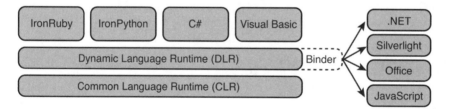

FIGURE 22.5
DLR architecture.

In a similar way to ADO.NET data providers, the DLR uses binders that encapsulate the language semantics and specify how operations are performed. This not only enables a consistent syntax but also enables statically typed languages to use the services provided by the DLR.

The language binders make use of LINQ expression trees to perform operations. To support this, the DLR extends LINQ expression trees to include control flow, assignment, and other language-specific nodes. Any location in code where you perform an operation on a dynamic object is considered a **dynamic call site**, and the DLR caches the metadata of the dynamic types involved and information about the operation being performed. If the operation is subsequently performed, the information is retrieved from the cache, improving performance.

Finally, to support interoperability with other languages, the DLR provides the `IDynamicMetaObjectProvider` interface and the `DynamicObject` and `ExpandoObject` classes.

NOTE

Understanding `IDynamicMetaObjectProvider`

The `IDynamicMetaObjectProvider` interface represents a dynamic object. If you have advanced scenarios for defining how dynamic objects behave, you should create your own implementation of `IDynamicMetaObjectProvider`; otherwise, you should derive from `DynamicObject` or use `ExpandoObject`.

If you need an object that enables you to dynamically add or remove members at runtime, you can create an instance of an `ExpandoObject`. Instances of an `ExpandoObject` can be shared between any languages that support the DLR. For example, you can create an instance in C# and use it as an argument to an IronPython function. Listing 22.4 shows a simple example of using an `ExpandoObject` to dynamically add a new property.

LISTING 22.4   Dynamically Adding a New Property to an `ExpandoObject`

```
dynamic expando = new ExpandoObject();

expando.ExampleProperty = "This is a dynamic property.";
Console.WriteLine(expando.ExampleProperty);
Console.WriteLine(expando.ExampleProperty.GetType());
```

Figure 22.6 shows the output from the code shown in Listing 22.4.

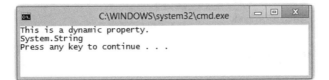

FIGURE 22.6
Output of using an `ExpandoObject`.

If you need to define specific operations for your class when it is used dynamically, you can derive your class from `DynamicObject`. Just as with an `ExpandoObject` instance, any languages supporting the DLR can share an instance of a derived `DynamicObject` type.

The code in Listing 22.5 shows a dynamic dictionary that enables you to access dictionary values by key as if they were actual properties. It overrides the `TrySetMember` and `TryGetMember` methods to provide this dynamic syntax.

LISTING 22.5   Creating a Custom Dynamic Object

```
public class CustomDictionary : DynamicObject
{
    Dictionary<string, object> internalDictionary =
      new Dictionary<string, object>();

    public int Count
    {
        get
        {
            return internalDictionary.Count;
        }
    }

    public override bool TryGetMember(GetMemberBinder binder, out object result)
    {
        return this.internalDictionary.TryGetValue(binder.Name.ToLower(),
          out result);
    }

    public override bool TrySetMember(SetMemberBinder binder, object value)
    {
        this.internalDictionary[binder.Name.ToLower()] = value;
        return true;
    }
}
```

Listing 22.6 shows how this new dictionary might be used.

LISTING 22.6   Using a Custom Dynamic Object

```
public class Program
{
    static void Main(string[] args)
    {
        dynamic contact = new CustomDictionary();
        contact.FirstName = "Ray";
        contact.LastName = "Manzarek";

        Console.WriteLine(contact.FirstName + " " + contact.LastName);
    }
}
```

The output from the code shown in Listing 22.6 is shown in Figure 22.7.

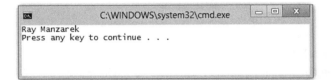

```
C:\WINDOWS\system32\cmd.exe                    _  □  X
Ray Manzarek
Press any key to continue . . .
```

FIGURE 22.7
Output of using a custom dynamic object.

TRY IT YOURSELF ▼

Creating a Custom Dynamic Type

To implement a custom dynamic dictionary and see how to use it at runtime, follow these steps:

1. Create a new console application in Visual Studio.

2. Add a new class named CustomDictionary that looks like Listing 22.5.

3. Modify the Main method of the Program class so it looks like Listing 22.6.

4. Run the application by pressing Ctrl+F5. The output should match what is shown in Figure 22.7.

5. Add additional dynamically defined properties to the contact class and output them in Console.WriteLine statements.

6. Run the application again by pressing Ctrl+F5 and observe that the output changes to show the additional properties added.

Interoperating with COM

Although the .NET Framework has always enabled you to interoperate with COM, particularly with the Office COM APIs, the DLR simplifies the code you have to write considerably. Because many COM methods return types as object, the dynamic type enables you to easily treat them as dynamic objects instead.

To interoperate with COM APIs, you make use of a Primary Interop Assembly (PIA), which forms a bridge between the unmanaged COM API and the managed .NET application. To do this, you add a reference to the PIA in your Visual Studio project, allowing your application access to the types defined. When the reference has been added, you can choose to embed only those types actually used by your application.

The code in Listing 22.7 shows a simple example of how to open a Microsoft Word document using COM interop.

NOTE

Embedded Primary Interop Assemblies

Because each PIA must contain a managed equivalent for every type, interface, enumeration, and so on defined in the COM API, some, such as the Office PIAs, can be quite large.

Only embedding the interop types used by your application can help reduce the size of your deployment and does not require the PIAs to be deployed at all. This also allows you to avoid a lot of the complexity of working with COM APIs by treating the `object` occurrences in the COM signatures as `dynamic` instead.

LISTING 22.7   COM Interop Without Dynamic Types

```
public static Main(string[] args)
{
    object missing = System.Reflection.Missing.Value;
    object readOnly = false;
    object isVisible = true;
    object fileName = "SampleDocument.docx";

    Microsoft.Office.Interop.Word.ApplicationClass wordApp =
        new Microsoft.Office.Interop.Word.ApplicationClass();
    wordApp.Visible = true;

    Document doc = wordApp.Documents.Open(ref fileName, ref missing, ref readOnly,
        ref missing, ref missing, ref missing, ref missing, ref missing, ref missing,
        ref missing, ref missing, ref isVisible, ref missing, ref missing,
        ref missing, ref missing);

    doc.Activate();
}
```

Compare that with the code shown in Listing 22.8, which performs the same actions but uses `dynamic` instead. This code also makes use of named parameters and implicit typing, showing how all these features come together, allowing you to write succinct code that is both easy to read and easy to maintain.

LISTING 22.8   COM Interop with Dynamic Types

```
public static Main(string[] args)
{
    var wordApp = new Microsoft.Office.Interop.Word.ApplicationClass();
    wordApp.Visible = true;
    string fileName = "SampleDocument.docx";

    Document doc = wordApp.Documents.Open(fileName, ReadOnly: true, Visible: true);
    doc.Activate();
}
```

Reflection Interoperability

Taking this a step further, suppose you wanted to invoke the `Multiply` method of a `Calculator` object. If the `Calculator` object was defined in C#, you could do this easily, as shown in Listing 22.9.

LISTING 22.9   Invoking a Method in a C# Object

```
var calculator = GetCalculator();
int sum = calculator.Multiply(6, 7);
```

If you didn't know the `Calculator` object was written in .NET, or needed to use Reflection because the compiler couldn't determine that the object implemented a `Multiply` method, you would need to use code like that shown in Listing 22.10.

LISTING 22.10   Invoking a Method Reflectively

```
object calculator = GetCalculator();
Type type = calculator.GetType();
object result = type.InvokeMember("Multiply", BindingFlags.InvokeMethod, null,
    calculator, new object[] { 6, 7 });
int sum = Convert.ToInt32(result);
```

As you can see, this is not nearly as simple. However, by utilizing dynamic types, the code becomes that shown in Listing 22.11.

LISTING 22.11   Invoking a Method Dynamically

```
dynamic calculator = GetCalculator();
int sum = calculator.Multiply(6, 7);
```

If the `Calculator` object were defined in a dynamic language such as IronPython, the same code shown in Listing 22.11 could still be used. The only differences would be in the implementation of the `GetCalculator` method, which would need to create an instance of the IronPython runtime and load the appropriate file, as shown in Listing 22.12.

LISTING 22.12   Getting a Dynamic Object from IronPython

```
dynamic GetCalculator()
{
    ScriptRuntime pythonRuntime = Python.CreateRuntime();
    return pythonRuntime.UseFile("calculator.py");
}
```

Summary

Including the dynamic language runtime (DLR) greatly expands the number of languages the .NET Framework can support. It also enables statically typed languages such as C# to easily access objects defined in a dynamic language. Using dynamic types allows you to access dynamic objects using code syntax that is essentially the same as you would use if the object were statically defined.

In this hour, you learned the basics of using dynamic types, including how to use `ExpandoObject` and create your own custom dynamic objects by deriving from `DynamicObject`. After exploring the basic architecture of the DLR, you then learned how to use dynamic types when working with COM APIs, such as the Office COM API, and objects defined in other languages, such as IronPython.

Q&A

Q. **What is a dynamic type?**

A. A dynamic type is one whose operations bypass the compile-time type checking and instead are resolved at runtime.

Q. **What is the benefit of `ExpandoObject`?**

A. `ExpandoObject` enables you to create an instance of an object that enables you to dynamically add or remove members at runtime.

Q. **Can you create your own dynamic objects?**

A. Yes, you can create your own dynamic object by deriving from `DynamicObject` or implementing `IDynamicMetaObjectProvider`.

Q. What are the benefits of embedding primary interop assembly types?

A. Embedding only the interop types used by your application can help reduce the size of your deployment and does not require the PIAs to be deployed at all. This also allows you to avoid a lot of the complexity of working with COM APIs by treating the `object` occurrences in the COM signatures as `dynamic` instead.

Workshop

Quiz

1. What is the static compile-time type of a dynamic type?

2. What LINQ functionality does the DLR use to perform dynamic operations?

Answers

1. A dynamic type is statically typed at compile time to be of type `dynamic`.

2. The DLR language binders utilize LINQ expression trees to perform dynamic operations.

Exercises

There are no exercises for this hour.

Memory Organization and Garbage Collection

What You'll Learn in This Hour:

▶ Memory organization

▶ Garbage collection

▶ Understanding the `IDisposable` interface

▶ Using the dispose pattern

▶ Declaring and using finalizers

In Hour 1, "The .NET Framework and C#," you learned that one of the benefits provided by the .NET Framework is automatic memory management. This helps you create applications that are more stable by preventing many common programming errors and enables you to focus your time on the business logic your application requires. Even with automatic memory management, it is still important to understand how the garbage collector interacts with your program and the types you create.

You briefly learned about value and reference types in Hour 3, "Understanding C# Types." The simple definition for a value type presented was that a value type is completely self-contained and copied "by value." A reference type, on the other hand, contains a reference to the actual data. Because variables of a value type directly contain their data, it is not possible for operations on one to affect the other. It is possible for two variables of a reference type to refer to the same object, allowing operations on one variable to affect the other.

In this hour, you learn some of the fundamentals of how memory is organized in the common language runtime (CLR), how the garbage collector works, and how the .NET Framework provides mechanisms for deterministic finalization.

Memory Organization

To better understand how types work, you need to have a basic understanding of the two mechanisms the CLR uses to store data in memory: the stack and the heap. Figure 23.1 shows a conceptual view of stack and heap memory.

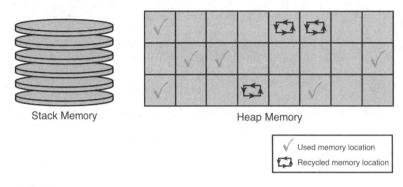

Stack Memory   Heap Memory

√   Used memory location

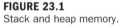 Recycled memory location

FIGURE 23.1
Stack and heap memory.

The simplest way to think of stack memory is that it is organized like a stack of plates in a restaurant. The last plate placed on the stack is the first one removed. This is also known as a last-in first-out (LIFO) queue. Stack memory is used by the .NET Framework to store local variables (except for the local variables used in iterator blocks or those captured by a lambda or anonymous method) and temporary values. You can think of stack memory as providing cheap garbage collection because the lifetime of variables placed on the stack is well known.

Heap memory, however, is more like a wall of empty slots. Each slot can indicate if it is already full or if it is no longer used and ready to be recycled. When a slot has been filled, its contents can be replaced only with something that is the same type as it originally contained. A slot can be reused (and have its type changed) only when it has been recycled.

Garbage Collection

A type defined by a class is a reference type. When you create an instance of a reference type using the new operator, the runtime actually performs several actions on your behalf. The two primary actions that occur follow:

1. Memory is allocated and initialized to its default value.

GO TO ▶ TABLE 3.12, **"DEFAULT VALUES,"** to determine the value used.

2. The constructor for the class is executed to initialize the allocated memory.

At this point, your object is initialized and ready to be used. Because the runtime allocated the memory on your behalf, it is reasonable to expect that it also deallocates that memory at some undetermined future point in time. The responsibility for deallocating memory falls to the garbage collector.

The simple view of how the garbage collector works is that when it runs, the following actions occur:

1. Every instance of a reference type is assumed to be "garbage."

2. The garbage collector determines which instances are still accessible. These types are considered "live" and are marked to indicate they are still reachable.

3. The memory used by the unmarked reference types is deallocated.

4. The managed heap is then compacted (by moving memory) to reduce fragmentation and consolidate the used memory space. As the "live" objects are moved, the mark is cleared in anticipation of the next garbage collection cycle.

NOTE

Object Lifetime

Every object instance has a lifetime, which is the length of execution time an object is pointed to by a valid reference. As long as an object has at least one valid reference, it cannot be destroyed. By creating more references to an object, you can potentially extend its lifetime.

Understanding the IDisposable **Interface**

Because memory deallocation occurs at an unspecified point in time, the .NET Framework provides a mechanism, through the IDisposable interface, that enables you to provide explicit cleanup behavior before the memory is reclaimed. This interface provides a way to perform deterministic resource deallocation. It also provides a consistent pattern that types needing to control resource allocation can utilize.

Listing 23.1 shows the definition of the IDisposable interface, which provides a single public method named Dispose.

LISTING 23.1   The IDisposable Interface

```
public interface IDisposable
{
   void Dispose();
}
```

Types that implement this interface, commonly called disposable types, give the code using that type a way to indicate that the type is eligible for garbage collection. If the type has any unmanaged resources it maintains, calling Dispose should immediately release those unmanaged resources; however, calling the Dispose method does not actually cause the instance to be garbage collected.

The using **Statement**

Even if a type implements IDisposable, there is no way for the .NET Framework to ensure that you have actually called the Dispose method. This problem is compounded when you consider the implications of an exception occurring. If an exception occurs, there is a possibility that, depending on how the calling code is written, the disposable type will never get the opportunity to actually perform its cleanup.

From Hour 11, "Handling Errors Using Exceptions," you learned that you could place the calling code in a try-finally block where the call to the Dispose method is placed in the finally handler. Although this is the correct implementation, it can be easy to get incorrect (particularly when you need to nest multiple protected regions) and can lead to code that is hard to read.

To alleviate these problems, C# provides the using statement. You saw examples of the using statement in Hour 14, "Using Files and Streams." The using statement provides a clean and simple way to indicate the intended lifetime of an object and ensures the Dispose method is called when that lifetime ends.

The syntax for the using statement is as follows:

```
using (resource-acquisition) embedded-statement
```

When the compiler encounters a using statement, it actually generates code similar to what is shown in Listing 23.2.

LISTING 23.2   Compiler Generated Expansion for the using Statement

```
{
   DisposableObject x = new DisposableObject();

   try
   {
      // use the object.
   }
   finally
   {
      if (x != null)
      {
         ((IDisposable)x).Dispose();
      }
   }
}
```

There are a few subtle, but important, things to note in this expansion. The first is the outermost enclosing braces. This defines a scope that contains the expansion but, more specifically, helps ensure that the variable defined in the using statement is accessible only from within that defined scope. The second is that the local variable declared for the resource acquisition is read-only and that it is a compile-time error to modify this variable from within the using block statement. Finally, because the compiler explicitly casts the object to the IDisposable interface (to ensure that it is calling the correct Dispose method), the using statement can be used only with types that implement the IDisposable interface.

Using the Dispose Pattern

To implement the dispose pattern, you provide an implementation of the IDisposable interface. However, implementing the IDisposable interface is actually only part of the pattern. The complete dispose pattern, in the context of the Contact class, is shown in Listing 23.3.

TIP

When Should You Implement the Dispose Pattern?

Typically, you should only implement the dispose pattern if

▶ You control unmanaged resources directly.

▶ You control other disposable resources directly.

LISTING 23.3 Basic Dispose Pattern

```
public class Contact : IDisposable
{
    private bool disposed;

    public void Dispose()
    {
        Dispose(true);
        GC.SuppressFinalize(this);
    }

    protected virtual void Dispose(bool disposing)
    {
        if (!this.disposed)
        {
            if (disposing)
            {
                // Release only managed resources here.
            }
```

```
        // Release only unmanaged resource here.
        this.disposed = true;
    }
  }
}
```

The public `Dispose` method should always be implemented as shown. The order of the two calls is important and shouldn't be changed. This order ensures that `GC.SuppressFinalize` is called only if the `Dispose` operation completes successfully. When `Dispose` calls `Dispose(true)`, the call might fail, but later on the garbage collector can call `Dispose(false)`. In reality, these are two different calls that can execute different portions of the code, so even though `Dispose(true)` fails, `Dispose(false)` might not.

All your resource cleanup should be contained in the `Dispose(bool disposing)` method. If necessary, you should protect the cleanup by testing the `disposing` parameter. This should happen for both managed and unmanaged resources. The `Dispose(bool disposing)` runs in two distinct scenarios:

▶ If `disposing` is `true`, the method has been called directly or indirectly by a user's code. Managed and unmanaged resources can be disposed.

▶ If `disposing` is `false`, the method has been called by the runtime from inside the finalizer, and you should not reference other objects. Only unmanaged resources can be disposed.

The benefit of using the dispose pattern is that it provides a way for users of the type to explicitly indicate that they are done using that instance and that its resources should be released.

Declaring and Using Finalizers

The dispose pattern is not the only way the .NET Framework enables you to perform explicit resource cleanup before the object's memory is reclaimed. The other way is using a finalizer, which is a special method called automatically after an object becomes inaccessible. It is important to realize that the finalizer method will not be called until the garbage collector realizes the object is unreachable.

A finalizer method looks like the default constructor for a class except the method name is prefixed with the tilde (~) character. Listing 23.4 shows how you would implement a finalizer for the `Contact` class.

LISTING 23.4   Implementing a Finalizer

```
public class Contact : IDisposable
{
    private bool disposed;

    public Contact()
    {
    }

    ~Contact()
    {
        Dispose(false);
    }

    public void Dispose()
    {
        Dispose(true);
        GC.SuppressFinalize(this);
    }

    protected virtual void Dispose(bool disposing)
    {
        if (!this.disposed)
        {
            if (disposing)
            {
                // Release only managed resources here.
            }

            // Release only unmanaged resource here.
            this.disposed = true;
        }
    }
}
```

There are several important rules about declaring and using finalizers:

▶ The exact time and order of when a finalizer executes is undefined.

▶ The finalizer method runs on the GC thread, not the application's main thread.

▶ Finalizers apply only to reference types.

▶ You cannot specify an access modifier for a finalizer method.

▶ You cannot provide parameters to a finalizer method.

▶ You cannot overload or override a finalizer method.

▶ You cannot call a finalizer method directly in your own code; only the garbage collector can call a finalizer method.

Although finalizers are typically used when you want to provide some assurance that resources will be released even if the calling code does not call `Dispose`, it is not necessary to provide a finalizer just because you implement the dispose pattern. However, if you do implement a finalizer, be sure to also implement the dispose pattern.

CAUTION

Finalizers

Finalizers are actually difficult to write correctly because many of the normal assumptions you can make about the state of the runtime environment are not true during object finalization.

Making your class finalizable means that it cannot be garbage collected until after the finalizer has run, which means your class survives at least one extra garbage collection cycle. In addition, if not written carefully, finalizer methods have the possibility of creating a new reference to the instance being finalized, in which case the instance is alive again.

Summary

The .NET Framework does an excellent job at handling memory allocation and deallocation on your behalf, enabling you to focus on the business logic required by your application. It is, however, beneficial to have at least a basic understanding of how the .NET Framework manages memory and, more important, what mechanisms it provides to enable you to influence that management.

In this hour, you learned about the different ways the .NET Framework manages memory, through the managed heap and the stack. You saw how the `using` statement enables you to ensure a disposable object has its `Dispose` method called and how to implement the `IDisposable` interface in your own classes through the dispose pattern.

Q&A

Q. What are the two mechanisms the CLR uses to store data in memory?

A. The CLR uses stack and heap memory to store data.

Q. What is object lifetime?

A. Every object instance has a lifetime, which is the length of execution time an object is pointed to by a valid reference.

Q. What is one purpose of the `IDisposable` interface?

A. The `IDisposable` interface is intended to provide a way to perform deterministic resource deallocation. It also provides a consistent pattern that types which need to control resource allocation can utilize.

Q. Can the `using` statement be used with types that do not implement `IDisposable`?

A. No, the `IDisposable` interface is required because the compiler-generated expansion of the `using` statement casts the object to the interface to ensure that the correct implementation of the `Dispose` method is called.

Q. When should you implement the dispose pattern?

A. Typically you should only implement the dispose pattern if

- ► You control unmanaged resources directly.

- ► You control other disposable resources directly.

Q. If you implement `IDisposable`, should you also implement a finalizer?

A. No, just because you implement the `IDisposable` interface does not mean that you should also implement a finalizer. However, if you do implement a finalizer, you should also implement the `IDisposable` interface.

Workshop

Quiz

1. What are the two primary actions that occur on your behalf when using the `new` operator?

2. Does calling `Dispose` immediately cause the disposable object to be garbage collected?

3. What is the implication on garbage collection of implementing a finalizer?

Answers

1. The two primary actions that occur are

   a. Memory is allocated.

   b. The constructor for the class is executed to initialize the allocated memory.

2. No, calling `Dispose` does not cause the object to be immediately garbage collected. It can, however, cause the object to immediately release any unmanaged resources it maintains.

3. Making your class finalizable means that it cannot be garbage collected until after the finalizer has run, which means your class survives at least one extra garbage collection cycle. In addition, if not written carefully, finalizer methods have the possibility of creating a new reference to the instance being finalized, in which case the instance is alive again.

Exercises

There are no exercises for this hour.

Understanding Threads, Concurrency, and Parallelism

What You'll Learn in This Hour:

▶ Understanding threads and threading

▶ Concurrency and synchronization

▶ Understanding the Task Parallel Library

▶ Working with Parallel LINQ (PLINQ)

▶ Potential pitfalls

So far, all the applications you have written, and most software that exists today, were designed for single-threaded execution. This is mainly because the programming model of single-threaded execution reduces complexity and is easier to code. However, as processor technology continues to evolve from single-core to multicore architectures, it is more common for applications to begin taking advantage of the benefits of multiple threads and multiple cores. Unfortunately, using multiple threads and cores brings with it an entirely new set of problems and complexity. The .NET Framework, through the parallel computing platform, simplifies the task of writing applications that can take advantage of multiple threads and cores. This platform forms the basis of the multithreading capabilities provided by the .NET Framework, such as the managed thread pool, and includes parallel implementations of the common loop instructions, LINQ to Objects, and new thread-safe collections.

In this hour, you learn the basics of writing multithreaded applications and how the parallel computing platform enables you to write efficient and scalable code that takes advantage of multiple processors in a natural and simple way.

Understanding Threads and Threading

The Windows operating system (and most modern operating systems) separates different running applications into processes; a process can have one or more threads executing inside it. Threads form the basic unit of work to which the operating system can allocate processor time.

A thread maintains its own exception handlers, a scheduling priority, and a way to save its context until it is scheduled.

The Windows operating system supports a threading strategy called **preemptive multitasking**, which creates the effect of simultaneous execution of multiple threads from multiple processors. To do this, the operating system divides the available processor time across each of the threads that need it, sequentially allocating each thread a slice of that time. When a thread's time slice elapses, it is suspended, and another thread resumes running. When this transfer, known as a **context switch**, occurs, the context of the preempted thread is saved so that when it resumes, it can continue execution with the same context. On a multiprocessor system, the operating system can take advantage of having multiple processors and schedule more threads to execute more efficiently, but the basic strategy remains the same.

The .NET Framework further expands processes into **application domains** (represented through the `AppDomain` class), which are lightweight managed subprocesses. A single process might have multiple application domains, and each application domain might have one or more managed threads (represented by the `Thread` class). Managed threads are free to move between application domains in the same process, which means you might have one thread moving among several application domains or multiple threads executing in a single application domain.

Using multiple threads is the most powerful technique available to increase the responsiveness of your application by allowing it to process data and respond to user input at almost the same time. For example, you can use multiple threads to do the following:

▶ Communicate to a web server or database.

▶ Perform long-running or complex operations.

▶ Allow the user interface to remain responsive while performing other tasks in the background.

This same application, when run on a computer with multiple processors, could also exhibit dramatic performance improvements without requiring modification.

There is, however, a trade-off. Threading consumes operating system resources to store the context information required by processes, application domains, and threads. The more threads you create, the more time the processor must spend keeping track of those threads. Controlling code execution and knowing when threads should be destroyed can be complex and can be a source of frequent bugs.

Concurrency and Synchronization

A simple definition for **concurrency** is simultaneously performing multiple tasks that can potentially interact with each other. Because of this interaction, it is possible for multiple threads to access the same resource simultaneously, which can lead to problems such as deadlocking and starvation.

A **deadlock** refers to the condition when two or more threads are waiting for each other to release a resource (or more than two threads are waiting for resources in a circular chain). **Starvation**, similar to a deadlock, is the condition when one or more threads are perpetually denied access to a resource.

NOTE

Thread Safety

Thread safety refers to protecting resources from concurrent access by multiple threads. A class whose members are protected is called thread-safe.

Because of these potential concurrency problems, when multiple threads can access the same resource, it is essential that those calls be synchronized. This prevents one thread from being interrupted while it is accessing that resource. The common language runtime (CLR) provides several different synchronization primitives that enable you to control thread interactions. Although many of the synchronization primitives share characteristics, they can be loosely divided into the following three categories:

▶ Locks

▶ Signals

▶ Interlocked operations

Working with Locks

What would happen if multiple threads attempted to access the same resource simultaneously? Imagine this resource is an instance of a `Stack<int>`. Without any type of protection, multiple threads could manipulate the stack at the same time. If one thread attempts to peek at the top value at the same time another thread is pushing a new value, what is the result of the peek operation?

Locks protect a resource by giving control to one thread at a time. Locks are generally exclusive, although they need not be. Nonexclusive locks are often useful to allow a limited number of threads access to a resource. When a thread requests access to a resource that is locked, it goes to sleep (commonly referred to as **blocking**) until the lock becomes available.

Exclusive locks, most easily accomplished using the `lock` statement, control access to a block of code, commonly called a **critical section**. The `lock` statement is best used to protect small blocks of code that do not span more than a single method. The syntax of the `lock` statement is as follows:

```
lock ( expression )
   embedded-statement
```

The expression of a `lock` statement must always be a reference type value.

CAUTION

Lock Expressions to Avoid

You should not lock on a public type, using `lock(typeof(PublicType))`, or instances of a type, using `lock(this)`. If outside code also attempts to lock on the same public type or instance, it could create a deadlock.

Locking on string literals, using `lock("typeName")`, is also problematic due to the string interning performed by the CLR. Because only a single instance is shared across the assembly, placing a lock on a string literal causes any location where that string is accessed to also be locked.

The best practice is to define a read-only private or private static object on which to lock.

Listing 24.1 shows an example of using locks to create a thread-safe increment and decrement operation.

LISTING 24.1   The `lock` Statement

```
public class ThreadSafeClass
{
    private int counter;
    private static readonly object syncLock = new object();

    public int Increment()
    {
        lock(syncLock)
        {
            return this.counter++;
        }
    }

    public int Decrement()
    {
        lock(syncLock)
        {
            return this.counter--;
        }
    }
}
```

The Monitor class also protects a resource through the Enter, TryEnter, and Exit methods, and can be used with the lock statement to provide additional functionality.

The Enter method enables a single thread access to the protected resource at a time. If you want the blocked thread to give up after a specified interval, you can use the TryEnter method instead. Using TryEnter can help detect and avoid potential deadlocks.

CAUTION

Monitor **and** lock

Although the Monitor class is more powerful than the simple lock statement, it is prone to orphaned locks and deadlocks. In general, you should use the lock statement when possible.

The lock statement is more concise and guarantees a correct implementation of calling the Monitor methods because the compiler generates the expansion on your behalf.

The compiler expands the lock statement shown in Listing 24.1 to the code shown here:

```
bool needsExit = false;
try
{
    System.Threading.Monitor.Enter(syncLock, ref needsExit);
    this.counter = value;
}
finally
{
    if (needsExit)
    {
        System.Threading.Monitor.Exit(syncLock);
    }
}
```

By making use of a try-finally block, the lock statement helps ensure that the lock will be released even if an exception is thrown.

A thread uses the Wait method from within a critical section to give up control of the resource and block until the resource is available again. The Wait method is typically used in combination with the Pulse and PulseAll methods, which enable a thread that is about to release a lock or call Wait to put one or more threads into the ready queue so that they can acquire the lock.

NOTE

SpinLock

If you hold a lock for a short period, you might want to use a `SpinLock` instead of `Monitor`. Rather than blocking when it encounters a locked critical section, `SpinLock` simply spins in a loop until the lock becomes available. When used with locks held for more than a few tens of cycles, `SpinLock` performs just as well as `Monitor` but uses more CPU cycles.

Using Signals

If you need to allow a thread to communicate an event to another, you cannot use locks. Instead you need to use synchronization events, or signals, which are objects having either a signaled or unsignaled state. Threads can be suspended by waiting on an unsignaled synchronization event and can be activated by signaling the event.

There are two primary types of synchronization events. Automatic reset events, implemented by the `AutoResetEvent` class, behave like amusement park turnstiles and enable a single thread through the turnstile each time it is signaled. These events automatically change from signaled to unsignaled each time a thread is activated. Manual reset events, implemented by the `ManualResetEvent` and `ManualResetEventSlim` classes, on the other hand, behave more like a gate; when signaled, it is opened and remains open until it is closed again.

By calling one of the `Wait` methods, such as `WaitOne`, `WaitAny`, or `WaitAll`, the thread waits on an event to be signaled. `WaitOne` causes the thread to wait until a single event is signaled, whereas `WaitAny` causes it to wait until one or more of the indicated events are signaled. On the other hand, `WaitAll` causes the thread to wait until all the indicated events have been signaled. To signal an event, call the `Set` method. The `Reset` method causes the event to revert to an unsignaled state.

Interlocked Operations

Interlocked operations are provided through the `Interlocked` class, which contains static methods that can be used to synchronize access to a variable shared by multiple threads. Interlocked operations are atomic, meaning the entire operation is one unit of work that cannot be interrupted, and are native to the Windows operating system, so they are extremely fast.

Interlocked operations, when used with volatile memory guarantees (provided through the `volatile` keyword on a field), can create applications that provide powerful nonblocking concurrency; however, they do require more sophisticated, low-level programming. For most purposes, simple locks are the better choice.

Other Synchronization Primitives

Although the `lock` statement and `Monitor` and `SpinLock` classes are the most common synchronization primitives, the .NET Framework provides several other synchronization primitives. A detailed explanation of the remaining primitives is beyond the scope of this book, but the following sections introduce the basic concepts of each one.

Mutex

If you need to synchronize threads in different processes or across application domains, you can use a `Mutex`, which is an abbreviated form of the term "mutually exclusive." A global mutex is called a named mutex because it must be given a unique name so that multiple processes can access the same object.

Reader-Writer Locks

A common multithreaded scenario is one in which a particular thread, typically called the writer thread, changes data and must have exclusive access to the resource. As long as the writer thread is not active, any number of reader threads can access the resource. This scenario can be easily accomplished using the `ReaderWriterLockSlim` class, which provides the `EnterReaderLock` and `EnterWriterLock` methods to acquire and release the lock.

Semaphore

A semaphore enables only a specified number of threads access to a resource. When that limit is reached, additional threads requesting access wait until a thread releases the semaphore. Like a mutex, a semaphore can be either global or local and can be used across application domains. Unlike `Monitor`, `Mutex`, and `ReaderWriterLockSlim`, a semaphore can also be used when one thread acquires the semaphore and another thread releases it.

Understanding the Task Parallel Library

The preferred way to write multithreaded and parallel code is using the Task Parallel Library (TPL). The TPL simplifies the process of adding parallelism and concurrency to your application, allowing you to be more productive. Rather than requiring you to understand the complexities of scaling processes to most efficiently use multiple processors, the TPL handles that task for you.

CAUTION

Understanding Concurrency

Even though the TPL simplifies writing multithreaded and parallel applications, not all code is suited to run in parallel. It still requires you to have an understanding of basic threading concepts, such as locking and deadlocks, to use the TPL effectively.

Data Parallelism

When the same operation is performed concurrently on elements in a source collection (or array), it is referred to as **data parallelism**. Data parallel operations partition the source collection so that multiple threads can operate on different segments concurrently. The System. Threading.Tasks.Parallel class supports data parallel operations through the For and ForEach methods, which provide method-based parallel implementations of for and foreach loops, respectively.

Listing 24.2 shows an example of using a traditional foreach statement and a Parallel. ForEach statement that will print out the numbers 1 through 9. The output is shown in Figure 24.1.

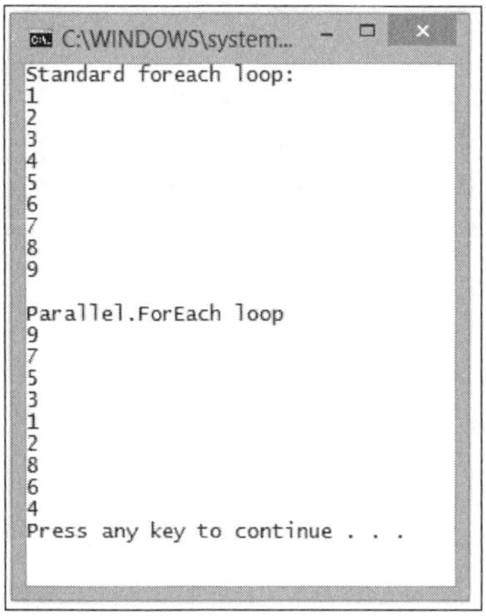

FIGURE 24.1
Output of a standard foreach loop and a Parallel.ForEach loop.

LISTING 24.2 Comparison of foreach and Parallel.ForEach

```
class Program
{
    static void Main(string[] args)
    {
        int[] source = new int[] { 1, 2, 3, 4, 5, 6, 7, 8, 9 };

        Console.WriteLine("Standard foreach loop:");
        foreach (var item in source)
        {
            Console.WriteLine(item);
        }
```

```
        Console.WriteLine();
        Console.WriteLine("Parallel.ForEach loop");
        System.Threading.Tasks.Parallel.ForEach(source, item => Process(item));
    }

    private static void Process(int item)
    {
        System.Threading.Thread.Sleep(1000);
        Console.WriteLine(item);
    }
}
```

Using `Parallel.For` or `Parallel.ForEach`, you write the loop logic in much the same way as you would write a traditional `for` or `foreach` loop. The TPL handles the low-level work of creating threads and queuing work items.

Because `Parallel.For` and `Parallel.ForEach` are methods, you can't use the `break` and `continue` statements to control loop execution. To support these features, several overloads to both methods enable you to stop or break loop execution, among other things. These overloads use helper types to enable this functionality, including `ParallelLoopState`, `ParallelOptions`, `ParallelLoopResult`, `CancellationToken`, and `CancellationTokenSource`.

Thread-Safe Collections

Whenever multiple threads need to access a collection, that collection must be made thread-safe. The collections provided in the `System.Collection.Concurrent` namespace are specially designed thread-safe collection classes that should be used in favor of their generic counterparts.

CAUTION

Thread-Safe Collections

Although these collection classes are thread-safe, this simply means that they won't produce undefined results when used from multiple threads. However, you still need to pay attention to locking and thread-safety concerns.

For example, using `ConcurrentStack`, you have no guarantee that the following code would succeed:

```
if (!stack.IsEmpty)
{
    stack.Pop();
}
```

Even in this example, you still need to lock the `stack` instance to make sure that no other thread can access it between the `IsEmpty` check and the `Pop` operation, as shown here:

```
lock(syncLock)
{
   if (!stack.IsEmpty)
   {
      stack.Pop();
   }
}
```

The concurrent collection classes are shown in Table 24.1.

TABLE 24.1 Concurrent Collections

Class	Description
BlockingCollection<T>	Provides blocking and bounding capabilities for thread-safe collections that implement IProducerConsumer Collection<T>
ConcurrentBag<T>	Represents a thread-safe, unordered collection of objects
ConcurrentDictionary<TKey, TValue>	Represents a thread-safe collection of key-value pairs
ConcurrentQueue<T>	Represents a thread-safe first in-first-out (FIFO) collection
ConcurrentStack<T>	Represents a thread-safe last in-first-out (LIFO) collection
OrderablePartitioner<TSource>	Represents a particular manner of splitting an orderable data source into multiple partitions
Partitioner	Provides common partitioning strategies for arrays, lists, and enumerables
Partitioner<TSource>	Represents a particular manner of splitting a data source into multiple partitions

Task Parallelism

You can think of a task as representing an asynchronous operation. You can easily create and run implicit tasks using the Parallel.Invoke method, which enables you to run any number of arbitrary statements concurrently, as shown here:

```
Parallel.Invoke(() => DoSomeWork(), () => DoSomeOtherWork());
```

`Parallel.Invoke` accepts an array of `Action` delegates, each representing a single task to perform. The simplest way to create the delegates is to use lambda expressions.

As Listing 24.3 shows, you can also explicitly create and run a task by instantiating the `Task` or `Task<TResult>` class and passing the delegate that encapsulates the code the task executes.

LISTING 24.3 Explicitly Creating New Tasks

```
class Program
{
    public static void Main(string[] args)
    {
        var task = new Task(() => Console.WriteLine("Hello from a task."));
        task.Start();
        Console.WriteLine("Hello from the calling thread.");
    }
}
```

Figure 24.2 shows the output of the simple console application from Listing 24.3.

FIGURE 24.2
Output of creating tasks.

If the task creation and scheduling do not need to be separated, the preferred method is to use the `Task.Factory.StartNew` method, as shown in Listing 24.4.

LISTING 24.4 Creating Tasks Using `Task.Factory`

```
Task<double>[] tasks = new Task<double>[2]
{
    Task.Factory.StartNew( () => Method1() ),
    Task.Factory.StartNew( () => Method2() )
};
```

Waiting on Tasks

To wait for a task to complete, the Task class provides a Wait, WaitAll, and WaitAny method. The Wait method enables you to wait for a single task to complete, whereas the WaitAll and WaitAny methods enable you to wait for any or all of an array of tasks to complete.

The most common reasons for waiting on a task to complete are as follows:

▶ The main thread depends on the result of the work performed by the task.

▶ You need to handle exceptions that might be thrown from the task. Any exceptions raised by a task will be thrown by a Wait method, even if that method was called after the task completed.

Listing 24.5 shows a simple example of waiting for an array of tasks to complete using the Task.WaitAll method.

LISTING 24.5   Waiting on Tasks

```
Task[] tasks = new Task[2]
{
    Task.Factory.StartNew( () => Method1() ),
    Task.Factory.StartNew( () => Method2() )
};

Task.WaitAll(tasks);
```

Handling Exceptions

When a task raises exceptions, they are wrapped in an AggregateException and propagated back to the thread that joins with the task. The calling code (that is, the code that waits on the task or attempts to access the task's Result property) would handle the exceptions by using the Wait, WaitAll, WaitAny method or the Result property. Listing 24.6 shows one way in which you might handle exceptions in a task.

LISTING 24.6   Handling Exceptions in a Task

```
var task1 = Task.Factory.StartNew(() =>
{
    throw new InvalidOperationException();
});

try
{
    task1.Wait();
}
```

```
catch (AggregateException ae)
{
    foreach (var e in ae.InnerExceptions)
    {
        if (e is InvalidOperationException)
        {
            Console.WriteLine(e.Message);
        }
        else
        {
            throw;
        }
    }
}
```

If you don't use the TPL for your multithreaded code, you should handle exceptions in your worker threads. In most cases, exceptions occurring within a worker thread that are not handled can cause the application to terminate. However, if a `ThreadAbortException` or an `AppDomainUnloadedException` is unhandled in a worker thread, only that thread terminates.

NOTE

AggregateException and `InnerExceptions`

It is recommended that you catch an `AggregateException` and enumerate the `InnerExceptions` property to examine all the original exceptions thrown. Not doing so is equivalent to catching the base `Exception` type in nonparallel code.

Working with Parallel LINQ (PLINQ)

Parallel LINQ is a parallel implementation of LINQ to Objects with additional operators for parallel operations. By utilizing the Task Parallel Library, PLINQ queries can scale in the degree of concurrency and can increase the speed of LINQ to Objects queries by more efficiently using the available processor cores.

The `System.Linq.ParallelEnumerable` class provides almost all the functionality for PLINQ. Table 24.2 shows the common PLINQ operators.

TABLE 24.2 Common `ParallelEnumerable` Operators

Operator	Description
AsParallel()	The entry point for PLINQ, indicating that the rest of the query should be parallelized if possible
AsSequential()	Specifies that the rest of the query should be run sequentially (nonparallel)
AsOrdered()	Specifies that PLINQ should preserve the ordering of the source sequence for the rest of the query or until the order is changed
ForAll()	Invokes the specified action for each element in the source sequence in parallel
Aggregate()	Applies an accumulator (aggregate) function over a sequence in parallel

To create a PLINQ query, you invoke the `AsParallel()` extension method on the data source, as shown in Listing 24.7.

LISTING 24.7 A Simple PLINQ Query

```
var source = Enumerable.Range(1, 10000);
var evenNums = from num in source.AsParallel()
               where Compute(num) > 0
               select num;
```

Potential Pitfalls

At this point, you might be tempted to take full advantage of the TPL and parallelize all your `for` loops, `foreach` loops, and LINQ to Objects queries; but don't. Parallelizing query and loop execution introduces complexity that can lead to problems that aren't common (or even possible) in sequential code. As a result, you want to carefully evaluate each loop and query to ensure that it is a good candidate for parallelization.

When deciding whether to use parallelization, you should keep the following guidelines in mind:

▶ Don't assume parallel is always faster. It is recommended that you always measure actual performance results before deciding to use PLINQ. A basic rule of thumb is that queries having few source elements and fast user delegates are unlikely to speed up.

▶ Don't overparallelize the query by making too many data sources parallel. This is most common in nested queries, where it is typically best to parallelize only the outer data source.

▶ Don't make calls to non-thread-safe methods and limit calls to thread-safe methods. Calling non-thread-safe methods can lead to data corruption, which might or might not go undetected. Calling many thread-safe methods (including static thread-safe methods) can lead to a significant slowdown in the query. (This includes calls to `Console.WriteLine`. The examples use this method for demonstration purposes, but you shouldn't use it in your own PLINQ queries.)

▶ Do use `Parallel.ForAll` when possible instead of `foreach` or `Parallel.ForEach`, which must merge the query results back into one thread to be accessed serially by the enumerator.

▶ Don't assume that iterations of `Parallel.ForAll`, `Parallel.ForEach`, and `Parallel.For` will actually execute in parallel. As a result, you shouldn't write code that depends on parallel execution of iterations for correctness.

▶ Don't write to shared memory locations, such as static variables or class fields. Although this is common in sequential code, doing so from multiple threads can lead to race conditions. You can help prevent this by using `lock` statements, but the cost of synchronization can actually hurt performance.

▶ Don't execute parallel loops on the UI thread because doing so can make your application's user interface nonresponsive. If the operation is complex enough to require parallelization, it should off-load that operation to be run on a background thread using either the `BackgroundWorker` component or by running the loop inside a task instance (commonly started by calling `Task.Factory.StartNew`).

Summary

Creating applications that efficiently scale to multiple processors can be quite challenging, can add additional complexities to your application logic, and can introduce bugs, in the form of deadlocks or other race conditions, which can be difficult to find.

The Task Parallel Library in the .NET Framework provides an easy way to handle the low-level details of thread management and provides a high level of abstraction for working with tasks and queries in a parallel manner. The managed thread pool used by the .NET Framework for many tasks (such as asynchronous I/O completion, timer callbacks, `System.Net` socket connections, and asynchronous delegate calls) uses the task and threading capabilities provided by the Task Parallel Library.

Through the course of this book, you have learned the fundamentals of the C# programming language. From those fundamentals, you learned advanced concepts such as working with files, streams, and XML data and learned how to query databases. You then used those skills to create a Windows desktop, Windows Store, and web application. After that, you were introduced to parallel programming with the Task Parallel Library, how to interact with dynamic languages, and how to interoperate with other languages and technologies, such as the component object model (COM) and the Windows application programming interfaces (APIs).

Although you have reached the end of this book, your career as a C# developer is just beginning. I encourage you to continue learning and expanding your knowledge just as the .NET Framework and the C# programming language continue to evolve.

Q&A

Q. What is the benefit of the Task Parallel Library?

A. The Task Parallel Library simplifies the process of adding parallelism and concurrency to your application, enabling you to be more productive by focusing on your application logic rather than requiring you to understand the complexities of scaling processes to most efficiently use multiple processors.

Q. What is an application domain?

A. An application domain is a lightweight managed subprocess.

Q. What are some common reasons for using multiple threads?

A. Some common reasons for using multiple threads follow:

   a. Communicate to a web server or database.

   b. Perform long-running or complex operations.

   c. Allow the user interface to remain responsive while performing other tasks in the background.

Q. What is concurrency?

A. Concurrency is simultaneously performing multiple tasks that can potentially interact with each other.

Q. What are locks?

A. Exclusive locks protect a resource by giving control to one thread at a time. Nonexclusive locks enable access to a limited number of threads at a time.

Q. What is the benefit of using one of the collections provided in the `System.Collection.Concurrent` namespace?

A. The collections provided in the `System.Collection.Concurrent` namespace are specially designed thread-safe collection classes and should be used in favor of their generic counterparts when writing multithreaded applications.

Q. What is Parallel LINQ (PLINQ)?

A. PLINQ is a parallel implementation of LINQ to Objects with additional operators for parallel operations.

Workshop

Quiz

1. What is a deadlock?

2. What are the three categories of synchronization primitives provided by the .NET Framework?

3. How is the `lock` statement in C# expanded by the compiler?

4. Why should you not lock on a string literal?

5. What are the three primary methods provided by the `Parallel` class?

Answers

1. A deadlock refers to the condition when two or more threads are waiting for each other to release a resource, or more than two threads are waiting for a resource in a circular chain.

2. The synchronization primitives provided by the .NET Framework can be loosely divided into the following categories:

   a. Locks

   b. Signals

   c. Interlocked operations

3. The `lock` statement is expanded by the compiler to the following code:

```
bool needsExit = false;
try
{
    System.Threading.Monitor.Enter(syncLock, ref needsExit);
    this.counter = value;
}
finally
{
    if (needsExit)
    {
        System.Threading.Monitor.Exit(syncLock);
    }
}
```

4. Locking on string literals is problematic due to the string interning performed by the CLR. Because only a single instance is shared across the assembly, placing a lock on a string literal causes any location where that string is accessed to also be locked.

5. The `Parallel` class provides the `For` and `ForEach` methods for executing parallel loops and the `Invoke` method for executing tasks in parallel.

Exercises

There are no exercises for this hour.

Index

custom dynamic types, 459

custom format strings, 195

specifiers, 195-197

CustomValidator control, 433

D

data binding, 385-387

adding binding expressions, 431

ASP.NET, 431-432

Bind method, 432

collection view, 388-390

collections, implementing, 390

components, 386

creating, 387-392

current item pointers, 392

Eval method, 431-432

OneTime, 386

OneWay, 386, 431-432

OneWayToSource, 386

SortDescription structure, 389

target, 386

TwoWay, 386, 431-432

Web applications, 431-432

WPF, 372

data conversion, 392-393

ConverterParameter property, 396

creating converters, 392-393

multivalue converters, 394-396

data hiding, 78-79

data parallelism, 482-484

concurrent collections, 484

guidelines, 488-489

thread-safe collections, 483-484

data providers, 347

data selection, 285-288

data streams. *See* streams

data templates, 399-400

associating, 400

defining, 399

data validation, 396-399

client-side validation

CompareValidator control, 433

CustomValidator control, 433

RangeValidator control, 433

RegularExpressionValidator control, 433

RequiredFieldValidator control, 433

controls, 433-435

ControlToValidate property, 434

Display property, 434

ErrorMessage property, 434

Text property, 434

Web applications, 432-435

client-side validation, 433-435

sample application, 433-435

security, 432-433

server-side validation, 432-433

databases, 343

ADO.NET, 346

connection pooling, 349

data providers, 347

DataSet class, 346

queries, 348-349

read-only database access, 348

required references, 348

sample application, 350

SQL injection attacks, 349

AdventureWorks sample database, 343-345

LINQ to ADO.NET, 351

LINQ to DataSet, 351-352

LINQ to Entities, 359-361

LINQ to SQL, 353-359

prerequisites for, 343-345

DataContext class, customizing, 358-359

DataSet class, 346

DataTips, 37-38

Date property, 55

DateTime type, 55-56

arithmetic methods, 55

properties, 55

Day property, 55

DayOfWeek property, 55

Days method, 57

deadlocks, 477

double type, 51

downcasting, 112-114

downloading

SQL Server, 343

SQL Server Express, 343

dynamic language runtime.
See **DLR (dynamic language
runtime)**

dynamic languages, 13

dynamic types, 52, 451-452

COM interoperability, 459-461

conversions, 454

creating, 459

custom, 459

overload resolution, 455-456

reflection interoperability,
461-462

runtime, determining dynamic
types at, 454

sample application, 453-452

E

editions, 26

Eiffel programming language,
254-255

embedded ASP.NET code
blocks, 432

Empty method, 56

empty strings, 182-183

encapsulation, 78-79

encoding and decoding characters
in XML (Extensible Markup
Language), 329

EndsWith method, 186

Enqueue method, 227

Enter method, 479

enterprise access to Windows
Store apps, 407

EntityClient data provider, 360

enumerable objects, 230-233

EnumerateDirectories method

Directory class, 311

DirectoryInfo class, 306

EnumerateFiles method

Directory class, 311

DirectoryInfo class, 306

EnumerateFileSystemEntries
method, 311

EnumerateFileSystemInfos
method, 306

enumerations, 129-132

defining, 130

flags, 132-135

multiple named values, 131

sample application, 133

underlying type, 132

zero value, 132

equality operator, 61

equals (==) operator, 62

ErrorMessage property, 434

errors. *See also* **exceptions**

compiler, 33-34

return codes used to
report, 237

runtime, 33-34

EscapeUriString method, 58

Eval method, 431-432

event handlers, 148-151

event target, 439

event-driven programming, 147.
See also **events**

events, 147-148

bubbling strategy to route
events, 368

declaring, 152-154

delegates, 148

direct strategy to route
events, 368

firing, 154-157

handlers

attaching to events,
148-151

multithreaded, 156

post-events, 154

pre-events, 154

publishing, 152-154, 157

raising, 154-157

routed, 368

subscribing, 148-151

tunneling strategy to route
events, 368

unsubscribing, 150-152

Exception Assistant, 34-35

exception points, 34-35

exceptions, 238. *See also specific
exceptions*

code contracts, 254-255

Contract.Result<T> class,
256-257

corrupted state, 250

guard statements, 253-254

handling, 242-240

catch handler, 242-244

finally handler, 242

task parallelism, 486-487

integer arithmetic operations,
overflowing, 252-253

invariants, 257-258

grouping data, 289-292

joining data, 291-294

lambdas, 297-300

  delegate replacement,
  297-298, 300

  expression, 298-299

  statement, 299-300

  variables, capturing, 298

lazy evaluation, 301

orderby clause, 289-290

ordering data, 289-292

standard query operator
  methods, 296-297

syntax, 285

Query property, 58

queues, 224, 226

Queue<T> class, 226

R

raising events, 154-157

RangeValidator control, 433

Read method, 315

ReadAllBytes method, 313, 320

**ReadAllLines method, 313,
  320-321**

ReadAllText method, 313

reader threads, 481

reader-writer locks, 481

reading and writing data, 314-321

ReadLines method, 313, 321

read-only database access, 348

read-only properties, 87

ReadOnlyCollection<T>, 219

reference parameters, 90

reference types, 14-15, 50, 465

  garbage collection, 466-467

  predefined reference
  types, 15

reflection, 447

**reflection interoperability,
  461-462**

Refresh method

  DirectoryInfo class, 306

  FileInfo class, 308

Regex class, 200

regular expressions, 199

  classes, 200-201

  compatibility, 199

  metacharacters, 199-200

  substrings, matching, 201

  validation with, 201

**RegularExpressionValidator
  control, 433**

**relational and type testing
  operator, 61**

relational operators, 62

  equals (==), 62

  greater than (>), 62

  greater than or equals
  (>=), 62

  less than (<), 62

  less than or equals (<=), 62

  not equals (!=), 62

  sample application, 64

relative paths, 304

Remove method, 187

  Dictionary<TKey, TValue>
  class, 220

  HashSet<T> class, 219

  SortedDictionary<TKey,
  TValue> class, 221

SortedList<TKey, TValue>
  class, 221

SortedSet<T> class, 219

XML modification, 339-340

RemoveItem method, 218

RemoveWhere method

  HashSet<T> class, 219

  SortedSet<T> class, 219

removing data, 339-340

Replace method, 187

  File class, 313

  FileInfo class, 308

ReplaceWith method, 339

replacing data, 339

required parameters, 94

required references

  ADO.NET, 348

  LINQ to DataSet, 352

**RequiredFieldValidator
  control, 433**

Resize method, 210

resource dictionaries, 381-382

rethrowing exceptions, 250-251

**return codes used to report
  errors, 237**

return statement, 175

return target, 439

Reverse method

  HashSet<T> class, 219

  SortedSet<T> class, 219

Root method, 306

routed events, 368

rows/columns

  creating, 376

  definitions for, 377

  star sizing, 378

Sams **Teach Yourself**

When you only have time
for the answers™

Whatever your need and whatever your time frame, there's a Sams **Teach Yourself** book for you. With a Sams **Teach Yourself** book as your guide, you can quickly get up to speed on just about any new product or technology—in the absolute shortest period of time possible. Guaranteed.

Learning how to do new things with your computer shouldn't be tedious or time-consuming. Sams **Teach Yourself** makes learning anything quick, easy, and even a little bit fun.

Windows 8 Apps with XAML and C# in 24 Hours

David Davis, Richard Crane, John Pelak
ISBN-13: 9780672336188

Visual Basic 2012 in 24 Hours
James Foxall
ISBN-13: 9780672336294

ASP.NET 4.0 in 24 Hours
Scott Mitchell
ISBN-13: 9780672333057

Windows Phone 7 Application Development in 24 Hours
Scott J. Dorman, Kevin Wolf, Nikita Polyakov, Joe Healy
ISBN-13: 9780672335396

Windows Phone 7 Game Programming in 24 Hours
Jonathan Harbour
ISBN-13: 9780672335549

informIT.com THE TRUSTED TECHNOLOGY LEARNING SOURCE

PEARSON

InformIT is a brand of Pearson and the online presence for the world's leading technology publishers. It's your source for reliable and qualified content and knowledge, providing access to the top brands, authors, and contributors from the tech community.

Addison-Wesley　Cisco Press　EXAM/CRAM　IBM Press.　QUE　PRENTICE HALL　SAMS　| Safari Books Online

---

LearnIT at InformIT

Looking for a book, eBook, or training video on a new technology? Seeking timely and relevant information and tutorials? Looking for expert opinions, advice, and tips? **InformIT has the solution.**

- Learn about new releases and special promotions by subscribing to a wide variety of newsletters.
  Visit **informit.com/newsletters**.

- Access FREE podcasts from experts at **informit.com/podcasts**.

- Read the latest author articles and sample chapters at **informit.com/articles**.

- Access thousands of books and videos in the Safari Books Online digital library at **safari.informit.com**.

- Get tips from expert blogs at **informit.com/blogs**.

Visit **informit.com/learn** to discover all the ways you can access the hottest technology content.

Are You Part of the IT Crowd?

Connect with Pearson authors and editors via RSS feeds, Facebook, Twitter, YouTube, and more! Visit **informit.com/socialconnect**.

---

informIT.com THE TRUSTED TECHNOLOGY LEARNING SOURCE

PEARSON

Addison-Wesley　Cisco Press　EXAM/CRAM　IBM Press.　QUE　PRENTICE HALL　SAMS　| Safari Books Online

Your purchase of **Sams Teach Yourself C# 5.0 in 24 Hours** includes access to a free online edition for 45 days through the *Safari Books Online* subscription service. Nearly every Sams book is available online through *Safari Books Online*, along with thousands of books and videos from publishers such as Addison-Wesley Professional, Cisco Press, Exam Cram, IBM Press, O'Reilly Media, Prentice Hall, Que, and VMware Press.

Safari Books Online is a digital library providing searchable, on-demand access to thousands of technology, digital media, and professional development books and videos from leading publishers. With one monthly or yearly subscription price, you get unlimited access to learning tools and information on topics including mobile app and software development, tips and tricks on using your favorite gadgets, networking, project management, graphic design, and much more.

Activate your FREE Online Edition at
informit.com/safarifree

STEP 1:   Enter the coupon code: UWOHDDB.

STEP 2:   New Safari users, complete the brief registration form.
Safari subscribers, just log in.

If you have difficulty registering on Safari or accessing the online edition,
please e-mail customer-service@safaribooksonline.com

Addison Wesley   Adobe Press   ALPHA   Cisco Press   FT Press TECHNICAL INDEX   IBM Press   Microsoft Press   New Riders   O'REILLY

Peachpit Press   PRENTICE HALL   Que   Redbooks   SAMS   SAS Publishing   vmware PRESS   WILEY   wrox